14th International Conference on ICT, Society, and Human Beings (ICT2021); 18th International Conference on Web Based Communities and Social Media (WEBC2021); and 13th International Conference on e-Health (EH2021)

Held at the 15th Multi-Conference on Computer Science and Information Systems (MCCSIS 2021)

Online
20 - 23 July 2021

ISBN: 978-1-7138-3580-6

Printed from e-media with permission by:

Curran Associates, Inc.
57 Morehouse Lane
Red Hook, NY 12571

Some format issues inherent in the e-media version may also appear in this print version.

Printed with permission by Curran Associates, Inc. (2021)

International Association for Development of the Information Society (IADIS)
Rua Sao Sebastiao Da Pedreira
No. 100, 30, 1050-209
Lisbon, Portugal

Phone: 351 21 3151373
Fax: 351 21 3151244

secretariat@iadis.org

Additional copies of this publication are available from:

Curran Associates, Inc.
57 Morehouse Lane
Red Hook, NY 12571 USA
Phone: 845-758-0400
Fax: 845-758-2633
Email: curran@proceedings.com
Web: www.proceedings.com

TABLE OF CONTENTS

MEASURING THE ENGAGEMENT OF IN-HOUSE CURRENCY SYSTEM USERS

Toshiomi Moriki[1], Hiroki Satoh[1], Shinpei Takami[1], Kie Yoshiji[1], Miho Kobayashi[1]
and Norihisa Komoda[2]
[1]*Research & Development Group, Hitachi, Ltd., 1-280, Higashi-koigakubo Kokubunji, Tokyo 185-8601, Japan*
[2]*Code Solutions, Co.,Ltd., Daidoseimei south building 9th floor, 1-2-11 Edobori Nishi-ku,Osaka, Osaka 550-0022, Japan*

ABSTRACT

With the recent outbreak of infectious diseases and the spread of remote work, there are concerns about the lack of communication among employees and the resulting loss of their motivation. In this paper, the design and effectiveness of the in-house currency system are reported, which is developed for the purpose of stimulating informal communication and mutual assistance among employees. In order to encourage employees to actively participate in the in-house currency system, user interactions are designed to foster empathy by visualizing the mutual aid behaviors of other employees in the system, in addition to small financial rewards. It has also a function that encourages solicitation among employees, inspired by events such as community contribution activities and other volunteer activities. The in-house currency system has been introduced to our R&D department on a trial basis and evaluated the level of employee participation for about a year. As a result of analyzing the usage of 118 registered employees, it is observed that user engagement increases in the order of following steps; recognition of the in-house currency system, daily use of the system, and involvement of other employees.

KEYWORDS

In-house Currency System, Mutual Assistance, Engagement Measurement

1. INTRODUCTION

In corporate activities focusing on intellectual labor, (Nomura, T., 2002) are looking for ways to share knowledge possessed by employees and initiate innovation as an organization. In the context of so-called intellectual management, it is important to have a place and a method for sharing knowledge among employees.

In conventional Japanese companies, employees have gathered in a large office and have worked in groups to help each other (Furukawa, Y., 1998). While this traditional form of work is advantageous for knowledge sharing as employees can naturally overhear the phone call conversation and chats of those around them, it is also a hotbed of long working hours due to peer pressure (Nishida, Y. and Terashima, N., 2019). To deal with this problem, work style reforms have been implemented, and due to the recent epidemic of infectious diseases, remote works from home, hotel, and remote office are rapidly spreading.

In response to this situation, in-house currency systems (Tamura, K., 2018), (Kamii, M., 2019) have been attracting attention as one of the reward systems to promote a good culture of interaction and mutual help among employees and to improve employee engagement. In an in-house currency system, employees are given small monetary incentives that are accepted only within a specific organization. When introducing an in-house currency system, it is desirable to create a system that complements, not conflicts with, the company's conventional incentive systems, such as bonuses and awards. Specifically, in addition to notification from top management and administrative departments, it is necessary to successfully combine the involvement of other employees by advanced users (early adopters) who can use the in-house currency system at an early stage. However, there is a problem that a mechanism to objectively measure the effects of the introduction measures has not been established.

Therefore, we have attempted to measure the amount of user engagement. In this paper, we describe the design of a service to promote the use of an in-house currency system, the construction of a user engagement measurement model, and an example of its application.

2. THE IN-HOUSE CURRENCY SYSTEM AND ITS CHALLENGES

2.1 Overview of the In-House Currency System

An in-house currency system is a reward system that issues a private currency, which is effective only within a specific organization. Although the amount of money in circulation and the scope of circulation are both limited, it is expected to promote actions that meet organizational goals, such as productivity improvement and organizational management facilitation, for employees and workers in the organization.

The functions of an in-house currency system are generally categorized into the following two types.

(1) Incentives to encourage favorable behavior from the company to the employees: incentive program type

(2) Message function to express gratitude for mutual help among employees: Peer bonus type

In this study, both functions will be included.

Figure 1 shows the overall picture of the services provided by the in-house currency system. The system is implemented on the mobile web application and the backend cloud service, which provides the intermediary between stakeholders and manages the currency. Users can access to this system via their own smartphone easily.

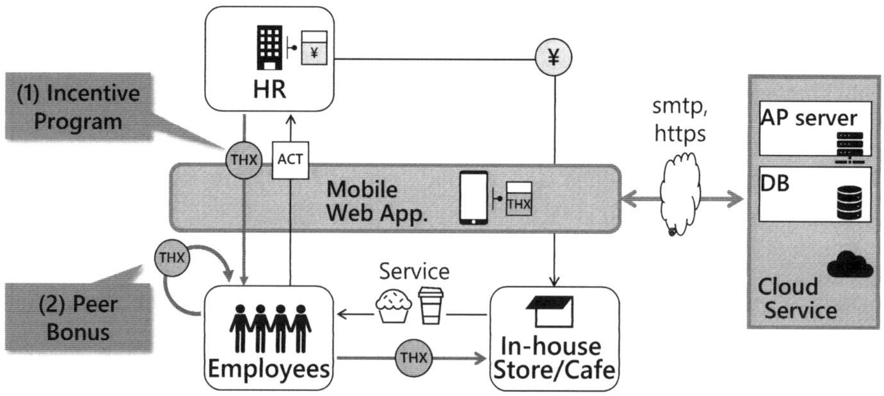

Figure 1. Service Overview of the In-house Currency System

The in-house currency insurance and consumption processes are like followings; (1) The company's management department, HR, issues virtual money named THX as an incentive program for employees' desirable mutual-help behavior (ACTION). Employees can be given THX for not only direct help but also for sympathetic behavior through (2) peer bonuses. The THX received can be used for payment at the company stores and cafeteria.

Figure 2. User Interface of the In-house Currency System

Figure 2 shows the screen images of the mobile web application that serves the user interface. At the App frontpage, users can see the timeline which contains recent mutual aid activities (ACT) by all users. If user get sympathies to other's ACT, he/she can make several reactions to others, such as "Like (I like this)", "Wanna (I want to do such a thing)", and "Done (I have done the same thing too)." Those reactions can be sent through this timeline with small THX attached – its for (2) peer bonus feature.

This frontpage has two main action buttons for subfunctions. Right one is for reporting ACTs and get THXs. This screen has a text area box to input the description of his/her ACT. Next, 39 ACT are sent to him/her a day for the reward – its for (1) incentive program.

Another button is for payment at in-house cafeteria and store. User can pay THXs for the service, like a cup of coffee, cookie, breads, and other daily materials. The application offers him/her the QR scan screen and he/she can pay any amount of THXs to get service.

2.2 Challenges in Promoting the Use of In-House Currency Systems

In this section, we examine the issues involved in implementing an in-house currency system. Table 1 shows a list of issues to be considered in order to increase the number of users who use this system on a daily basis (i.e., active users).

(a) Regarding the low threshold for starting to use the system, many people said that it would be good if there was some kind of mechanism to encourage participation from the company side. Specifically, it would be desirable if the work line of the employee's supervisor recommends participation, or if the benefits of participation are clearly stated for individual employees.

(b) It is difficult to devote a lot of time and effort to programs related to the in-house currency system because it is different from the main business. It is desirable to make it as easy as possible for novices to use the system in order to prevent them from leaving.

(c) Considering that it is a means of communication among employees, it is desirable to be able to see at a glance that others are using it even in a remote environment. It is also good to have an incentive to involve other employees.

Table 1. Issues in implementing an in-house currency system

#	Issues	Description
(a)	Barriers to involve new users	They need a good mechanism to encourage participation. Participation should be encouraged via command channel, the benefits of participating as an individual are easy to understand, etc.
(b)	Difficulties to continue to use the app	Since the program is different from the main task, it should be as easy to use as possible.
(c)	Challenges of sharing their activities	It is desirable to be able to see at a glance that other people are using it, even in a remote environment. It is better if there is an incentive to involve other employees.

The following are service policies to deal with the above issues and to increase the number of active users.

(a) Easy to enter: We make the service known on the company intranet and install signs as a permanent guide. We recommend that employees use nicknames instead of their real names, assuming that they are highly sensitive to others' opinions and privacy.

(b) Easy to use: Implemented as a mobile web application that does not require installation of any application as a touch point for users.

(c) Easy to spread to others: In order to feel the mutual activities of other users even in non-contact situations such as working from home, we can observe the timeline of all users' ACT reports, peer bonus sympathy, and THX giving. In addition, we provide time-limited reward program for recruiting new users.

3. USER ENGAGEMENT MEASUREMENT MODEL

An in-house currency system is generally a mechanism to promote communication among employees. It can be viewed as a network service closed to the company. In this section, we examine how to measure user engagement in order to promote the use of internal currency services by employees.

Research on user recognition of general services and promotion of their use has been widely conducted in the marketing field. AIDA (Rehman, F. U., Nawaz, T., Ilyas, M., & Hyder, S., 2014) and AISAS (Xu, C., Hao, Q., & Han, G., 2017) are well known as representative models. We refer to SIPS (Dentsu, 2011), (Luo, Z. 2018) a consumer behavior model derived from AISAS and published by Dentsu Co. Ltd. They assume that users recruit and involve other users by word of mouth and sympathy among themselves.

We were inspired by SIPS and assumed the following four steps in the usage of an internal currency service. We assume that user engagement will increase in the order from (i) to (iv).

(i) Employees are aware to the in-house currency service via intra media.
(ii) Registered as a user of the in-house currency service.
(iii) Reported ACT and earned incentives (THX).
(iv) Promoted the in-house currency service to other employees to attract new users.

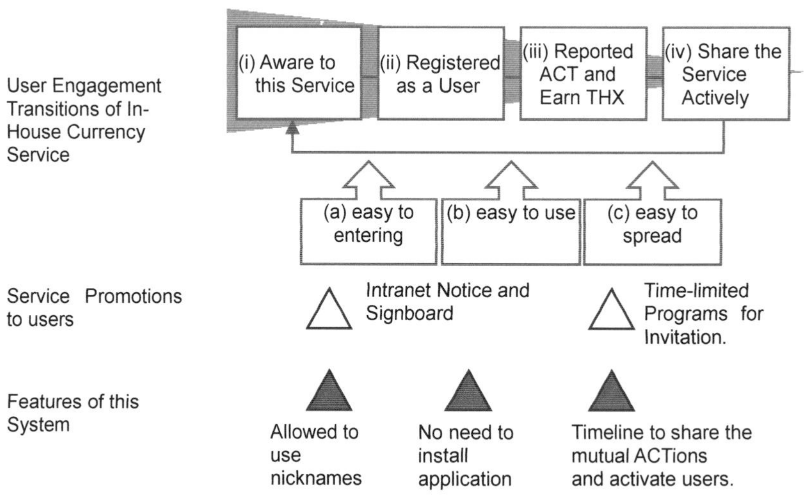

Figure 3. Measurement steps of Engagements of In-house Currency System

Figure 3 shows the relationship between the transition in user engagement and the measures taken to introduce the in-house currency system. We have planned the following (a)-(c) as measures for user acquisition.

As a measure (a) to promote the transition from (i) to (ii), announcements are made on the company intranet and signs are installed as service measures. In addition, the use of nicknames in the system is recommended to prevent users from leaving the system.

As a measure (b) to promote the transition from (ii) to (iii), implement the system as a mobile web application that does not require the installation of an application, and make the operation as simple as possible.

As a measure (c) to promote the transition from (iii) to (iv), we offer rewards for soliciting other employees through a time-limited program. In addition, the timeline on the front page should be used to increase the number of active users by sharing the mutual aid activities of other users.

4. ANALYSIS OF IN-HOUSE CURRENCY SYSTEM USAGE

Based on the engagement measurement model described in Section 3-2, we analyzed the effect of the trial introduction of the in-house currency system.

The assumptions of the environment in the test are shown in Table 2. The test period started at April 2020, when work was basically prohibited due to the declaration of a state of emergency against the spread of COVID-19. The target office is the research and development division, and almost all of the approximately 700 employees are researchers and white-collar workers.

Table 2. Trial Environment of the In-house Currency System

Trial Period	2020/4/1～2021/3/29 (continued)	
Target Organization	Type of organization	Research and Development
	# of employees	700 persons (approx.)
	Types of workers	White-collar workers
Incentive Setting	Incentive Amount	39 THX per ACT (once a day rewarded)
	Peer Bonus Amount	1 THX per Like (no limitation per day)
	Incentive Amount for Inviting a new user	110 THX per each program.
	Where to use	In-house store and cafeteria

The incentive for the operation of the in-house currency system is to add 39 THX points for each act of mutual aid (ACT). This is equivalent to 39 yen. Peer bonus is given by returning three types of responses ("Like", "Wanna", "Done") to the ACT of others, and 1 THX is given for each responses. In general, the monetary incentives given are limited, and it is thought that users use this system mainly to enjoy communication with other employees.

Table 3 shows the transition of the status of user engagement during the test operation period. The number of user registrations (ii) and ACT-reported users (iii) increased rapidly from April 1, just after the service was launched, and increased to (ii) 84 and (iii) 55 as of May 27, when the emergency declaration corresponding to the infectious disease epidemic was lifted. During the declaration of the state of emergency, the business units to be tested were almost in a state of lockdown, but it is thought that effective advertising and promotion measures (a) and (b) were carried out.

After that, telecommuting was half enforced until the end of July, but from August 17, (c) a program to recruit new users was started. In October, several timed programs was conducted led by the administration department (HR) in order to encourage employees' volunteer and CSR activities. 7 users eventually shared and spread the program to other users, contributing to the acquisition of a total of 12 new users.

Table 3. Transition of User Engagement Status

Date	(i) Aware to this Service	(ii) Registered as a User	(iii) Reported ACT and Earn THX	(iv) Share the Service Actively
2020/4/1	700	17	5	0
2020/5/27	700	84	55	0
2020/8/5	700	92	57	0
2020/10/14	700	104	60	6
2021/3/29	700	118	61	7
Note	(Approx.)	# of users registered.	# of users reported an ACT or more.	# of users invited new users.

Figure 4 shows the engagement breakdown of the number of users during the test implementation period of the in-house currency system.

Within the first month of the test introduction of the in-house currency system, the number of users who completed the registration (ii) reached 84, and the number of users who reported the ACT and participated (iii) reached 55, indicating that the initial measures (a) to lower the threshold for starting to use the system and (b) to make the system easy to use were generally successful. After that, the number of newly registered users of (ii) increased steadily due to (c) measures to make it easier to spread the service to other people, and finally 118 users were acquired.

On the other hand, the number of users in the stage (iii) after May did not grow much, and it turned out that almost half of the registered users in the stage (ii) had never reported an ACT finally. This implied that the users might be fixed who reports ACTs and sends Likes repeatedly.

In order to understand the transition to the step (iv): sharing and spreading, we added a function in mid-August that allows new employees to report the email address of the solicitor when they register as a user. As a reward for solicitation, 110 THX is distributed to both new registrants and solicitors. As with the step (iii) users, we have not observed any new transitions to the state (iv) since December, and it is necessary to take act including advertising measures.

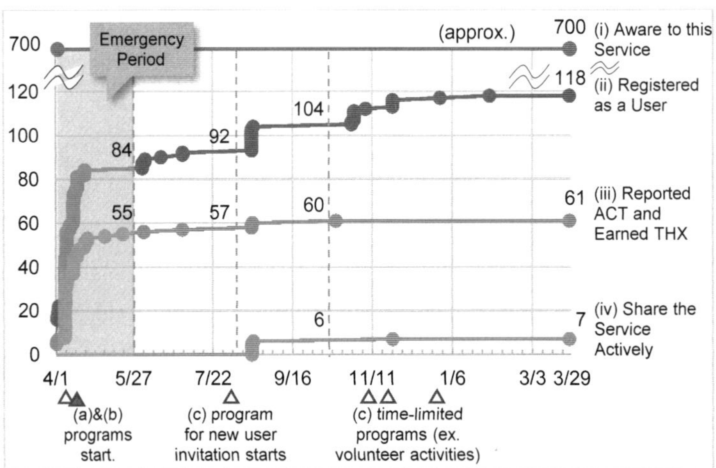

Figure 4. Trends in the breakdown of the number of users

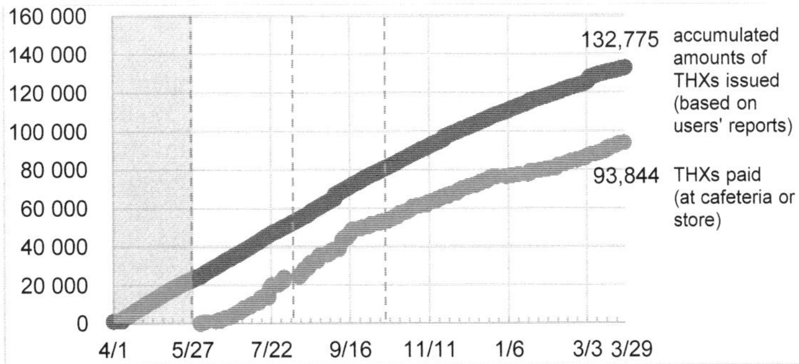

Figure 5. Trends of accumulated THXs issued and paid by the in-house currency system

Figure 5 shows the trend of THX issuance and paid by users throughout the experimental period. Throughout the experimental period, users reported ACTs stably, and the issuance of THX increased almost linearly. The company paid out 366 THX per day on average, which means that 9 to 10 people reported their ACTs. Payments by users at the cafeteria and concession stands have been made since June, after the state of emergency was lifted.

The payments have been made sequentially following the issuance of THX, but some of the payments are still pending and have not been paid from user accounts. As a result of the user interviews, some users answered that they look forward to acquiring THX itself, and it is possible that user preferences are leading to the withdrawal of THX.

Figure 6 shows the frequency distribution of the price per unit of THX acquisition and payment by users. 39 THX/day was used in most cases for THX acquisition, but some users paid a higher price due to the timed program (c) for acquiring new users and interviews with users about their usage. In addition, many users reported ACTs with THX=0 (i.e., more than two reports per day), suggesting that employees report each other's supportive behavior even when there is no monetary reward.

Payments at the cafeteria and store peaked between 120 and 150 THX, and continued to grow steadily thereafter to around 570 THX/payment. This suggests that users are making THX payments for every 3 to 10 or more ACT reports.

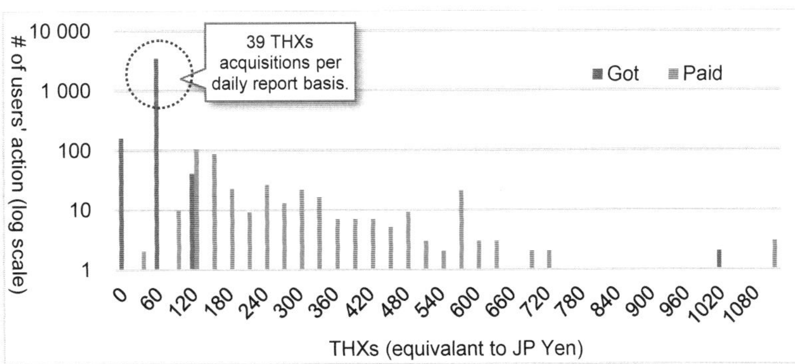

Figure 6. THX amounts per each action (got or paid)

5. CONCLUSION

An in-house currency system has been developed and implemented at a research and development department. More than 100 employees are involved though a 12-month trial. By analysis of the usage of the system, it is suggested several findings such as that more than 70% of user registrations were done during the first 2-month, even under the emergency declaration period. It might be a good aspect of the in-house currency system implementation, which needs no face-to-face communication between users.

By the analysis of issuance and usage of the in-house currency, active users reported several mutual activities a day regardless the financial rewards. Their payment amounts varied depending on users. With the invitation program for new user acquisition, highly engaged users have involved new users but the number of them were limited throughout the trial period.

REFERENCES

Dentsu, 2011, SIPS, [online] Available at https://www.dentsu.co.jp/news/release/pdf-cms/2011009-0131.pdf [Accessed 24 May 2021]. (in Japanese)

Furukawa, Y., 1998, Office Design and Communication in Japanese Corporations, Journal of Policy Studies 6, 1-20. (in Japanese)

Kamii, M., 2019, Introduction of intra-facility currency to enhance social participation and proactive behavior, Congress of the Japanese Physical Therapy Association 46S1(0), G-78_2. (in Japanese)

Kijima, K., 2015. Translational and trans-disciplinary approach to service systems. in Service systems science (pp. 37-54). Springer.

Luo, Z. 2018, The Consumer Behavior Analysis under Large Data Environment. in Proc. of 2017 5th International Education, Economics, Social Science, Arts, Sports and Management Engineering Conference (IEESASM 2017), pp.334-339.

Nishida, Y. and Terashima, N., 2019, Japanese work style and "Work-style reform": The problem of reducing long working hours and introducing telework, Psychologist: bulletin of the Graduate School of Professional Clinical Psychology, Kansai University, (9), 61-69. (in Japanese)

Nomura, T., 2002, Design of 'Ba' for successful Knowledge Management? how enterprises should design the places of interaction to gain competitive advantage, Journal of Network and Computer Applications, 25(4), pp.263-278.

Novani, S., Cintyawati, C., & Mayangsari, L., 2018, Back to the Future: A Revelation of Conventional Platform Preference of Digital Creative Ecosystem Entities in Bandung. in Collaborative Value Co-creation in the Platform Economy (pp. 247-268). Springer.

Rehman, F. U., Nawaz, T., Ilyas, M., & Hyder, S., 2014, A comparative analysis of mobile and email marketing using AIDA model. Journal of Basic and Applied Scientific Research, 4(6), 38-49.

Tamura, K., 2018, Eliminating waste and optimizing manpower and equipment! DISCO's mysterious " in-house currency operation", *Nikkei Top Leader*, 402, pp.76-82. (in Japanese)

Xu, C., Hao, Q., & Han, G., 2017, Research on the marketing strategy of the new media age based on AISAS model: A Case study of micro channel marketing. in Proc. of the Fourth International Forum on Decision Sciences (pp. 477-486). Springer.

DIGITAL HYBRID LEARNING INDIVIDUAL QUALITY ASSESSMENT IN EUROPEAN AND ORIENTAL LANGUAGES PROGRAMS: STUDENT CASE STUDY IN UKRAINE

Rusudan Makhachashvili and Ivan Semenist
Borys Grinchenko Kyiv University
Bulvarno-Kudryavska-st., 18/2, Kyiv, Ukraine

ABSTRACT

The global pandemic and subsequent quarantine measures and restrictions have posed an array of challenges to the structure and procedure of higher education workflow, which significantly influenced the scope of individual experiences, projected outcomes and estimated quality of higher education in countries across the world. This study focus is the in-depth assessment of the case of individual digital distance and blended learning experiences by students of different tiers (Bachelor's level, Master's level, Graduate school level) in European (French, Italian, Spanish, English) and Oriental (Mandarin Chinese, Japanese) Languages university level programs at Borys Grinchenko Kyiv University of Ukraine through the span of educational activities in the time-frame of COVID-19 quarantine measures of March 2020 to January 2021. The survey and analysis of different ICT tools is used to assess the parameters and challenges of individual quality and efficiency of translation of the real life Foreign Languages Acquisition practices into digital hybrid format, involving activation of interdisciplinary skills and cross-sectorial activities, assisted by ICT tools. The online survey of over 300 students of European and Oriental Languages programs provides for disclosure of a comprehensive case of student satisfaction with digitized foreign languages education, systematized individual experiences and quality estimation of e-learning and hybrid learning in the framework of COVID-19 lockdown; assessment of individual experiences and quality of e-learning and hybrid learning in the framework of COVID-19 lockdown as compared to traditional, face-to-face learning formats for foreign languages; individual quality assessment of learning process design, programmed learning outcomes and projected competencies for university programs of Oriental and European languages in the framework of COVID-19 lockdown and quarantine measures.

KEYWORDS

Hybrid Learning, e-Learning, Digital Literacy, Quality Assessment, Oriental Languages, European Languages, Survey Study

1. INTRODUCTION

In the educational domain, according to our estimations, the result of fundamental Technospheric shift, induced by the COVID-19 pandemic development and enhanced by subsequent digitalization measures, was the need to take quick comprehensive action (Makhachashvili, Semenist et al 2020) in order to achieve such desirable results: a) to adapt the existent educational scenarios to digital, remote and blended formats; b) to activate complex interdisciplinary skill-sets, otherwise latent or underutilized in the educational process; c) to boost ICT competence and digital literacy of all participants of the educational process relocated to computer being.

The global pandemic and subsequent quarantine measures and restrictions have posed an array of challenges to the structure and procedure of higher education workflow, which significantly influenced the scope of individual experiences, projected outcomes and estimated quality of higher education in countries across the world.

Foreign Languages Acquisition at university level major programs is a rigorous process (Law OHE 2019) that involves different stages and a regimen of activities and competencies across interconnected interdisciplinary domains. The presented study is a parcel of comprehensive institutional inquiry into the toll digitalization and amplified use of ICT tools put on different aspects of Oriental (Mandarin Chinese and Japanese) as well as European (French, Italian, Spanish, English) languages acquisition efficiency, assessment management, programmed results, communicative and digital competency formation in COVID-19 lockdown paradigm.

The research project to date spans the following areas: 1) full survey datasets on in-depth subjective experiences of students in e-learning and blended learning in COVID-19 timeframe for stakeholders of Oriental languages (Mandarin Chinese and Japanese) and European Languages (French, Italian, Spanish, English) major programs in capital city and regional universities of Ukraine; 2) full survey datasets on in-depth subjective experiences of faculty and staff in e-learning and blended learning in COVID-19 timeframe for stakeholders of Oriental languages (Mandarin Chinese and Japanese) and European Languages (French, Italian, Spanish, English) major programs in capital city and regional universities of Ukraine.

The accumulated data so far has been seminal for a range of publications (Makhachashvili, Semenist et al 2020; Makhachashvili, Semenist, Bakhtina 2020), covering the issues of ICT tools efficiency rating regimen for foreign languages programs, isolated and comparative case studies of Oriental and European languages acquisition digitization procedures and best practices.

The estimations of digital distant education quality, conducted across various studies in the pre-COVID-19 inquiry framework have spanned, among others, assessment of satisfaction with distance learning experience (Bekele 2010; Bolliger 2009); added value of online learning (Thiessen, Ambrock 2011); evaluation of learning outcomes (Costareie 2011; Ni 2013); overall attitudes to distance learning (Salyers et al 2014); challenges of online education (Markova et al 2017), networking principles in e-learning (Smyrnova-Trybulska, Kommers et al 2019).

These issues require a comprehensive revisit in terms of the toll the global pandemic took on individual learning experiences and subsequent shift in quality estimations of linguistic education in universities due to the abrupt transition to exclusively distant, digital distant or hybrid learning formats as a mode of formal education and university degree acquisition (as opposed to being a mostly auxiliary learning method or an informal learning format).

This **study objective**, henceforth, is to critically review the satisfaction parameters of via in-depth assessment of individual digital distance and hybrid learning experiences and best practices by students of Oriental (Mandarin Chinese, Japanese) and European (French, Italian, Spanish, English) Languages university level programs in Borys Grinchenko Kyiv University (BGKU) through the span of educational activities in the time-frame of COVID-19 quarantine measures of March 2020 to January 2021. The survey and analysis of different ICT tools is used to assess the parameters and challenges of individual quality and efficiency of translation of the real life Foreign Languages Acquisition practices into digital blended format, that Borys Grinchenko Kyiv University adopted comprehensively across the board, involving activation of interdisciplinary skills and cross-sectorial activities, assisted by ICT tools.

The study premise is based on identification of various digital distant learning formats (u-learning, m-learning, hybrid learning) (Crowe 2007) and modes for university educational programs and projected digital literacy requirements (EC 2020; DGR 2019; WEF 2020). Within the parameters of this study we estimate digitally enhanced or electronic learning (e-learning) as a form of ubiquitous learning (u-learning) that involves learning in an environment with full access to digital devices and services at any given moment (Van't Hooft 2007).

The framework evolution and innovation of e-learning as a complex system of human activity in the digital age, is determined by a range of qualifying conditions of its emergence, existence and transformation in the COVID-19 timeframe, including: 1) exhaustive synchronization of the object, phenomenological and anthropological planes of educational activities and proceedings processes ICT development; 2) exhaustive output of parameterization isomorphism of ontological (substance phenomenological), anthropic and digitized structures of reality and educational activity; 3) flexibility, adaptability and dynamic potential of the educational activities enhanced by ICT tools and digital technology (that is fulfilled, in particular through info-capacity, sign hybridization, the evolution of the basic ontological and functional features of the learning process).

COVID-19 quarantine measures, put in place country-wide in educational institutions Ukraine in the time spans of March-June 2020, October-December 2020 and January 2021 have demanded the simultaneous employment and overlap of the following structurally complex learning formats: e-learning 1.0 (direct synchronous computer assisted distant instruction); e-learning 2.0 (mostly asynchronous computer-supported collaborative learning, also known as "networked collaborative learning") (Trentin 2010); blended learning (in-person teaching with asynchronous ICT assisted learning methods) (Voorn, Kommers 2013; Dos Reis 2015; Boyarsky 2020); hybrid learning (synchronous instruction of in-presence and remote students via ICT tools) (Duff 2020).

Modelling of the comprehensive framework of educational activities and experiences in foreign language acquisition transformation into digitally enhanced format (Makhachahshvili, Semenist 2021) is, therefore, possible through an interoperable set of parameters (Figure 1): Time; Space; Communicative distance; Dependence on ICT tools and infrastructure; Level of complexity:

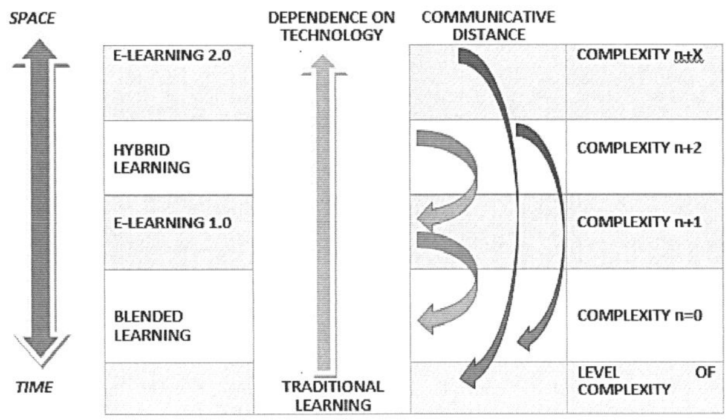

Figure 1. Modelling of Complex Digitally Enhanced Learning Formats

Based on the level of quarantine alert, adopted in the capital city of Kyiv at different intervals, different level of complexity was utilized for educational activities at Borys Grinchenko Kyiv University: e-learning 1.0/2.0 (for red and orange zones of quarantine) and hybrid learning (for yellow zones) formats were implemented.

2. DIGITAL DISTANT AND HYBRID LEARNING STUDENT INDIVIDUAL QUALITY ASSESSMENT: SURVEY RESULTS

2.1 Method Overview

The study employs the combination of mixed methods (Almalki 2016) – a proportional arrangement of quantitative and qualitative inquiry to assess in-depth aspects of subjective and individual quality estimation of digital distant and hybrid learning. The comprehensive study design methodology included the following consecutive steps: 1) distant digital learning activity, experience and application profiling; 2) The online survey method - based on D. Dillman's concept of mixed media and mixed mode surveys (Dillman 2014) - applied to conduct in-depth assessment of individual digital distance and blended learning experiences and practices by relevant groups of stakeholders in Oriental and European Languages university level programs at Borys Grinchenko Kyiv University, Kyiv, Ukraine; 3) digital content analysis of individual associations with different modes of learning by relevant groups of stakeholders in Oriental and European Languages university level programs in regions of Ukraine (via corpus and text-mining tools); 4) digital distance and blended learning models and procedures adaptation and customization, tailored to the individual and group needs of stakeholders in Foreign Language Acquisition on university level.

Based on the activity profile (digital distance and blended learning in Foreign Language Acquisition) an online survey was devised to assess in-depth subjective experiences of e-learning and hybrid learning in COVID-19 timeframe (March 2020 – January 2021) for students of Oriental languages (Mandarin Chinese and Japanese) and European Languages (French, Italian, Spanish, English) major programs.

The online questionnaire comprised of 21 questions total (multiple choice, ranking/scoring and open-end/short answer types), divided into such categories: 1) questions on overall assessment of individual experiences and quality estimation of e-learning and hybrid learning in the framework of COVID-19 lockdown and quarantine measures (March 2020 – January 2021) for university programs of Oriental (Mandarin Chinese, Japanese) and European (English, French, Spanish, Italian) and languages; 2) questions on assessment of individual experiences and quality of e-learning and hybrid learning in the framework of COVID-19 lockdown as compared to traditional, face-to-face learning formats; 3) questions on individual quality assessment of learning process design, programmed learning outcomes and projected competencies for university programs of European (English, French, Spanish, Italian) and Oriental (Mandarin Chinese, Japanese) languages in the framework of COVID-19 lockdown and quarantine measures (March 2020 – January 2021).

2.2 Data Gathering

A sizable sample of 337 respondents total across Oriental (Mandarin Chinese, Japanese) and European (English, French, Spanish, Italian) languages at Borys Grinchenko Kyiv University took part in the survey. The following groups of stakeholders of the digital distant education in the timespan of COVID-19 pandemic measures were respondents of the survey overall languages on all three tier of educational levels according to the legislature of Ukraine (Law OHE 2019): undergraduate, graduate and post-graduate: 1) students of Bachelor's programs for Oriental (Mandarin Chinese, Japanese) and European (French, Italian, Spanish, English) languages (1st, 2nd, 3rd and 4th years of study) – 92.5%; 2) students of Master's programs for Oriental (Mandarin Chinese, Japanese) and European (English, French, Spanish, Italian) languages (1st and 2nd years of study) – 5.7%; students of Post-graduate programs for Oriental (Mandarin Chinese, Japanese) and European (French, Italian, Spanish, English) languages (1st, 2nd, 3rd and 4th years of study) – 1.8%.

For the purposes of this paper the survey results were scaled to accommodate the sample of students of Oriental (Mandarin Chinese, Japanese) and European (French, Italian, Spanish, English) languages programs of Borys Grinchenko Kyiv University of Ukraine (Kyiv being the capital city). This limitation was adopted to assess the case of best practices of educational digitization to estimate the parameters and challenges of the individual experiences and quality assessment of e-learning and hybrid learning in the framework of COVID-19 lockdown, comprehensively implemented at Borys Grinchenko Kyiv university since the first days of the global lockdown in March of 2020 and thereon, as a parcel of the university overall digital campus implementation policy.

The overarching research project hypothesis is the observable variation in the individual perception of e-learning and hybrid learning quality of foreign languages acquisition programs by different groups of stakeholders in different regions of Ukraine and in the capital city due to an arrangement of educational (core competencies, soft skills proficiency), social and psychological (information fatigue, stress, community influence) and technological factors (digital literacy, digital divide, digital gap, pre-existing level of educational process digitization and e-learning experiences).

2.3 Survey Results and Discussion

Group 1 of survey questions - *overall assessment of individual experiences and quality estimation of e-learning and hybrid learning in the framework of COVID-19 lockdown and quarantine measures (March 2020 – January 2021) for university programs of European (English, French, Spanish, Italian) and Oriental (Mandarin Chinese, Japanese) languages* - yielded the following representative results across the board.

The assessment of overall comprehensive individual experience (or a take-away) of e-learning and hybrid learning in the framework of COVID-19 lockdown by different groups of stakeholders was conducted according to the 5-Point Likert Scale (a response scale in which responders specify their level of engagement with a statement or a parameter in five points: (1) Strongly disagree; (2) Disagree; (3) Neither agree nor disagree; (4) Agree; (5) Strongly agree (Handbook 2010). The extremum points for evaluation were 1 (maximum negative overall experience of e-learning and hybrid learning) and 5 (maximum positive overall experience of e-learning and hybrid learning).

Students of European and Oriental languages programs of all levels at Borys Grinchenko Kyiv University evaluated their comprehensive individual experience of e-learning as predominantly 4 – mostly agreeable (35.3% of respondents), 3 – Average (30.9%), 5 – most agreeable – 20.8%. The average estimation of the overall individual satisfaction with e-learning and hybrid learning experience on Oriental and European Languages programs by students of Borys Grinchenko Kyiv University is 4>3 – ***mostly agreeable to average***.

Qualitative assessment of the e-learning and hybrid learning was conducted through the retrospective evaluation of respondents' individual experience through the span of March 2020 to January 2021, in order identify and select the preferred features and elements of e-learning and hybrid learning among the following (Figure 2): Ability to work from home; Ability to customize of the study space (video conferencing or LMS); Adaptability and flexibility of the work schedule; Time saving for commute; Parallel performance of several tasks and activities; Opportunity to technologically diversify educational activity, educational materials and methods; Ability to adapt the structure and content of curricula of disciplines to the conditions of online learning; Ability to activate and improve different types of soft skills; Opportunity to improve digital literacy; Ability to work independently in the learning process; No need for constant interpersonal communication; Ability to engage international professionals through digital means.

Quantitative assessment demonstrated that students of European and Oriental languages programs of all levels in the surveyed university have distributed preferred features and elements of e-learning and hybrid learning and identified the significantly top ranking ones as follows (Figure 2): Saving time for commute – 83.70% of respondents; Ability to work from home – 75.10%; Parallel performance of several tasks and activities – 60.20%; Adaptability and flexibility of the work schedule – 50.40%; Ability to work independently in the learning process – 48.10%.

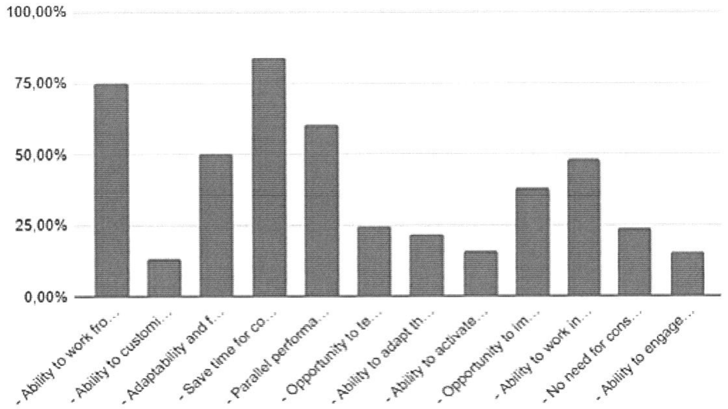

Figure 2. Top ranking of preferred features and elements of e-learning and hybrid learning: students of Oriental and European Languages programs (BGKU)

It is notable that most common preferred features of e-learning and hybrid learning by all groups of students of Oriental and European languages programs of all levels in the capital city university of Ukraine are two-fold: 1) time management due to the necessity to commute across a megapolis; 2) framework soft skills (WEF 2020), identified as relevant for the job market of the 2021-2020 timespan – flexibility, adaptability, active learning, multi-tasking.

Evaluation of respondents' individual experience through the span of March 2020 to January 2021 allowed to identify and select the features and elements of e-learning and hybrid learning, considered drawbacks, challenges or a hindrance among the following (Figure 3): Forced need to work at home (uncomfortable living conditions); Impossibility / difficulty of adaptation and flexibility of the work schedule; The need for specialized technical means of training and online communication / technical limitations; Lack of interpersonal communication with students and colleagues on a regular basis; Emotional burnout; The need to activate and improve different types of soft skills; The need to improve digital literacy; Increasing the amount of workload in preparation for training sessions and ensuring the learning process; The need to adapt the structure and content of curricula of disciplines in terms of online learning; The need to organize and control the independent work of students; Availability of mechanisms for control and accounting of the educational process

Students of Oriental and European languages programs of all levels at Borys Grinchenko Kyiv University of Ukraine have distributed drawback features and elements of e-learning and hybrid learning and identified the top ranking ones as follows (Figure 3):

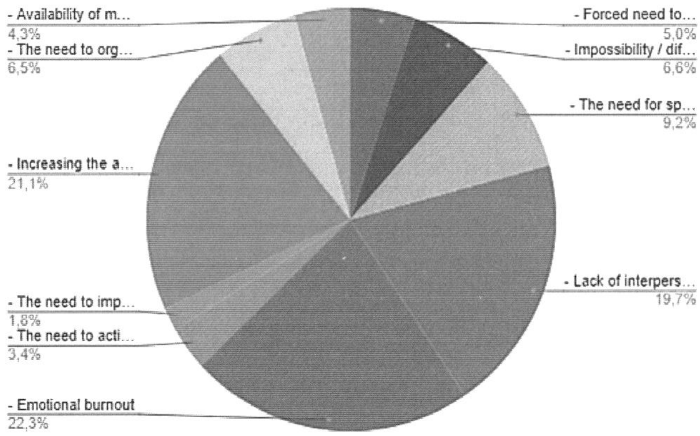

Figure 3. Distributed drawback features and elements of e-learning and hybrid learning: students of Oriental and European Languages programs (BGKU)

Top scoring features and elements of e-learning and hybrid learning, considered drawbacks, challenges or a hindrance by all groups of students of Oriental and European languages programs of all levels at Borys Grinchenko Kyiv University are: Emotional burnout – 70.80% of respondents; Increasing the amount of workload in preparation for training sessions and ensuring the learning process – 67.20%; Lack of interpersonal communication with students and colleagues on a regular basis - 63%.

The following prominent elements of educational process were identified and selected by respondents across all groups and Foreign Language Programs: Conducting lectures; Conducting practical classes; Development of training materials and materials for assessment; Execution of tasks (volumes, format, method of presentation); Organization of group work of students; Organization of independent work of students; Organization of creative work of students; Organization of research work; Communication with students (current); Communication with students (advisory); Informal communication outside the learning process / mentoring and moderation; Assessment (formative, summative, qualification).

Each element of the educational process was subjected to ranking by all groups of students according to the 5-point Likert Scale in terms of its efficiency for e-learning and hybrid learning quality assurance.

Students of Oriental and European languages programs of all levels have identified the following elements of the educational process and management as ranking highest (*5 - most conductive for quality of e-learning and hybrid learning in individual experience*): Conducting lectures (54.3% of respondents); Organization of independent work of students (45.6%%); Development of training materials and materials for assessment (34.6%); Conducting practical classes (34.1%).

The following elements of the educational process and management were identified as ranking 2nd highest by all groups of students (*4 - mostly conductive for quality of e-learning and hybrid learning in individual experience*): Summative assessment (37.1%); Formative assessment (35.9%); Qualification assessment (33.5%); Execution of tasks (volumes, format, method of presentation) (29.1%); Communication with students (current) (30.26%).

The overall workload of educational activities for Foreign languages programs in the framework of e-learning and hybrid learning mode (Figure 4) was estimated by all groups of respondents as *overwhelmingly increased* (in terms of 10% increments) as compared to the years of study, proceeding 2020: Increased by a 100% - 27.6% of respondents; Increased by 80% - 17.5%; Increased by 90% - 15.3%; Increased by 70% - 11.3%.

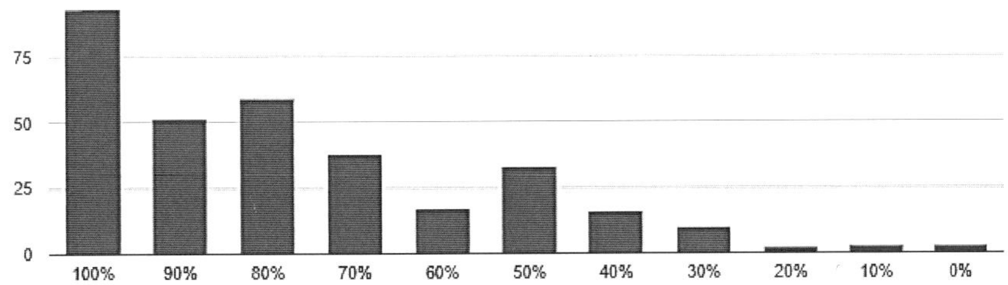

Figure 4. Increase of workload across educational activities for European and Oriental Languages programs (BGKU, Ukraine): students survey

Respondents of Oriental and European languages programs of all levels were asked to identify the e-learning and hybrid learning educational process elements that are conductive to quality of learning experiences outside of the COVID-19 framework and are preferable to be retained and implemented on a regular basis (Figure 5): Online classes through video conferencing systems; Online advisory sessions; Online implementation and defense of final / diploma projects; Use of electronic learning management system (LMS Moodle, Google Class etc.); Electronic tests and assessments online; Cloud technologies for collaboration; Cloud technologies for project presentation; Communication through electronic resources (mail, video, chat services, social networks); Use of e-textbooks and materials; Online interaction with the administration and methodological support; Time management; Possibility of study / research work at home or without binding to a place (ubiquitous learning); Ability to build an individual learning trajectory; Opportunity to utilize informal education resources.

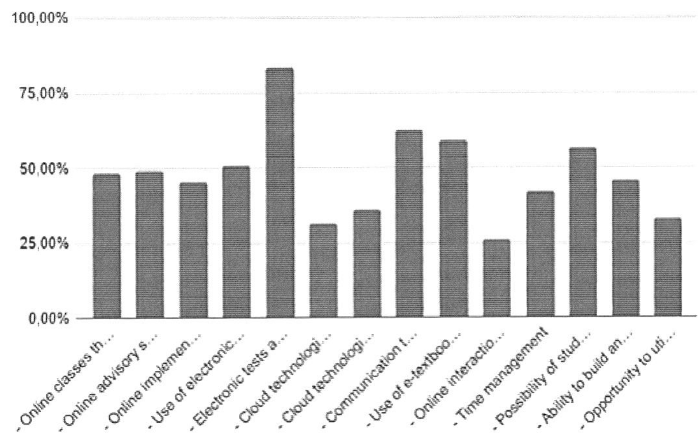

Figure 5. Elements that are conductive to quality of learning experiences outside of the COVID-19 framework: students survey (BGKU)

The following elements of hybrid and e-learning scored highest by students of European and Oriental languages programs at Borys Grinchenko Kyiv University scored highest as desirable to be retained and further implemented in the educational process outside of the COVID-19 limitation measures: Electronic tests and assessments online – 83.30% of respondents; Communication through electronic resources (mail, video, chat services, social networks) – 62.30%; Use of e-textbooks and materials – 59.30%; - Possibility of study / research work at home or without binding to a place (ubiquitous learning) – 56.80%; Use of electronic learning management system (LMS Moodle, Google Class etc.) – 50.80%.

Group 2 of survey questions - *assessment of individual experiences and quality of e-learning and hybrid learning in the framework of COVID-19 lockdown as compared to traditional, face-to-face learning formats* - yielded the following representative results across the board.

Respondents of all groups were asked to compare the individual experiences and estimations of quality and efficiency of traditional, face-to-face in-presence learning and hybrid or e-learning in the timeframe of the COVID-19 lockdown (respondents were instructed to disregard their individual assessment of blended learning or online learning prior to 2020).

The comprehensive comparison of individual experiences of traditional learning (TL) and e-learning (EL) was ranked according to the 5-point Likert Scale (5 – maximum quality and efficiency, 1 – minimum quality and efficiency). Students of Oriental and European languages programs of all levels at BGKU of Ukraine have ranked the comparative quality of traditional and e-learning in the following way: 4 – mostly qualitative and efficient (TL – 46%, EL – 32.6% of respondents); 5 – most qualitative and efficient (TL – 33.82%, EL – 22.8% of respondents); 3 – average in quality and efficiency (TL – 12.5%, EL – 27.6% of respondents).

The average score of individual quality and efficiency comparison for traditional learning (TL) and e-learning (EL) by all groups of students in regional universities of Ukraine is 4 – mostly qualitative and efficient.

The students of all groups were prompted to contrast their individual assessment e-learning and hybrid learning against the prior to COVID-19 timeframe paradigm of experience of traditional in-presence learning. In-presence learning (TL) was estimated as a conventional 100% of potential quality of education process and learning outcomes for European and Oriental languages programs. Accordingly, the respondents were to scale their assessment of e-learning and hybrid learning quality from 0% (no correspondence to TL quality in individual experience) to 100% (full correspondence to TL quality in individual experience) in 10% increments (Figure 6):

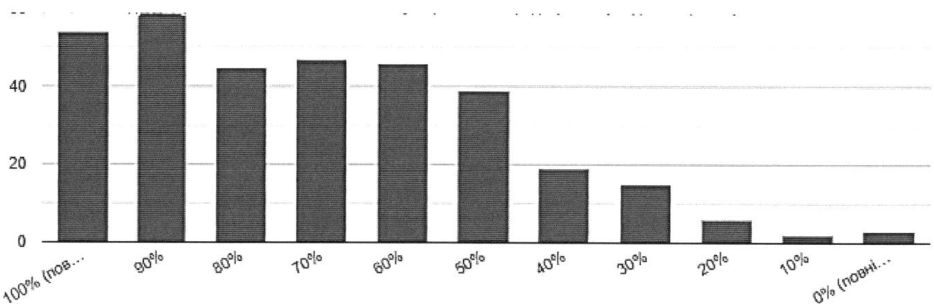

Figure 6. Distribution of contrastive assessment of e-learning and hybrid learning quality by students of European and Oriental languages programs (BGKU)

According to survey data of students of Oriental and European languages programs of all levels, e-learning and hybrid learning satisfaction in the timespan of COVID-19 score the highest quality approximation to traditional learning in such proportions: 90% of quality correspondence between EL and TL – 17.5%; 100% of quality correspondence between EL and TL – 16.02%; 70% of quality correspondence between EL and TL – 14%.

Therefore, the average estimation of the quality correspondence between hybrid learning and traditional learning by students of Foreign Languages major programs at Borys Grinchenko Kyiv University is 85% - majorly correspondent quality.

The accompanying social, educational and technological factors that contributed to this results in case of Borys Grinchenko Kyiv University are estimated as follows: 1) High level of digitalization (prior to quarantine measures), implementation of a functional e-learning environment (digital campus); 2) High level of blended learning implementation in the classrooms of European and Oriental languages surveyed (the implementation of a practice and applied skills oriented educational strategy at the university); 3) High level of digital literacy of students (individual and institutional – implemented through consistent digital literacy training at the university for all stakeholders); 4) High level of international mobility prior to quarantine measures that informed implementation of e-learning techniques and habitual usage of LMS.

Group 3 of survey questions - *individual quality assessment of learning process design, programmed learning outcomes and projected competencies for university programs of European (French, Italian, Spanish, English) and Oriental (Mandarin Chinese, Japanese) languages in the framework of COVID-19 lockdown and quarantine measures (March 2020 – January 2021)* - yielded the following representative results across the board.

Respondents of all groups were prompted to assess the degree of adaptation efficiency of each element of the educational process, heretofore identified as conductive to quality of e-learning and hybrid learning format in the framework of COVID-19. The scale of 5 (most efficiently adapted for e-learning and hybrid learning format) to 1 (least efficiently adapted for e-learning and hybrid learning format) was applied. Students of Oriental and European languages programs of all levels have identified the adaptation of the following elements of the educational process and management as ranking proportionately efficiently and mostly efficiently adapted for e-learning and hybrid learning format): Conducting lectures (77% of respondents); Organization of independent work of students (75% of respondents); Formative, Summative and Qualification Assessment (69.1% of respondents); Conducting practical classes (67% of respondents).

For the purposes of the survey inquiry, students of Oriental and European languages programs of all levels were prompted to evaluate the effectiveness of the formation of program competencies and learning outcomes in philology in the process of online and hybrid learning (from individual experience through the timespan of COVID-19 lockdown). The set of program competencies was estimated according to the official curriculum and syllabi, normative for the major programs in Oriental and European languages of any given year (Figure 7): Reflective practice; Self-development; Research activities; Time-management; Self-organization; Interpersonal skills; Teamwork; Stress management; Professional international mobility; Analysis of linguistic and communicative phenomena; Proficiency in oral foreign communication; Proficiency in written foreign communication; Public speaking skills; Intercultural competence; Translation (oral and written); Digital literacy; Literary competence; Pedagogical and methodological competence; Critical thinking in a professional context; Practical application of analytical conclusions based on linguistic and communicative data.

Each programmed competence was ranked according to the 5-point Likert Scale (5 – maximum quality and efficiency in achievement through online and hybrid learning, 1 – minimum quality and efficiency in achievement through online and hybrid learning) – Figure 7:

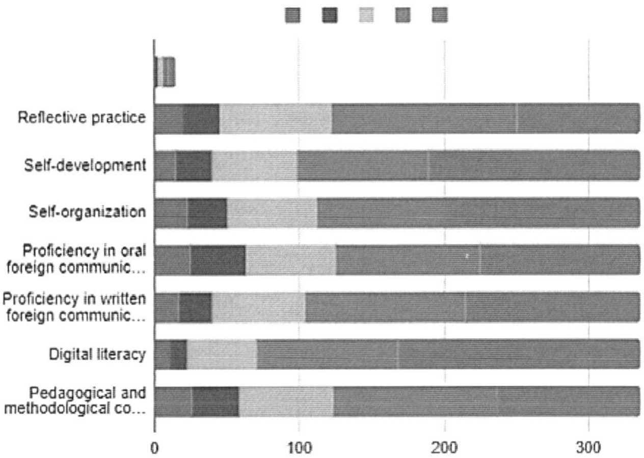

Figure 7. Effectiveness of the formation of program competencies and learning outcomes in philology in the process of online and hybrid learning (BGKU). Sample evaluation

Program competencies and learning outcomes in philology in the process of online and hybrid learning scoring highest (5 maximum quality and efficiency in achievement through online and hybrid learning) in individual estimation of students of Oriental and European Languages Programs through the timespan of spring and fall semesters of 2020 in COVID-19 lockdown) are as follows: Digital literacy- 50.1% of respondents; Self-development - 44% of respondents; Self-organization - 40.3%; Proficiency in written foreign communication – 36.5% ; Proficiency in oral foreign communication – 33.5% ; Pedagogical and methodological competence – 30%.

Respondents of all groups were prompted to identify the key challenges that impaired effective and qualitative adaptation of the learning process design into hybrid and digital distant format (Figure 8):

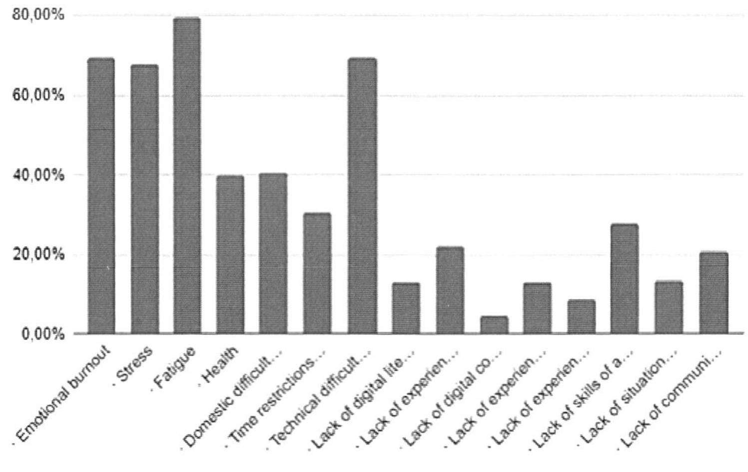

Figure 8. Ranking of challenges derived from the individual experiences of Oriental and European languages students in hybrid and e-learning (BGKU)

The following generic types of impediments (Figure 8) were derived from the individual experiences of Oriental and European languages programs students in the timeframe of COVID-19 in universities of Ukraine:

- *Social and psychological:* Emotional burnout; Stress; Fatigue; Health; Domestic difficulties / limitations; Time restrictions in connection with the introduction of quarantine restrictions.
- *Technical challenges and digital literacy:* Technical difficulties (lack of stable Internet connection, lack of necessary equipment, capacity of household computer equipment); Lack of digital literacy skills; Lack of experience in transforming the curriculum and training materials into an online format; Lack of digital communication experience; Lack of experience with electronic learning management systems (Moodle, GoogleClass, etc.); Lack of experience with auxiliary ICT tools for organizing the learning process (video conferencing, testing, surveys, online boards, etc.).
- *Soft skills:* Lack of skills of adaptation and self-organization; Lack of situational learning and training skills; Lack of communication and cooperation skills.

Students of Oriental and European languages programs of all levels at Borys Grinchenko Kyiv University of Ukraine have identified the following top scoring challenges and limitations (technical and socio-psychological) in efficient and qualitative transformation of educational elements into hybrid and e-learning format in their individual experience: Fatigue – 79.60% of respondents; Emotional burnout – 69.60%; Technical difficulties (lack of stable Internet connection, lack of necessary equipment, capacity of household computer equipment) – 69.30%; Stress – 67.80%.

It is notable that most of the challenges of the 'digital literacy' group feature as relatively insignificant (>13% score) in individual experiences of students of all levels at a university of the capital city of Ukraine. Such distribution of technical challenges estimation testifies to the phenomenon of *digital gap* (DGR 2019; WEF 2020), pervasive in various areas of educational activities in the framework of Covid-19 lockdown. That placed students as an age group, as mostly representatives of the "*digital native*" generation - term by M. Prensky (2001) - people born or grown up through early formative years into the digital society (1995 year of birth onwards), at a significant advantage in the hybrid and digital educational process through the implementation of emergency quarantine measures of in 2020 and 2021.

3. CONCLUSION

The global pandemic and subsequent quarantine measures and restrictions have significant influence on the structure and procedure of higher education workflow, which informed significantly the scope of individual experiences, projected outcomes and estimated quality of higher education in the realm of Foreign languages acquisition in all regions of Ukraine.

The survey results on the individual experiences and quality assessment of e-learning and hybrid learning in the framework of COVID-19 lockdown yield comprehensive data on the parameters and challenges of e-learning and hybrid learning transformation of Oriental and European languages programs, common for students of higher educational institutions of the capital city of Ukraine - Kyiv.

Overall individual experiences and quality estimation of e-learning and hybrid learning in the framework of COVID-19 lockdown and quarantine measures (March 2020 – January 2021) for regional university programs of European (English, French, Spanish, Italian) and Oriental (Mandarin Chinese, Japanese) languages are assessed as mostly agreeable to most agreeable by all groups of students across educational levels.

The qualitative assessment of the e-learning and hybrid learning was conducted through the retrospective evaluation of respondents' individual experience that helped identify the comparative coordinates of positive and negative dimensions of the latter. The invariant positive quality indicators for e-learning and hybrid learning across all groups of students surveyed are the opportunity for multitasking, digital skills improvement and lack of commute expenditure. The invariant negative quality indicators for e-learning and hybrid learning across all groups of students surveyed are the lack of interpersonal communication, technical impediments and psychological states (fatigue, burnout, stress).

The contrastive exposure of individual experiences and quality of e-learning and hybrid learning in the framework of COVID-19 lockdown against the backdrop of traditional, in-presence learning formats identify e-learning and hybrid learning as mostly to average comparative in quality for foreign languages stakeholders at Borys Grinchenko Kyiv University of Ukraine.

Assessment of learning process design, programmed learning outcomes and projected competencies for university programs of Oriental (Mandarin Chinese, Japanese) and European (French, Italian, Spanish, English) languages in the framework of COVID-19 lockdown allowed to identify the types of challenges that impaired effective and qualitative adaptation of learning process design into hybrid and digital distant format as predominantly socio-psychological for students of all groups surveyed.

The presented study is limited in scope to the indicative survey results, exemplifying the outlined quality assurance dimensions of e-learning and hybrid learning implementation for Oriental and European languages programs in the capital city university of Ukraine, induced by COVID-19 measures. The perspectives of the inquiry include fine-tuned estimation of the in-depth subjective quality assessment and subsequent efficiency assessment of hybrid and e-learning in different regions of Ukraine; contrastive case studies of Oriental and European languages programs emergency digital distance format adaptations in the COVID-19 timespan in universities of regional and national status; contrastive case studies and best practices of Oriental and European languages programs transformation to hybrid and e-learning format in countries of Europe and Asia upon alleviation of COVID-19 restrictive measures.

ACKNOWLEDGEMENT

Empirical findings and survey procedures have been conducted under the auspices of Integrated Research framework of Romance Languages and Typology Chair of Borys Grinchenko Kyiv University European Languages And Literatures Development In Cross-Communication Context (0116U006607) and Integrated Research framework of Oriental Languages and Translation Chair of Borys Grinchenko Kyiv University Oriental Studies Development in the framework of Higher Education Internationalization (0116U007073).

REFERENCES

Almalki, S. 2016. Integrating Quantitative and Qualitative Data in Mixed Methods Research - Challenges and Benefits. *Journal of Education and Learning*, 5(3), pp. 288-296.

Bekele, T. A., 2010. Motivation and satisfaction in internet-supported learning environments: A review. *Educational Technology & Society*, 13(2), pp. 116–127.

Bolliger, D. U. & Wasilik O., 2009. Factors influencing faculty satisfaction with online teaching and learning in higher education. *Distance Education*, 30(1), pp.103–116.

Boyarsky K., 2020. What is Hybrid Learning. eThink. Retrieved from: https://www.owllabs.com/blog/hybrid-learning

Costareie, S., 2011. Assuaring quality based on the assessment of learning outcomes. *5th International Technology, Education and Development. Conference (INTED)* Mar. 07-09, 2011, pp. 3235–3236.

Crowe, A. R., 2007. Learning to teach with mobile technology: A teacher educator's journey. In M. van 't Hooft & K. Swan (Eds.), *Ubiquitous computing in education*. Mahwah, New Jersey: Lawrence Erlbaum Associates, pp. 127–144.

Dillman, D. A., Smyth, J. D., Christian, Leah Melani, 2014. Internet, Phone, Mail and Mixed-Mode Surveys: The Tailored Design Method, 4th edition. John Wiley: Hoboken, NJ.

Dos Reis A., 2015. To Be a (Blended) Teacher in the 21st Century - Some Reflections. *International Journal of Research in E-learning,* 1(1), pp. 11-24.

DQ Global Standards Report, 2019. *World's first global standard for digital literacy, skills and readiness launched by the Coalition for Digital Intelligence*. Retrieved from: https://www.dqinstitute.org/ (accessed July 2020).

Duff C., 2020. *Everything you need to know about education, technology and distance learning*. eThink, Retrieved from: https://www.owllabs.com/blog/hybrid-learning

European Commission, 2020. *European E-Competence Framework Guideline*. Retrieved from: https://www.ecompetences.eu/ (accessed July 2020).

Handbook of Disease Burdens and Quality of Life Measures, 2010. Springer Science+Business Media, pp 4288-4288.

Law of Ukraine, 2019. *On Higher Education*. Retrieved from: https://zakon.rada.gov.ua/laws/show/1556-18#Text (accessed July 2020).

Makhachashvili, R., Semenist, I., 2021. Complex Framework of Digital Learning Quality Assessment in Covid-19 Context: Survey Study for European and Oriental Languages Programs. *Proceedings of the 6th International Conference on Complexity, Future Information Systems and Risk*. Lisbon, Portugal, pp. 107-116.

Makhachashvili, R., Semenist, I., & Bakhtina, A., 2020. Digital Skills Development And Ict Tools For Final Qualification Assessment: Survey Study For Students And Staff Of European And Oriental Philology Programs, *Electronic Scientific Professional Journal "Open Educational E-Environment Of Modern University*, (9), 2020, pp. 54-68. https://doi.org/10.28925/2414-0325.2020.9.5

Makhachashvili, R., Semenist, I., & Bakhtina, A., 2020. ICT Tools and Practices for Final Qualification Assessment in the Framework of COVID-19 Lockdown, *Innovative Educational Technologies, Tools and Methods for E-learning Monograph*. University of Silesia in Katowice, Poland, Katowice, pp. 183-194.

Markova, T., Glazkova, I., & Zaborova, E. 2017. Quality Issues of Online Distance Learning. *Social and Behavioral Sciences*, (237), pp. 685 – 691.

Ni, A. Y., 2013. Comparing the effectiveness of classroom and online learning: Teaching research methods. *Journal of Public Affairs Education,* 2013, 19(2), 199–215.

Prensky, M. 2001. Digital Natives, Digital Immigrants. *On the Horizon*, Vol. 9 No. 5.

Salyers, V., Carter, L., Carter, A., Myers, S., & Barrett, P., 2014. The search for meaningful e-learning at Canadian universities: A multi-institutional research study. *The International Review of Research in Open and Distributed Learning*, 15(6), 2014, 313–347.

Smyrnova-Trybulska, E., Kommers P. et al (Eds). 2019. *Universities in the Networked Society*. Springer.

Thiessen J & Ambrock V. 2011. Value Added – The Editor in Design and Development of Online Courses. *The Theory and Practice of Online Learning*, AU Press, Athabasca University. Retrieved from: https://read.aupress.ca/read/the-theory-and-practice-of-online-learning/section/7b34c0dd-89ad-4280-9c95-137c1e2aa471#ch11

Trentin G. 2010. *Networked Collaborative Learning: Social Interaction and Active Learning.* Springer.

Tu, Pierre N. V. 1994. *Dynamical systems : an introduction with applications in economics and biology*. Berlin New York: Springer.

Van 't Hooft, M., Swan, K., Lin, Y-M., & Cook, D. 2007. What is ubiquitous computing? *Ubiquitous Computing in Education*, pp. 3–17.

Voorn, R. J., & Kommers, P. A. 2013. Social media and higher education: introversion and collaborative learning from the student's perspective. *International Journal of Social Media and Interactive Learning Environments*, *1*(1), pp. 59-73.

World Economic Forum, 2020. *The Future of Jobs Report*. Retrieved from: http://www3.weforum.org/docs/WEF_Future_of_Jobs_2020.pdf (accessed November 2020).

A COMPARATIVE ANALYSIS OF THE E-GOVERNMENT DEVELOPMENT INDEX (EGDI)

Eltahir F. Kabbar
School of Computing, Electrical and Applied Technology
Unitec Institute of Technology
Auckland, New Zealand

ABSTRACT

During the past two decades, the United Nations Department of Economic and Social Affairs (UN DESA) published series of reports. Each report presents global survey results that measure e-government development in the 193 UN Member States. The surveys are intended to periodically assess e-government development progress in each of the UN Member States. One of the critical e-government development indicators used in these reports is the E-Government Development Index (EGDI). This quantitative study compares and contrasts the EGDI results (and its principal components indicators) during the past ten years.

The study compares the recent two e-government survey results (2018 and 2020) with the (2008 and 2010) results using correlations analysis and cluster analysis. The comparison is performed to achieve two main objectives: first, to measure the degree of EGDI indicators association during the past ten years and detect any significant changes in the overall Member States ranking during the same period. Second, to measure the degree of variation in cluster memberships. The study results show that there is a strong correlation between EGDI scores during the study period. Also, the results show minor changes in cluster membership, indicating that despite the apparent EGDI overall improvements for almost every UN Member State, the situation remains as before. The finds of this study will be of interest to both e-government academics and practitioners.

KEYWORDS

E-government, EGDI, United Nations, Online Government Services

1. INTRODUCTION

Internet technologies are used to provide a broad variety of online resources, ranging from simple educational websites to advanced platforms for managing communications within government agencies and between government agencies, individuals, and firms (Janowski, 2015; Sivarajah, Irani, & Weerakkody, 2015). The World Bank (2006) states that the primary aim of e-government is to fundamentally alter government relations with individuals, corporations, and other government entities. Many counties are working towards achieving such a transformative relationship with their citizens by introducing new e-government initiatives regularly (Eggers, W. D., & Bellman, J. (2015); OECD. (2016); Di Maio, A., & Howard, R. (2017); Gil-Garcia, J. R., Helbig, N., & Ojo, A. (2014); Williams, M., & Valayer, C. (2018)). The United Nations produces one of the well-publicized global periodical reports which monitor e-government development progress worldwide. The report is based on measuring e-government developments using a UN E-Government Development Index (EGDI) (UN 2016). The High-Level Panel on Digital Cooperation, which the UN Secretary-General convened in July 2018 to advance proposals to improve digital cooperation among governments, and other relevant stakeholders, has emphasized the importance of the EGDI. The panel recognized the E-Government Survey as a key ranking, mapping, and measuring tool, supporting the digital transformation of countries.

The EGDI metric is made up of three different parts. First, the Online Service Index (OSI) assesses the maturity of a country's e-government websites, including its national website and related portals, and related websites from departments such as education, labor, social services, and health economy, and the environment. Second, the Telecommunication Infrastructure Index (TII) assigns a ranking to a country's telecommunications infrastructure based on five factors: Internet customers, fixed telephone lines, smartphone subscribers, fixed Internet subscriptions, and fixed broadband services. Finally, the Human Capital Index (HCI) is measured using adult literacy levels and education enrollment in a region. In addition, the UN created an e-participation index (EPI) as a supplementary index to the UN E-Government Survey. EPI broadens the scope of the survey by concentrating on the use of online resources to help governments provide information to people. It focuses on three elements: (1) E-information: Enabling citizen engagement by supplying public information and access to information on demand, (2) E-consultation: Involving people in feedback to and deliberation on public policies and services, and (3) E-decision-making: Empowering citizens by co-designing some policy options and co-producing services. Thus the EGDI and its main components are geared not only to measure the maturity of a country's e-government services but also the capacity of Member States to deliver online services both in terms of the telecommunications infrastructure and the skills required by citizens to engage with the online services offered.

This quantitative study investigates the level of changes that counties participated in the United Nations e-government survey experienced during the last decade using correlation analysis and cluster analysis. The EGDI score data (and its principal components) was used in this investigation.

2. THE EGDI IN THE LITERATURE

Different scholars and government officials increasingly use the EGDI and its three components in a variety of contexts. The indices scores and ranking positions benchmark/compare and set ranking improvement targets even in some cases. For example, the Ministry of Telecom and Mass Communication of the Russian Federation used the UN EGDI to benchmark Russia's e-government development against other countries in the region and beyond (Ministry of Communications of Russia, 2017; Sukhankin (2017. Further, in Greece, the country's EGDI score and ranking position was used to show how Greece "lags" behind its neighboring EU counterparts (Zafiropoulos et al., 2012). In addition, several Middle Eastern countries often quote their ranking positions to demonstrate how they have improved from their previous lower ranking or aim at set ranking positions to aspire to achieve a better ranking (KSA National Transformation Plan (2016); Ducass (2017)).

Another context in which EGDI was used is related to examining the impact of e-government development on government corruption from an economic perspective Máchová; Volejníková; Lněnička, (2018). In addition, the EGDI was also used to measure the impacts of e-government on the shadow economy (Rohman and Veiga, 2017) and the impacts of national culture on e-government development (Zhao, 2011).

Despite the EGDI's undeniable popularity and ranking systems, some academics have expressed reservations about the methodology used to assess e-government growth using the EGDI. Whitmore (2012), for example, argues that the EGDI's calculation should be modified and suggests that factor analysis be used to ensure that the index accurately calculates what it is meant to measure. Kabbar and Dell (2013) proposed a revised EGDI called E-Government Development by GDP (EGDGDP) that incorporates the Gross Domestic Product (GDP). They argue that the adjusted EGDGDP provides a better assessment of the countries' e-government development because it measures a country's performance relative to what would be expected of that country according to its GDP rather than the absolute measure currently to each country.

The EGDI's widespread usage and success, as well as its vocal detractors, prompted this investigation. The aim of the study and the research methods used in this investigation are described in the following section.

3. RESEARCH METHODS

To meet the research objectives, first, Pearson Product-Moment correlation analysis was conducted using four datasets, 2008, 2010, 2018, and 2020 surveys dataset (UN, 2008; UN, 2010; UN, 2018; UN, 2020). These four datasets were used to enable the researcher to gauge the level of EGDI correlation using two intervals (2008-2010) and (2018-2020) with a ten-year duration. The correlation analysis was performed using SPSS version 24 to detect and measure the association between the indices scores during the study period. Second, to fully explain the correlation analysis results, the study used the Cluster Analytical method, which allowed the researcher to identify hidden patterns and natural groupings (segments) in the dataset that would have otherwise not been identifiable (Punj and Stewart, 1983; IBM, 2017).

The results of both the correlation and cluster analysis are described in the next section.

4. ANALYSIS, RESULTS, AND DISCUSSION

Using 2008, 2010, 2018, and 2020 UN survey datasets, the Pearson Product-Moment correlation analysis results showed a strong positive correlation between all corresponding e-government indices, as shown in Table 1. The results show that correlating the 2008 EGDI with the related 2010, 2018, and 2020 EGDI scores produces strong R2 (0.9680, 0.8670, and 0.8720, respectively). Similar results were obtained when the EGDI principal components were correlated with each other during the same period (see Table 1 for the detailed correlation scores).

Table 1. Correlation Results for E-Government Development Indices

		2008	2010	2018	2020
EGDI Correlation Results					
EGDI 2008	Pearson Correlation	1	.968**	.867**	.872**
N = 192	Sig. (2-tailed)		.000	.000	.000
EGDI 2010	Pearson Correlation	.968**	1	.876**	.875**
N = 192	Sig. (2-tailed)	.000		.000	.000
EGDI 2018	Pearson Correlation	.867**	.876**	1	.980**
N = 193	Sig. (2-tailed)	.000	.000		.000
EGDI 2020	Pearson Correlation	.872**	.875**	.980**	1
N = 193	Sig. (2-tailed)	.000	.000	.000	
OSI Correlation Results					
OSI 2008	Pearson Correlation	1	.873**	.826**	.833**
N = 192	Sig. (2-tailed)		.000	.000	.000
OSI 2010	Pearson Correlation	.873**	1	.797**	.790**
N = 192	Sig. (2-tailed)	.000		.000	.000
OSI 2018	Pearson Correlation	.826**	.797**	1	.924**
N = 193	Sig. (2-tailed)	.000	.000		.000
OSI 2020	Pearson Correlation	.833**	.790**	.924**	1
N = 193	Sig. (2-tailed)	.000	.000	.000	
TII Correlation Results					
TII 2008	Pearson Correlation	1	.971**	.882**	.824**
N = 191	Sig. (2-tailed)		.000	.000	.000
TII 2010	Pearson Correlation	.971**	1	.911**	.851**
N = 189	Sig. (2-tailed)	.000		.000	.000
TII 2018	Pearson Correlation	.882**	.911**	1	.958**
N = 193	Sig. (2-tailed)	.000	.000		.000
TII 2020	Pearson Correlation	.824**	.851**	.958**	1
N = 193	Sig. (2-tailed)	.000	.000	.000	
HCI Correlation Results					
HCI 2008	Pearson Correlation	1	.994**	.947**	.940**
N = 182	Sig. (2-tailed)		.000	.000	.000
HCI 2010	Pearson Correlation	.994**	1	.946**	.938**
N = 183	Sig. (2-tailed)	.000		.000	.000
HCI 2018	Pearson Correlation	.947**	.946**	1	.990**
N = 193	Sig. (2-tailed)	.000	.000		.000
HCI 2020	Pearson Correlation	.940**	.938**	.990**	1
N = 193	Sig. (2-tailed)	.000	.000	.000	

EPI Correlation Results					
EPI 2008	Pearson Correlation	1	.744**	.580**	.578**
N = 192	Sig. (2-tailed)		.000	.000	.000
EPI 2010	Pearson Correlation	.744**	1	.677**	.683**
N = 192	Sig. (2-tailed)	.000		.000	.000
EPI 2018	Pearson Correlation	.580**	.677**	1	.906**
N = 193	Sig. (2-tailed)	.000	.000		.000
EPI 2020	Pearson Correlation	.578**	.683**	.906**	1
N = 193	Sig. (2-tailed)	.000	.000	.000	

**. Correlation is significant at the 0.01 level (2-tailed).

A two-step cluster analysis method was performed to understand the correlation analysis results better. The researcher used SPSS 24.0 to segment the 2008-2010 and the 2018-2020 datasets. The clusters obtained using these datasets were built using the EGDI index score for each country as the input variables. In addition, all of the EGDI sub-components (OSI, TII, and HCI) and the EPI were used as the evaluation fields. The model summary for both periods presented in Figure 1 and Figure 2 shows that the solutions obtained by SPSS were adequate. The silhouette measure of cohesion and separation measure, the cluster size results, and the ratio of sizes of the largest cluster to the smallest cluster are acceptable, and no single factor is predominant.

The 2008-2010 and 2018-2020 cluster analysis results reveal that the datasets are naturally grouped into four distinct segments. The countries with very high to high EGDI scores fall in cluster 3 and cluster 4, representing 22.4% and 38.5% of the participating countries, followed by the middle and low EGDI countries, which fall in cluster 2 and cluster 1 and represents 33.3% and 5.7% of the participating countries.

In comparison, the 2018-2020 cluster analysis results show that cluster 3 and 4 represents 31.3% and 26.0% while cluster 2 and cluster 1 represents 23.4% and 19.3%. The cluster comparison analysis shows that cluster 1 membership has increased (from 5.7% to 19.3%) in 2018-2020 compared to the cluster size in 2008-2010. This increase in the cluster size indicates that despite the apparent improvement in the EGDI score of counties in this cluster, these counties are still considered relatively low EGDI compared to other countries. We argue that with the increased investment in telecommunication infrastructure and improved online services, countries' EGDI scores are bound to improve continually. Eventually, most counties will be classified as high to very high EGDI countries. Therefore, instead of relying on a cut-off score classification system, perhaps a relative cluster-based classification approach is adequate.

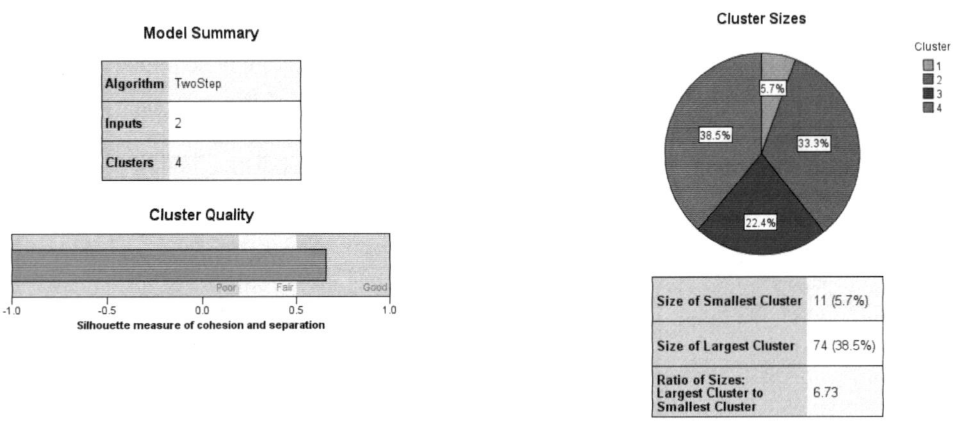

Figure 1. Model Summary and Cluster Sizes 2008-2010

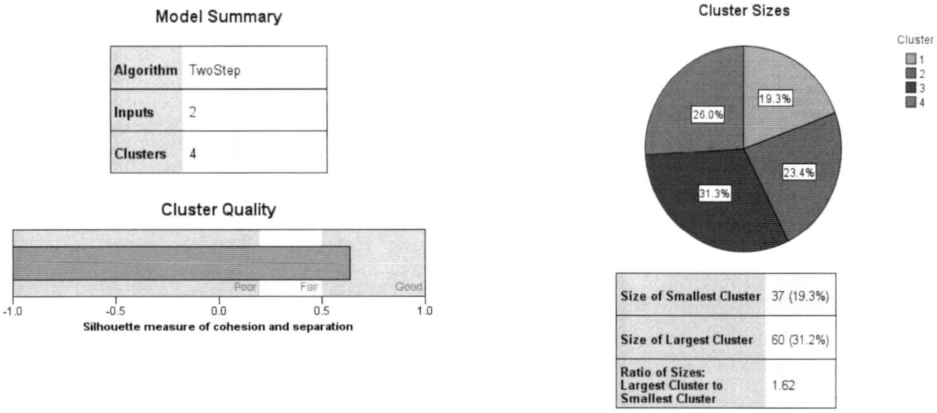

Figure 2. Model Summary and Cluster Sizes 2018-2020

The cluster analysis results also showed that the four clusters' membership distribution in 2008-2010 and 2018-2020 are comparable, as shown in Figure 3. A closer look at the movement of countries between clusters revealed that the vast majority of countries (66%) in 2018-2020 retained the remained in the same cluster-group that they belonged to 2008-2010. Only 33% of the studied counties experienced a change in a cluster in 2018-2020 compared to 2008-2010, and 1% of the countries studied had no cluster classification in 2008-2010.

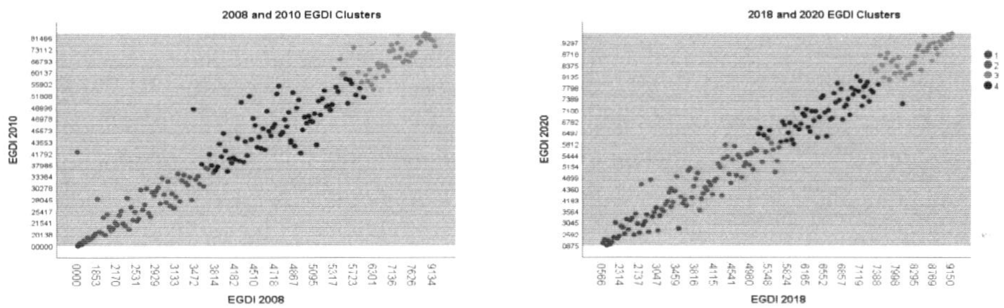

Figure 3. Cluster Segmentation Using EGDI for 2008-2010 and 2018-2020

The recent United Nations 2020 report showed that Denmark, the Republic of Korea, and Estonia lead the 193 UN Member States regarding the scope and quality of online services, the status of telecommunication infrastructure, and the existing human capacity. Finland, Australia, Sweden, the United Kingdom, New Zealand, the United States of America, the Netherlands, Singapore, and Iceland round out the top ten. As expected, all the top ten counties retained their cluster membership despite minor changes in their rank and EGDI scores. In contrast, and among the least developed countries (Bhutan, Bangladesh, and Cambodia) celebrated in the recent United Nations 2020 report as the counties that have become leaders in digital government development, advancing from the middle to the high EGDI. The cluster analysis conducted in this study shows that despite the improvement in these counties' ranks and EGDI scores, all three counties remain in the same cluster they were part of previously, as shown in Table 2.

Table 2. Cluster Membership Comparison of Selected Developed and Developing Countries

Country		Rank and EGDI Score				Cluster Membership	
		2008	2010	2018	2020	2008-2010	2018-2020
Denmark	Rank	2	7	1	1	3	3
	EGDI	0.9134	0.7872	0.9150	0.9758		
Republic of Korea	Rank	6	1	3	2	3	3
	EGDI	0.8317	0.8785	0.9010	0.9560		
Estonia	Rank	7	20	16	3	3	3
	EGDI	0.7600	0.6965	0.8486	0.9473		
Bangladesh	Rank	142	134	115	119	2	2
	EGDI	0.2936	0.3028	0.4862	0.5189		
Bhutan	Rank	134	152	126	103	2	2
	EGDI	0.3074	0.2598	0.4274	0.5777		
Cambodia	Rank	139	140	145	124	2	2
	EGDI	0.2989	0.2878	0.3753	0.5113		

While the EGDI and its principal components are valuable indicators of how countries worldwide track e-government development endeavors, the results obtained in this study suggest that the measure can be tweaked. Perhaps incorporating indicators on the actual usage of e-government services, government corruption measures, and economic indicators such as GDP into the EGDI provides a more accurate measurement of e-government development.

5. CONCLUSION

This quantitative study compared the most recent two e-government survey data (2018 and 2020) with the (2008 and 2010) datasets. The comparison is carried to measure the degree of correlation of the EGDI scores over the past decade. In addition, the degree of variation in cluster memberships was measured. The findings of this study suggest that there is a high association between EGDI scores. Furthermore, the results demonstrate minor changes in cluster membership for most countries studied over the last decade. Despite the popularity of the EGDI among practitioners, we argue incorporating actual online government services usage, economic indicators, and government corruption index into each country's EGDI to produced an adjusted EGDI provides a more accurate measure of e-government development.

REFERENCES

Di Maio, A., & Howard, R. (2017). *Introducing the Gartner Digital Government Maturity Model 2.0.* Gartner. [Online], [Retrieved May 25, 2021], https://www.gartner.com/doc/3764382/introducing-gartner-digital-government-maturity

Ducass, A. (2017). 'E-Gov Development in Africa.' *The Electronic Journal of e-Government15 (2)* pp. 59-62.

Eggers, W. D., & Bellman, J. (2015). *The journey to government's digital transformation*. Deloitte.

Gil-Garcia, J. R., Helbig, N., & Ojo, A. (2014). Being smart: Emerging technologies and innovation in the public sector. *Government Information Quarterly*, 31, I1-I8.

IBM. (2017). TwoStep Cluster Analysis. [Online], [Retrieved May 20, 2021],https://www.ibm.com/support/knowledgecenter/en/SSLVMB_21.0.0/com.ibm.spss.statistics.help/idh_twostep_main.htm

Janowski, T. (2015). 'Digital government evolution: From transformation to contextualization,' *Government Information Quarterly, 32*(3), 221-236.

Kabbar, E.F & Dell, P. (2103). Weaknesses of the E-Government Development Index. In Uesugi, S. (Ed.),*IT Enabled Services*. Springer, ISBN: 978-3-7091-1424-7, pp. 111-124.

KSA National Transformation Plan. (2016). National Transformation Plan, [Online], [Retrieved December 07, 2017], http://vision2030.gov.sa/en/goals

Máchová, Renáta; Volejníková, Jolana; Lněnička, Martin (2018): Impact of E-Government Development on the Level of Corruption: Measuring the Effects of Related Indices in Time and Dimensions, *Review of Economic Perspectives*, ISSN 1804-1663, De Gruyter, Warsaw, Vol. 18, Iss. 2, pp. 99-121, http://dx.doi.org/10.2478/revecp-2018-0006

Ministry of Communications of Russia. (2017). [Online] [Retrieved May 25, 2021], http://minsvyaz.ru/en/activity/statistic/rating/index-razvitiya-elektronnogo-pravitelstva/#tabs|Compare:Place

OECD. (2016). *Comparative Studies Report: Digital Government Strategies for Transforming Public Services in the Welfare Areas.* OECD Comparative Study.

Punj, G., & Stewart, D. W. (1983). 'Cluster Analysis in Marketing Research: Review and Suggestions for Application,' *Journal of Marketing Research, 20*(2).

Rohman, I; & Veiga, L. (2017). *Against the shadow*. In: Proceedings of the 18th Annual International Conference on Digital Government Research. Association for Computing Machinery, New York, NY, USA.

Sivarajah, U., Irani, Z., &Weerakkody, V. (2015). 'Evaluating the use and impact of Web 2.0 technologies in local government,' *Government Information Quarterly, 32*(4), pp. 473-487.

Sukhankin, S. (2017). Russia Adopts New Strategy for Development of Information Society. [Online], [Retrieved December 06, 2017], https://jamestown.org/program/russia-adopts-new-strategy-development-information-society/

UN, 2008. *United Nations e-Government Survey 2008: From E-Government to Connected Governance*. United Nations, NY. ISBN 9789211561364. DOI: https://doi.org/10.18356/047afd3a-en

UN, 2010. *United Nations e-government survey 2010: Leveraging E-Government at a Time of Financial and Economic Crisis*. United Nations, NY. ISBN 9789210544320. DOI: https://doi.org/10.18356/0e749d15-en

UN, 2018. *United Nations e-Government Survey 2018: Gearing E-Government to Support Transformation Towards Sustainable and Resilient Societies*. United Nations, NY. ISBN 9789210472272. DOI: https://doi.org/10.18356/d54b9179-en

UN, 2020. *United Nations e-government survey 2020: Digital Government in the Decade of Action for Sustainable Development (With addendum on COVID-19 Response).* United Nations NY. ISBN 9789210051453. DOI: https://doi.org/10.18356/8bdf045f-en

Whitmore A, 2012. A statistical analysis of the construction of the United Nations E-Government Development Index, *Government Information Quarterly 29 (1),* pp. 68-75.

Williams, M., & Valayer, C. (2018). *Digital Government Benchmark Study on Digital Government Transformation.* DG Joint Research Centre, European Commission.

World Bank, 2006. *A Definition of E-Government*,[Online], [Retrieved May 07, 2021],http://web.worldbank.org/

Zafiropoulos K et al., 2012. Assessing the Adoption of e-Government Services by Teachers in Greece, *Future Internet,* Vol. 4, No. 4, pp 528-544.

Zhao, F. (2011). Impact of national culture on e-government development: a global study, *Internet Research,* Vol. 21, No. 3, pp. 362-380. https://doi.org/10.1108/10662241111139354.

E-VOTING AND NON-RESIDENT CITIZENS' VOTER TURNOUT: A QUASI-EXPERIMENT IN ECUADOR

Régis Dandoy[1,2,3] and Sebastián Umpierrez de Reguero[4,5,6]
[1]Universidad San Francisco de Quito, Quito, Ecuador
[2]Université Libre de Bruxelles, Brussels, Belgium
[3]Waseda University, Tokyo, Japan
[4]Leiden University, Leiden, The Netherlands
[5]Diego Portales University, Santiago, Chile
[6]European University Institute, Fiesole, Italy

ABSTRACT

Over the last decades, e-voting has been used in a large number of countries and its impact on voter turnout has been closely scrutinized. Regardless, scholarly attention has largely focused on turnout in the domestic arena, and the link between e-voting and external voting have been scarcely explored. Based on a quasi-experimental design of the 2021 Ecuadorian elections, we investigate the effect of both on-site electronic voting and Internet voting on non-resident citizens' voter turnout. This paper shows that, while on-site electronic voting seems to have no significant impact on turnout, turnout of non-resident citizens using Internet voting significantly increased as compared to prior elections and to neighboring electoral districts.

KEYWORDS

E-voting, Internet Voting, Turnout, Ecuador, External Voting

1. INTRODUCTION

In preparation of the 2021 presidential, legislative and Andean elections in Ecuador, the electoral management body – the National Electoral Council – decided to run pilots regarding different voting modalities for Ecuadorian voters living abroad. These pilots consisted in organizing binding elections in three different electoral districts located abroad based a voting modality different that in-person voting in the polling stations hosted in consulate and diplomatic venues: postal voting, on-site electronic voting (direct-recording electronic or DRE voting) and Internet voting. In the form of a quasi-natural experiment, these pilots constituted a unique opportunity to investigate the impact on the voting modality on the decision of some voters to participate in elections.

Compared to the analysis of e-voting in the participation of non-resident voters, empirical studies analyzing the impact of e-voting on voter turnout in domestic electoral districts are relatively frequent. Yet, their conclusions diverge. On-site e-voting (DRE voting) leads to higher turnout in Japan (Tsukiyama, 2018) and Switzerland (Petitpas et al, 2020), to lower turnout in Belgium (Dandoy, 2014; Dejaeghere & Vanhoutte, 2015) and India (Debnath et al, 2017), while other scholars find no statistically significant effect of DRE voting on turnout in Brazil (Fujiwara, 2015), in India (Desai & Lee, 2019) and in the Netherlands (Allers & Kooreman, 2009). Similarly, contributions on Internet voting leads to divergent findings as various scholars suggest that internet voting has no effect on domestic voter turnout in Estonia (Bochsler, 2010) and in Switzerland (Germann & Serdült, 2017) while others find out that internet voting increases voter turnout in Brazil (Spada, Mellon, Peixoto, & Sjoberg, 2016) and in Canada (Goodman & Stokes, 2020).

Even if numerous scholars have already suggested the importance of Internet voting in long distance elections, notably for increasing electoral turnout since it facilitates the act of voting, turnout among non-resident voters has not been the focus of much research (Petitpas et al, 2020). Exceptions are to be found in the recent works of Fowler (2020) and Germann (2021), who found out that internet voting increased turnout – respectively – by 3 to 5% in the United States of America (West Virginia) and by 5% in

Switzerland. In the French case, Dandoy and Kernalegenn (2021) observed that Internet voter turnout among French non-residents is more likely to be higher in large and developed countries as well as in European countries.

The research objective of this short paper is to explore the impact of DRE voting and Internet voting on turnout for voters living abroad in an overlooked country case (Ecuador) at the occasion of the 2021 presidential, legislative and Andean elections and to contribute to the burgeoning literature on the consequences of different modalities of e-voting on voter's behavior. Based on the short literature review presented above, our hypothesis is that the voting modality has an impact on turnout: a higher turnout should be observed among non-resident Ecuadorians using Internet voting, while no significant difference in turnout should be observed among non-resident Ecuadorians using DRE voting.

In what follows, we present in a first section the characteristics of the Ecuadorian external voting system and we discuss the measurement of voter turnout. A second section analyses turnout figures in the two electoral districts where e-voting (DRE voting and internet voting) was used and compares then with previous elections, whereas considering gender and the type of elections. A third section compares turnout figures for four different types of voting modalities in the two analysed electoral districts as well as in neighbouring districts. This note concludes that while DRE voting seems to have no significant impact on turnout, Internet voting had a positive effect on turnout. Compared to districts using ballot box voting, overall turnout increased respectively by 13,09% and 12,12% in the district using Internet voting.

2. E-VOTING AND TURNOUT IN THE 2021 ELECTIONS IN ECUADOR

2.1 External Voting in Ecuador

External voting (i.e., voting from abroad or out-of-country voting) can be defined as the provisions and procedures that allow voters who are temporarily or permanently outside the country of citizenship to exercise their voting rights. Since 2006, Ecuador permits its non-resident nationals to participate in the presidential elections and these voting rights have been since 2008 enlarged to four other types of elections: legislative elections, in both a nation-wide district (the so-called 'national seats') and in three overseas districts the so-called 'territorial seats';[1] supra-national elections (i.e., for the Andean Parliament); elections for the Citizen's Council; and in referenda and popular consultations. These elections are often organised simultaneously, and turnout figures tend to be very similar across types of elections.

Although voting in Ecuador is compulsory[2], active electoral rights of non-resident Ecuadorians are facultative. Overall, non-resident citizens' voter turnout is relatively high compared to other Latin American countries; still, akin eligibility rights.[3] Non-resident citizens' voter turnout in Ecuador (from about 20% up to 60%, depending on the type of election) is higher than in Argentina and Mexico, and very similar to Bolivia and Peru (Bermúdez et al, 2017; Burgess, 2018). Furthermore, voter registration is fairly easy – permanent and one-off – but the voting method have been somehow been restrictive until 2019. One the one hand, non-resident Ecuadorian must change their domicile once living abroad and thereafter, they can vote in national- and supranational-level elections any time they want. Over the last years, registration is not only channelled at consular offices by the electoral management body, but also online. Additionally, consular staff has often mobilised, including in rural areas, in the main destination countries of Ecuadorians (for instance in Italy, Spain or the USA) in order to facilitate their enrolment prior to each election (Ramírez, 2018). On the other, in-person voting was the only method for non-resident Ecuadorians to partake in homeland elections, and it was largely contingent upon the presence of consular offices. The combination of these electoral rules and consular practices increased the number of non-resident Ecuadorians inscribed to vote from abroad in an exponential manner (from 143.352 voters in 2006 to 410.145 in 2021). Yet, non-resident citizens' voter turnout has decreased over time (Umpierrez de Reguero & Dandoy, 2020).

[1] Non-resident Ecuadorians can elect their six emigrant representatives in their national legislature, two in each overseas electoral district.

[2] Turnout in mainland Ecuador is often above 80%. Despite the Covid-19 crisis, turnout for the 2021 elections reached 81%.

[3] In Ecuador, such as in most Latin American countries, eligibility rely on both *jus sanguinis* and *jus soli* modes of citizenship acquisition.

In this paper, we differentiate between two main operationalizations of turnout. First, the overall turnout measures the percentage of voters that participated in the elections based on the total number of registered voters in a district. Second, the effective turnout takes into account the invalid votes (i.e., the blank and null votes) in the calculation of turnout: it is measured as the number of valid votes divided by the total number of registered voters. This differentiated operationalization of the electoral participation into overall and effective turnout follows recent works on turnout (see for instance Barnes & Rangel, 2018; Dandoy & Kernalegenn, 2021). The use of voting machines instead of traditional paper ballots constitutes an effective method to reduce voter errors and uncounted ballots (Álvarez & Hall, 2008) and Germann (2020) concluded that internet voting reduced the risk of voters making mistakes in Switzerland.

The analysis of effective turnout is particularly relevant in the case of Ecuadorian elections. Unlike in many other countries, Ecuadorian voters have the legal possibility to express a blank or invalid vote, independently on the chosen voting modality. There are no specific provisions for paper voting (i.e., the voter can leave his/her ballot empty in order to express a blank vote while the voter can indicate '*nulo*' or even make a large mark on the ballot in order to express a null vote). However, the e-voting system provides the voter with two additional options: two additional buttons appear on the screen – usually at the bottom of the list of parties or candidates – allowing the voter to express a blank or an invalid vote instead of a vote for a specific party or candidate.

Moreover, the share of invalid and/or blank vote is traditionally high in Ecuadorian elections – usually around 10% for the presidential elections and even higher in second-order elections. This is partly explained by the fact that voting is compulsory for large segments of the Ecuadorian voting population and that voters may express their discontent with this obligation by emitting a blank or an invalid vote. During the 2021 electoral campaign, several prominent political actors called voters to 'annul' their votes in order to protest against the fact that some parties and candidates were not allowed to participate in the elections. Altogether, these elements indicate the importance of distinguishing overall and effective turnout in our analyses.

2.2 Voter Turnout Abroad: Differences Over Time

The analyses presented in this short paper rely on official election results at the district level. To our knowledge, there have been no attempts to collect data at the individual level in the two districts using e-voting in the 2021 Ecuadorian elections. We are aware of the limitations of our findings since they are solely built on descriptive statistics. The small number of overseas districts does not allow for more in-depth quantitative analysis. Yet, given that male and female citizens vote separately, we are able to present results across gender for the different types of voting modalities.

We first turn to the observed differences in non-resident citizens' voter turnout in the 2021 presidential, legislative and Andean elections compared to previous elections for the two districts that adopted an e-voting modality (in the 2017 elections, these districts used paper-based voting). In the Buenos Aires district (DRE voting), 2.082 Ecuadorians were registered, whereas only 567 enrolled in the Phoenix district (Internet voting). This is a significant increase since previous elections were only 1.481 and 304 were registered respectively, meaning that many voters were potentially first-time voters. However, it is important to notice that the decision of electoral management body to run e-voting pilots in these districts was taken after the closing of the registration of Ecuadorians living abroad. This prevents the occurrence of two potential sample selection biases: non-resident Ecuadorians that would not have registered knowing that e-voting would be used in their electoral district, or that would have registered only in order to participate electronically to the elections.

Strikingly, we observe noteworthy differences between the two districts using different e-voting modalities. In the Buenos Aires district (DRE voting), overall turnout figures dropped by more than 10% (see Table 1) compared to previous elections. Conversely, overall turnout increased by more than 11% in the Phoenix district where Internet voting was used, compared to previous elections. There are no significant differences depending on the type of elections as turnout figures are by definition fairly similar given that they occur on the same day.

These observations are verified when using an alternative measure of turnout that considers null and blank votes. Effective turnout dropped by almost 10% in the electoral district using DRE while it increased by almost 10% in the electoral district using Internet voting. Yet, the effect of e-voting on participation decision in both districts is slightly lower than for overall turnout as there were – on average – less blank and null votes in 2021 compared to previous elections. Since non-resident Ecuadorians had the opportunity to participate in three different elections[4], we can also analyze the differentiated impact on e-voting on turnout for each type of elections. In the electoral district using DRE voting, the e-voting penalty is higher for the presidential and district-based legislative elections (reserved seats) and there are proportionally less blank and null votes in the legislative elections (national seats). In the electoral district using Internet voting, the benefits of e-voting in terms of political participation are particularly large in the presidential elections (+10.97%) whereas they are relatively more modest for the legislative elections (reserved seats) with an effective turnout bonus of +9.03%.

Table 1. Average turnout in the 2017 and 2021 elections in Ecuador

	Overall turnout (average)			Effective turnout (average)		
	2017 (Paper voting)	2021 (E-voting)	Difference	2017 (Paper voting)	2021 (E-voting)	Difference
Buenos Aires (DRE voting)	46.70 %	39.95 %	-10.75 %	41.90 %	31.96 %	-9.94 %
Phoenix (Internet voting)	19.49 %	30.65 %	+11.05 %	18.43 %	28.35 %	+9.92 %

We also replicated the analyses per gender as female voters in Ecuador traditionally tend to display higher turnout figures than male voters. Both measures of turnout drop significantly in the electoral district using DRE voting machines but its negative impact on overall turnout is slightly higher for female voters. Since the share of blank and null votes is higher for male voters, the negative impact of DRE voting on effective turnout is larger in the case of this group of voters (-10.48%) compared to female voters (-9.57%). In the electoral district using Internet voting, the positive impact on turnout strongly depends on the gender of the voter. On average, the measure of overall turnout increases by 8.31% among male voters and no less than 13.80% among female voters. In other words, the Internet voting bonus in overall turnout is higher for female than for male voters. This differentiated impact loses some its strength when looking at effective turnout, even if we still observe relevant differences between male voters (+8.70%) and female voters (+11.14%).

2.3 Voter Turnout Abroad: Differences Across Types of Ballots

We also compared our measures of overall and effective turnout across four different types of ballots (see Table 2): paper ballots emitted in-person in the consulate building (i.e., ballot box votes), postal paper ballots (i.e., postal votes), electronic ballots filled in-person in the consulate building (i.e., DRE votes) and internet ballots (i.e., Internet votes). We included in our analyses the three electoral districts where pilots have been running by the Ecuadorian electoral management body and their average figures for the two geographically closest electoral districts using ballot box voting. This geographical proximity allows us to limit the socio-demographic variation of the characteristics of the electorate in various abroad districts.[5] But more importantly, it allows us to control for similar trends observe in the neighboring districts and for the potentially differentiated impact of the Covid-19 situation on voter mobilization. There are indeed relevant geographical variations of turnout among districts that relied on ballot box voting: turnout is significantly higher in South American than in North American electoral districts.

Table 2. Different types of ballots used for the 2021 Ecuadorian elections

	Consulate	Distance
Paper	Ballot box voting	Postal voting
Electronic	DRE voting	Internet voting

[4] Voters were given four different ballots: one for the presidential elections, two for the legislative elections (one for the national seats, one for the reserved seats for Ecuadorian living abroad) and one for the Andean parliamentary elections.

[5] The nine analyzed electoral districts are: Buenos Aires (DRE voting), Montevideo and Santiago (ballot box voting); Phoenix (Internet voting), Houston and Los Angeles (ballot box voting); and Ottawa (postal voting), Montreal and Toronto (ballot box voting).

We observed that the introduction of alternative modalities of voting affected turnout figures compared to neighboring districts (see Graphs 1 and 2). In the electoral district where DRE voting was used, the average overall turnout for the three different elections (presidential and Andean[6] elections as well as the two ballots for the legislative elections) is slightly lower than in neighboring districts using ballot box voting while the average effective turnout is slightly higher. Differences are within the margin of standard errors, meaning that we do not observe differences in turnout between districts using DRE voting and districts using ballot box voting. This finding also helps us relative the observed decline of turnout declined compared to previous elections as this trend is similar in neighboring South American electoral districts. Regarding gender, the average negative difference in overall turnout is larger among male voters, while the average positive difference in effective turnout is larger among female voters.

Contrary to DRE voting, the impact of Internet voting on turnout is significantly more important and positive. On average, overall turnout is higher by 13% in the electoral district using Internet voting compared to neighboring districts using ballot box voting. Effective turnout is similarly higher (+12%) in the electoral district using Internet voting compared to neighboring districts using ballot box voting. Therefore, we can affirm that Internet voting seems to have a significant and positive impact on turnout in the US electoral districts. Regarding gender, average differences in both overall and effective turnout indicate that Internet voting has a larger positive impact on women than on men. More specifically, there are proportionally more blank and null votes in the group of male voters compared to neighboring districts using ballot box voting.

Finally, postal voting has a similar positive impact on turnout as the electoral district implementing this voting modality displays an overall and effective turnout more than 20% superior compared to turnout in neighboring districts based on ballot box voting. There are no significant differences regarding gender in both types of turnout measurement.

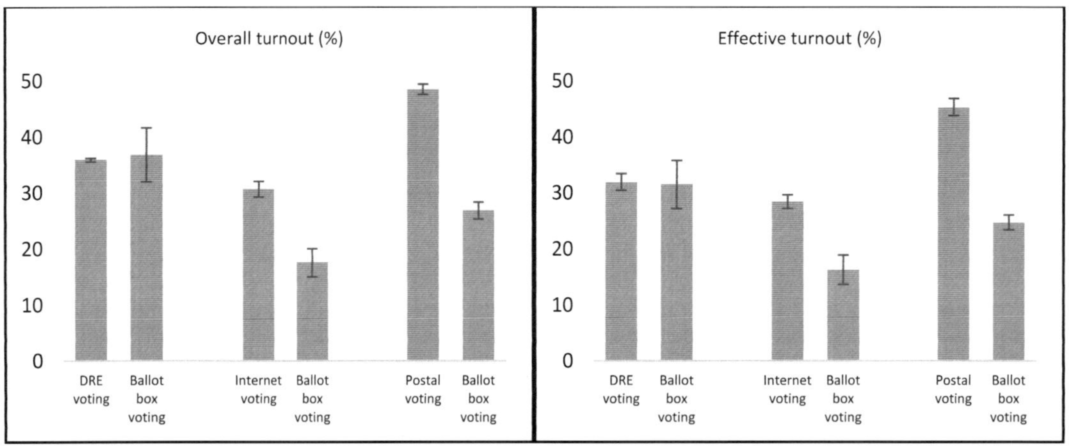

Graphics 1 and 2. Average turnout per voting modality in the 2021 elections in Ecuador

3. CONCLUSION

The elections of 7 February 2021 in Ecuador constituted a quasi-natural experiment as - for the first time in the political history of this country - two electoral districts abroad used e-voting (one relied on DRE voting while the other relied on Internet voting) while neighboring districts kept using on-site paper voting. This situation allowed us to evaluate the impact of these different voting modalities on turnout in abroad district. Even if the gathered data may appear modest (overall it concerns only a few thousand voters), our two main findings seem in synchrony with the blooming literature linking technology and external voting. Based on the burgeoning literature on turnout among non-resident voters, our hypothesis was that the voting modality had

[6] Given the late sending of the ballot papers in abroad districts, voters from the Ottawa district could not vote for the Andean parliament. As a proxy for these elections are calculated as the average figures of the two other plurinominal elections (the two ballots for the legislative elections).

an impact on turnout: we expected to observe a higher turnout among non-resident Ecuadorians using Internet voting, while we expected no significant difference in turnout among non-resident Ecuadorians using DRE voting.

Based on descriptive statistics, the findings presented in this short paper confirm our hypotheses. First, we observed that DRE voting seems to have no significant impact on non-resident citizens' voter turnout, even this measure drops compared to previous elections (2017). The effect of DRE voting is negative when evaluating overall turnout while it is positive when using effective turnout. However, both differences across electoral districts are poorly significant. Accordingly, our findings are in line with the diverging conclusions from previous scholarly contributions based on a diversity set of countries, and more particularly with the Brazilian case where no statistically significant effect of on-site e-voting on turnout was found (Fujiwara, 2015).

Second, we report that Internet voting had a positive and significant impact non-resident citizens' voter turnout. Voter turnout using Internet voting increased as compared to previous elections and neighboring electoral districts. Compared to districts using ballot box voting, overall and effective turnout increased respectively by 13,09% and 12,12% in the district using Internet voting. This increase is even higher in the case of the presidential elections and in the case of female voters (+15,31% and +13,3% respectively). These findings are also in line with the literature as it confirms (and even surpasses) the positive effect of Internet voting on non-resident citizens observed in Switzerland (Germann, 2021) and in the USA (Fowler, 2020).

These findings call for further research on the impact of voting modalities on turnout across non-residents. First, we encourage researchers to duplicate their analyses by distinguishing between overall and effective turnout. Distinct electoral dynamics could be at play depending on the voting modality and this distinction could be particularly relevant when voting is compulsory or in the case of an election characterized by a large share of invalid votes. Second, our analyses indicated that the type of elections may also have a role in the interplay between e-voting and turnout. The comparison of the Ecuadorian elections with other cases would confirm if the positive impact of Internet voting is larger in the case of first-order elections, as opposed to other types of elections. Finally, the Ecuadorian case seems to indicate that gender is an important variable in the explanation of turnout: the positive impact of Internet voting on turnout is higher among female voters while the negative impact of DRE voting on turnout is higher among male voters. We therefore call for a closer look at gender dynamics in future voter surveys investigating the impact of e-voting on voter's behaviour.

ACKNOWLEDGEMENT

The authors thank the three anonymous reviewers for the useful comments.

REFERENCES

Allers, M.A. & Kooreman, P. (2009). More evidence of the effects of voting technology on election outcomes. *Public Choice*, 139(1-2), 159–170.

Alvarez, M. R., and Hall, T.E. (2008). *Electronic Elections: The Perils and Promises of Digital Democracy*. Princeton: Princeton University Press.

Barnes, T.D. & Rangel, G. (2018). Subnational Patterns of Participation: Compulsory Voting and the Conditional Impact of Institutional Design. *Political Research Quarterly*, 71(4): 826-841.

Bermúdez, A., Lafleur, J.M. & Escrivá A. (2017). Contribuyendo a la democracia en países de origen: El voto externo de los migrantes andinos, *América Latina Hoy*, 76, pp. 35–54.

Bochsler, D. (2010). Can internet voting increase political participation? Remote electronic voting and turnout in the Estonian 2007 parliamentary elections. *Paper prepared for presentation at the "Internet and Voting" conference*. Fiesole (Italy), June 3-4.

Burgess, K. (2018). States or Parties? Emigrant Outreach and Transnational Engagement, *International Political Science Review*, 39(3), pp. 369–383.

Dandoy, R. (2014). The impact of e-voting on turnout: Insights from the Belgian case. *Proceedings of the 2014 International Conference on eDemocracy & eGovernment (ICEDEG)*. Quito (Ecuador), 29-37.

Dandoy, R. & Kernalegenn, T. (2021). Internet Voting from Abroad: Exploring turnout in the 2014 French consular elections, *French Politics* (published online).

Debnath, S., Kapoor, M. & Ravi, S. (2017). The Impact of Electronic Voting Machines on Electoral Frauds, Democracy, and Development. Retrieved from https://ssrn.com/abstract=3041197

Dejaeghere, Y & Vanhoutte, B. (2016). Virtuous villages and sinful cities? A spatial analysis into the effects of community characteristics on turnout and blank/invalid voting in local elections in Belgium 2006–2012. *Acta Politica*, 51, 80–101.

Desai, Z. & Lee, A. (2019). Technology and protest: the political effects of electronic voting in India, *Political Science Research and Methods* (published online).

Fowler, A. (2020). Promises and perils of mobile voting. *Election Law Journal*, 19(3), 418–431.

Fujiwara, T. (2015). Voting Technology, Political Responsiveness, and Infant Health: Evidence from Brazil. *Econometrica*, 83(2), 423-464.

Germann, M. & Serdült, U. (2017). Internet voting and turnout: Evidence from Switzerland. *Electoral Studies*, 47, 1–12.

Germann, M. (2020). Making votes count with internet voting. *Political Behavior* (published online).

Germann, M. (2021). Internet voting increases expatriate voter turnout. Government Information Quarterly (published online).

Goodman, N.J. & Stokes, L.C. (2020). Reducing the cost of voting: An empirical evaluation of internet voting's effect on turnout. *British Journal of Political Science*, 50 (3), 1155–1167.

Petitpas, A., Jaquet, J.M. & Sciarini, P. (2020). Does E-Voting matter for turnout, and to whom?. *Electoral Studies* (published online).

Ramírez, J. (2018), Estado, migración y derechos políticos: El voto de los ecuatorianos desde el extranjero, *Foro Internacional*, 4(234), pp. 755–804.

Spada, P., Mellon, J., Peixoto, T., & Sjoberg, F.M. (2016). Effects of the internet on participation: Study of a public policy referendum in Brazil. *Journal of Information Technology & Politics*, 13(3), 187–207.

Umpierrez de Reguero S. & Dandoy, R. (2020). Extending the incumbency presence abroad. The case of MPAIS in Ecuadorian elections, in Kernalegenn T., van Haute E. (eds.), *Political Parties Abroad. A New Arena for Party Politics*, Routledge, London and New York, 115-132.

A RANDOM CHOICE, LATE DISCOVERY, AND PENALTY ROUNDS: MAPPING WOMEN'S PATHWAYS TO INFORMATION TECHNOLOGY EDUCATION

Hilde G. Corneliussen
Western Norway Research Institute, Norway

ABSTRACT

What leads women to information technology (IT)? Successful recruitment is often perceived as relying on interest in IT. This study, however, identifies the pathways bringing women to IT that only partly rely on interest in IT and also involve other factors. In-depth interviews with 24 women in IT education and early research positions in Norway provide the empirical material for this qualitative study. Feminist technology studies and research on gender and technology provide a framework for the study, and the analysis is guided by the grounded theory method. The findings show that IT is a highly gendered field in Norway and that gender stereotypes affect women's expectations toward, and choices of, IT. Women enter the fields of IT despite stereotypes. However, for many such women, this follows a coincidence or a late discovery of IT as interesting, and some women have been on a "penalty round" in a different field before finally entering the fields of IT.

KEYWORDS

Educational Choices, IT Education, Women, Penalty Round, Safe Platform

1. INTRODUCTION

Of all the people employed in information technology (IT) jobs in Europe in 2018, more than 80% were men (EUROSTAT, 2019). The continually low proportion of women in IT has led to many studies exploring the factors that motivate women to enter the IT fields (Frieze & Quesenberry, 2019; Makarem & Wang, 2020). The challenge has been conceptualized as "*an 'input problem,' wherein women do not enter IT, and a 'throughput problem,' wherein women enter IT but then leave*" in greater numbers than men (Branch, 2016; McKinney et al., 2008; Pantic & Clarke-Midura, 2019). This study focuses on the first by exploring what makes women choose IT. Via analysis, five pathways leading women into IT education are identified. These pathways provide important insights about the particular ways in which women move through a landscape that they experience as unfamiliar and masculine.

This paper reports on a study conducted for the Norwegian Centre for STEM Recruitment in 2020 that aimed to build knowledge for future strategies to recruit women to the field of IT (Corneliussen, 2020, 2021). The study is based on qualitative, in-depth interviews with 24 women, students, and researchers in IT programs at science and technology faculties and universities in Norway. It is an explorative study that uses grounded theory as an analytical tool for identifying new patterns rather than relying on previous findings. Thus, the aim is not to generalize but rather to explore the *variations* in how women find their way into the fields of IT and to learn more about how and why these patterns develop. This paper contributes to literature in the field of gender and technology studies by expanding the knowledge of how women are recruited to fields of IT.

2. BACKGROUND

Research on the low proportion of women who choose IT education and careers has been ongoing for decades and has revealed barriers and drivers for women's entry into IT (Cohoon & Aspray, 2006; Google Inc. & Gallup Inc., 2016; Misa, 2010). Today, there is widespread agreement that the main challenges for women's entry into IT are the institutional cultures and structures (Frieze & Quesenberry, 2019) and the gendered stereotypes about IT (Master et al., 2016), making it a rather "bumpy road" for women (Branch, 2016). Studies from western countries have identified that youth lack knowledge about IT education and careers and that this lack of knowledge has more negative consequences for girls than for boys (Grover et al., 2014; Jethwani et al., 2016). Moreover, IT education is strongly associated with gaming and programming, making it more attractive for boys than for girls (Corneliussen, 2021; Denning & McGettrick, 2005; Jethwani et al., 2016). Stereotypes associating IT competence more with men than with women (Blum et al., 2007; Cheryan et al., 2015) make it challenging for women to identify themselves with fields of IT (Cheryan et al., 2009; Jethwani et al., 2016; Margolis & Fisher, 2002; OECD, 2016; Rommes et al., 2007).

This study focuses on the recruitment of women and their entry point to fields of IT. International studies suggest that the interest in and the ability-belief related to IT are important factors that are weighed more than many other factors for women's recruitment to IT (Master & Meltzoff, 2020). Research suggests that interest in IT needs to be sparked early in girls, before gender stereotypes reduce their likeliness to express such interest (Armoni & Gal-Ezer, 2014; DiSalvo et al., 2014). Important educational choices are made during high school, and Vainionpää et al. (2019) claim that "senior high school is the last opportunity to influence girls' major and career choice." However, studies on women attending boot camps for programming show that some women find such alternative pathways to IT more available than attending a university course (Lyon & Green, 2020; Seibel & Veilleux, 2019). Hyrynsalmi and Hyrynsalmi (2019) find that women also make career changes after high school to enter fields of IT and software. Thus, recent findings suggest that the ways in which men and women are recruited to IT careers may be different and that women might rely more on alternatives to traditional "college paths" (Seibel & Veilleux, 2019). This study contributes to research in this field by exploring the pathways that bring women in Norway into fields of IT.

3. THEORETICAL AND METHODOLOGICAL FRAMEWORK

3.1 Feminist Technology Studies

This study is based on theories from feminist technology studies emphasizing gender and technology as socially constructed and co-constructed (Cockburn, 1992; Corneliussen, 2011). Gender is a reflection of the socially constructed differences between men and women, which are developed through cultural discourses and negotiated in many different arenas (Connell, 2005). Women, however, are not a uniform group, as emphasized in the individual difference theory (Trauth & Quesenberry, 2007). This theory points to how factors such as ethnical background, age, and cultural and economic situations differentiate women from each other. Technology is also part of a gendered cultural discourse; it includes images of who work with technology, what they do, and what they know (Cheryan et al., 2015). The analysis below brings these perspectives together to explore how women navigate from early youth through the stage of high school and until entering higher IT education.

3.2 Informants and Interviews

This study is based on in-depth explorative interviews conducted with 24 women attending IT education programs in faculties of science and technology across different locations in Norway. The interviewees attended various IT programs, including informatics or computer science, bioinformatics, computer engineering, computer technology, cybersecurity, and business informatics. Overall, fourteen interviewees were students at bachelor level, five were students at master level, and five had a research or recruitment position in academia. Sixteen of the participants were between the ages of 20 and 24, and the average age was 27. The interviews began with a questionnaire aimed at confirming the factors identified by previous research as relevant for women's choice of entering IT education. This allowed for a more explorative interview, encouraging the interviewees to describe their experiences and explain their choices from childhood until they entered a university-based IT degree course. All informants are anonymized. The study has been approved by the Data Protection Services at the Norwegian Centre for Research Data.

3.3 Grounded Theory Method

The analysis is based on the grounded theory method inspired by Charmaz (2006). Grounded theory represents a systematic and flexible scientific method covering the entire research process, from formulating research questions to writing the analytical text (Strauss & Corbin, 1998). Charmaz (2006) describes the method as a strategy for exploring data while answering the question: "What is going on here?" Grounded theory supports explorative research because it starts with the data and the phenomenon being studied and not with a predefined understanding. The findings presented below were obtained by coding the interview transcripts, sorting the codes and developing categories, writing analytical notes (memos), and, finally, developing the notes into scientific text. The main codes and categories developed for this study relate to the *changes* and *movements* in the women's narratives about their experiences from childhood until entering IT education and aim to answer the question, "what made the women move into IT?"

4. FINDINGS: WOMEN'S PATHWAYS TO IT EDUCATION

The interviews commenced with the women drawing their chronological story from youth to entering IT education (see Corneliussen, 2020). This drawing worked as a map for discussing what affected each new turn on their way through the stages from being unfamiliar with IT, to becoming interested in IT, and finally to deciding to enter the fields of IT. The discussion revealed that only few women had established an interest in IT before attending high school. The majority had developed a gradual familiarity and interest during or after high school. Interestingly, some of the women did not recognize that they had any interest in IT at all before applying for IT education. Thus, although interest in IT has been identified in international studies as one of the most important factors for the recruitment of women to IT (Master & Meltzoff, 2020), 19 out of the 24 women interviewed in this study described other factors as more important for their entry into IT education. Furthermore, 21 women perceived IT as a masculine field before entering and expected men to dominate not only in numbers but also in terms of competence, which the women associated with boys' leisure time use of computers for playing and programming (Corneliussen, 2021). Thus, most of the women recognized IT as a highly gendered landscape. The findings shared below show how the women's pathways can be described according to the different ways of moving through this landscape. The pathways identified here are not entirely exclusive, and six women present two different pathways in their narrative (cf. Table 1 and Figure 1).

Table 1. Features defining women's pathways to IT education

Pathways	Features
1) Early interest in IT (17%)	Early interest, friends with IT interest; programming, HTML, and web design; early decision to study IT
2) Late discovery of IT (20%)	Limited knowledge and initially limited interest for IT; discovered IT as relevant; changed direction or education into IT
3) An alternative platform (33%)	Limited knowledge and initially limited interest for IT; platform in familiar subject; interest in combining IT with other fields; IT as an alternative to sciences
4) A random choice (20%)	Limited knowledge, no interest, and no intention of attending IT education before suddenly finding herself there
5) Invited because it suits girls (10%)	IT culturally defined as suitable for women; mathematics as a gateway; suitable for the best students

4.1 Early Interest in IT

Only five interviewed women described an early interest in IT. This interest had developed from playing with computers, coding in HTML, and learning to program. Some had started to think about studying IT already during secondary school: "I remember at secondary school, my brother asked what I wanted to be when I grew up, and I answered that I wanted to study something to do with IT. [I had] best friends who were very interested in programming, and that sort of 'infected' me too." They described the importance of IT interest in their environment and among friends for developing their own interest in IT. The women were interested in controlling technology because technology is important in today's society. This made programming one of the most valued skills for them to learn: "If you want to have a computer in your home, then you have to know how to use it one hundred percent. Not just two percent." One of the women had taught herself to program in high-level programming languages, such as Python and C++: "It started in high school, when friends started making video games. I was inspired and wanted to learn a little myself, since I was also playing video games. That made me want to take it to a professional 'level'." For some of these women, programming defined their interest in IT, and this also affected their educational choice; they moved directly from high school to higher IT education.

4.2 Late Discovery of IT

The next group of women have little knowledge of IT before they "discovered" IT as interesting. Some had this realization just in time for applying to higher education, whereas some changed their study program to IT at a later stage. Two of the women realized their interest in IT when participating in activities to recruit high school girls to IT at university level: "We were on the 'Girls days,' a conference we were invited to since we were enrolled in the science program. [...] We heard presentations by people working in IT [...]. That's when I got interested and decided that I wanted to apply."

Another woman had already decided to apply for either finance or law when she attended a presentation on IT education, and this presentation changed her mind: "I didn't think about IT as a possibility before we were supposed to apply for higher education. Back then I knew what to do [finance or law], so I just joined a friend who was going to a presentation of engineering, and that's when I found out that this was an option." Her newfound interest strengthened when she met someone working in IT, and she decided to apply to an IT program. Note that the two women described above were the only women in our sample who referred to recruitment activity organized by educational institutions as relevant for their choice of entering the IT field. Five other women "discovered" IT after they had already started at another bachelor's degree course. One of them had started at a different engineering degree course where she learned to program: "I remember, in the beginning we had programming and I did not understand the way of thinking, but I was forced to have that subject, so then I began to understand more. In the end I had a lot of fun, and that was the subject I did best. And then I wanted to change to computer science." This illustrates how interest develops after becoming familiar with IT; the interest is also related to establishing her ability-belief: recognizing that she could understand programming (Master & Meltzoff, 2020). Several women followed this pattern. One of them fell in love with programming while learning about it through an interdisciplinary program: "I can't explain the joy I got from the introduction to programming. [...] For me, it has been one of the best things. It's like no other subject I've ever had. It was the most wonderful thing about joining that study." These narratives, however, also involve a change of direction or even a delayed entry into IT, as the women had to restart on a new degree, a phenomenon I have labeled as a "penalty round for women" (Corneliussen, 2021). Many of the interviewed women described this penalty round; they did not enter IT in the first place because they did not know enough about it when leaving high school, which suggests a missed opportunity to recruit women: "I think that since I thought IT was so much fun when I started here, I probably would have felt the same at high school." Common to the women discovering IT late is that they had little interest in IT during high school because they knew little about it. Learning about IT from a different perspective or through practice—for instance, in programming—was crucial to their discovery of IT as interesting.

4.3 Alternative Platform

The next group of women also had little interest in and limited knowledge about IT at high school. However, their interest had developed from a "platform" within another discipline that they already knew and had mastered. Thus, they could approach IT as a new field while ensuring professional security and with a certain level of ability-belief (Eccles, 2015). For most of these women, science was an important platform: "Mathematics was probably the strongest subject I had ever since I was a child." While feeling safe owing to the familiar platform, they could give IT a try and test whether they liked it but in combination with other subjects: "Since I looked both at biology and computer science, it was the mixture of the two that seemed interesting."

Several of the women saw IT as an alternative to a pure science program: "In high school, I had science and liked it, but I didn't like science so much that I wanted a bachelor in math or chemistry alone. [...] I saw technology as a middle ground where you could both be creative and use sciences." There was still a level of uncertainty in their choice due to limited exposure to IT at school; therefore, many of them initially started by considering the disciplines they already knew: "I was on the 'chemistry day,' and I was like 'no, this was kind of old-fashioned, maybe a little boring.' And then I found that program online: bioinformatics. These are two topics that I'm interested in, like the bio part and the chemical part, and you can connect it with some IT."

Although they had learned about sciences in high school, IT was new and unfamiliar, making them uncertain about the choice. However, unlike traditional science subjects, many of the women recognized IT as more relevant in today's digital society; a cybersecurity student illustrates: "I have worked with security for many years [...]. So I was interested in IT and I needed that perspective [at work]. Because it is a lot about being able to understand the digital society. [...] For me, it has been a way of preparing myself for the new digital society." The societal perspective was important for the women: "It has to do with the framework for society, in a way." One was concerned with "how we choose to set boundaries for technology [because this] will determine what society will look like in the future, including what values and what rights people will have." Although this group of women expressed various motivations for attending IT education, a common point is that they became interested in IT when they realized that it can be combined with a subject they already knew well, functioning as a safe and well-known platform for entering IT.

4.4 A Random Choice

Similar to the previous group, the next group had limited interest in and knowledge about IT education. They had no intention of applying for IT education—not until they, by chance, ended up in IT: "I put a list of studies in front of me, and then I just let my finger slide down and it stopped at something called [an IT degree]. I turned up at the first class; it said I had to bring my own laptop. I had minimal knowledge about that, but I went to buy myself a laptop and turned up at school and the first thing the teacher said was 'Today we will program in Visual Basic.' I had no idea what programming or Visual Basic was, so I hurried to Google it while sitting there. I understood nothing, and went to see my brother-in-law, who helped me get started with Visual Basic. And then I was really hooked after the first class. Thus, it was totally random." Her entry into IT relied on a coincidence rather than a thoughtful choice. Another woman hardly knew that she had applied to an IT program: "I didn't know anything about the discipline until I started. I didn't know I had applied for it, even; I had only searched for a lot of subjects at [university]." Her goal was to attend a particular university and therefore she had applied for any study program that seemed slightly relevant, including IT, but had since forgotten about it and was surprised when she realized she had been enrolled. A total of six women described their pathway to IT education as a result of random events rather than a deliberate choice, and they applied to IT education without identifying an interest in IT. However, once they started, most of them developed such interest, as they mentioned during the interviews, with one even becoming "hooked" to programming on the first day.

4.5 Invited Because it Suits Girls

"It is something cultural; it was one of the most appropriate studies for girls in [her homeland]. I knew about it because of my sister, and she encouraged me." Three women expressed a similar experience with IT education, having been "recommended and encouraged" to study IT because it was considered "appropriate for women." None of them were born in Norway. In their homeland, IT had been presented as a natural choice for students, such as them, who were good at mathematics. One of them explained that IT attracted the best students: "That is also why I chose to go to IT, because it was a trend, but also because the best students go there. I had the best results at school, and that's how I chose the direction." These women were surprised to find so few women in IT in Norway—not because of the expectations of Norwegian gender equality but because they were used to seeing more women attending IT education: "It was a shock, for me: 'Really, am I the only girl in this class?'" We do not find this pathway to IT education among the women who grew up in Norway.

4.6 A Fragile Choice

Whereas interest in IT is often treated as a decisive factor for both girls and boys choosing IT education (Master & Meltzoff, 2020), the five identified pathways show that only some of the women considered interest in IT as important for their choice of entering the field of IT. The majority rather claimed that their pathway to IT was a coincidence or based on interest in other subjects. The women interviewed here also recognized that they had little knowledge about different IT disciplines, and only few had been encouraged in the direction of IT. For some, the unknown became a motivational factor: "It was because I thought it seemed pretty open and it seemed like you had a lot of opportunities and I just really wanted to try it out." One of the women used the motto of Pippi Longstocking (a children's book character, "the strongest girl in the world," by Astrid Lindgren) to illustrate how difficult it was to know what to expect in this unfamiliar field: "I've never done this before, so I'm probably really good at this."

Owing to the women's lack of insights about IT, several of them described IT as a fragile choice and that upon entering, they considered it a test to find out if it suited them: "After high school, when I started looking at studies, I didn't quite know what it was, but I thought it seemed interesting [...]. There wasn't much information about bioinformatics either, so I didn't really know what I was going for. [...] After all, I knew nothing about programming and computer science." Some of the women were still not certain after enrolling that IT education was right for them: "To be completely honest, I would say that I was not really interested until I started [...]. When I started here, I was a little skeptical too [...]. So it was like, ok, if I absolutely do not like it then I can always switch." The lack of knowledge about IT made entering the field of IT a fragile choice because they were prepared from the start to leave if IT did not turn out to be a good fit for them.

5. DISCUSSION

This study suggests that many women are not recruited to IT education through the expected route of moving from high school to university with a dedicated wish to study IT. Rather, for the majority of women in this study, their pathways to IT are characterized by the discovery of IT as relevant and interesting through other channels than those at high school. The findings suggest that although the women might initially have had low motivation to study IT, they established an interest when they realized that IT can be combined with something familiar, such as science, or something they find interesting, such as societal challenges. This finding is in line with research suggesting that a feeling of belonging is important for developing interest in IT (Master & Meltzoff, 2020). A surprisingly large group of women, one out of four, described how they had ended up in the IT field owing to random incidents and with no initial intention of studying IT. This also illustrates the difficulty in considering IT as a relevant field of study before being confronted with it. The last pathway, taken by women from other cultures, shows that women are invited and encouraged to choose IT education partly because it is considered appropriate for women. This installs a different pathway for women's entry into IT, one that is not recognized among the women born in Norway. This pathway also helps to identify the cultural character of the Norwegian women's narratives, highlighting some of the challenges and barriers for women's decisions to attend IT education in Norway.

6. CONCLUSION: AN INVISIBLE OPTION

This study reminds us that women are not a unified group; they have different backgrounds and interests, and they have found different pathways to IT education that also illustrate how educational patterns are shaped by culture. Although IT education is a varied field with many different disciplines, the trend identified here shows that many young women in Norway do not see IT as a relevant educational choice while they move from high school to higher education. Women's limited knowledge about IT at this point also includes little knowledge about the different IT disciplines. Consequently, many women rely on the stereotypical images of IT before attending an IT program. This suggests that women choose IT education *despite* barriers, in particular, a close association between IT and men (Corneliussen, 2020). The findings show that women know few people who work in IT, they identify few female role models in IT, and only few of them are encouraged to take up IT. They have to negotiate a culture recognized for causing low self-confidence in women and challenging women's feelings of belonging in IT (Corneliussen, 2020). The long list of barriers experienced by the women suggests that the right question might not be why there are so few women in IT but rather how women, despite all the experienced barriers, still find their way into IT. The many detours and coincidences that lead women to IT education indicate a significant unused potential for recruiting women to IT. The main challenge seems to involve women's lack of experience and insights into IT during high school. We also saw that many of the women became interested in, fascinated with, and found great joy in IT and that several women believed that they would have become interested earlier if they had only been introduced to it. The extra round many of them go before establishing sufficient insights into IT to attend an IT program is what I have termed women's "penalty round" (Corneliussen, 2021). Paradoxically, in many ways, the detour they have taken has helped them to identify IT education as a relevant opportunity for them. The detour has not only made them better acquainted with IT but also less afraid to enter a professional field that remains deeply rooted in the cultural notions of IT as a male-dominated field.

ACKNOWLEDGMENT

The study was conducted on behalf of the Norwegian Centre for STEM recruitment in 2020. This publication was funded by Nordwit, the Nordic Centre of Excellence studying women in tech-driven careers in the Nordic countries.

REFERENCES

Armoni, M., & Gal-Ezer, J. (2014). Early Computing Education - Why? What? When? Who? *ACM Inroads,* 5(4), 54-59.

Blum, L., Frieze, C., Hazzan, O., & Dias, M. B. (2007). A Cultural Perspective on Gender Diversity in Computing. In C. J. Burger, E. G. Creamer, & P. S. Meszaros (Eds.), *Reconfiguring the Firewall. Recruiting Women to Information Technology across Cultures and Continents* (109-133). Wellesley, MA: A K Peters, LTD.

Branch, E. H. (Ed.) (2016). *Pathways, potholes, and the persistence of women in science: Reconsidering the pipeline.* Lanham MD: Lexington Books.

Charmaz, K. (2006). *Constructing grounded theory: A practical guide through qualitative research.* London: Sage Publications.

Cheryan, S., Master, A., & Meltzoff, A. N. (2015). Cultural Stereotypes as Gatekeepers: Increasing Girls' Interest in Computer Science and Engineering by Diversifying Stereotypes. *Frontiers in psychology,* 6(49), 1-8.

Cheryan, S., Plaut, V. C., Davies, P. G., & Steele, C. M. (2009). Ambient Belonging: How Stereotypical Cues Impact Gender Participation in Computer Science. *Journal of Personality and Social Psychology,* 97(6), 1045-1060.

Cockburn, C. (1992). The circuit of technology: gender, identity and power. In R. Silverstone & E. Hirsch (Eds.), *Consuming Technologies: Media and Information in Domestic Spaces* (32-47). London: Routledge.

Cohoon, J. M., & Aspray, W. (Eds.). (2006). *Women and information technology: Research on underrepresentation.* Cambridge, MA: MIT Press.

Corneliussen, H. G. (2011). *Gender-Technology Relations: Exploring Stability and Change.* Basingstoke: Palgrave Macmillan.

Corneliussen, H. G. (2020). *"Dette har jeg aldri gjort før, så dette er jeg sikkert skikkelig flink på" – Rapport om kvinner i IKT og IKT-sikkerhet.* Sogndal: VF-rapport 8/2020.

Corneliussen, H. G. (2021). Women empowering themselves to fit in ICT. In E. Lechman (Ed.), *Technology and Women's Empowerment.* London: Routledge.

Denning, P. J., & McGettrick, A. (2005). Recentering computer science. *Communications of the ACM,* 48(11), 15–19.

DiSalvo, B., Guzdial, M., & Bruckman, A. (2014). Saving Face While Geeking Out: Video Game Testing as a Justification for Learning Computer Science. *The journal of the Learning Sciences,* 23(3), 272-315.

Eccles, J. S. (2015). Gendered Socialization of STEM Interests in the Family. *Journal of Gender, Science and Technology,* 7(2), 116-132. Retrieved from http://genderandset.open.ac.uk/index.php/genderandset/article/view/419/692

EUROSTAT. (2019). *ICT specialists in employment: statistics explained.* https://ec.europa.eu/eurostat/statistics-explained/index.php/ICT_specialists_in_employment [Accessed 10 May 2021].

Frieze, C., & Quesenberry, J. L. (2019). *Cracking the Digital Ceiling: Women in Computing Around the World.* Cambridge: Cambridge University Press.

Google Inc. & Gallup Inc. (2016). *Diversity gaps in computer science: exploring the underrepresentation of girls, Blacks and Hispanics.* http://goo.gl/PG34aH [Accessed 16 June 2021].

Grover, S., Pea, R., & Cooper, S. (2014). Remedying misperceptions of computer science among middle school students *Proceedings of the 45th ACM technical symposium on Computer science education* (343-348): ACM.

Hyrynsalmi, S., & Hyrynsalmi, S. (2019). What motivates adult age women to make a career change to the software industry? *2019 IEEE International Conference on Engineering, Technology and Innovation (ICE/ITMC)* (1-8): IEEE.

Jethwani, M. M., Memon, N., Seo, W., & Richer, A. (2016). "I Can Actually Be a Super Sleuth": Promising Practices for Engaging Adolescent Girls in Cybersecurity Education. *Journal of Educational Computing Research,* 55(1), 3-25.

Lyon, L. A., & Green, E. (2020). Women in coding boot camps: an alternative pathway to computing jobs. *Computer Science Education,* 30(1), 102-123.

Makarem, Y., & Wang, J. (2020). Career experiences of women in science, technology, engineering, and mathematics fields: A systematic literature review. *Human Resource Development Quarterly,* 31(1), 91-111.

Margolis, J., & Fisher, A. (2002). *Unlocking the clubhouse. Women in computing.* Cambridge, Mass.: MIT Press.

Master, A., Cheryan, S., & Meltzoff, A. N. (2016). Computing Whether She Belongs: Stereotypes Undermine Girls' Interest and Sense of Belonging in Computer Science. *Journal of Educational Psychology,* 108(3), 424-437.

Master, A., & Meltzoff, A. N. (2020). Cultural Stereotypes and Sense of Belonging Contribute to Gender Gaps in STEM. *International of Gender, Science and Technology,* 12(1), 152-198.

McKinney, V. R., Wilson, D. D., Brooks, N., O'Leary-Kelly, A., & Hardgrave, B. (2008). Women and Men in the IT Profession. *Communications of the ACM,* 51(2), 81-84.

Misa, T. J. (Ed.) (2010). *Gender Codes: Why Women are Leaving Computing.* Hoboken, New Jersey: IEEE Computer Society and John Wiley & Sons, Inc.

OECD. (2016). *PISA 2015 results (Volume I). Excellence and equity in education.* Paris: OECD Publishing.

Pantic, K., & Clarke-Midura, J. (2019). Factors that influence retention of women in the computer science major: A systematic literature review. *Journal of Women and Minorities in Science and Engineering,* 25(2), 119-145.

Rommes, E., Overbeek, G., Scholte, R., Engels, R., & De Kemp, R. (2007). 'I'm not interested in computers': Gender-based occupational choices of adolescents. *Information, Communication & Society,* 10(3), 299-319.

Seibel, S., & Veilleux, N. (2019). Factors influencing women entering the software development field through coding bootcamps vs. computer science bachelor's degrees. *Journal of Computing Sciences in Colleges,* 34(6), 84-96.

Strauss, A., & Corbin, J. (1998). *Basics of qualitative research: Techniques and procedures for developing grounded theory.* London: Sage Publications.

Trauth, E. A., & Quesenberry, J. L. (2007). Gender and the information technology workforce: issues of theory and practice. In P. Yoong & S. Huff (Eds.), *Managing IT Professionals in the Internet Age* (18-36). Hersey, PA: Idea Group Publishing.

Vainionpää, F., Kinnula, M., Iivari, N., & Molin-Juustila, T. (2019). Gendering and Segregation in Girls' Perceptions of IT as a Career Choice: A Nexus Analytic Inquiry. In A. Siarheyeva et al. (Eds.), *Information Systems Development: Information Systems Beyond 2020 (ISD 2019 Proceedings)* (1-12). Toulon, France: ISEN Yncréa Méditerranée.

RECORD THE TRANSCRIPT OF STUDENT ACTIVITY IN HIGHER EDUCATION BASED ON BLOCKCHAIN TECHNOLOGY

Meyliana[1], Yakob Utama Chandra[1], Cadelina Cassandra[1], Surjandy[1],
Henry Antonius Eka Widjaja[1], Erick Fernando[1] and Harjanto Prabowo[2]
[1]*Information Systems Department, School of Information Systems, Bina Nusantara University Jakarta, Indonesia, 11480*
[2]*Computer Science Department, BINUS Graduate Program – Doctor of Computer Science, Bina Nusantara University Jakarta, Indonesia, 11480*

ABSTRACT

Apart from the core competency, learning in the organization also brings students opportunities to improve their soft skills. Good soft skills can help students when working in a company with many people. Students can get soft skills by participating in various non-academic activities such as new student orientation, Student organization, seminar, and workshop. For every non-academic activity participated by students, they will get points and recorded in Student Academic Transcript (SAT). SAT is an integral part of a diploma certificate. The research method used in this research is a user-centered design to build an education value chain model for recording student activity transcripts based on blockchain technology. Blockchain technology is used to ensure data validity, reliability, and integrity for all student non-academic activities.

KEYWORDS

Blockchain, Higher Education, Student, Transcript, Activity, Point

1. INTRODUCTION

Learning in university is carried out by learning the hard skill (core competency) according to the major and leaning the soft skill. Soft skill learning is currently considered very important, especially in the industrial era of 4.0. The World Economic Forum in 2019 has predicted that several skills will grow and will disappear in 2022 (*5 things to know about the future of jobs | World Economic Forum*, no date). Some skills such as analytical thinking and innovation, active and strategy learning, creativity, originality, and initiative, etc., will still exist and needed in this era, while some skills such as manual dexterity, endurance, and precision, memory, verbal, auditory and spatial abilities, management of financial, material resources, etc. will be no longer needed because they can be replaced by technology / robots. This situation needs to be responded quickly by universities in providing students with the suitable soft skills according to industry needs (Ekaterina, Anastasya and Ksenya, 2015). Problem solving is one soft skill that needed the most by industries. Problem solving is not instant, it must be trained continuously, because of that, this skill must be taught in both academic and non-academic learning processes from the first semester. More creativity is needed to improve students' ability in solving problems (Škėrienė and Jucevičienė, 2020).

Apart from problem solving, creative thinking is also important because creative thinking makes students have high adaptive abilities in various situations. In addition, creative thinking can produce unique outcomes and it can be a differentiator from its competitors. This will be an added value for students (Cheng, 2019). Students also need to improve their self-management. Self-management can be formed from a student mindset while study so they can explore and manage themselves, this soft skill can give students the ability to become an intrapreneur or entrepreneur, and be able to face various kinds of obstacles (Almeida, Daniel and Figueiredo, 2019).

Humans are social creatures who cannot live individually, so they really need social skills to interact with others. One skill that is very important to interact with other people is a communication skill. Humans are highly valued based on the way they communicate with others.

With good communication skills, students can "sell themselves" which has a positive connotation. Other people can consider the good potential of the students based on the way they communicate. Communication skills must be trained from students entering the university until they graduate, both orally and writing (Tseng, Yi and Yeh, 2019). The implementation of hard skill and soft skill learning is integrated into the academic curriculum document, so for every learning carried out by students, there is a guarantee that students get hard skill and soft skill learning simultaneously. Evidence of hard skills learning outcomes is recorded in student transcripts, while evidence of soft skills learning outcomes is recorded in student activity transcripts (Rebele and St. Pierre, 2019).

Learning activities in university must be able to answer the challenges that occur in society. The participation of the community, including the industry, in learning activities is expected. The active involvement of the community in learning activities will significantly improve students' hard skills and soft skills (Singh Dubey and Tiwari, 2020). The challenge from the community can be a mini case in higher education (Ng, 2020).

To maintain data validity and data integrity in increasing industry and public trust in universities, it is necessary to have technology that can provide the assurance of data security to ensure the record of non-academic learning activities and points are valid recorded in the student activity transcript. The number of points earned by students is confirmed according to the activities carried out by students (Bongiovanni, 2019).

Blockchain technology can be a solution in recording student activity points and providing the data validity and integrity. Thus, companies or organizations will trust the results that have been made on blockchain technology. Companies or organizations will see through the student activity transcript for the data validity of non-academic learning activities held by university (Grech and Camilleri, 2017).

The research question of this research is how to build a blockchain model for university to maintain data integrity in recording student activity into student activity transcript?

This research used a qualitative approach, and the research method is using a user-centered design framework to answer the research questions. The result of this research is the education value chain model for the process of recording student activity transcript based on blockchain technology, which is suitable for business processes in university, starting from the student registration for non-academic learning activities in universities.

2. LITERATURE REVIEW

2.1 Education Value Chain

Students take teaching and learning processes in both intra-curricular and extra-curricular activities. Intra-curricular is an academic learning activity followed by students and lecturers and is managed by the department at university. While extra-curricular is a non-academic learning activity followed by students and is managed by student activity unit.

Exhibit in figure 1, the value chain starts with prospective students entering the university through admission process. Prospective students will take the entrance test. If the result is accepted, the prospective students will become students and take part in intra-curricular and extra-curricular activities.

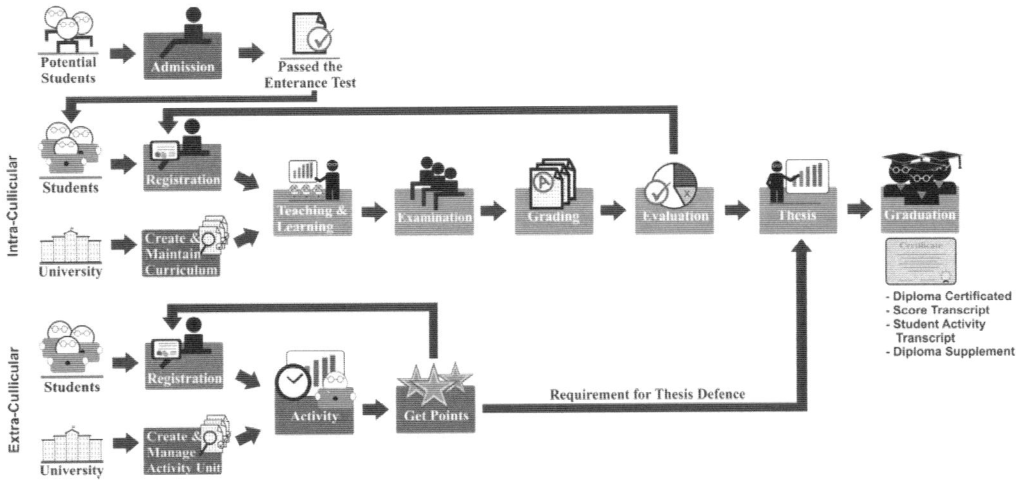

Figure 1. Education Value Chain (Meyliana *et al.*, 2019)

Intra-curricular activities or academic activities begin from the university create and maintain curricula in each department. Students register for each lecture for every semester and follow the teaching and learning process with lecturer and laboratory staff.

Students will take the exam twice in each semester (mid exam and final exam) to determine their comprehension on the course. After students take the exam, they will receive the exam and assignment scores. After that, the grading and evaluation process will be carried out for these students. This process will be repeated until students enter the final semester and take the thesis course. One of the requirements for students to be able to take the thesis defense is students must take part in extra-curricular activities to earned points. These points will be recorded in the student activity transcript. After student passed their thesis defense and graduate, student will get the diploma certificate, transcript score, student activity transcript, and diploma supplements (Meyliana *et al.*, 2019).

Student must also take extra-curricular learning activities. Students can register for activities organized by the student activity unit. The attendance and participation will be verified, and the points will be given to the students. These points will be collected and become a requirement for the thesis defense. The standard amount of point is determined by the university (Meyliana *et al.*, 2020) (Chandra *et al.*, 2019).

2.2 Student Activity Transcript

Non-academic learning activities will increase student soft skills. The points given to the student for their participation need to be managed and recorded properly. This recording process is very important because the data recorded is evidence of non-academic learning activities. It will be recorded in student activity transcript (SAT) (Meyliana *et al.*, 2019).

2.3 Blockchain in Education

Currently, not many blockchain research for university has been discussed, because blockchain is generally implemented in companies for finance and data security (Singh and Singh, 2016).

Blockchain is possible to be implemented in various fields after smart contracts was found, all business processes can be recorded into blockchain technology and this implementation ensures data integrity and data security. The capability of blockchain such as unchangeable, undeletable, and not easy be manipulated, makes Blockchain easily detect diplomas or official university documents that require data verification and authenticity (Devecchi *et al.*, 2017)(Palma *et al.*, 2019).

3. RESEARCH METHODOLOGY

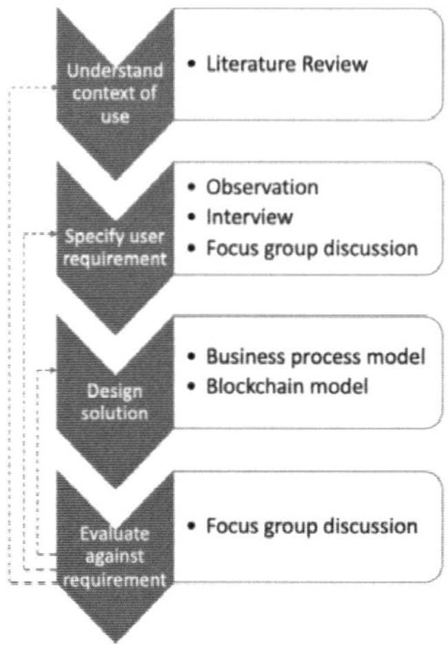

Figure 2. Research Methodology (User-Centered Design)

This research used User Centered Design Method (*What is User Centered Design? | Interaction Design Foundation (IxDF)*, no date). Exhibit in figure 2 shows the initial stage starts from understanding the context of use. In this case, the method used is to literature study about student activity in universities and how blockchain technology can maintain data integrity in universities related to that student activity.

After literature study, the research was continued by specifying user requirements by doing observations, interviews, and focus group discussions. Regarding student activity data that needs to be maintained by blockchain technology, an observation is done to see how the process from the beginning to the end until the student activity data can be recorded to student activity transcript. In addition, interviews and focus group discussions was conducted to confirm the processes from several universities so the results could be generalized to facilitate implementation in many universities.

The next stage is the design solution. At this stage, the education value chain model based on blockchain technology was designed focuses on certain business processes and according to focus group discussions result, especially on recording student activity transcript data.

The model was evaluated on the next stage. Focus group discussion was conducted again to get the feedback. The results of this focus group discussion also validate the education value chain model based on blockchain technology.

4. RESULT AND DISCUSSION

This research focuses on extra-curricular activities or non-academic learning activities in university, starting from the activity created and managed Student Activity Unit. Students can register and take part on the activities. The student participation will be rewarded as points and student can collect them. These points are recorded into a student activity transcript which will be distributed to students along with diploma certificate and academic transcripts when students graduated from the university. This process can be seen in figure 3.

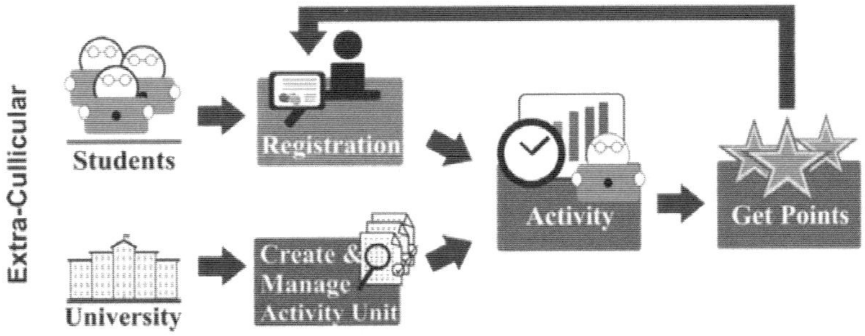

Figure 3. Focus of Research (Meyliana *et al.*, 2019)

Non-academic learning activities aim to improve soft skills and provide real experiences for students. Figure 4 shows a detailed business process of recording student activity transcript using blockchain technology. Student activity units / departments / universities can propose making non-academic learning activities by submitting activity proposals to the student affairs section. If the activity proposal is approved, the student activity unit / department / university can create activities in the event management system and input the event name, description, location, time, and how many SAT points can be earned by student. This data is stored in a blockchain technology database. Then the student activity unit / department / university will publish the event on social media platforms and university digital media.

After published, students can register on the application provided by the committee. If the event is a paid event, students are asked to make payments to the university account number. In this case, the payment is received by the university finance unit. The finance unit then confirms the payment to the event organizer. After Student activity units / departments / universities receive payment, the unit will confirm and validate the registration and payment (if any) from student and send the proof of registration and payment (if any) to the student. Activities to validate registration and payment (if any) from students are also stored in the blockchain technology database.

On the day of the event, students will attend the event and give the proof of registration and payment. The committee will input the evidence into event management system and add the SAT points. Student attendance data SAT points are stored in the blockchain technology database. The report will be given to the student. This will continue to be repeated until students reach the minimum number of points according to the standard of university. If the student has passed the thesis defense, the student grading unit will print the student activity transcript which will be distributed to students along with diploma certificate and academic transcripts. From the business processes described above, there are four main activities for data recording in blockchain technology databases, they are:

a. Record event

The data recorded is event code, event name, description, event type, time, location, event organizer name, target of participant, and amount of SAT Points. Event type is the scale of the event (international / national / local).

b. Record registration and payment from student

In this section, the data recorded is the student name, student ID, student major, student campus location, event code, payment type (if any), payment amount (if any).

c. Record student data and SAT Point

In this section, the data recorded is student name, student ID, student major, student campus location, event code, event name, description, event type, time, location, SAT points earned, SAT points cumulative.

d. Record student activity transcript

In this section, the data recorded is student name, student ID, student major, event code, event name, along with each point earned.

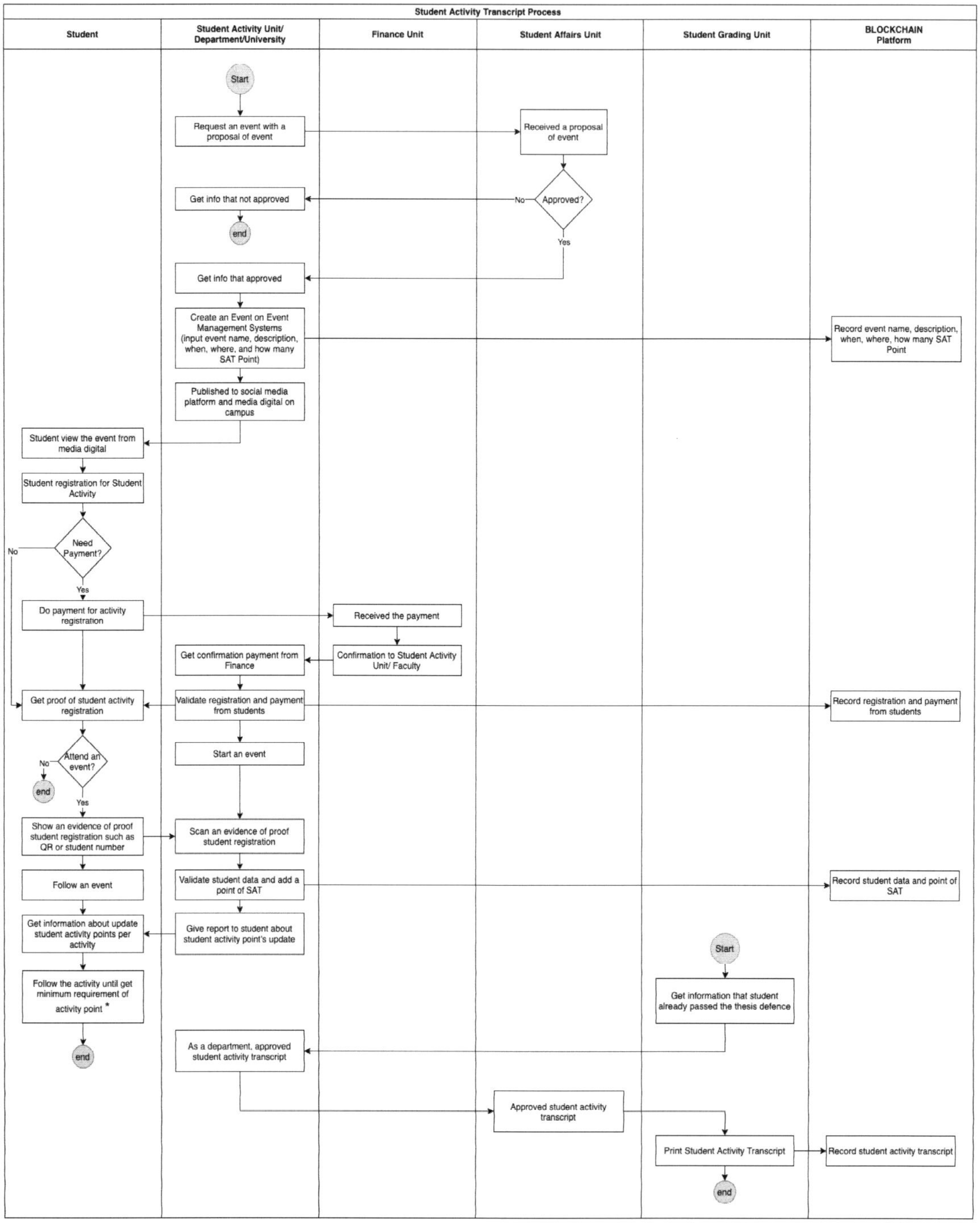

* *requirement for thesis defence and graduation judicial process*

Figure 4. Business Process Model with Blockchain

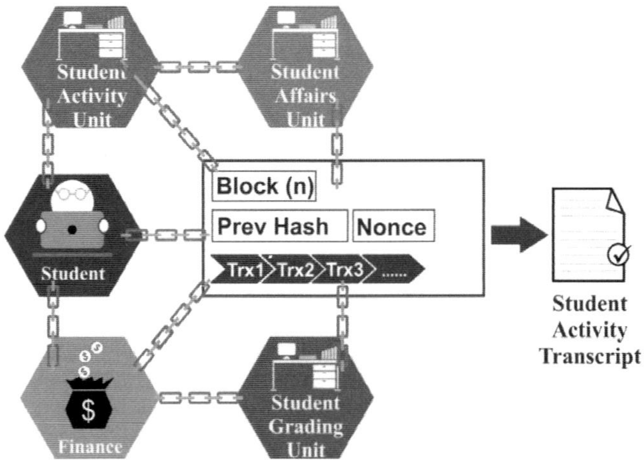

Figure 5. Transaction Illustration of Education Value Chain Model for student activity transcript record

Exhibit in Figure 5 is an illustration of transactions from the education value chain model for recording student activity transcript based on blockchain technology. The part involved in this transaction are student, student activity unit / department / university, student affairs unit, finance unit, and student grading unit. All parts are integrated with each other to produce correct and valid data points thus the point record into the student activity transcript has good data validity.

5. CONCLUSION

The process of student non-academic learning activities in university produces points that can be collected cumulatively as a standard for achieving soft skills for a student. All data points collected by students are recorded into a student activity transcript and recorded in blockchain technology.

The implementation of blockchain technology provides benefits and data integrity. It will increase public dan industry for the quality of the graduates. This is consistent with the characteristics of blockchain technology which makes data undeletable, unchangeable, not easy to be manipulated, peer to peer, and distributed. If there is data adjustment, new data can only be added and linked to the old data, the previous data cannot be replaced.

ACKNOWLEDGEMENT

This work is supported by the Directorate General of Strengthening for Research and Development, Ministry of Research, Technology, and Higher Education, Republic of Indonesia as a part of Penelitian Terapan Unggulan Perguruan Tinggi Research Grant to Binus University entitled "Implementasi Blockchain Platform untuk Menciptakan "Good Governance" pada Perguruan Tinggi" or "The Implementation of Blockchain Platform to Create "Good Governance" in Higher Education" with contract number: 12/AKM/PNT/2019 and contract date: 27 March 2019.

REFERENCES

5 things to know about the future of jobs | World Economic Forum (no date). Available at: https://www.weforum.org/agenda/2018/09/future-of-jobs-2018-things-to-know/ (Accessed: 25 November 2020).

Almeida, J., Daniel, A. D. and Figueiredo, C. (2019) 'The future of management education: The role of entrepreneurship education and junior enterprises', *International Journal of Management Education*. Elsevier, (November 2018), p. 100318. doi: 10.1016/j.ijme.2019.100318.

Bongiovanni, I. (2019) 'The least secure places in the universe? A systematic literature review on information security management in higher education', *Computers and Security*. Elsevier Ltd, 86, pp. 350–357. doi: 10.1016/j.cose.2019.07.003.

Chandra, Y. U. *et al.* (2019) 'Smart E-badge for Student Activities in Smart Campus', *Proceeding - 2019 International Conference on ICT for Smart Society: Innovation and Transformation Toward Smart Region, ICISS 2019*. doi: 10.1109/ICISS48059.2019.8969806.

Cheng, V. M. Y. (2019) 'Developing individual creativity for environmental sustainability: Using an everyday theme in higher education', *Thinking Skills and Creativity*. Elsevier, 33(April 2018), p. 100567. doi: 10.1016/j.tsc.2019.05.001.

Devecchi, C. *et al.* (2017) 'Blockchain Educational Passport Blockchain Educational Passport: Decentralised Learning Ledger (DLL) Preceding white papers Proof-of-Concept: Authors', *Development Heads: Sajin Abdu (Technology)*, (Dll). Available at: https://github.com/seratio/whitepaper%0Ahttps://issuu.com/seratio/docs/social_value_and_intangibles_review_3109c1666e0df2%0Ahttp://mypad.northampton.ac.uk%0Ahttp://eepurl.com/cCQgJv%0Ahttp://eepurl.com/cnrY7L%0Awww.cceg.org.uk/lab%0Ahttp://blockchain.sera.

Ekaterina, G., Anastasya, B. and Ksenya, G. (2015) 'Sociocultural Competence Training in Higher Engineering Education: The Role of Gaming Simulation', *Procedia - Social and Behavioral Sciences*. Elsevier B.V., 166(d), pp. 339–343. doi: 10.1016/j.sbspro.2014.12.533.

Grech, A. and Camilleri, A. F. (2017) 'Blockchain in Education', *JRC Science for Policy Report*. doi: 10.2760/60649.

Meyliana *et al.* (2020) 'A Proposed Model of Secure Academic Transcript Records with Blockchain Technology in Higher Education', (Conrist 2019), pp. 172–177. doi: 10.5220/0009907401720177.

Meyliana, M. *et al.* (2019) 'Defying the Certification Diploma Forgery with Blockchain Platform: A Proposed Model', in *Proceedings of the International Conferences ICT, Society, and Human Beings 2019; Connected Smart Cities 2019; and Web Based Communities and Social Media 2019*. IADIS Press, pp. 63–71. doi: 10.33965/ict2019_201908L008.

Ng, L. K. (2020) 'The perceived importance of soft (service) skills in nursing care: A research study', *Nurse Education Today*. Elsevier, 85(April 2019), p. 104302. doi: 10.1016/j.nedt.2019.104302.

Palma, L. M. *et al.* (2019) 'Blockchain and smart contracts for higher education registry in Brazil', *International Journal of Network Management*, (June 2018), pp. 1–21. doi: 10.1002/nem.2061.

Rebele, J. E. and St. Pierre, E. K. (2019) 'A commentary on learning objectives for accounting education programs: The importance of soft skills and technical knowledge', *Journal of Accounting Education*. Elsevier Ltd, 48, pp. 71–79. doi: 10.1016/j.jaccedu.2019.07.002.

Singh Dubey, R. and Tiwari, V. (2020) 'Operationalisation of soft skill attributes and determining the existing gap in novice ICT professionals', *International Journal of Information Management*. Elsevier, 50(May 2019), pp. 375–386. doi: 10.1016/j.ijinfomgt.2019.09.006.

Singh, S. and Singh, N. (2016) 'Blockchain: Future of financial and cyber security', *Proceedings of the 2016 2nd International Conference on Contemporary Computing and Informatics, IC3I 2016*, pp. 463–467. doi: 10.1109/IC3I.2016.7918009.

Škėrienė, S. and Jucevičienė, P. (2020) 'Problem solving through values: A challenge for thinking and capability development', *Thinking Skills and Creativity*. Elsevier, 37(May), p. 100694. doi: 10.1016/j.tsc.2020.100694.

Tseng, H., Yi, X. and Yeh, H. Te (2019) *Learning-related soft skills among online business students in higher education: Grade level and managerial role differences in self-regulation, motivation, and social skill*, *Computers in Human Behavior*. Elsevier B.V. doi: 10.1016/j.chb.2018.11.035.

What is User Centered Design? | Interaction Design Foundation (IxDF) (no date). Available at: https://www.interaction-design.org/literature/topics/user-centered-design (Accessed: 13 November 2020).

PHISHING, TRUST AND HUMAN WELLBEING

John Ayooluwa Adejobi[1], Fiona Carroll[1] and Liqaa Nawaf[1] and Reza Montasari[2]
[1]*Cardiff Metropolitan School of Technologies*
Cardiff Metropolitan University, Llandaff Campus, Western Avenue, Cardiff, CF5 2YB, Wales, UK
[2]*Hillary Rodham Clinton School of Law, Swansea University*
Swansea University, Singleton Park, Swansea, SA2 8PP, Wales, UK

ABSTRACT

The more time we spend online, the more our global connections grow and frighteningly, the more we are susceptible to cyberattacks. In particular, 2020/ 2021 has seen a significant increase in successful phishing attacks mainly due to the rise in human vulnerabilities caused by the global COVID-19 situation. In this paper, we consider the human factors of the phishing attack. We explore the evolution of the phishing attack with particular reference to its many different guises. Following that, the paper discusses the concept of trust and the human trust issues resulting from a phishing attack; it will focus on human vulnerability and the idea of phishing awareness. The findings from the study show that people feel that they can confidently recognize a phishing attack but it also highlights how personal attitudes and situational influences can make certain online users more susceptible than others. The findings also clearly detail how the phishing attack makes them and others feel and they assertively suggest ways to counter the attack. After portraying this picture, the question lies around the degree to which the everyday person is adequately equipped to psychologically deal with the sophisticated and contemporary phishing attack, and whether their thinking and methods of detection/ coping are so outdated that this (in itself) is creating an even greater risk.

KEYWORDS

Phishing, Trust, Wellbeing, Cyber Security, Vulnerability

1. INTRODUCTION

The COVID-19 pandemic has brought with it an avalanche of cyber-attacks and in particular phishing attacks. Cyber criminals are targeting people's vulnerabilities caused by the uncertainty of the virus as well as their increased dependence on remote working and digital tools. This last year, the UK Department for Digital, Culture, Media & Sport (2020) has experienced a rise in businesses experiencing phishing attacks (from 72 % to 86 %) (DCMS, 2020). Indeed, whether corporate or personal, the phishing attack is on the rise and many people, all over the world, are battling to detect and cope with these threats and attacks. Despite the fact that the phishing has been around a long time (i.e. as long as email has existed), it continues to present a substantial risk to people and their wellbeing. The question arises: why are we still so susceptible and vulnerable to the phishing attack? In this paper, we take a glimpse into the everyday online user's understanding and experience of the phishing attack. We will focus on trust and human trust issues resulting from a phishing attack and in doing so, we will build a more human centric picture of where the problem/s lie. This paper is organized as follows. Section 2 discusses the evolution of the phishing attack focusing on the changing anatomy of the phishing attack. Section 3 discusses trust, vulnerability and human wellbeing. Section 4 documents the study and its main findings. Finally, section 5 reviews future investigations and concludes the paper.

2. THE CHANGING ANATOMY OF THE PHISHING ATTACK

Phishing attacks evolved with the introduction of various technology. For example, the introduction of mobile phones and application software have made users much more vulnerable to phishing attacks, giving criminals/ phishers more opportunities for exploitation. In particular, a major part of application software being exploited by phishers is the email. 'In terms of scope, physical infrastructure, usage, and accessibility, email is of killer application proportions'(Tassabehji & Vakola, 2005, p.70). The phisher's objective, generally, is to lure their victim to another interface to gain sensitive information and often, to obtain financial data. In fact, the phishing email is a 'subset of spam which is related to social engineering schemes, which depends on forged e-mails (i.e. it claims that originated from a legitimate company or bank) and then through an embedded link within the e-mail, the phisher tries to redirect users to fake websites' (Almomani et al., 2013, p.1). Concisely, phishing attacks have evolved from 1) the email with wrong spellings and grammar to 2) the email presenting a desperate urgency to click a link to 3) the email with professional and very sophisticated ways of obtaining data. And social media has a huge impact on the success of these more sophisticated attacks. For example, social media has made spear phishing much easier. Spear phishing is a more targeted version of phishing 'where an adversary conducts online reconnaissance against an individual or organization in order to construct an email which appears to be of significant interest to those targeted' (CPNI, 2021, p.1). The email is strategically designed to persuade the person to open a file attachment or click on a website link. Indeed, the art is in the persuasion and as we have seen particularly during COVID-19, phishers have been evolving their methods and techniques to persuade, they capitalise on human vulnerabilities and manipulate people's trust to achieve their malicious objectives.

Some of the earliest techniques (human and technical) that have been used to detect phishing attacks have centred on the presentation and appearance of the emails. These include things like: misspelled URLs, grammatical errors, hidden URLs, etc. However, this becomes much more difficult today as phishers have improved on these basic inaccuracies and mistakes, it is now a lot harder for a human and machine to detect a syntax pattern used by phishers. Indeed, using semiotic mechanisms, phishing attackers can make victims believe that they are communicating with a trusted entity or brand, this is often executed through websites displaying official logos to obtain sensitive information. In fact, a visual deception can make many technical securities redundant as the onus is on the users to identify contents of such signs and symbols being used. As Dhamija (2006, p.1) highlight 'some visual deception attacks can fool even the most sophisticated users. These results illustrate that standard security indicators are not effective for a substantial fraction of users and suggest that alternative approaches are needed'.

A phishing attack has been described as a clever array of three forms of pattern: authority, time pressure and tone (Wanca & Cannon, 2016). Trusted brand logos create and provide the necessary illusion of legitimacy (and authority) to users and they open them up to phishing attacks. As Wanca and Cannon (2016, p.8) show 'Phishing scams claim to be from a trusted source by using a corporate logo or name as the sender to attempt to create legitimacy and credibility'. Time is another important factor used to lure victims into making decisions without thinking it through. Time can put them under a lot of pressure especially when needing to make a decision on whether to trust or not trust. Finally, the tone in which the message is delivered is another crucial component. For example, a formal tone with a combination of persuasive and courteous statements has the power to influence and manipulate the user's decision making (Wanca & Cannon, 2016). In line with this, it is no longer about sending a single isolated phishing email. Social engineering is a complex approach now used by attackers to mislead and manipulate users to ensure a more successful phishing attack. It is less predictable and often more calculated: 'Social engineering is a type of psychological manipulation. The attacker will persuade you to undertake a number of actions or to provide information that may seem innocent to you, by pretending to be someone else' (BDO, p.4). There are many types of social engineering approaches that can all link up to ensure a more convincing attack and in terms of phishing, these are no longer surface 'syntax' deep. They are now a deeper and more studied psychological attack which probes and persuades the human in clever ways.

3. TRUST AND HUMAN WELLBEING

Trust is a key player in the phishing attack. The question remains, why, despite receiving wide media coverage, has the globally discussed and known phenomenon of the phishing attack continued to be effective? For example, during COVID-19, the preying on people's vulnerabilities and the securing of people's trust was/is the main trigger for a continued successful phishing attack landscape. People tend to believe/ accept familiarity, as discussed, they trust professional looking brands and emails. However, it goes without saying that 'email has always been a casual communications medium: email content is not authenticated, and forging an email is an easy operation' (Adida et al.,2005, p. 2). By researching a person presence online (i.e. life), phishers can gather not only people's history but also their current interests, hobbies, beliefs, likes, dislikes etc. A lot of valuable data can easily be obtained from online platforms; in fact, sufficient information can be collected to fool them into thinking that they are in contact with a familiar person. Like a spider, this information can help attackers to fabricate environments in the form of convincing interfaces and links to lure victims into giving out sensitive information. 'Human intellectual and social life is based on the production, use, and exchange of signs. When we gesture, talk, write, read, watch a TV program, listen to music, navigate through YouTube, or look at a painting, we are engaged in sign-directed or meaning-based behavior' (Danesi, 2019, p.37). The phishing experience can be built from these signs and can seem very authentic. Hence it's detection can be very difficult. 'One of the biggest challenges facing businesses in their fight against cyberthreats is the breadth of phishing scams used' (Rutherford, 2018, p6-8). With a world of private data being freely uploaded on social media, attackers can apply their skills in many different ways to gain sensitive information. 'In today's technologically connected society, social engineers have begun to focus and apply their skills onto the cyber realm in hopes of gaining access to unauthorized or private information' (Walker, 2016). Research has shown that an emphasis on persuasive scams and social engineering are key elements to ensuring phishing attack success (Ferreira & Lenzini, 2015).

As the UK Department for Culture, Media & Sport (DCMS, 2020) highlight from 2017 to 2020 there has been a rise in phishing attacks (it increased by around 14 percent). Anti-phishing tools are becoming more and more ineffective when attackers use human behaviors and trust mechanisms to carry out such fraudulent attacks. As Abroshan et al. (2018) show phishers invest a lot of time in the design of phishing techniques solely around human behaviours. With that, there is an interplay of emotion which often impacts users' judgments on phishing attacks; these attacks strategically use enticing and emotive information to lure victims into giving sensitive information. Indeed, emotions have a strong impact on trust decisions: 'It has long been known that the principal determinant of human behavior is emotion, that when the emotions and intellect are in competition for control of will, it is usually that emotion that win' (Arnold, 1970, p31). To the extent, social-psychological research has determined ineffective cognitive processing as a key reason for individual victimization (Harrison et al., 2016). And social media tends to create a culture of false trust which drives relationships and promotes the sharing of excess information. Unfortunately, this façade of false trust and hence humans consciously and often unconsciously sharing their information (i.e. users habits and social lives) is having an impact on human wellbeing and in doing so, also appears to be the root to many phishing susceptibilities. In detail, human wellbeing is a complex ecosystem including emotional and intellectual aspects. Phishing attacks that deceive and take an advantage of human emotions can lead to fear and distrust which in turn leads to isolation and a loss of relationships and lower quality of life (Drevitch, 2021).

4. STUDY

The goal of this study was to explore the human factors of the phishing attack experience and to share a glimpse of phishing through the eyes of the everyday online user. The study took place at Cardiff Met University in Autumn 2020 and aims to give insight into individuals' understanding and feelings around the phishing attack and the impact that it has on a person. Ninety-two participants from both the UK and Nigeria completed the study. The study took approximately twenty minutes in duration. The study was approved by the Ethics Board of School of Technologies, Cardiff Met University and subjects provided online consent for study participation and the academic use of de-identified data.

4.1 Data Collection

The study was conducted using the Qualtrics online survey software. Participants were presented with a series of quantitative and qualitative questions. To detail, some of these questions included: In your opinion, how would you spot a phishing attack? Do you think phishing attacks has changed since you have been online? Why do you think you were a victim to phishing attack? The study also collected data on participants descriptions of the phishing attack: How would you describe a phishing email attack to a friend? Participants were also asked: In general, how did you/ how do you think people feel when they get a phishing email attack? And in your opinion, what is the impact/outcomes of a phishing attack on a person?

4.2 Methodology

A survey was carried out via questionnaires on Qualtrics software to get different perspective to phishing attacks. It examined different ages, educational groups, race, gender and two counties. During the research, samples of the participant were collected which was used to represent the group. Probability sampling was used, making strong statistical inferences about the whole group. Data gathered were analyzed using excel. Social media (twitter) analysis was carried out checking sentiments of key words such as Phishing email, scam, financial loss etc. Participants were presented with a series of quantitative and qualitative questions in other to get their perception to phishing attacks. Data collected were analyzed thus, bringing several findings to the survey.

4.3 Findings

After an analysis of the collected data, several interesting findings were identified. For starters, most participants (82%) shared that they depend on grammatical errors, spelling mistakes and obvious irregularities in emails to spot phishing attacks. In detail, many of participants felt they could spot such attacks:

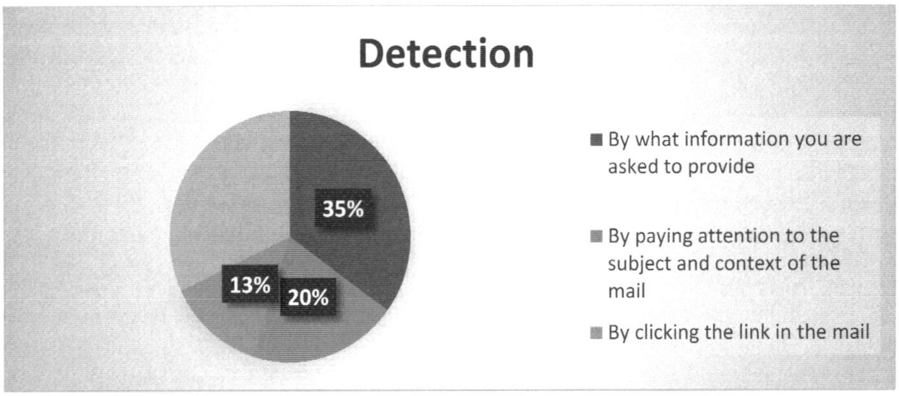

Figure 1. Detection of the phishing email attack

By what information you are asked to provide (35% participants)

- Asking for personal information (participant 54)
- Through the info being sent to me and what I am being asked to provide(participant 79)
- Usually when they request for personal information such as bank details claiming to be a representative of my bank (participant 80)
- They tend to want immediate response with threats (participant 87)
- Combination of things such as grammar, the address it was sent from, the content on the email and what it is asking for, whether I was addressed by name and also whether I was expecting that particular email (participant 31)

By paying attention to the subject and context of the mail (20% participants)

- Spelling mistakes- Dodgy email accounts - non-relevant information (participant 19)
- Formatting, grammar, but also the context and reasoning given for personal data requests (participant 22)
- Incorrect sender address, missing details like starting the email with "Dear user" instead of the person's name. Spelling errors or missing data from the email or website. (participant 40)
- Negative perceptions, unnecessary distractions and fake news (participant 58)
- Their emails are usually not encrypted (i.e. not secure), appear in your spam box and websites that lack a secure connection (participant 72)
- There's always a sort of bait, sometimes it's obviously too good to be true (participant 77)

By clicking the link in the mail (13% participants).

- spelling errors, looking behind the email picture / name, looking - without clicking - as to where the link points to (participant 20)
- Links asking for personal information (participant 55)
- The link (participant 56)
- Email or web link from unknown source (participant 83)

When participants were asked if they think the phishing attack has changed since they have been online? All participants agree that phishing attacks have evolved from when they first started to go online. The findings show that the majority of participants within the age bracket 17-24 years old (85 %) receive 0-5 malicious emails per week. This compares with the 36% of the 25-35 age group, the 20 % of 36-45 age group and 50% of 46-55 age group. Interestingly, when participants were asked why do they think they were a victim to phishing attack? The findings shows that around 60% of participants ignored this question. Around 15% stated they were victims out of curiosity, negligence, and a weak security. In all responses, it is clear that participants were blaming their own actions for being phished: 'Because I was looking for something online. Or I was trying to get a Job' (participant 57); 'My account was hacked after getting an email' (participant 61); 'My security wasn't strong enough' (participant 78) and 'There was no prize as the link suggested' (participant 84).

In more detail, three participants claimed it was as a result of their impatience. As one participant (40) highlighted 'I rushed into things - was foolish and did not take time to check. May have been to tiredness'. Others claimed it was because 'I was in a hurry' (participant 64) and 'I was in a haste' (participant 76). The study also highlighted participant's descriptions of the phishing attack (see Figure 1). Words like 'loss', 'financial loss', 'trust issues', 'attack', 'money', 'account' and 'bad spelling' are featuring most frequently in their descriptions of the phishing attacks.

Figure 2. Descriptions of the phishing email attack

Furthermore, a large number of participants discussed the deception in the emails particularly in how the attackers tried to obtain their personal information. Participants were strongly feeling that they were 'Fake emails to trick you for information' (participant 12); 'Mass email sent out appearing legitimate trying to bait individuals into a scam or downloading malicious software' (participant 13); 'legit looking email that intends to gain access to sensitive information' (participant 14); 'Looks like it comes from a legit business, will ask for personal info or ask you to click a link within the email or download an attachment' (participant 18); 'An email that copies as much as it can about a real trustworthy company, but it steals your information when you submit it' (participant 35) and finally, 'When the content of the mail includes a link that directs you to a different webpage. Or when a link pops up on your browser. It could also be an SMS telling you to confirm login details and the likes' (participant 47). When participants were probed about how they feel/ think people feel when they get a phishing email attack? Participants aged thirty-five years old and below who answered, believed that people feel nervous, insecure, unaware and less confident after receiving a phishing attack email. Interestingly, the data shows that only two participants aged thirty-six years old and above (1.94 % of overall sample) answered the question. Are these questions too close for comfort? Is there a disconcerted feeling in being fooled (i.e. losing control of one's emotions and trust in people?). Moreover, all the participants from Nigeria (36 participants in total) didn't answer this question. This raises another interesting question: are different cultures more sensitive (and possibly more vulnerable) to phishing attack emails than others?

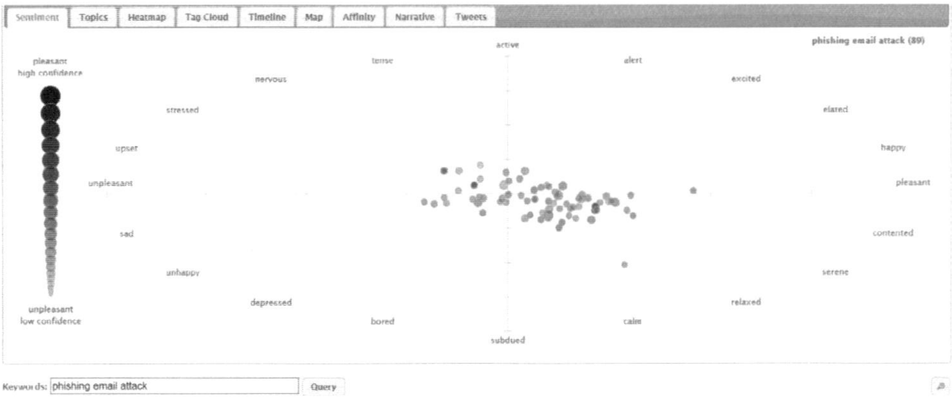

Figure 3. Twitter sentiment

An additional short analysis was carried out on social media data (2nd of February 2021, from 11:00 to 12 midnight) to more generally probe people's feelings to the phishing email attacks. Using the key words "phishing email attacks", the findings highlight that the overall sentiment across all the tweeters was quite negative with words like 'malicious', 'obfuscation', 'warning', 'targeted', 'ransomware' and 'scam' appearing most frequently. It is clear from this data that phishing email attacks afford negativity, the challenge is that even for the more cautious users it is difficult to detect the threat. In many ways, they are alone in this digital threat landscape. Moreover, when participants were asked how confident they were that the government/banks would compensate them for losses due to phishing attack emails. The findings show that all participants from Nigeria seemed to show little trust or confidence in getting a compensation from their government/ banks (i.e. they selected options of 'probably not', 'definitely not' and 'might or might not'). In contrast, participants from the UK felt a bit more confident in getting a compensation from their government/banks (i.e. selecting 'probably yes', 'definitely yes' and a few 'might or might not').

4.4 Discussion

From this study, some interesting questions emerge: why are people still susceptible to phishing attacks? And how is this lack of power and lack of knowing what is a threat or not, having on people's wellbeing? The paper shows that a lot of people receive and are still victims to phishing attacks. Indeed, the increase of public awareness on phishing email attacks has reduced the human's contribution to the successful phishing attack campaigns.

However, as the study highlights, even with awareness of these threats, people do still fall to the more sophisticated scams; this is mainly the result of their natural human characteristics such as curiosity, emotions, impatience, laziness and others. As humans, we just can't help ourselves and we fall victim to the psychological tricks, we succumb to the temptation despite often feeling that it could be an inherent risk. Indeed, the impact or outcome of this on a person's wellbeing can be catastrophic. In the study, participants believed that people can feel a lot of stress as a result of a phishing attack, that they can develop anxiety, or have long term trust issues afterwards. As one participant (22) mentioned 'it can make them feel less secure online, and less likely to trust what comes into their inbox'. Another participant (24) highlighted that there might be 'a sense of stupidity/ blaming oneself for falling for it. Afterwards, a well-deserved feeling of caution and distrust'. It could be said that people from countries with little support from the government after a successful phishing email scam, tend to be more alert and vigilant, however, this still does not guarantee that they will not become victims.

The psychological based methodologies used to persuade, coerce, or manipulate can be very convincing. As discussed, the phishing email attack has evolved and is now presenting in various sophisticated forms (combining affective, behavioral and cognitive processes) and thus making it more and more difficult for the human alone to detect. When we asked participants about what they think is needed for them to avoid or to detect a phishing email attack. The findings clearly highlighted that participants felt they and others needed a support such as an alert system and/ or pop-up warnings. They suggested several forms of possible alerts: 'possibly an IP address scanner' (participant 16); 'A security notification of some sort? Detailing the dangers and things to look out for?' (participant 12); 'traffic light system?' (participant 22) and 'I don't think a general user interface would be sufficient enough to warn a person about a phishing attack (this by itself could be used to inform a user to look out for phishing attacks). However, the implementation of a UI and algorithm (maybe antivirus) could be utilized to warn a user about a phishing attack by including a small alert section above the email/text to inform the user that the email is suspicious. Thus, allow users the option to listen to the alerts or to ignore them (if it is a false positive)' (participant 30).

In terms of detecting phishing email attacks, we have definitely moved on from using 'misspelling and bad grammar' to identify a possible attack, we now need to look at the pragmatics of the email (i.e. the meanings behind the emails and most importantly the context). This study has highlighted that people want and need support to protect themselves from the phishing attack. It is clear that training, education and awareness are only part of the solution, we need to equip people with the systems that will directly enhance their threat perception. Anti-phishing tools need to take a pragmatic approach to understanding the psychological and sociological factors being played as a form of attack. In adopting this practice, future research will be best placed to design 'alert systems' for not only human online safety but also human wellbeing.

5. CONCLUSION

Phishing email attacks which have been prolific since the mid-2000's can no longer solely be detected from their presentation and appearance. The authors of this paper believe that exposing the deeper and often hidden meanings afforded by phishing email attacks is the only way to provide people with a better chance in identifying potential threats. Moreover, they feel that it is only when we start to look at the pragmatics of the email attack that we will truly be in a position to curb and protect against the phishing attack. As the paper highlights, people need support to protect themselves against the phishing attack. The focus here needs to be on identifying and understanding the intent of such emails, rather than just identifying poor spelling and grammar. Despite humans being the biggest risk to organizations, we can't and shouldn't want to take them out of the picture. To ensure a flourishing business we need humans to interact, to communicate and to receive and send emails. Trust and human wellbeing are key players in this mix and to further nurture this trust and wellbeing, we need to adopt an approach that looks at the wider context of these attacks. In fact, more attention needs to be placed on the pragmatics of the attack; people's trust/engagement is one of the main triggers to a successful phishing attacks especially during a trendy event or situation across the world (i.e. Covid-19). Realizing the wider trends and context is crucial to understanding the threat. No doubt, and as we have experienced, the form/medium of communication amongst people may change but the fact remains that people will continue to want to interact and trust one another. This is a good thing, interaction and trust are fundamental to our lives and our businesses, we just need to ensure that people are fully equipped and supported to protect themselves (wellbeing), their businesses, and their trust online.

REFERENCES

Abroshan, H., Devos, J., Poels, G. and Laermans E. (2018). *Phishing attacks root causes. In Lecture Notes in Computer Science (including subseries Lecture Notes in Artificial Intelligence and Lecture Notes in Bioinformatics).*

Adida, B., Hohenberge, S. and Rivest, R. L. (2005). *Fighting Phishing Attacks: A Lightweight Trust Architecture for Detecting Spoofed Emails.* Available from: http://people.csail.mit.edu/rivest/AdidaHohenbergerRivest-FightingPhishingAttacks.pdf

Almomani, A., Gupta, B. B. Wan, T.-C., Altaher, A. and Manickam, S. (2013). *Phishing Dynamic Evolving Neural Fuzzy Framework for Online Detection "Zero-day" Phishing Email.* Technical report.

Arnold, M. B. (1970). *Feelings and Emotions: The Loyola Symposium*. Google Books.

BDO (2019). *A Pragmatic Approach to Enhancing Cyber Security.* Available from: https://www.bdo.ky/en-gb/insights/insights-2016-2019/a-pragmatic-approach-to-enhancing-cyber-security

CPNI (National Centre for the Protection of National Infrastructure) (2021). *Spear phishing - Understanding the threat.* Technical report. Available from: www.cpni.gov.uk/advice/cyber/online-reconnaissance

Danesi, M. (2019). *Understanding Media Semiotics*. Google Books.

DCMS (Department for Culture & Media & Sport) (2020). *Cyber Security Breaches Survey 2020*. Technical report.

Dhamija, R., Tygar, J. D. and Hearst, M. (2006). *Why phishing works. In Conference on Human Factors in Computing Systems - Proceedings*. DOI 10.1145/1124772.1124861

Drevitch, G. (2021). *How Does Fraud Impact Emotional Well-Being?* Available from: https://www.psychologytoday.com/us/blog/the-fraud-crisis/202101/how-does-fraud-impact-emotional-well-being

Ferreira, A. and Lenzini, G. (2015). *An Analysis of Social Engineering Principles in Effective Phishing.* In Proceedings - 5th Workshop on Socio-Technical Aspects in Security and Trust, STAST 2015.

Harrison, B., Svetieva, E. and Vishwanath, A. (2016). *Individual processing of phishing emails: How attention and elaboration protect against phishing*. Online Information Review.

Rutherford, R. (2018). *The changing face of phishing*. Computer Fraud and Security.

Tassabehji,R. and Vakola, M. (2005). *Business email: The killer impact.* Commun. ACM. 48. 64-70. 10.1145/1096000.1096006.

Walker, L. E. (2016). *Deception of Phishing: Studying the Techniques of Social Engineering by Analyzing Modern-day Phishing Attacks on Universities*. Available from https://etd.auburn.edu/bitstream/handle/10415/5175/LEW%20Thesis.pdf?sequence=2&isAllowed=y

Wanca, I. and Cannon, A. (2016) *How human behavior and decision-making expose users to phishing attacks.* Technical report. Available from: http://www.nycrimecommission.org/pdfs/CCC-How-Human-Behavior-and-Decision-Making-Expose-Users-to-Phishing-Attacks.pdf

GEN MZ TOWARD SUSTAINABLE FASHION PRACTICES - ALTERNATIVE SERVICES AND BUSINESS MODELS

Alma Leora Culén and Swati Srivastava
Department of Informatics, University of Oslo
P. Boks 1080, 0316 Blindern, Oslo, Norway

ABSTRACT

As information emerges on the scale and seriousness of environmental, economic, and socio-cultural challenges related to the fashion industry, millennials and Generation Z (Gen MZ) consumers direct their attention to sustainable fashion. Their perspective and possible influence on the future of more responsible consumption is not fully explored, especially in terms of 1) understanding of the complexities of industry's unsustainability, 2) what it implies concerning sustainable fashion consumption, and 3) using the opportunities that ICT provides to create platforms, services, and business models that align with their visions, demands, and needs. This paper describes two small qualitative studies tackling these gaps – an action research intervention and an open questionnaire, both focusing on already sustainability-aware consumers, to gain insights about their thoughts on sustainable fashion, including acquisition and dispossession decisions, the importance of understanding production challenges, awareness/action gap, and their visions in terms of novel services and business models. Using transition design framework, and in conjunction with our previous work, findings served to envision local, community-based alternative services and business models that support more responsible consumption and continued, dynamic creation of sustainable fashion practices among Gen MZ consumers.

KEYWORDS

Sustainable Fashion, Green Choices, Responsible Consumption, Transition Design, Service Design, Gen MZ

1. INTRODUCTION

Growing awareness of the heavy environmental impact of the fashion industry led to particular urgency in rethinking the industry's unsustainable practices, business models, and opacity regarding its life cycle stages. The latter has been perceived as an essential barrier for consumers, retailers, and designers in understanding life cycle processes and their negative impact on the environment (*Environmental indicator report*, 2014). Every stage of the fashion life cycle (growing plants to extract fibers/artificial fiber production, manufacturing, distribution, use, and disposal) has a high environmental impact. The European Environmental Agency (ibid.) ranked the industry fourth by negative environmental impact. Despite recognition of the above challenges, we are witnessing a substantial increase in fashion consumption. This increase is linked, at least partially, to the success of the fast fashion business model, which promotes inexpensive and trendy clothing with a short lifespan manufactured in developing countries under unfavorable or unethical conditions (Niinimäki *et al.*, 2020). Ellen MacArthur Foundation reports that hundreds of billions of dollars are lost annually on underused clothes (*A New Textiles Economy: Redesigning fashion's future*, 2017), indicating the need to extend the lifespan of clothing, find appropriate business models to mitigate the trend set by fast fashion, and support responsible consumption.

A better understanding of the industry's challenges has led some fashion brands, designers, retailers, and consumers to start making socially responsible choices (Jacobs *et al.*, 2018). Consequently, the term *sustainable fashion* has become widely discussed, with discussion extending beyond social responsibility toward long-term systemic, sustainable solutions that consider all life cycle stages of the fashion industry. A holistic understanding of sustainable fashion is complex – its production and consumption represent wicked problems (Rittel and Webber, 1973) that are interconnected, incomplete, contradictory, and where solutions are difficult to find. For example, if the amount of water or chemical dyes needed to produce a pair of jeans is reduced, how does it impact energy use or garment color? Transparency is needed to make appropriate, socially responsible decisions. Fashion brands are still reluctant to disclose this information fully (Chun *et al.*, 2021). Gaps in consumers' understanding of life cycle stages and a lack of transparency have been identified as two of the most significant barriers to the discussion of systemic changes (e.g., toward circular economy) (Camacho-Otero, Boks and Pettersen, 2018) and diffusion of circular business models.

Millennials and the older segment of Generation Z (Gen MZ) are often seen as a leading force in transitions toward sustainable fashion. They are consistently increasing their awareness of the complexities of fashion production and consumption. Still, increasing awareness and transparency of fashion production does not necessarily translate into more sustainable actions and practices (Peirson-Smith and Evans, 2017; Turunen and Halme, 2021) when Gen MZ uses its substantial spending power (Moran, 2020). However, they have already changed the ways of advertising, sales, and information sharing by abandoning traditional media for Instagram, Facebook, YouTube, event sales, and other channels (Park, Ciampaglia and Ferrara, 2016; Stein, Spinler and Vanthournout, 2020). Gen MZ consumers use these channels (DeVaney, 2015; Serazio, 2015) to influence other age groups and promote new trends, consumption patterns, and lifestyles (Thelwall, 2021).

Recently, transition design (Escobar, 2018; Irwin, 2018) emerged as a design-led approach to tackling wicked problems and supporting transitions to more sustainable lifestyles. We use the transition design framework (Irwin, 2018) in this work to reflect on our mindset and values, theories that might support design for social change at scale, visions of sustainable fashion consumption, and new ways of designing (e.g., multi-stakeholder co-design, use of different design approaches). We used the framework previously to discuss a future-oriented service, Zygo, which aims to mitigate the consumption of durable goods among millennials by extending the lifespan of goods (Srivastava, 2017; Srivastava and Culén, 2018, 2019a, 2019b).

In this work, we describe two small qualitative studies that aim to gain insights into how Gen MZ consumers understand sustainable fashion and responsible consumption, in particular: 1) the complexity of the fashion industry's unsustainability 2) what it implies regarding sustainable fashion consumption 3) the opportunities that information and communication technologies (ICT) provide for creating supporting platforms, services, and business models that align with Gen MZ's visions, demands, and needs. The insights from these studies, and three other design projects that we supervised in the context of a larger funded project that sought to understand greener consumption more generally are then related to Zygo. This paper contributes to transition and interaction design by providing a perspective on how Norwegian Gen MZ understands sustainable fashion, the meaning of adopting sustainable practices related to clothing, and their thoughts on desirable services for the future that support their efforts to be responsible fashion consumers. Furthermore, we show how to extend Zygo to include local communities of practice concerned with fashion that offer sustainable services and business models toward responsible consumption and the continued, dynamic creation of sustainable fashion practices among Gen MZ consumers.

Next, we address some relevant literature and our previous work on sustainable consumption for Gen MZ and the digital solutions that were suggested. Then, we present our method, followed by the insights gained. Finally, we show how to integrate these insights with Zygo to provide services and business models for Gen MZ consumers.

2. BACKGROUND

This section is divided into four parts: 1) relevant work discussing consumers' mental model of sustainability and sustainable consumption, 2) designing for change, 3) Zygo, and 4) findings from the three small design projects that are related to the research described in this paper.

2.1 Consumers' Mental Models of Sustainability and Sustainable Consumption

Studies report that Gen MZ consumers increasingly make conscious and green choices (McDonald and Oates, 2006), showing a clear preference for brands that conduct their business with regard to environmental and social safety – in other words, products, services, and economies that could be described as being within the safe and just space for development (Rockström *et al.*, 2009; Steffen *et al.*, 2015; Raworth, 2017).

The mental concepts around sustainability and sustainable product attributes may differ between the fashion industry and consumers. Hanss and Böhm (2012) studied the latter (i.e., how Norwegian consumers understand sustainability and attributes of sustainable products). Their study found that consumers' general understanding of sustainability covered its five dimensions: environmental, social, economic, temporal, and developmental. Consumers focused on recyclable packaging, ecological production, fair payment for production, humane animal treatment, low energy use, and low carbon dioxide emissions during production and shipping. For the fashion industry specifically, the most important aspects of sustainability were fair and ethically made garments and accessories (e.g., no child labor, transparent production and fair pay (social and economic sustainability), sustainable production methods, and responsible waste management (environmental sustainability)).

Sustainable fashion practices are uniquely challenging because they extend beyond the utilitarian notion of fashion and into personal identity, need for distinction, status, and social acceptance (Niinimäki and Hassi, 2011). The novel practices and business opportunities suggested in the literature often have to do with upcycling, recycling, reconstruction, and zero waste (Khandual and Pradhan, 2019), or collaborative use and custom-made fashion, including Do-it-Yourself (DiY). De Angelis, Amatulli, and Pinato (2020) investigated differences in luxury and fast fashion consumption, concluding that luxury fashion brands activate a higher intention to purchase than sustainability associated with fast fashion brands. The authors attribute this to the intrinsic characteristics of luxury products: high quality, long life cycle, and limited quantities – all consistent with the consumers' ideas of sustainability. They argue further that these findings open for novel opportunities for both mass and luxury fashion. Previous research also shows that Gen MZ is open to new business models, such as sharing economies in luxury fashion consumption, as the study by Jain and Mishra (2020) finds.

Within sustainable interaction design, Pierce and Paulos (Pierce and Paulos, 2011) discussed consumption in terms of acquisition, possession, dispossession, and reacquisition. In particular, they paid attention to reacquisition, the use of secondhand goods, as a way to extend the lifetime of products and possibly lead to more sustainable consumption practices, especially when dispossession is linked to reacquisition. Another take-away from this work is related to the importance of designing for and with communities of reacquisition and that designing from communities of reacquisition generally works towards seeking and shaping radically different alternatives to the existing ones. In (Odom *et al.*, 2009), the authors present an interesting perspective on the strength of attachments to products, linking it to the function of the product, its meaning, and materials, all influencing the length of the use of the product.

2.2 Designing for Change

Design and fashion designers are, in part, responsible for our (over)consumption, continuously persuading with new trends and aggressive marketing. They are also increasingly called upon to focus on values beyond profit and to work for the greater social good (Papanek, 1971; Chick and Micklethwaite, 2011; Niedderer, Clune and Ludden, 2017). To counter the challenges in the industry, several directions have been proposed, both through design and consumer behavior change, for example, slow fashion, behavior change (Becker-Leifhold, 2018; Brewer, 2019), or transition design (Kossoff, 2015; Irwin, 2018) – the latter approach chosen for this work because of its holistic perspective, which also looks into the design practice itself, theories that support design for change, values, and the ability to focus on the future by generating visions of preferred lifestyles.

The design practice used in our previous work that aimed to mitigate overconsumption among millennials (Srivastava and Culén, 2018) was based on integrated research through design (Zimmerman and Forlizzi, 2014) and service design, while the theory chosen to support the transition in most of the described design projects was social practice theory (Shove and Pantzar, 2005; Ingram, Shove and Watson, 2007; Kuijer, 2014). The main elements that configure practices (shown in Figure 3 within the context of the master's thesis project (Hilde, 2019)) whose re-combination leads to new practices, are material things (both digital and physical), skills (knowledge), and meanings (e.g., creating a more sustainable lifestyle).

2.3 Zygo – Design Led Reframing of Secondhand Marketplaces

Zygo is a future oriented, integrated service designed to reframe secondhand marketplace for millennials and Generation Z and propose an adequate business model, community building model, and privacy and safety (suggesting a membership-based model for participation). To design Zygo, in depth research on the lifestyle of young consumers (aged 16-27) was central (Srivastava and Culén, 2019a) to establishing pathways for the flow of goods between consumers in different life phases and with distinct consumption habits (Srivastava and Culén, 2019b). The service opened for the building of small local communities of practice, which might include repair, redesign, or upscaling. Importantly, Zygo was designed so that new community-based consumption practices could be shaped dynamically and continuously – a feature that we use in this work.

The evaluation of Zygo was carried in two separate workshops with four millennials and three experts (see Figure 1). The workshop with millennials confirmed that Zygo meets their lifestyles, while experts found that the concepts that Zygo embodied offered opportunities for future extensions and support sustainable practices.

Figure 1. a) Evaluation of Zygo with millennials b) millennials making suggestions for new Zygo services c) the expert evaluation covered the service, branding, business model, strategies for community building. Photos: Culén

2.4 Supervised Projects that Provided Insights used in this Research

As mentioned, a large, funded research project served as an umbrella for several smaller design projects in the context of research-based teaching or supervision of master's thesis design projects with a focus on fashion consumption. We briefly present three projects and their main findings.

Conserve and Consume student project (Fosser *et al.*, 2017) (a course project) engaged millennials in workshops and interviews to identify design opportunities. The first idea was an *Interactive Wardrobe*. By scanning the garments, one could find out which items were not used and nudged to resell garments that were not used over a certain amount of time, e.g., a year. During the *Interactive Wardrobe* prototype evaluation, the participants said that clothes were very personal. They felt attached to them and were not interested in selling or sharing their unused clothes. They liked the idea of using secondhand clothing but acting on it was different – only a few bought secondhand. They were more interested in being environmentally friendly and wanted garments with good production information.

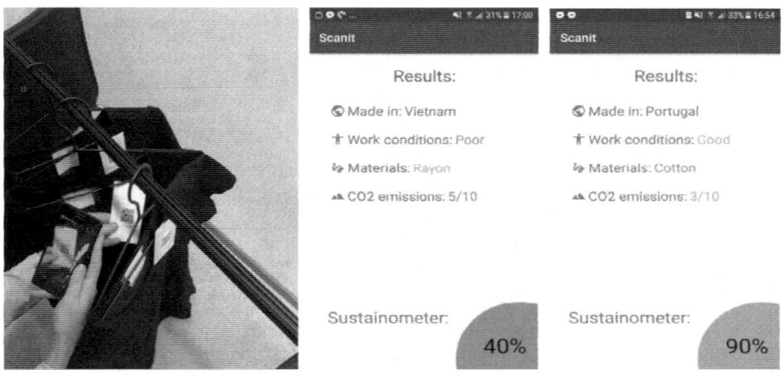

Figure 2. Scanning the tag of a t-shirt, to find out about the place of origin, work conditions, material, and CO_2 emissions. The information was combined into a sustainability percentage (in the bottom right corner). Images: (Fosser *et al.*, 2017)

This led to the second prototype *ScanIt* (see Figure 2), based on making such information readily available. In the evaluation of *ScanIt*, the team focused on exploring how knowing this information could affect purchasing practices. Their explorations revealed that almost all participants would change their initial choices after finding out issues with garment production, particularly its environmental impact and materials. Many commented that it felt good to select fair-made and environmentally friendly products.

Transitions to more sustainable fashion (Hilde, 2019), a master's thesis project, looked into possibilities to connect consumers and fashion designers, different business model concepts for niche audiences. Hilde examined how new practices around fashion could be developed and how access might be given to consumers to the process of design and garment production. Hilde collaborated with a fashion designer, and they used woven QR codes that were sewn onto garments, linking the garment to a video showing how reconstruction (the use of old material to make an entirely new design) was implemented, how the item was priced, and other relevant production and material information (see Figure 3). Follow-up with consumers was possible.

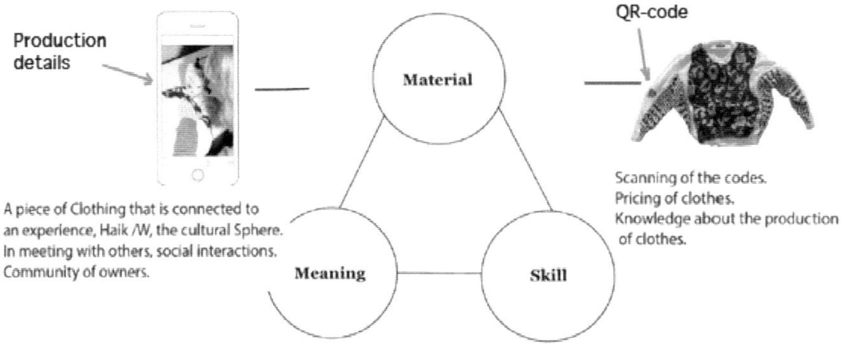

Figure 3. Adopted from (Hilde, 2019), showing how the sweater was made, scanning the woven QR-codes that are a part of the sweater. Sweaters are sold through events and a consumer could then interact with the designer

Scaffolding secondhand fashion consumption among adolescent girls (Fjeldstad and Leonardsen, 2017), was a master's thesis project. Fjeldstad and Leonardsen noted a lack of platforms targeting young girls (15–20) for secondhand fashion sharing. In the fashion-focused age, girls were more prone to sharing garments than older consumers. At that age, they experience occasions like confirmations, balls, and end of high school celebrations. Fjeldstad and Leonardsen designed and evaluated a service for this age group, aiming for the app design itself to be cool, use familiar interactions, and be simple, safe, and enjoyable to use.

3. METHODS

Two qualitative studies were carried out with Gen MZ participants (aged 19–35), *an action research intervention*, and an *online, open questionnaire* (instead of in-person interviews, which were not possible due to COVID-19). The study participants were selected based on their interest in sustainability, such as taking a transition design course to learn about the design of technologies within a safe and just space for the development of humanity (Rockström *et al.*, 2009; Raworth, 2017). In contrast, Zygo and student projects that we supervised did not focus on participants' a priori stance favoring sustainable design, just on their age.

The action research intervention was chosen to observe actions rather than what participants say they would do regarding the acquisition of secondhand garments. The study had four participants, three of whom participated in person, while the fourth used video conferencing. Notes were taken. A room was arranged in one of the researcher's homes with clothing organized into three categories: giveaways (placed into large plastic bags), borrow/trade (one side of the wardrobe), and rent/buy (the other side of the wardrobe). Items were inspected for faults prior to the intervention. All clothes were medium in size, and the participants were chosen accordingly. Participants were chosen from among acquaintances of the person who provided clothing items for the study to mitigate hesitation about items of unknown origin. The items were a good mix of luxury, mid-range, and lower-end fashion brands in all three categories. As the participants walked into the room, the researcher explained the arrangement and asked them to talk aloud while they looked at different sections and items (see Figure 4). After they were done looking, they were asked a few questions about possible services and business models that they might want to use. The interventions took between 30 minutes and an hour, a shorter amount of time than expected.

Figure 4. The images show the participants getting garments out of the bags containing free items. Photos: Culén

The online, open questionnaire had fourteen open-ended questions. It was implemented using Nettskjema, an online service that provides questionnaires. It was anonymous, and the answers to each question were randomized. The link to Nettskjema was sent to 25 people, and ten responses were received and analyzed using text analysis. The participants were students in a transition design course, design students, and a few others within the age group who we knew cared about the environment and social justice, but for whom we did not know anything about their attitude toward sustainable fashion.

The questions probed the thought process when buying a new piece of clothing, the length of use, how old the pieces were, and why they kept them. Further, we asked about dispossession practices, secondhand markets, and business models, such as luxury goods rental for special occasions. A range of questions addressed the importance of the material composition of garments and factors required for purchase (information on garment's production, identity, repair, or upcycling opportunities). Finally, we asked what participants considered the most interesting aspect related to sustainable fashion.

4. INSIGHTS AND IMPLICATIONS FOR DESIGN

This section has three parts: 1) insights from the action intervention, 2) insights from the questionnaire, and 3) implications for design, where we integrate the findings with Zygo toward sustainable fashion practices.

4.1 Insights from the Action Intervention Study

Being able to observe the body language of the participants while they engaged with clothing and talked through different choices while looking at or holding a particular garment was quite important. We, and the participants, could clearly relate our observations to the awareness/action gap that the literature addresses (Peirson-Smith and Evans, 2017; Turunen and Halme, 2021). For example, one participant, taking a cotton corduroy jacket out of a plastic bag with free items, said: *"I would probably take this."* The researcher pointed to some empty shopping bags and told the participant to take one and pack whatever she likes. *"Ha? Hmmm. No, maybe not."* Taking out the next item, a viscose dress (a more environmentally friendly material), she said: *"Maybe this? No, this is not me."* Neither the materials nor the brand status impacted her willingness to take a garment home – the participant chose nothing. When asked if anything would make any of the options more appealing, she replied in the negative: *"Gosh! I have so much stuff myself."* Another participant responded similarly, adding that thinking that someone does not want these free items does not help – it made her not want them either. Their way of being sustainable in this situation was to not take any clothes with them.

One participant was happy with many free things and of the four participants, she spent the longest time selecting items. She filled the purses found inside the black plastic bags and added a couple of smaller shopping bags to take home: *"This is great, I can give some of these to friends also, they look new. I love stuff like this and what turns out not to fit me, I have someone else to hand it down to."* The video conferencing participant had a green brand preference. A few items that were of that brand were selected from giveaway bags. They were than shown to her and she decided if she wanted them or not.

Participants showed no interest in the shared consumption (borrowing, renting, or trading) of ordinary, everyday clothing. They were worried that garments could get accidentally ruined, or that picking up and returning items would be inconvenient: *"If I think of borrowing, I think that things would be a hassle with returning and so on, so it is best to buy [own]."* Knowing the person whose clothes were for rent/trade/borrow was, on the one hand, positive, but on the other hand, there were worries about social consequences – as part of a circle of friends, they were familiar with each other's clothing, and it would feel awkward unless done by all. Furthermore, participants were not sufficiently interested in buying secondhand clothes, consistent with the findings from the *Conserve and Consume* student project.

One apparent limitation of this study is the small number of participants. However, we felt that we did gain insights, especially on the awareness/action gap, and found the participants' actions consistent concerning all options except for giveaway clothing. As that category got depleted, we stopped the interventions – a different approach would be needed to understand the actions and use of such secondhand clothing.

4.2 The Insights from the Questionnaire

We analyzed the questionnaire answers by looking for the themes related to 1) the level of understanding of the unsustainability of the fashion industry and how it affected practices around acquisition and dispossession, 2) opportunities for creating sustainable practices, 3) what interested participants most with sustainable fashion.

On the first topic, our findings were similar to those of the Conserve and Consume project, (Hilde, 2019), or (McDonald and Oates, 2006). The participants were interested in better and more understandable production information and found that the transparency still needed improvement: *"Ideally, I would like to think more about the production of clothing, but that always seems so abstract."* Most of the participants said that they try to make sustainable choices consistently. That includes concern with materials, the country of origin, care instructions, durability, fair and green production. Nevertheless, they also said that due to the non-transparency of many brands, they could not be sure that their choices were actually sustainable. Furthermore, half of the participants said that the basis for deciding on a purchase was the real need for an item of clothing. These participants valued this way of thinking as their way of acting sustainably in everyday life. With only one exception, participants liked to donate their used clothes to secondhand stores; alternatively, they placed them in recycling bins for clothing. Most participants do not consider selling clothes using either digital or physical secondhand markets (only three said that they might try to sell nicer items). While using secondhand markets to dispossess, the participants did not find them equally interesting for purchasing. Only one person said that they preferred to buy secondhand. Some said that they like secondhand markets and think that they do represent a sustainable choice. Others saw them as a sort of treasure hunt, where one might find unique pieces though nothing could be expected – it was a matter of luck. Two participants were not excited about them: *"Not something that excites me"* and *"I would consider visiting one."* In conclusion, we see the need to focus both on alternative ways to prolong use-life of clothing, for example, by creating stronger attachments (Odom *et al.*, 2009) and aim to move secondhand markets from niche to mainstream for Gen MZ consumers. As mentioned earlier, Zygo's aim was to fulfill the latter (Srivastava and Culén, 2019a).

As for the second topic, ideas related to possible alternative and more sustainable choices, such as luxury rentals, were met with some enthusiasm, although most participants said that they had not tried them. One shared their rental experience: *"I've rented a tuxedo once, and that was okay. I had to go to the store and get fitted, and then return later to get the stuff, and then again to return it after the event. So, it is too much hassle to do it often."* The thinking in favor of rentals included the fact that dresses for special occasions can be really expensive, and once the expense is incurred, one feels that the dress has to be worn on many occasions (unless, of course, the individual's resources are plentiful). On the other hand, rental shops offer a variety of choices that might fit the exact occasion for which they are rented. In the long term, the rental approach was seen as offering benefits of choice, quality, personal savings, and environmental benefits.

Regarding sustainable practices like upcycling, restyling, or reconstructing, only two participants were not interested. About half tried upcycling and restyling, with mixed results. The skilled ones reported it as a very satisfying experience. The less skilled participants were open to learning. Thus, in line with (Khandual and Pradhan, 2019), supporting sustainable practices is worth pursuing beyond DiY – and, as mentioned, perhaps in the context of services such as Zygo.

As for the third topic, one participant took a systemic swipe:

"Define interesting! I think the entire fashion industry needs a major systemic overhaul, from the rate of change with fashion houses outputting a minimum of two collections a year to fast fashion existing at all. I'm curious to see what kind of model can be built that keeps fashion interesting without making it financially inaccessible to the working class on the one hand and destroying the environment on the other."

Another participant pointed to social media as the source of the bad mindset taking hold:

"I think the trend-cycle is very interesting. Lately, there has been a surge in people buying fast-fashion brands and doing 'hauls' on the internet (on sites like TikTok and brands like Shein) with super-trendy items. When people are commenting that it is very unsustainable to be using 500$ on polyester clothing that's going to go out of style in a month, the buyers are excusing themselves by saying "there is no ethical consumption under capitalism" and that they cannot afford to buy more sustainably, even though they spend hundreds of dollars on cheap clothing. I think it is a really unhealthy mindset, and it is exaggerated by social media where you have to be trendy and appear cool."

Further, a couple of participants mentioned greenwashing and mistrust of green brands until the government makes regulatory decisions that such companies would be required to comply with. Several mentioned fast fashion as a problem, and some referred to slow fashion as a sustainable alternative. Someone made a distinction between style and trend, where style is accentuated as something that fits the personal identity, while the trend is something that everyone should follow. Thus, focusing on style is better (more sustainable) than following trends. One participant liked the emerging technologies, like the technology that makes it possible to extract fibers from used items and make new clothes with recycled fibers.

4.3 Implications for Design

Discussing what might work in terms of sustainable practices, in line with findings from (De Angelis, Amatulli and Pinato, 2020; Jain and Mishra, 2020), the participants thought that luxury rentals made sense economically, and services that would provide quality, age appropriate rentals were viewed favorably.

Many participants said that they would like to use secondhand clothes for DiY re-construction, or at least easy upcycling or restyling. Two participants in the intervention and several questionnaire participants acknowledged that the skills needed for this way of using secondhand clothing might be a barrier to doing it. Skills had to go beyond the ability to fix a missing button. Thus, workshops to gain or improve skills were seen as interesting. Engaging in such practices had a potential to increase the attachment (Odom *et al.*, 2009) and extend the life-span of textiles while reducing the textile waste.

One intervention participant returned to the idea of trading. The participant described the situation when she opened her overfilled wardrobe and thought that she had nothing to wear. She related this to not paying enough attention to how new items fit with the rest, making it difficult to create desirable styles later. Thus, if someone had something that would fit with something she loved, she would be happy to trade to get that item: *"Maybe even, an idea would be to make an app where a stylist would help people to select clothes from their own wardrobe that fit well together – sometimes the potential of this is missed."*

Some of the ideas discussed could be reconceptualized as services and business models in the context of Zygo. For example, a local Gen MZ fashionista might give styling advice for a small fee. Alternatively, as the basis for trade, Zygo social media (which is safe as membership is required) might be used to post the selfie of a person in an item that is in want of matching items or cool accessories. Members could then respond with images of items they own and think would fit well with the posted garment. If a match is found, a favorable trade or sale might be initiated. Furthermore, a service where a sustainability-oriented stylist is invited to come home and reduce the size of the wardrobe, leaving only environmentally friendly items that match other items in the wardrobe (and suit the owner well, both in terms of the fit and style), would work well with Zygo. The Zygo community members would have a variety of options to engage with sustainable fashion practices. For example, one might start by reducing the wardrobe, where no longer needed items are further used for learning to upcycle, restyle, or reconstruct clothing through community-organized workshops. As the community members move through different life stages, their needs change. Finding patterns related to clothing use with such life stage changes can uncover new dispossession pathways (Pierce and Paulos, 2011) and allow new sustainable business models to emerge dynamically.

5. CONCLUSION

Two small qualitative studies were implemented to explore the understanding of sustainable fashion among already sustainability aware Norwegian Gen MZ consumers. The studies show that there is still a lot of room to develop sustainable fashion practices, in particular when making purchasing or dispossession decisions, or obtaining information concerning the fashion production. However, this situation implies numerous opportunities for design of new services and business models. As an umbrella service, we have used our future-oriented service Zygo, which supports local communities that actively contribute to development of sustainable practices and dynamically open pathways between different services and members in different stages of life.

While these studies, in part, confirmed the findings from the literature, they also shed a new light on some of the ways these young consumers liked to engage with sustainable fashion, generating ideas for new services and business models that support their visions and aspirations toward sustainable practices related to fashion that include personal style (and not trends), high aesthetics, comfort, and proper fit – in items that they actually need. Gen MZ consumers are getting ready for more responsible fashion consumption.

REFERENCES

Becker-Leifhold, C. V. (2018) 'The role of values in collaborative fashion consumption - A critical investigation through the lenses of the theory of planned behavior', *Journal of Cleaner Production*, 199, pp. 781–791.

Brewer, M. K. (2019) 'Slow Fashion in a Fast Fashion World: Promoting Sustainability and Responsibility', *Laws*, 8(4), pp. 24.

Camacho-Otero, J., Boks, C. and Pettersen, I. N. (2018) 'Consumption in the circular economy: A literature review', *Sustainability*, 10(8), pp. 2758.

Chick, A. and Micklethwaite, P. (2011) *Design for Sustainable Change: How Design and Designers Can Drive the Sustainability Agenda*. AVA Publishing.

Chun, E. *et al.* (2021) 'Business transparency and willingness to act environmentally conscious behavior: Applying the sustainable fashion evaluation system "Higg Index"', *Journal of Global Scholars of Marketing Science*, pp. 1–16.

Circular Fashion - A New Textiles Economy: Redesigning fashion's future (2017). Available at: https://www.ellenmacarthurfoundation.org/publications/a-new-textiles-economy-redesigning-fashions-future (Accessed: 21 June 2021).

De Angelis, M., Amatulli, C. and Pinato, G. (2020) 'Sustainability in the Apparel Industry: The Role of Consumers' Fashion Consciousness', in Muthu, S. S. and Gardetti, M. A. (eds) *Sustainability in the Textile and Apparel Industries: Consumerism and Fashion Sustainability*. Cham: Springer International Publishing (Sustainable Textiles: Production, Processing, Manufacturing & Chemistry), pp. 19–33. doi: 10.1007/978-3-030-38532-3_2.

DeVaney, S. A. (2015) 'Understanding the millennial generation.', *Journal of financial service professionals*, 69(6).

Environmental indicator report - European Environment Agency (2014). Available at: https://www.eea.europa.eu/publications/environmental-indicator-report-2014 (Accessed: 28 April 2021).

Escobar, A. (2018) *Designs for the Pluriverse: Radical Interdependence, Autonomy, and the Making of Worlds*. Durham: Duke University Press Books.

Fjeldstad, V. and Leonardsen, M. R. (2017) *Scaffolding secondhand fashion consumption among adolescent girls-Cool and sustainable app design for better user experience of redistribution of clothing*. Master's Thesis. University of Oslo.

Fosser, M. *et al.* (2017) *Conserve and Consume - INF2260 - Høst 2017 - Universitetet i Oslo*. Available at: https://www.uio. no/studier/emner/matnat/ifi/INF2260/h17/projects/conserve-and-consume/index.html (Accessed: 28 June 2021).

Hanss, D. and Böhm, G. (2012) 'Sustainability seen from the perspective of consumers: Sustainability seen from the perspective of consumers', *International Journal of Consumer Studies*, 36(6), pp. 678–687.

Hilde, M. (2019) *Transitions to more sustainable fashion: relational, transparent, and community building*. Master's Thesis. University of Oslo.

Ingram, J., Shove, E. and Watson, M. (2007) 'Products and Practices: Selected Concepts from Science and Technology Studies and from Social Theories of Consumption and Practice1', *Design issues*, 23(2), pp. 3–16.

Irwin, T. (2018) 'The Emerging Transition Design Approach', in *DRS 2018. Design Research Society 2018: Catalyst*, 3, pp. 968–989. doi: 10.21606/drs.2018.210.

Jacobs, K. *et al.* (2018) 'Green thinking but thoughtless buying? An empirical extension of the value-attitude-behaviour hierarchy in sustainable clothing', *Journal of Cleaner Production*, 203, pp. 1155–1169.

Jain, S. and Mishra, S. (2020) 'Luxury fashion consumption in sharing economy: A study of Indian millennials', *Journal of Global Fashion Marketing*, 11(2), pp. 171–189.

Khandual, A. and Pradhan, S. (2019) 'Fashion Brands and Consumers Approach Towards Sustainable Fashion', in Muthu, S. S. (ed.) *Fast Fashion, Fashion Brands and Sustainable Consumption*. Singapore: Springer (Textile Science and Clothing Technology), pp. 37–54.

Kossoff, G. (2015) 'Holism and the reconstitution of everyday life: a framework for transition to a sustainable society', *Design Philosophy Papers*, 13(1), pp. 25–38.

Kuijer, S. C. (2014) *Implications of Social Practice Theory for Sustainable Design*. Doctoral dissertation. Delft University. Available at: http://resolver.tudelft.nl/uuid:d1662dc5-9706-4bb5-933b-75704c72ba30 (Accessed: 30 June 2021).

McDonald, S. and Oates, C. J. (2006) 'Sustainability: Consumer Perceptions and Marketing Strategies', *Business Strategy and the Environment*, 15(3), pp. 157–170. doi: 10.1002/bse.524.

Moran, G. (2020) 'Gen Z and Millennials 2020 report', *Drapers*, 9 September. Available at: https://www.drapersonline.com/insight/drapers-bespoke/gen-z-and-millennials-2020-report (Accessed: 28 April 2021).

Niedderer, K., Clune, S. and Ludden, G. (2017) *Design for Behaviour Change: Theories and practices of designing for change*. Routledge.

Niinimäki, K. *et al.* (2020) 'The environmental price of fast fashion', *Nature Rev. Earth &Environment*, 1(4), pp. 189–200.

Niinimäki, K. and Hassi, L. (2011) 'Emerging design strategies in sustainable production and consumption of textiles and clothing', *Journal of Cleaner Production*, 19(16), pp. 1876–1883. doi: 10.1016/j.jclepro.2011.04.020.

Odom, W. *et al.* (2009) 'Understanding why we preserve some things and discard others in the context of interaction design', in *Proceedings of the SIGCHI Conference on Human Factors in Computing Systems*. New York, NY, USA: ACM (CHI '09), pp. 1053–1062. doi: 10.1145/1518701.1518862.

Papanek, V. (1971) *Design for the Real World - Human Ecology and Social Change*. First American Edition. Pantheon.

Park, J., Ciampaglia, G. L. and Ferrara, E. (2016) 'Style in the age of instagram: predicting success within the fashion industry using social media', in *Proceedings of the 19th ACM Conference on computer-supported cooperative work & social computing*, pp. 64–73.

Peirson-Smith, A. and Evans, S. (2017) 'Fashioning Green Words and Eco Language: An examination of the user perception gap for fashion brands promoting sustainable practices', *Fashion Practice*, 9(3), pp. 373–397.

Pierce, J. and Paulos, E. (2011) 'Secondhand Interactions: Investigating Reacquisition and Dispossession Practices Around Domestic Objects', in *Proceedings of the SIGCHI Conference on Human Factors in Computing Systems*. New York, NY, USA: ACM (CHI '11), pp. 2385–2394. doi: 10.1145/1978942.1979291.

Raworth, K. (2017) *Doughnut Economics: Seven Ways to Think Like a 21st-Century Economist*. White River Junction, Vermont: Chelsea Green Publishing.

Rittel, H. W. J. and Webber, M. M. (1973) 'Dilemmas in a general theory of planning', *Policy Sciences*, 4(2), pp. 155–169.

Rockström, J. *et al.* (2009) 'Planetary boundaries: exploring the safe operating space for humanity', *Ecology and society*, 14(2). doi: 10.5751/ES-03180-140232.

Serazio, M. (2015) 'Selling (Digital) Millennials: The Social Construction and Technological Bias of a Consumer Generation', *Television & New Media*, 16(7), pp. 599–615. doi: 10.1177/1527476413491015.

Shove, E. and Pantzar, M. (2005) 'Consumers, producers and practices: understanding the invention and reinvention of Nordic walking', *Journal of consumer culture*, 5(1), pp. 43–64.

Srivastava, S. (2017) 'ZYGO: Design led reframing of secondhand marketplaces', *Nordes*, 7(1).

Srivastava, S. and Culén, A. L. (2018) 'Transition-oriented Futuring: Integrated Design for Decreased Consumption amongst Millennials', in *DRS 2018: Catalyst. DRS 2018*, 3, pp. 927–940.

Srivastava, S. and Culén, A. L. (2019a) 'From Niche to Mainstream Transitions: Digital Secondhand Markets for Millennials', in *Proceedings of the International Conference ICT, Society and Human Beings 2019. ICT 2019*, IADIS Press, pp. 19–27. doi: 10.21606/drs.2018.210.

Srivastava, S. and Culén, A. L. (2019b) 'Implications for Transitions to Sustainable Consumption: Finding Millennials' Behavior Archetypes', in *IASDR 2019: Design Revolutions,* pp. 1–12.

Steffen, W. *et al.* (2015) 'Planetary boundaries: Guiding human development on a changing planet', *Science*, 347(6223), pp. 1259855.

Stein, N., Spinler, S. and Vanthournout, H. (2020) 'Face-to-face communication as a tool to support secondhand fashion sales: a field experiment at Fashion Week in Berlin', *Sustainability*, 12(5), pp. 1758.

Thelwall, M. (2021) 'Lifestyle information from YouTube influencers: some consumption patterns', *Journal of Documentation*. doi: 10.1108/JD-02-2021-0033.

Turunen, L. L. M. and Halme, M. (2021) 'Communicating actionable sustainability information to consumers: The Shades of Green instrument for fashion', *Journal of Cleaner Production*, 297, pp. 126605. doi: 10.1016/j.jclepro.2021.126605.

Zimmerman, J. and Forlizzi, J. (2014) 'Research Through Design in HCI', in Olson, J. S. and Kellogg, W. A. (eds) *Ways of Knowing in HCI*. Springer New York, pp. 167–189.

@RE-ART. HOW TO MIX A VIRTUAL TOUR, ARCHIVING AND A SOCIAL MEDIA STRATEGY ON THE WEB TO INVOLVE A NEW PUBLIC AND BRING AWARENESS TO THE MUSEUM AND THE EXHIBITION

Dalia Gallico
Università San Raffaele Roma, Italy

ABSTRACT

The forced closure of cultural realities, dictated by the Coronavirus emergency, generated new needs for urgent solutions. Italy has heavily suffered as everything has been interrupted: exhibitions, trade fairs and museums, between more or less hard lockdowns and #iorestoacasa. From the spread of the virus, that thanks to vaccines sooner or later will begin to wane, to the spread of beauty that will help us revive the world. This is the path to follow and Italy a generator of beauty since ancient times, will have to be at the forefront of this mission. The reason is soon to be said. The aesthetic emotion brings man closer: the first sensation we experience in front of something beautiful - whatever it is - is that of not being alone. To encourage the meeting of beauty and people, many have done their utmost, let's think for example of the campaigns #museichiusimuseiaperti, #laculturanonsiferma, #MuseumFromHome, so well organized as to successfully substitute real life visits to museums and galleries, at least for the moment. Thanks to digital technology that allows activities to be carried out in places of art and culture and the distribution of content by all the main cultural institutions through social media. For the first time, the doors of the Web open wide and present to the public, through viewing rooms and virtual exhibition spaces, shows of all kinds. Broadening the horizon, the same choice is made by art galleries around the globe. Changing only the exhibition spaces, no longer physical but digital. Thanks to immersive 3D technology, one can enjoy the sensations and atmospheres of traditional visits. Therefore, the cultural mission of museums is not interrupted, rather it is strengthened and new projects are born exclusively for the Web that follow the themes of the moment. The @Re-Art project fits into this scenario which aims to combine the dynamism of multimedia and digital means of communication (webinar, podcast, social network, virtual tour, and exhibitions intended for the Web) with the uniqueness of the carefully archived heritage from Milanese exhibitions of the past two decades. A way to make them accessible, galvanize them and bring them into circulation, making them live again.

KEYWORDS

Virtual Tour, Exhibition, Web, Social Media, Covid, Digital Archive

1. INTRODUCTION

The Covid-19 Emergency has had a dramatic and unprecedented impact on museums around the world. On several occasions, the drastic personnel cuts in the sector have already been written about, as well as the hypothesis of new strategies for a less "standardized" museum fruition. To better understand the effects of the pandemic on museums around the world, NEMO - Network of European Museum Organizations – launched a survey (between March 24th and April 30th 2020) which involved around 1.000 museums from 48 countries including Italy, the United Kingdom, France, Germany and the United States. This analysis is part of a context that is dramatic in itself given that 93% of museums around the globe have been forced to close their doors as a result of state provisions, generating losses which, compared to pre-virus volumes, range from 75% to 80% per week. If we want to translate these figures, it is around € 10.000 per week for smaller museums, up to hundreds of thousands of euros for the larger ones. To be more precise, three out of five museums reported losses of around € 20.000 per week. Institutions including the Rijksmuseum and the Stedelijk in Amsterdam and the Kunsthistorisches Museum in Vienna have lost between €100.000 and €600.000 per week. In any case, among these, the ones that suffered most were those museums that support themselves thanks to private financing, that are more susceptible to changes and unforeseen events. Museums have suffered the consequences of the tourism blockade - according to the European Commission in this sector a decrease of between 50% and 70% is estimated - and, if we consider that 40% of European tourism is cultural, the prospects for the future are not the best.

The good news is that compared to American museums, most of those in Europe did not have to lay off their employees but, three out of ten museums have suspended their contracts with freelancers, and three out of five have stopped volunteer projects. 25% of museums said they will have to reduce staff in the future. Smart working appears to have been used in a widespread way: nearly half of the museums that responded to the NEMO survey stated that 80% of their staff work from home. With Regard to the emergency funds made available by governments, the panorama is varied. Museums from 15 countries said measures to address the emergency are still under discussion while special funds have already been made available in 12 countries. This difference is due to several factors, ranging from the development in the spread of Covid-19 to the typology of museum. The aid is intended to cover wages or lost earnings. Only 15% of museums are evaluating the possibility of finding alternative resources to make up for the huge losses. Of these, 7% trust in the possibility of making money through online programming.

2. DIGITAL SERVICES & VIRTUAL TOURS

Four out of five museums have upgraded their digital services to reach the public, often giving employees new tasks and duties. Nearly half of the museums that responded to the survey said they had promoted at least one new online business. 70% of the museums have increased their presence on Social Networks (see Figure 1). The platform most used by 602 museums is Facebook compared to only 183 who have chosen Instagram. Then they use YouTube, Twitter, LinkedIn and TikTok. Two out of five museums have seen an increase in online visits, between 10% to 150%. Products such as podcasts and direct online learning have increased significantly and, among the most popular contents, we see those dedicated to the various museum collections, with the availability of insights and information of more or less known works.

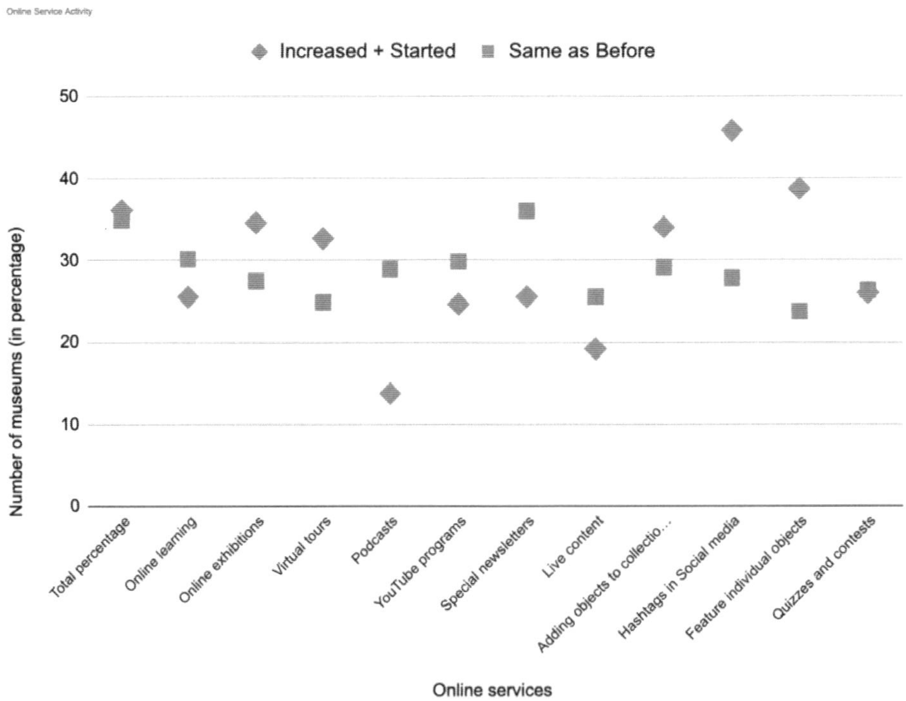

Figure 1. Increased online anctivity of museum during lockdown

For a few days in March 2020, the world focused its attention on virtual museum tours. His attention was driven by museum closures, major media coverage, and a mighty social media effort by museums to offer an online experience to audiences. And then, just as quickly, the attention disappeared and museums were left in what might be the greatest struggle for short-term relevancy they have ever faced. The data shows that we are past peak interest in virtual museum tours. The mainstream market isn't interested in seeing these world class institutions in virtual 3D spaces or photo galleries. As the Director of the Rubin Museum of Art, Jorrit Britschgi, said: "*There is nothing that can replace in-person encounters with art.*" However, just as interest peaked for virtual museum tours, it is now starting to peak in other areas that museums can serve. In this article, I'll share the data I mentioned and also the areas of opportunity. Google is one of the most data rich organizations ever to exist, and makes a portion of this data available to the public. Anyone can go to Google Trends, type in a query, and see search interest on Google's platform for the last 16 years. This data has several limitations, for example:

- The data is limited to Google's platform, which is popular but not quite ubiquitous. China, for example, has over 1.3 billion people that can't access Google without a VPN.
- The site does not provide number of searches and instead graphs on normalized and relative data. This structure allows for relative comparisons, without knowing whether you are analyzing in the thousands or millions.

Google provides related trends, but to a degree you still need to pinpoint an accurate search. It is possible, for example, that "online museum tours" could be a more relevant search than "virtual museum tours." It's not. Still, the data is accurate enough that we use it to make decisions on product development, marketing, staffing and other important aspects of our business. And to write blog posts. For example the results of Google's search data for "virtual museum tours" from 2019 to 2020 shows that interest in virtual museum tours started to surge on March 14th peaked on March 17th and has been on decline ever since. Related searches, such as "free virtual museum tours", "virtual museum tours for kids", and "online museum tours", show a similar trend. One notable exception is "best virtual museum tours" which continues to fluctuate. Data from other sources shows that the search volume with the "best" modifier is much lower than the other keywords. Some important notes:

1. With the wild fluctuations in the market, it is possible that we will see another surge in interest for virtual museum tours soon. My best guess is that for as long as the pandemic lasts, some interest in virtual museum tours will remain, but that we are still past peak.
2. This analysis is about the market size of virtual museum tours, and not otherwise a judgement of their quality or importance. For example, virtual museum tours are one way to make a museum and its collection more accessible.

3. PROJECT @ RE ART THE OBJECTIVES

Also in light of the fact that for some time it will not be possible to use the exhibition spaces except for very limited numbers of people, the need to produce narrative contents that rework the contents of past exhibitions and collect new ones designed for the digital. It is about collecting ideas and contents from the scientific committee to be reworked and conveyed on social networks. Alongside the strategy will be direct actions, that is writing and editing actions (written, video, audio, production of the collected contents). The aim is to increase the "followers" of the exhibitions and create a real community of enthusiasts who also actively participate with comments and ideas. The @ RE ART Multimedia platform aims to stimulate and disseminate a critical approach to the culture of the exhibition project through the 'collateral' content that is produced for exhibitions, catalogs, seminars and meetings. @ RE ART aims to broaden the territorial public ranges, lower the age of users and make the proposed contents more durable and in-depth. @ RE ART wants to present itself to young audiences through a channel that can be used interactively from anywhere, and become a place of study for young people, attractive and attentive to their requests, as well as a stimulus for the promotion and sharing of the exhibition activity which also includes a curatorial and realization dimension. With @ RE ART we want to broaden its impact outside the exhibition spaces (Palazzo Reale, Pac, Rotonda della Besana, Palazzo della Ragione) by virtually bringing people into the spaces and settings. From exhibition and traditional cultural institutions (where you can enter exhibitions with the purchase of a ticket) to ever-changing, open and welcoming international movement. The contents of the exhibitions stored in over 20 years of archive will become multimedia products hosted by a dedicated platform linked to an on and off line site. From exhibitions to conferences, from photos of installations to graphics, it will also be possible to experience the schedule of exhibitions (past, present and future) through a daily production of contents relating to individual initiatives. The artists, curators, fitters, graphic designers, technicians will hold webinars on their work, on the context in which they live and work, on the contents of the exhibition (past or future). The webinar will be dedicated to university and academy students, critics, young curators, visitors to Italian and international exhibitions (in English) but also to an audience of lovers of art and exhibitions. Postcasts will be made for the exhibitions (past and present), with interviews with the protagonists in order to expand the impact of the contents beyond the small number of visitors who can participate. The exhibition materials will also be translated into a language suitable for dissemination through Instagram and Facebook on the model of the "Harvard Business Review", with ad hoc daily editorial work followed by professional editors.With financing help by Fondazione Cariplo.

Figure 2. Timeline and details (video, photo, graphics, informations) Exhibitions in Royal Palace _Milan

4. THE ACTIVITIES

The activities must be articulated starting from some new rules that define contemporary communication. The first rule is that of relevance that sees a virtuous meeting between uniqueness, substance and distinction. It expresses the ability of art to emphasize passions, from the beating of hearts but also to ideas and their imagination. Artistic projects must make a difference in the everyday experience of life, with visions and messages that will be remembered and that are worth sharing in a virtual or physical space. Experiences that leave their mark allowing for the distinction of special and particular messages: Artistic UltraMessage. The second rule is that of resonance which we can consider on the other side of relevance. When you are unique and distinctive, you need to activate your So.na.r (acronym for sound navigation and ranging) intercepting the signals of widespread creativity. The phenomena are evaluated on the ability to overcome the wall of attention. For this purpose, it is interesting to understand the world of infrasound and ultrasounds perceived by dolphins and bats, which guarantees the perfect knowledge of a context through the bounce of an echo. On the web - with regard to the world of art - this will be the challenge of all-round resonance, which will go far beyond critics and industry experts.

The steps to take could therefore be:

- conceive and design a multimedia archiving project aimed at safeguarding and enhancing the material and intangible heritage of the exhibition;

- prepare new audiovisual, graphic and multimedia materials useful for a better use of the public with information and insights related to the exhibition activity of each individual exhibition (for all types of materials produced, translation into English is provided for); for an indicative estimate, about 30/35 exhibitions per year are calculated, so about 500 exhibitions in total in 15 years;
- to contribute to the development of new public-private partnership networks that favor the establishment of the Palazzo Reale and exhibitions in order to translate information relating to their history and structure into usable content in graphic and multimedia mode;
- design and implementation of the material produced, recovered and processed within the audiovisual and computer equipment of an innovative teaching platform;
- invest on cultural amplification of contents and the blooming of inventiveness not only for the few.

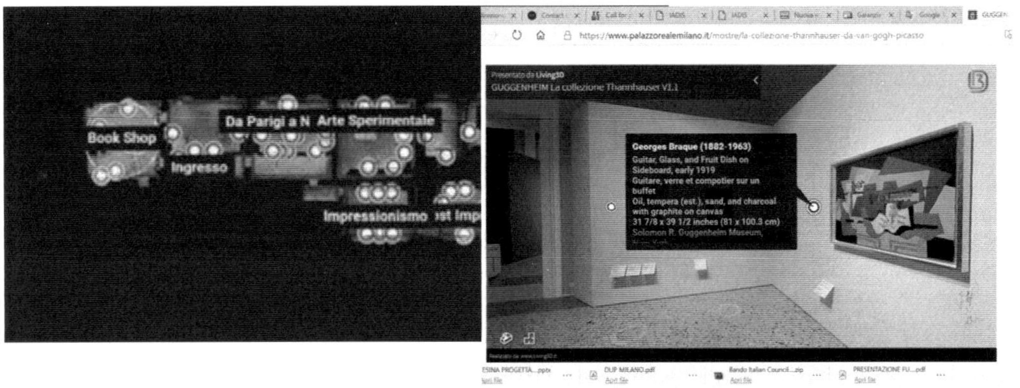

Figure 3. Virtual Exhibitions tour in Royal Palace _Milan

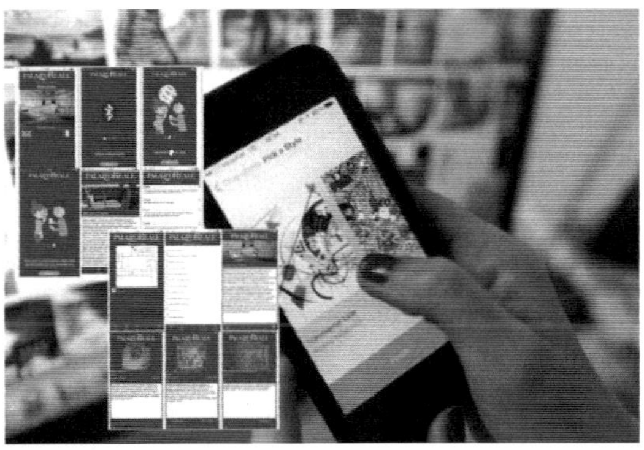

Figure 4. App Audio guide Exhibitions in Royal Palace _Milan

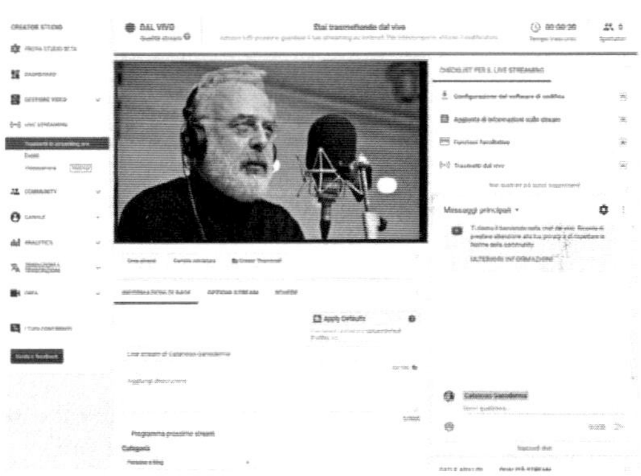

Figure 5. Live streaming curators, exhibit designers, art directors Exhibitions in Royal Palace _Milan

5. HOW TO MIX UP VIRTUAL TOUR & SOCIAL MEDIA STRATEGY: SOME INTERNATIONAL CASES HISTORIES

It's easy to get caught in social media posting patterns; particularly when a majority of other museums doing the same thing. Many museums are focused on the immediate metrics following a post, i.e. how many likes and new followers. However, it's important to step back and look at overall social media strategy. Is it cohesive? It is in line with museum's mission? Look at museum's social media short-term and long-term goals alongside the strategy to determine new guidelines that help you identify alternative measures of success.

Keep captions to a minimum as modern attention spans appreciate shorter text. The words you use to accompany an image can be a chance to tease followers. Release the title of an exhibition word by word on social media. Build up a wall of visuals to add impact to a big announcement like The Barbican in London did with their iconic brutalist architecture.

If you're feeling like audience might be tired of hearing museum's organisational voice and perspective over and over, then you're probably right. Mix things up by inviting guests to take over one of social media accounts for the day to see collection or a special event through their eyes. Today there are many cases in the world that follow the path of experimentation between art, technology, different disciplines proposing partnerships between public institutions, private companies and citizen associations. Let's view some and from each we can draw a key that will then be useful in the development of the @ RE ART project.

Art & Citizenship

#MuseumInstaSwap_is an initiative that was originally born in London but has now been adopted by New York City. In 2018, a whopping 42 New York City museums, galleries and arts and culture organisations participated in the now annual social media initiative aimed at highlighting the breadth of arts and culture institutions within the city. The premise is that organisations are coupled together based on their collections, interests and aims. For example, the art-deco Neue Galerie was partnered with NYC's Poster House in 2018 and the duo's posts beautifully complemented one another as there was a genuine shared interest and passion. Identify an organisation or individual with a similar ethos and social media presence and give them a shout! You may find that other museums are looking to switch up their social media as well.

Entire dissertations have been written about cat memes on the internet. The time of the meme and the GIF is now.

Instant Art Occasion

LACMA Los Angeles County Museum of Art has been a cheeky presence on social media for years with their comedic Snapchat stories and Instagram posts. They use their collection to connect with audiences and share their artworks with the world. Humour is a great way to connect with those who may find museum inaccessible either physically or mentally. Invite people to experience collection in a new way and engage digitally. Another example is the Brooklyn Museum that has a social media series featuring their staff called BKM WAY which stands for "Brooklyn Museum, We Are You". The series highlights the various departments and talented staff members behind every museum visit. Glimpsing what happens behind the scenes can help visitors to understand the bigger picture for organisation and allow them to feel more connected. Featuring staff, trustees and volunteers is something museums can do year-round, not just on the annual appreciation days. hether it be to commemorate Valentine's Day like the Royal Academy did in their cupid-inspired tweet or to take part in a new trend that's been bobbing round in newsfeed, it's important to use social media to mark special days and months.

Civil Engagement & Involvement

Use Women's History Month (March) to highlight female artists in collection. Photography Day (19th August) could be used to either highlight photographs in collection, or you could explore collection through the eye of a lens. There are lots of possibilities to get creative and engage with national and international audiences. Engage followers in a social media challenge. This can be anything from an invitation for comments on a post to a full-blown curated exhibition like Seattle's Frye Museum posed to the world in 2015 for the curation of their exhibition.

Single Artist Story

If you're aiming to operate on a smaller scale, then take inspiration from the Van Gogh Museum in Amsterdam that has a dedicated Instagram story to highlighting how visitors from across the world pronounce the museum's namesake, "Van Gogh". The story puts visitors front and centre, mixing up the content from institutional voices and objects. Take some inspiration from both inside and outside museum to switch up visuals. An easy way to do this is to look a bit closer at some elements of museum's collection, architecture and/or grounds. Post some magnified images and challenge followers to identify the contents or even better, go on a scavenger hunt within museum! Chicago's Field Museum posted a magnified photo of turkey feathers around the American holiday of Thanksgiving and used the opportunity to educate visitors about the iconic birds. To change things up, look for interesting patterns, colours, textures and details within collection, then create a strategy to showcase them and engage followers in museum's collection and mission.

Artistic Tours

With Tour [AR]T, Apple in collaboration with the New Museum in New York, is experimenting with new experiences for passionate consumers, somewhere between technological innovation and art. These are experiential tours to iconic places in cities of the United States where to discover installations by a selection of famous artists, such as Nick Cave, Nathalie Djurberg and Hans Berg, Cao Fei, John Giorno, Carsten Höller and Pipilotti Rist, made using AR. *«We hope attendees are inspired... we can't wait to see what our visitors learn to create in the [AR]T Lab»* affirmed Apple's Deirdre O'Brien.

Art & AI

Los Angeles-based studio Ouchhh combines artificial intelligence with data learnt from the pre-pottery neolithic period to create DATAMONOLITH AI, a 3 billion-pixel digital monolith. Built using 6-meter-high led screens, the architectural piece of art aims to breathe new life into the world's oldest and most ancient origins. Dating back to 9600–7000 b.C., it displays visuals produced by machine learning, which surveys data from Göbekli Tepe, an archaeological site in the southeastern Anatolia region of Turkey. It takes images collected from the site and translates them into data sculptures in the form of graphic visuals that illuminate the otherwise dark obelisk. Ferdi Alici, founder and Director of Ouchhh, explains "Our main question is: what would happen if the consciousness of the world's oldest ancient origins data and AI come together for hybrid architectural public art?" The piece is on display as part of the "Future and the Arts: AI, Robotics, Cities, Life – How Humanity Will Live Tomorrow" exhibition at the Mori Art Museum in Tokyo.

Music & AI

In her personal research, Bjork the Icelandic artist has never neglected to take care of a positive interaction with technology. Kórsafn is an installation inside the Sister City hotel in New York that combines her creativity in the musical field with artificial intelligence, through a Microsoft program. Referring to the Icelandic word Kórsafn, made up of "kór" = "choral" and "safn" = "archives", some of her choral arrangements that she's created over the course of her 17 year career are combined using technology to give value to the Icelandic choral culture. The algorithms of the program generate exciting musical variations in real time with the passage of birds, clouds, planes and pressure changes which envelop visitors, who can listen in the lobby or online.

Public Installation

Portuguese designer Vanessa Barragão uses ecological weaving techniques to make collections of modern rugs and tapestries, using industry-wasted yarns. Lately she has created a huge map, the Botanical Tapestry installation: a large tapestry, which resembles a textile sculpture, and represents the world with references to the flora of the various continents precisely to make the public aware of pollution and the increase in water temperature. The work, commissioned from London Heathrow airport and the Royal Botanic Gardens at Kew, was positioned in the area destined for departures at London Heathrow airport, where during the month of August a large number of travellers were able to admire it. To complete the tapestry, 20 meters long, Vanessa Barragão needed 520 hours of work.

Art & Science

With the exhibition Power *Pixels 2020*, taking place at the Wood Street Galleries in Pittsburgh until April 5th 2020, the french artist Miguel Chevalier (a pioneer of digital art) interprets abstract and complex phenomena in a unique and personal way, creating amazing experiences, between art and science. Of the two installations in virtual reality proposed, *Complex Meshes* allows the spectator to view the scientific concepts of flow and networks, intrinsically difficult to perceive, giving them form and consistency. The work is an interactive projection in which everything branches out, it intertwines and transforms according to how the spectators move in the hall.

6. CONCLUSION

In the new era of onlife that we live, @ RE ART is the art of remembering and telling with an innovative storytelling, aimed at creating and developing a network of information, relationships and knowledge to support the use of the exhibition activity. The peculiarity and its innovative character reside in the "transversal" approach to art, and in the activation of new communication tools to create a network of ideas and connections that cross the whole "system" between the public with the activities and exhibition venues connected to it. The platform will be attractive and interactive, motivating projects, areas of interest and broad surveys, creating different levels of accessibility and "narration" of the exhibition heritage, through the use of the most advanced multimedia and communication technologies. Objective: to memorize, reorganize and rationalize the information contents of the exhibitions, placing them within a path that contextualizes the temporary information (the exhibition, the layout, the graphics ...) with their cultural background (the author, the curator, the works, his history). The system will be able to manage different types of output. This means that all information can be published in the formats and through the most appropriate communication channels on the platform (such as archives or live streaming). The platform does not only want to document but to memorize, promote, communicate the exhibition reality in its daily development. We do not contemplate, we interact. The contents designed, archived and produced will become usable multimedia products hosted by a very technologically innovative platform, welcoming to a large and dedicated number of visitors. Past and future exhibitions will always be possible to experience and visit them through interviews, installations, videos, graphics, photos, virtual tours. Through a daily production of content relating to individual initiatives - to make it possible to carry out thematic researches and routes and virtual realities in the Archive of the unique exhibition heritage (set-ups, graphics, videos… etc.) of the most important exhibitions of the last twenty years. On the horizon that awaits us, some essential values clearly emerge: respect and responsibility that also in artistic and museum production imply a new management ethic. The artistic vision of *t*hose who produce works and then communicate them must take charge of a system of values, presenting, supporting and implementing their idea of quality of life, indicating the sense of experience. The new paradigms of sustainability, of personal dignity, relational empathy must be considered, as renewed playing fields on which to produce credible creative design. Relevance – the primary source of communication and resonance - must measure itself against the yardstick of respect and responsibility. Engagement then constitutes the keystone in the authentic relationship with visitors and their community, allowing the equal exchange of opinions and experiences that can and must consolidate the open discussion with one's interlocutors. The circle closes with recognition, which implies - only at the end of the process - a permanent mirroring in the observer, with interlocutors who become daily partners and who must be known and re-known, based on a common vision, a memorable message, a correct tone of voice and an ability to listen beyond the normal. The communication strategies of a museum thus enter a new dimension in which nothing is enough and everything is necessary.

REFERENCES

#SocialMedium https://fryemuseum.org/exhibition/5631/

@ RE ART http://www.artpalazzoreale.it/

Barbican https://www.barbican.org.uk/

Field Museum https://www.fieldmuseum.org/

Floridi, L., 2020. *Pensare l'infosfera. La filosofia come design concettuale.* Raffaello Cortina Editore, Milano.

Floridi, L., 2017. *La quarta rivoluzione. Come l'infosfera sta trasformando il mondo.* Raffaello Cortina Editore, Milano.

Kórsafn Björk https://www.microsoft.com/inculture/musicxtech/bjork/

LACMA Los Angeles County Museum of Art https://www.lacma.org/

Mandarano, N., 2019. *Musei e media digitali.* Carocci Editore, Roma.

Morace, F. , 2018. *Futuro più umano. Quello che l'intelligenza artificiale non potrà mai darci.* Egea, Milano.

Mori Museum Tokyo https://ouchhh.tv/AI-DATAMONOLITH-1

MuseumInstaSwap https://www.museuminstaswap.org/

NEMO Network of European Museum Organizations https://www.ne-mo.org/news/article/nemo/nemo-survey-onmuseums-and-covid-19-increasing-online-activities-of-museums.html

New Museum https://www.newmuseum.org/pages/view/ar-t

Vanessa Barragão https://www.vanessabarragao.com/html/ArtworkProjects/artworkP_Botanical.html

Wood Street Galleries http://woodstreetgalleries.org/portfolio-view/miguel-chevalier/

LEGAL PERSONALITY OF INDIVIDUALS IN THE SYSTEM OF DIGITAL RELATIONS: SCIENTIFIC UNDERSTANDING AND LEGAL REGULATION IN RUSSIA

Evgeny Mamay
Nizhny Novgorod Academy of the MIA of Russia
3, Ankudinovskoe shosse, Nizhny Novgorod, Russia

ABSTRACT

The essence of many social relations transferred from the real world to the virtual one is changed radically due to rapid development of ICT. Legislative framework of digital relations cannot get in time with digital innovations and occurs with a significant time lag. In recent years the Russian Parliament enacted dozens of bills targeted to Information Policy, Software and Communications, but the Russian Digital legislation still stays fragmented and unsystematic. It is especially clear in the context of legal personality of Natural Persons and other participants of digital relations.
The purpose of the publication is to integrate general legal approach with specific features of digital law and determine the legal personality of individuals as a basic point of legal regulations in the digital sphere.
The research methodology is based on doctrinal analysis, comparative legal and legal-technical approaches to research of texts of laws and regulations.
The article analyzes the phenomenon of legal personality of participants in digital relations, Russian and foreign legal experience. According to the author, the lack of comprehensive solutions and well-formed approaches to regulations of digital relations has long-term negative consequences. He sees the comprehensive solution to relevant problems in the united legislative act (Digital Code) aimed to common and system regulation of digital relations. Digital rights and obligations of Internet users should be legally linked, first of all, with the age and civil status of a person. At the level of laws, it is necessary to determine the requirements for identification of Internet users, the relevant criteria and procedures, to set up the system for protecting personal information and calculated data that allows identifying the person. The solution of these tasks is impossible without basic legal solutions, including the requirements for legal personality.

KEYWORDS

Natural Person, Individual, Legal Personality, Legal Capacity, Liability, Digital Rights

1. INTRODUCTION

In order to build the full-fledged relations between society and the State in the digital era, the technological development should be predicted and followed by a well-thought-out, harmonious legal regulation. Only over the past decade, societies in several countries have been shaken by scandals related to illegal use of digital technologies by commercial companies and private. So, in 2018, a high-profile investigation against the Cambridge Analytica company, which collected and subsequently sold personal information about users of the social network Facebook, led to the termination of the activities of this company and casted a shadow on all Tech Giants.

The rapid development of technologies has an increasing impact on the ways and means of interactions between individuals, society and the state. The leading states awared long time ago the value of information possession and the importance of IT for the purpose to applicate the potential of that resource to the goals of public administration. In this context, Russia looks like as a “catching up” state, although due to its significant intellectual potential, primarily represented by specialists in the field of information technologies, this lag is gradually decreasing.

In the field of law and public administration, the problem of comprehending new realities is characterized by systemic problems caused by the rapid development of digital technologies caught-up by domestic legislation. The evolving circumstances represent a paradoxical situation. On the one hand, the Russian legal doctrine, due to its inertia and inherent conservatism, instead of directing the development of normative regulation, is compelled to follow up it, trying to adapt itself to the already existing realities and assemble a single picture of law in the digital world from initially scattered and unrelated fragments. On the other hand, the legislation and subordinate regulations following the rapid growth of ICT are forced to be developed at a pace that outstrips domestic legal science, which entails a fragmentary, scattered, unsystematic regulation of digital relations.

The classical theory of law considers the law as "a set of rules governing the relations that develop between subjects about a certain object" (Talapina, 2018, p. 6), but in the digital age it needs to be changed fundamentally or at least significantly clarified. One of the main problems of law in the digital sphere is related to the determining of the essence and place of a person and personality in the world of Internet technologies. The special attention to a person as an actor of social relations is of the undeniable interest due to several circumstances. Firstly, any system of regulation is ultimately focused on human behavior. In Russian legal science, it is customary to subdivide all norms in force in society into two large groups. The first group are "social norms" which include legal, moral and religious norms, customs and traditions, etc. The second group of norms, "technical" ones, covers purely technical, sanitary, hygienic, environmental and other «non-social» norms (Matuzov, 2009, pp. 212-213). If the first group regulates relations between people and their collectives, for the technical norms the subject of regulation is the relationship between human and objects of the external world, nature, technology (relationship of the "human-machine", "human-nature" type, etc.). Secondly, information technologies change the person in his habits and features of behavior, creating a new environment of existence in which a person spends a significant part of his life and forced to adapt to. Finally, the gradual development of technologies leads to a change in the very essence of the relationship in which a person exists: despite the preservation of their subject-object character, the conditional “person” and the conditional “device” change places in them, and the person increasingly becomes an object of influence from the neural networks and artificial intelligence. The range of problems associated with these circumstances is not limited to issues of digital inequality, the availability of public services or execution of political authority, but, in its most extreme manifestation, can pose an immediate threat to the person himself, his honor, dignity, health and even life. This set of circumstances requires substantive understanding in legal science and adequate reflection in law of the place of the individual in the system of legal relations of the digital era.

2. MAIN CONTENT

2.1 Literature Review

Scientific literature covers quite extensively the problems of personality in the digital space. Bell predicted changes as a result of the formation of a post-industrial society (Bell, 1973, p. 32) find their real expression in the modern world. Researchers note the paradoxical trend: due to the impact of digital technologies even methods of communication between people are simplified, the initial components of the communication itself (information, message and understanding) are degraded (Bechmann, 2000), consciousness, style and nature of decisions are radically changed (Howes, 2001, p. 42). At the same time, the Internet continues to be perceived as a space of personal freedom and freedom of expression, which leads the fear of losing privacy becoming the subject of most discussion.

The focus of scientific publications in this area concentrates, on the one hand, on the problem of the ability of legal means to protect a person in a situation when digital technologies carry out breakthrough development, on the other hand, on the dangers arising from the misuse of digital technologies by states and third parties, who have opportunities to invade citizens' privacy.

A significant part of scientific articles in the first of these categories notes the inability of national legislation to adequately protect the rights of citizens in the digital environment. The fear of scientists, in particular, is caused by the initial problem of the legal status of information posted by users on the Internet, as well as the possibility of its use by “digital giants” and authorities (Peppet, 2014; Roberts, 2015). Cyberpsychologists and cyber-criminologists are actively studying the psychological aspects of citizens' victimization in the digital sphere (Alonso & Romero, 2017; Hadlington, 2017). Many researchers strive for the creation of legal mechanisms for the protection of citizens on the Internet as the development of the normative provisions of democratic constitutions that guarantee the individual's right to privacy. So, for the United States, the specified problems are discussed in the light of the implementation of the Fourth Amendment to the US Constitution (Kerr, 2010). Since digital data stored by telecom operators make it possible to disclose a person's life (e.g., day-to-day routs, places of purchases, list of calls, etc.), researchers pay attention to both legality of mass surveillance as whole (Golubok, 2015) and interception of data relevant to particular person (Desai, 2014). In European literature, mass surveillance on the Internet is widely discussed due to the adoption of landmark decisions on this issue by the European Court of Human Rights and the Court of Justice of the European Union (Rusinova, 2018). The recent trend has also become a discussion of the legislative aspects of face recognition technologies (FRT) (Ruhrmann, 2019).

The Russian jurisprudence, following the general trend of science, also explores the objective regularities of the influence of ICT on the legal status of an individual, however, as a rule, these issues are studied in the second place as a consequence arising from the author's interest in the problems of the information society, e-democracy, electronic government, information security, personal data protection and related phenomena of modern socio-political development. The study of literature on legal issues allows us to talk about disproportionate attention of scientists, on the one hand, to narrow problems of a civil, criminal and administrative nature and, on the other hand, insufficient general theoretical understanding of the legal personality in the system of digital relations. Oddly enough, the second statement is true even in relevance to the standpoints of information law and digital law which occupy particularly new place in the system of branches of the Russian law. Thus, most publications of both domestic and foreign authors are characterized by either superficial, generalized relation to the status of an individual in the digital era, or, on the contrary, a pinpoint attention to the sideshows and peripheral issues.

2.2 Place of a Natural Person among the Subjects of Legal Relations in the Digital Sphere

In legal literature the issue of the subjects of legal relations is covered by the authors in different ways. The Russian academic textbooks on information and digital law are mainly based on the general legal understanding of the subjects of legal relations. V.A. Kopylov (2002) singles out legal entities, natural persons, state and municipal bodies as the general subjects of information law. A.A. Tedeev (2021) supplements the specified list including the State of the Russian Federation, regions of the Russian Federation and municipalities. However, most often, scientists, who speak about the subjects of law, differentiate them into individual and collective, paying special attention to their functional differentiation. For example, I.A. Tsindeliani (2020), referring to the traditional definition of individual and collective participants in legal relations, then refers to "virtual" or "digital personalities", robots and other special subjects of digital law, but does not integrate them into the general system of subjects of law.

For understanding the specifics of legal relations in the digital sphere a functional classification is more significant, insofar as it distinguishes producers, consumers and owners of information, information resources, information products, information services, information systems, technologies and means of their support. Functional classification can be combined with the basic differentiation of legal subjects, in which the above roles are assigned to natural persons and legal entities. Of particular interest is the establishment of the place of electronic persons (Yastrebov, 2018), artificial intelligence (Morhat, 2018), robots (Gabov & Havanova, 2018) and other participants in legal relations in the digital sphere.

Speaking about the place of individuals among other subjects of legal relations in the digital sphere, it is necessary to be based on two important theoretical premises.

First, we see it as quite controversial to single out different legal subjects for different branches of law. As S.I. Arkhipov (2005, p. 23) states, legal personality is a generic connection of a person with the rule of law, carrying out different legal functions in various types of legal relations, the subject of law is endowed with additional properties that determine the features of his legal personality, but at the same time retains its integrity regardless of the susceptibility to branch regulation. For example, the individual can act as an author, supplier, owner of information or information resource, as well as its end user. Based on the foregoing, it is important to determine how the legal personality of an individual changes when he is involved in the sphere of digital legal relations.

Secondly, we consider it fundamentally important to separate the concepts of "subject of legal relationship in the digital sphere" and "subject of digital law". All persons who are targeted by the legal norms of digital law can be called subjects of digital law, however, some individuals cannot enter into specific legal relations regulated by digital law, and moreover, it's justified in relation to some persons to purposefully introduce such restrictions. For example, minors, like all individuals, are subjects of digital rights, but their participation in certain types of relationships on the Internet can and should be limited, in particular, to ensure their morality and physical health.

2.3 Legal Personality of a Natural Person in the Digital Sphere

With regard to the persons, jurisprudence traditionally operates with several concepts: "individual", "natural person", "citizen", "foreign citizen", "stateless person", "bipatride", however, in the digital sphere the attention should be paid to the both sides of the humans' essence: as a biological and as a social being what is equally important in relevance with the system of Internet relations.

The natural qualities of a person in social communication acquire a special meaning and endow him with the status of a personality. The dialectical unity of the personality structure is formed by consciousness, will and the ability to act. Each of these components in the digital space is undergoing significant change.

First of all, researchers-futurologists warn about the danger of the transhumanistic enhancement of humanity, as a result of which the "new man" will appear, created by merging his own physical body with electronic mechanisms and resulting in a wider range of certain possibilities.

Secondly, the socially conditioned structure of personality under the influence of information technologies also undergoes significant changes. V.V. Mironov (2017, p. 36) argues: "The constant use of digital technologies changes the very style of thinking of people, more and more of them acquire the so-called clip consciousness, which inevitably affects the style and nature of decision-making in the legal sphere". Researchers predict that as cyberspace becomes more interactive, more sensual and more ubiquitous, the way in which the legislation is conceptualized and presented over time may become less and less textual (written) and more like traditional forms of expressing norms of behavior in oral societies (such as for example, song or dance) (Howes, 2001, p. 42).

Finally, the basic feature of the virtual space is expressed in a change in the very identity on the human personality. The legal sphere is traditionally inherent in the differentiation of the statuses of citizens of their state, foreign citizens and stateless persons. In a general humanistic context, in the field of respect for personal rights, this division is not significant, however, in the sphere of political life, national security, a special political and legal relationship between a person and the State acquires fundamental importance, determining the very possibility of the existence of the state, defining the essence of national sovereignty. For example, the right of the natural person to participate in the system of political relations, elections or referendem is strictly involved with the citizenship or the place of permanent residence of the person.

The issue of the Legal Personality (in Russian – *правосубъектность* (pravosub"ektnost')) of the natural person in the system of digital relations must be approached taking into account the above mentioned. Traditionally, the Russian legal science defines Legal Personality as a triunity of such components as the Legal Capacity for Enjoying Rights (in Russian - *правоспособность* (pravosposobnost')), the Capacity for Performing Juristic Acts and Duties (in Russian - *дееспособность* (deesposobnost')) and the Capacity to be held accountable for wrongdoing (delictual or criminal accountability, in Russian – *деликтоспособность* (deliktosposobnost')). Since the responsibility for any activity is close linked with the performing of Juristic Acts and considered as the obligation of a person to undergo certain deprivations of a moral, physical or material nature, delictual accountability (the ability to bear responsibility stipulated by the law for one's actions) can be considered as an element of Capacity for Performing Juristic Acts.

2.4 The Legal Capacity of the Natural Person for Enjoying Rights and Capacity of the Natural Person for Performing Juristic Acts in the Digital Sphere

The Legal Capacity for Enjoying Rights is understood as the ability of an individual to have subjective rights and legal obligations due to the law. This ability is defined as an abstract, postulated possibility of carrying out certain actions in the future. According to Part 2 of Article 17 of the Civil Code of the Russian Federation, the legal capacity of a natural person arises at the time of his birth and terminates by death.

The Capacity of the subject of law for Performing Juristic Acts and Duties means the ability of the natural person to exercise subjective rights and bear legal obligations by his personal actions. For establishing the capacity of a person in the legal sphere, it is fundamentally important to determine his age and mental state. The capacity for Performing Juristic Acts in Civil relations begins from the age of 18 when the person is considered as an adult (clause 1 of article 21 of the Civil Code of the Russian Federation), bringing to administrative responsibility is possible from the age of 16 (article 2.3 of the Administrative Code of the Russian Federation), the age of criminal responsibility is also 16 years, and for a number of crimes from 14 years (article 20 of the Criminal Code RF).

In the digital sphere, the implementation of regulatory provisions that determine the legal capacity of a natural person for enjoying rights and the capacity for performing juristic acts and duties is faced with the specific features of digital reality, what requires a solution to the problem of personal identification. At first glance, this difficulty does not concern legal capacity. But if we are talking not only about its interpreting in Civil Law , but, for example, about Electoral Law , then the moment of capacity occurrence is inevitably linked with the person's acquisition of citizenship or a residence permit in Russia. So, Clause 10 of Article 4 of the Russian Federal Law "On Basic Guarantees of Electoral Rights and the Right to Participate in a Referendum of Citizens of the Russian Federation" provides for the possibility of participation in elections not only for Russian citizens, but also for foreign citizens permanently residing in the territory of the respective municipality (in relation to elections to local self-government bodies or participation in a local referendum). Nowadays the solution of this issue is becoming more and more urgent, because the elections are conducting more and more often in the electronic form.

With regard to capacity for performing juristic acts and duties, the situation is becoming even more complicated. Despite the relative simplicity of many actions on the Internet their commission requires users to understand the legal essence and consequences of happening, starting from the performance of civil transactions, for example, purchases on the online shops, and ending with acts bordering on the criminal law, for example, cyberbullying. The urgency of this problem is vividly emphasized by the number of pages that search engines give out to the query "child bought ... how to get the money back", which speaks of the massive nature of what is happening, but not regulated by law in many countries, including Russia.

Thus, the establishing in the digital space both the Legal Capacity of the natural person for Enjoying Rights and the Capacity for Performing Juristic Acts and Duties is required in order to ensure the admission of individuals to a wide range of social relations arising on the Internet.

First of all, it should be noted that a person can create many digital counterparts and virtual doubles on the Internet that do not coincide with objects of the real world. There is no direct relationship between an individual and his digital image: a man can impersonate a woman, a child - an adult, etc. (Howes, 2001, p. 43). Many proponents of the Net society advocate the importance of preserving the key characteristics of cyberspace as a sphere in which people are able to escape the constraints of the physical and cultural conditions of their lives, creating images of who they want to be, rather than who they are (Wilson, 1997, p. 145). As a result, there is a multiplier effect of digital technologies: there can be tens and hundreds of times more digital personalities on the Internet than there are real personalities on the planet (even if we take into account the exclusion of a significant part of the population from Internet communications).

In addition to the admission of people to freedom of self-identification, declared by the liberals, the effect of multiplication also gives rise to obvious negative aspects. The list of such problems starts with the difficulty of limiting the access of minors to resources that can harm their moral state, health and life, and ending with the need to suppress the commission of wrongdoings by subjects whose identity is difficult to establish. The identification problem can be resolved in two fundamentally opposite scenarios. According to one scenario the Internet is viewed as a zone of absolute freedom that does not allow interference by the State, Internet corporations or anyone else. On the contrary, the otherwise decision obliges the authorities to solve the problem of personal identification by providing access to the Internet exclusively by personal identifiers.

The problem of user identification arose simultaneously with the realization of the need for legal regulation of Internet relations, but so far it has not found its solution. On the technical side, the identification of a user is possible in various ways, ranging from one-factor identification by login/password and ending with multifactor verification through several interconnected channels, including verification by biometric data. At the same time any methods for solving this problem are not free from the risks of information leakage, loss of meaningful information and their seizure by third parties. Technical means can only create a legal fiction of certainty of the Internet user, but they are not able to finally identify the subject of legal relations. This legal fiction reduces the question of fact (a reliably established person) to a question of law (a person recognized as legally defined and established). In practice of modern conditions the problem of identifying the subject of legal relations is solved either by methods of Private Law (electronic signature) or methods of Public Law (admission to the Internet by identification data). The identity of the user in both cases is presumed to be established, since the identification procedure is recorded only from the formal side, and the probabilistic establishment of a personal identity is given the character of a legally reliable fact, i.e. a legal fiction is created.

In the commercial sphere the problem of user identification has been tested for a long time due to the need to ensure the commercialization of manufactured products. As an example we can mention the provision of access for users of technical products or software products through a single account that stores all data associated with a specific user (for example, Apple-ID, Google account, Huawei-ID, etc.). At the same time, this solution is not universal in nature, since in a business environment the identification is primarily aimed at obtaining funds from users and advertisers, which does not imply the absolute reliability of information about the user. Moreover, in the case of using encryption algorithms and decentralized networks built on the principle of anonymity, it becomes almost impossible to establish the identity of users.

At the same time, we see a promising development of domestic legislation along the way of registering individuals to provide users with access to the Internet. Scientific and legislative discussion has already begun in this direction. In particular, in 2018, the State Duma of Russia (the lower chamber of the Russian Parliament) considered the draft on amending the Federal Law "On Information, Information Technologies and Information Protection" (draft No. 369029-7), which obliged owners of social networks to provide access for individuals by registering them on passport data. At the current time the implementation of such initiatives is faced with the absence of personal electronic documents of citizens of the Russian Federation, however, in the future the possibility of identification can be carried out using the portal of public services as a single access point. This procedure has already been tested in software products of commercial enterprises (Sberbank, Renaissance Insurance, etc). In addition, there is being discussed the possibility of technical creation and legislative regulation of a unified biometric system, access to which can be obtained by state bodies, local authorities, individual entrepreneurs, notaries and other organizations.

The additional problem of personal identification is closely related with the issue of acquiring rights and obligations not only under one's own name, but under a fictitious name (pseudonym) in cases when it is prescribed by law. In accordance with Articles 18 and 1265 of the Civil Code of the Russian Federation the natural person has the right to do it, but special legal regulation of this area has not yet been developed. In their essence pseudonyms are closely related to the subject of copyright legislation which in accordance with the Berne Convention (1886) and the clause 4 of Article 1259 of the Civil Code of the Russian Federation doesn't require the need for registration or other formalities for obtaining copyright protection. The absence of clear rules led the Russian judicial practice to protecting pseudonyms and nicknames used on the Internet by means of industrial property legislation and registering these identifiers as trademarks. As a result the Russian Intellectual Property Court annually considers dozens of disputes on invalidating decisions of the Federal Service for intellectual property (Rospatent) on the granting of legal protection to such trademarks.

Another issue that needs to be addressed on the Internet is the problem of the continued existence of the virtual doubles of the natural persons even after the death of a human in the real world. Such an "experience" can have both positive (neutral) consequences (for example, the citation index of deceased authors continues to grow, despite the termination of their scientific activities) and a pronounced negative connotation (use of the good name, reputation of the deceased for illegal purposes by other people).

Already now, the legislation of some countries, including Russia, has reflected the so-called "right to be forgotten", but in the Russian Federation it is realized by the active behavior of the right holder (self-initiative approach). Thus, in 2015 the special amendment to the Federal Law "On Information, Information Technologies and Information Protection" introduced the right of a citizen (individual) to require the operator of a search engine that distributes advertising on the Internet to stop issuing information allowing access to information about the applicant. Meanwhile, taking into account the obligation of the applicant to prove the fact of violated Russian legislation, the inaccuracy, irrelevance of the information, the loss of its meaning for the applicant due to subsequent events or his actions, the discussed norm of law can be characterized rather as "an obligation to be on the Internet", but not "the right to be forgotten".

Also, modern Russian legislation does not in any way regulate the right to "digital death". This legal concept found the place in foreign legislation and been based on the understanding of the virtual double as an object of personal data relevant to particular natural person. In particular, in France, the Law on the Digital Republic (Loi pour une République numérique, 2016) imposes an obligation on online communication service providers to inform users about data sorting after their death. From our point of view the preferable way on the development of digital legislation is to establish the obligation for the internet search engine operators and any other controller of personal data to prevent human rights violations by ensuring both "the right to be forgotten" and "the right to digital death". The ensuring of this rights should not be linked with the removal of the relevant data from the Internet only by the initiation of right owner especially if such personal data revealing health or sex life, racial or ethnic origin, political opinions, religious or philosophical beliefs, trade-union membership. The certain exceptions and derogations are possible as regards the processing of data relating to offences, criminal convictions or security measures, which are carried out under the control of official authorities.

Thus, we find significant gaps even in the basic, initial categories of the legal personality of a natural person in the digital environment, which already at the current time gives rise to problems in the implementation of many citizens' rights. A significant part of such problems is of a latent nature, they either are not realized by citizens or deliberately ignored, which in the future can create an avalanche effect of the growth of social regulation problems, ranging from interpersonal conflicts in social networks and ending with massive leaks of personal data of users of various software products and technical products.

3. CONCLUSION

The above mentioned gaps in the Russian legislation and related problems of unsettled legal status of subjects of digital relations indicate not a lack of attention to them from legislators or law enforcers, but the high complexity of these circumstances and the resulting legal consequences. The lack of comprehensive solutions and common approaches to regulation the legal personality of individuals, as well as the legal status of other participants in digital relations has long-term negative effects. In this regard, it seems necessary to develop common legislative and law enforcement approaches based on the following key theses:

The legal personality of a person in the digital space is a natural continuation of his legal personality in the real world. In this regard, the situation requires not a simple statement of this fact, but specific, balanced decisions that take into account the peculiarities of the digital environment and resulting legal consequences with regard to the legal capacity of a person for enjoying rights and capacity for performing juristic acts and duties in the digital sphere. These decisions should be reflected in a single legislative act aimed at systemic and comprehensive regulation of digital relations (for example, the Digital Code of Russia). This act should prohibit of mass surveillance of citizens, segregation depending on their desire or ability to use the digital tools, the diminution of human rights and freedoms, which are established by the norms of international law and the Constitution of Russia, the use of AI to resolve legally significant cases related individuals, etc.

From our point of view, the legislative decision regarding the identification of users on the Internet should provide, as a maximum, generally access to the digital space or, at least, access to the most significant resources (for example, state and municipal services) through confidential personal identifiers and mechanisms that include multifactor authentication, including biometric data. Technological solutions to this problem must also find their legal legalization.

Personal identifiers of the individual who is realizing his legal personality in the digital space, including the user's name (nickname), must be protected by legal means to ensure that they can be used only by those to whom they belong. We believe discussible the solution worked out by judicial practice to protect personal data by analogy with trademarks and industrial property rights, where the legal protection is granted to registered objects holding patents. In the essence the data generation on the Internet closely related with mechanisms of copyright law, but existing copyright litigation practices were crafted in the analog age and don't take into account new technological achievements.

In addition to the regulation of personal data, Russian legislation should be supplemented with norms that determine the nature and application procedures for so-called "calculated data", which also make it possible to identify a person by ensuring the collection of indirect information. The existing realities of building relationships in the digital environment imply practically unlimited opportunities for search engines and other operators of personal data to get data generated by Internet users, while the State and its agencies in significant way limited by the legislation. These circumstances complicate the law enforcement activity, identification, disclosure and investigation of crimes and other offenses committed by Internet users.

Digital rights and obligations of Internet users should be brought into a system linked, first of all, with the age and civil status of a person. The paradox of the existing regulation is that many social relations inaccessible to minors in the real world (for example, certain goods, services and information containing age restrictions) become completely open to them in the digital space. Relations arising on the Internet require parallel solutions of legal status of individuals regarding possible administrative offences and criminal acts.

The right "to be forgotten", the right "to digital death" and other digital rights should have system reflection in national legislation along with other rights of citizens. Ensuring their protection should be the duty of the operators who processing personal data, but not the obligation of Internet users. Otherwise, the protection of digital rights becomes an unrealizable task for citizens, and the possibility of their practical implementation is negated for a reason of difficulties of law enforcement and proactive use.

Thus, in the context of the ICT rapid development, legislative regulation of the legal personality of individuals in the system of digital relations is becoming an urgent need for modern Russian society. With regret, we have to state that a person, the value of whose rights is declared as the highest priority of the modern states and societies, fades into the background despite the opportunities determined by the achievements of scientific and technological progress. The existing trend is not unique and exclusive for Russia, since the value priorities of the Internet environment are faced with a duality and inconsistency for cyberspace self-regulation that is the frightening experience for many people, who appeal for the authorities to establish law and order even in "the space of full freedom". In the absence of any alternative developed by the humanity through its history only the states and democratic governments can be entrusted the achievement of a balance between national interests and the freedom of individuals.

REFERENCES

Alonso, C., Romero E. (2017). Aggressors and Victims in Bullying and Cyberbullying: A Study of Personality Profiles using the Five-Factor Model. *The Spanish Journal of Psychology*. 20, E76.

Arhipov, S.I. (2005). Sub"ekty prava (teoreticheskoe issledovanie). Ekaterinburg. (In Russian)

Bechmann, G. (2000). Concepts of Information Society and the Social Function of Information. In Banse, G. et al. (Eds.). *Towards the Information Society: The Case of Central and Eastern European Countries* (pp. 37-52). Springer Verlag GmbH Deutschland.

Bell, D. (1973). The Coming of Post-Industrial Society. A Venture of Social Forcasting. New York: Basic books.

Tsindeliani, I.A. (2020). Sistema sub"ektov cifrovyh otnoshenij. In V.V. Blazheev & M.A. Egorova (Eds.) *Cifrovoe pravo* (pp. 83-92). Moscow: Prospekt. (In Russian)

Desai, D.R. (2014). Constitutional Limits on Surveillance: Associational Freedom in The Age of Data Hoarding. *Notre Dame Law Review*. 90(2). pp. 579-632.

Tedeev, A.A. (2021). Informacionnye pravootnosheniya. In M.A. Fedotov (Ed.), *Informacionnoe pravo* (pp. 27-31). Moscow: Yurajt. (In Russian)

Gabov, A.V., Havanova, I.A. (2018). Evolyuciya robotov i pravo XXI v. *Vestnik Tomskogo gosudarstvennogo universiteta*. 435. pp. 215-233. (In Russian)

Golubok, S. (2015). Roman Zakharov v. Russia: Big Brother Under Control? *Journal for Constitutionalism and Human Rights*. 34(8). pp. 20-26.

Hadlington, L. (2017). Human factors in cybersecurity; examining the link between Internet addiction, impulsivity, attitudes towards cybersecurity, and risky cybersecurity behaviours. Heliyon. 3(7). Retrived from https://www.sciencedirect.com/science/article/pii/S2405844017309982

Howes, D. (2001). e-Legislation: Law-Making in the Digital Age. *McGill Law Journal*. 47. pp. 39-57.

Kerr, O.S. (2010). Applying The Fourth Amendment to The Internet: A General Approach. *Stanford Law Review*. 62(4). pp. 1005-1049.

Kopylov, V.A. (2002). Informacionnoe pravo: uchebnik. Moscow: Yurist. (In Russian)

Loi pour une République numérique. (2016, October). Retrived from https://wipolex.wipo.int/ru/text/420578

Matuzov, N.I., Mal'ko, A.V. (2009). Teoriya gosudarstva i prava: uchebnik. Moscow: Yurist. (In Russian)

Mironov, V.V. (2017). Transformaciya kul'tur ot klassicheskoj k elektronnoj. *Filosofiya iskusstvennogo intellekta. Trudy vserossijskoj mezhdisciplinarnoj konferencii*. pp. 28-36. (In Russian)

Meints, M., Gasson, M. (2009). High-Tech ID and Emerging Technologies. In K. Rannenberg et al. (Eds.) *The Future of Identity in the Information Society: Challenges and Opportunities* (pp. 130-189). London: Springer.

Morhat, P.M. (2018). Pravosub"ektnost' iskusstvennogo intellekta v sfere prava intellektual'noj sobstvennosti: grazhdansko-pravovye problemy. Moscow. (In Russian)

Peppet, S.R. (2014). Regulating the Internet of Things: First Steps Toward Managing Discrimination, Privacy, Security, and Consent. *Texas Law Review*. 93(1). pp. 85-178.

Roberts, A. (2015). Privacy, Data Retention and Domination: Digital Rights Ireland Ltd v Minister for Communications. *Modern Law Review*. 78(3). pp. 535-548.

Ruhrmann, H. (2019). Protecting human rights in policy strategies for facial recognition technologyin law enforcement. Case Studies from the United Kingdom and the United States. *CITRIS Policy Lab*. Retrived from https://citrispolicylab.org/wp-content/uploads/2019/09/Facing-theFuture_Ruhrmann_CITRIS-Policy-Lab.pdf

Rusinova, V. (2018). Legalizatsiya “massovoy slezhki” Evropeyskim Sudom po pravam cheloveka: chto stoit za postanovleniem po delu Big Brother Watch and Others v. the United Kingdom? *Mezhdunarodnoe pravosudie*. 4(28). pp. 3-20. (In Russian)

Talapina, E.V. (2018). Pravo i cifrovizaciya: novye vyzovy i perspektivy. *Zhurnal rossijskogo prava*. 2(254). P.5-17. (In Russian)

Willson, M. (1997). Community in the Abstract: A Political and Ethical Dilemma? In D. Holmes (Ed.) *Virtual Politics: Identity and Community in Cyberspace*. London: Sage.

Yastrebov, O.A. (2018). Pravosub"ektnost' elektronnogo lica: teoretiko-metodologicheskie podhody. *Trudy Instituta gosudarstva i prava RAN*. 13(2). pp. 36-55. (In Russian)

ETHICAL RESPONSIBILITY DIRECTIVES AIMED AT BIG SOCIAL DATA RESEARCH

Charmaine du Plessis
Professor, Department of Communication Science, University of South Africa, Pretoria, South Africa

ABSTRACT

Despite the ongoing debate about ethics about big data and big social data, there are still no universal directives how to ethically deal with largescale datasets. Even big social data that is anonymous and seemingly harmless may have ethical implications and impacts that have not been previously anticipated. Hence, this paper explores the idea that, in the absence of universally agreed-upon ethical principles for big social data studies, researchers must adopt an ethical maturity focal point for such research projects. It is argued that researchers, who deal with big social data, must be ethically responsible and apply autonomous moral reasoning during all phases of the research process. To support the arguments, the study was conducted in two phases. The concept of ethical maturity was first extended to big social data research, after which some ethical directives are proposed, based on an inductive analysis of documents on the topic of ethics of big data and social data. The findings indicate that being ethically responsible could instill a greater appreciation of the current and new big social data context in researchers to justify ethical decision-making while becoming more aware of the manipulated reality of big social datasets.

KEYWORDS

Big Social Data, Inductive Analysis, Fourth Industrial Revolution, Ethical Maturity, Research Ethics, Ethical Responsibility

1. INTRODUCTION

This paper aims to contribute to the ongoing debate on ethics about big data with a focus on big social data research. The volume of big social data generated in the Fourth Industrial Revolution (4IR) concerns areas of business, society and even existence, and remains a controversial topic. Big social data is the direct result of the 4IR and the way such data is harvested and used is inherently ethics unfriendly. Concerns about ethics regarding big data and big social data have focused predominantly on aspects such as privacy, identity, ownership and reputation from scholars' and practitioners' different perspectives and epistemologies (Zook et al., 2017; Richterich, 2018).

Consequently, this paper explores the idea that, while it is difficult to apply ethics to big social data, researchers must, apart from being knowledgeable about ethics, also become ethically responsible. This means that researchers, who deal with big social data, must adopt an ethical maturity approach, anchored in autonomous moral reasoning during all phases of the research process.

The first aim of this paper is to explore how the concept of ethical maturity can be extended to big social data research. Second, the paper addresses the question of how being ethically mature can direct big social data research in the (4IR) by proposing some ethical directives. Framed by Klaus Schwab, founder and executive chairman of the World Economic Forum in 2016, the 4IR entails the fusion of technologies by blending the online and offline world, providing researchers with research opportunities previously unimaginable (Schwab, 2016). The 4IR brings a "Zetta flood of zettabyte data", which is the equivalent of a billion terabytes (Barnett, 2016). Specifically, the 4IR has made harvesting of data for research more widespread, because of ease of access and availability. For example, innovative technologies such as the internet of things (IoT), robotics and artificial intelligence (AI), among other things, generate large volumes of big social data (Floridi, 2014; Van den Hoven, 2017).

The past few years have seen the rapid development of new technologies during the 4IR, slowly dissolving the barriers between humans and technologies, while providing ample research opportunities to not only shape government, but also business and the quality of humans' connected lives (Marcus, 2015). As a direct result of the 4IR, large volumes of data have become readily available in the public domain, which can be routinely collected and analysed for purposes of research, without asking for informed consent (Herschel & Moir, 2017). Ethics of big social data research is increasingly a vital concern, but universally agreed upon guidelines on how to ethically deal with large social media datasets for research are still lacking, mainly due to the level of difficulty to conform with ethical theory (Richterich, 2018; Herschel & Moir, 2017; Zook et al., 2017). One of the most significant current discussions in big social data research is what ethics entails when using big data for purposes of research or strategic decision-making (Zook et al., 2017).

Furthermore, concerns about misusing big social data are rising, including issues about human rights, global governance and property. For example, organisations collect consumers' data, without their knowledge or consent, to not only monetise but also to provide tailor-made services to current and potential new customers (Marcus, 2015).

The paper is structured as follows: The concept of big social data is first explained, followed by an explanation of the concept of ethical maturity. Thereafter big social data is extended to ethical maturity followed by an explanation of the research method, findings, discussion and conclusion.

2. BIG SOCIAL DATA

Although the concept of big data is well-documented in the literature, there is still no universal agreement about its nature and is best understood as an umbrella concept that refers to emerging technologies, but also includes the infrastructure, practices, networks and even politics surrounding their use. Big data is thus networked data in such volumes that data cannot be processed by conventional computer or database systems (Kitchin & McArdle, 2016; Schwab, 2016). Big data has characteristics such as volume (being an enormous quantity), velocity (harvested in real-time), variety (having different formats) and veracity (contains uncertainty and errors), but also has value (can provide much insight and be repurposed) and variability (the meaning of the data can change in accordance with the context) (Kitchin & McArdle, 2016).

Social media data is an application of big data and is defined as "generated from technology-mediated social interactions and actions in the digital realm, and which can be collected and analyzed to model social interactions and behavior" (Olshannikova et al., 2017).

There is no single template of how to apply ethics in social media research since studies differ. This means that ethical problems are context-dependent and subject to different interpretations by researchers. Researchers can harvest big social data via social media sites, devices, machines and endless other applications, which are often unstructured, spread around and noisy (Olshannikova et al., 2017; Zook et al., 2017). However, human reality is not the same as a decade ago, as we only observe online information in accordance with how we personalise devices, the internet and social media, based on our interests and connections (Just & Latzer, 2017). Since all these new technological devices of the 4IR help to construct reality and create new responsibilities for researchers, when harvesting and using big social data, it is important to acknowledge how this affects ethical theory.

It is thus argued in this paper that in the absence of some clear guidelines, researchers are compelled to think differently about how to harvest and use big social data in the 4IR. Not only are researchers faced with more complicated and larger social media datasets, but ethical considerations are also becoming more urgent since it is not practical to obtain informed consent. This urgency is thus embedded in how to address the sensitive aspects of human behaviour and interactions, without informed consent. Research agendas, using big social data, now include a network that connects humans and communities with technologies with the potential to cause harm, since most data represents or impacts humans (Metcalf & Crawford, 2016; Zook et al., 2017). Importantly, ethics around big social data deals with less visible concepts such as information privacy and data discrimination, which might impact an individual or a larger grouping of people (Metcalf & Crawford, 2016). It is hence argued that the concept of ethical maturity could direct researchers in how to become ethically responsible when dealing with large social media datasets.

3. ETHICAL MATURITY

The concept of ethical maturity is widely applied in health sciences and the helping professions (see, for example, Caroll & Shaw, 2013; Caroll, 2014; Lategan & Van Zyl, 2017), and reflected on in organisational studies (Wickham & O' Donohue, 2012; Steven & Godkin, 2017). Also referred to as moral or human maturity, there are diverse views about what ethical maturity entails and, consequently, there is no universally agreed-upon definition. One of the most prominent scholars that has written about ethical maturity, Caroll (2011, p.12), defines ethical maturity as "the reflective, rational and emotional capacity to decide actions are right and wrong, or good and better; the resilience and courage to implement those decisions; being accountable for ethical decisions made." On the other hand, Wickham and O' Donohue's (2012) support Kohlberg's (1984) theory of moral development who defines ethical maturity as "the highest level of moral development at which an individual is capable of autonomous moral reasoning using abstract universal principles, such as human rights and justice, to determine what is ethical." Vivian-Burne and Hunt's (2014, p.5) definition focuses more on the complexity of ethics, namely "the increasing capacity to embrace ethical complexity and deal with appropriate respect to all parties involved in a situation."

Although there are different views about what ethical maturity entails, as evident in these definitions, collectively, scholars agree that ethical maturity leads to better ethical decision-making when facing an ethical dilemma that enables one to not only take but also to sustain the right practice (Caroll, 2011; Caroll & Shaw, 2013; Wickham & O' Donohue, 2012).

3.1 The Concept of Ethical Maturity Extended to Big Social Data Research

For the empirical part of the study, the perspectives of Wickham & O' Donohue (2012) and Caroll (2011) were adopted as a theoretical point of departure, to position ethical maturity within a big social data research context. These scholars' work on ethical maturity has attracted attention and is widely cited. Firstly, Caroll (2011) argues that when it comes to ethical maturity, developing ethical sensitivity and vigilance to alert researchers of the presence of ethical dilemmas are important. This alertness will assist in researchers' understanding of why particular ethical decisions were taken. Similarly, Wickham and O' Donohue (2012) argue that being socially intelligent is essential to not only understand but also to interpret different social situations and interactions. Therefore, researchers, who deal with big social data, must be able to interpret and understand social situations, interactions, roles and norms embedded in the data, based on the purpose of the data. This could help researchers to become sensitive to the potential ethical dilemma of harvesting and using big social data. Secondly, for Caroll (2011), it is important to be able to rationalise all ethical decisions and then to implement them. To be able to do this, it is important to think individually, relationally and systematically. Researchers must endeavour to become more experienced in ethical decision-making. In this regard Wickham and O' Donohue (2012) refer to cognitive intelligence, namely being able to interpret information rationally and to adapt to the environment. This means that the researcher must access, process and interpret big social data in a focused, methodical and logical manner while being cognizant of potential ethical issues. Thirdly, Caroll (2011) puts forward that it is essential to not only learn from the ethical decision that was taken but also to be able to justify the decision. Equally important is that ethical decision-making must be aligned to researchers' ethical principles and values. For Wickham and O' Donohue (2012), emotional intelligence is important, since, having this ability not only regulates one's emotions but also allows us to sense and respond to others' emotions. Thus, for the researcher, this means that they must continuously learn from ethical experiences and regulate any bias towards the big social dataset while staying respectful because of the human-related aspects behind human interactions. Table 1 below summarises how the ethical maturity concept can be extended to big social data research.

Table 1. The concept of ethical maturity extended to big social data research

Ethical maturity aspects	Proposed meaning within the context of big social data research
Social intelligence: ethical sensitivity, vigilance	Understanding of social situations, interactions, roles and morals embedded in the data, the privacy of individuals
Cognitive intelligence: justification, implementation	Access, process and interpret social media data in a focused, methodical and logical manner
Emotional intelligence: Learning, outcomes	Learn from the experience and regulate any bias about the data and stay respectful, adopt a human-centred approach

Sources: Wickham & O'Donohue (2012); Carroll (2011).

4. METHOD

This quality study adopted an interpretivist worldview and was done in two different phases. Firstly, the concept of ethical maturity was extended to big social data research, based on the frameworks of two well-cited scholars. Secondly, an inductive approach was adopted for a qualitative textual analysis by considering the ethical aspects in table 1 as well as their proposed meaning within the context of big social data research. For the analysis, a purposive sample of a corpus of 51 electronic reports on big data and big social data ethics, in the public domain, was used and searched for with keywords using search engines and Google scholar (see van Dijck 2010). These reports, with an average length of 30 pages, and consisting of 997 475 words and 35 486 unique word forms, were compiled by industry experts, regulating bodies in the private and public sectors, and universities. The unit of analysis was thus social artefacts. To be included in the study, the reports had to make proposals of how to ethically deal with big data or big social data research in the 4IR.

Coding and theme development were guided by existing ideas and concepts, as reflected in table 1 (see Braun & Clarke, 2013). In addition to Braun and Clarke's (2013) guidelines, the eight-step planning process of a quality study, as proposed by O'Leary (2014), was also considered.

Following an iterative data collection approach, data saturation was attained, in other words, no new data and, thus, no new themes became available with further reports (Fusch & Ness, 2015). Well-adopted criteria for inclusion and exclusion of documents for analysis, such as authenticity, credibility, representativeness and meaning of the reports, were applied (Bowen, 2011; Tight, 2019).

The documents were subjected to a systematic review, as proposed by Tight (2019) and Braun and Clarke (2013). Reading and understanding of the documents were also facilitated by robust qualitative data analysis software such as NVivo for Windows and Voyant Tools (a web-based application for text visualisation and analysis). A reflexive inductive thematic analysis followed, keeping in mind the ethical issues and their proposed meaning within the context of big social data research, as depicted in table 1. The researcher thus imposed this structure on the data to analyse it (Braun & Clarke, 2013).

The data analysis meets the criterion of trustworthiness, because a well-known systematic and exhaustive process, based on the frameworks of well-cited scholars, was followed (Tight, 2019).

5. FINDINGS

Three themes emerged from the inductive thematic analysis and which can be explained as follows.

5.1 Theme 1: Appreciation of the Current and New Context of the Big Social Dataset

Theme 1 deals with a greater appreciation of and reflection on the current and new context of the dataset, before harvesting and using it for studies. Appreciation of the current and new context of the data refers to researchers being vigilant and ethically sensitive about human-related social situations, conversations, roles and norms that cannot be separated from the data (Carroll, 2011; Wickham & O' Donohue, 2012). This appreciation is important because researchers must understand that, without exception, all big social datasets pose an ethical dilemma, since human participants and communities' conversations are naturally embedded in the data (Metcalf & Crawford, 2016). Because ethics about big social data is inherently complex and difficult to apply (Herschel & Moir, 2017), researchers must become sensitive to the current and new context of the big dataset by being more aware of the social context of the data. For example, the analysis reveals that researchers must not be distracted by how public the data is, but rather understand where the data originates from and how the data may cause harm when used in another context. In this regard boyd and Crawford (2012) argue that researchers cannot justify their research as being ethical just because the data is public, but that research ethics for the dataset must still be evaluated. Also, an understanding of how the handling of the data in another context adheres to researchers' values becomes essential. This means that researchers must acknowledge the purpose of the original data and first reflect on how the data will fit the new context of the research study, without changing the intended meaning thereof and without causing any harm. Also, the new context in which the data will be used should ideally contribute to new knowledge about a phenomenon and benefit society. Ethical sensitivity and vigilance will ensure that a researcher not only interprets the data appropriately but also becomes more aware of the human elements embedded in the data and the importance of protecting the privacy of human participants. Greater awareness could thus ensure proper usage of big social data and prevent potential harm to human participants (Zook et al., 2017). Hence at the start of a research study, the following questions are important: Where does the data come from? Is lawful to obtain the data? Will the data fit into the new context of the study? What harm can the data inflict upon humans when used in a study? What new knowledge will the data generate that will improve society?

5.2 Theme 2: Justification of the Reasons for Ethical Decision-Making

Theme 2 addresses the justification for the implementation of ethical decisions about harvesting big social data for use in a new context. This means that the researcher must not only access and process but also interpret, big social data methodically and logically while being aware of potential harm to human participants. Also, the researcher must be able to adapt to address potential ethical issues detected during the research process. Justification for ethical decision-making, before the start of the project and during the entire research process, is essential (Carroll, 2011; Wickham & O' Donohue, 2012), which is also revealed by the analysis in terms of ethics being a conscious consideration whenever a new research project commences. This means that ethical issues can emerge at every new development of a study which researchers must be aware of. For example, studies of a sensitive nature or of interest to national security, could affect the personal security and integrity of the researcher (Van Baalen, 2018). Furthermore, how human rights are affected by harvesting and using big data could substantiate and justify all ethical decisions and actions. It is important to always assess the potential impact of big social data on human participants (see Beninger et al., 2014). The researcher must also display ethical resilience during the implementation of the research project, guided by logical decision-making. Hence, the following questions are important: How is ethics applicable to all the phases of the study? Are there any ethical issues that have emerged not previously being aware of? Are there any risks involved for the researcher when using the data? How can the researcher become more experienced in ethical decision-making? How can decisions about the ethical implications of using this data be justified to others?

5.3 Theme 3: Awareness of the Tailored Reality of the Big Social Dataset

Theme 3 addresses awareness of how to regulate bias about the human-related information, embedded in the big data, which does not necessarily reflect the entire truth (Carroll, 2011; Wickham & O' Donohue, 2012). This means that researchers must adopt a human-centred approach, they must always learn from the experience and stay respectful throughout the entire research process. Knowledge and cognizance about matters such as algorithm bias, data discrimination and the non-neutrality of technology, which may alter human reality, are imperative.

The analysis reveals that issues such as algorithm bias, data discrimination and living in a "filter bubble", because of personalised searchers on the internet, are all realities that hide some information from researchers; thereby, limiting their views about the world and the data (see Just & Latzer, 2016; Philbeck et al., 2018). Also, big social datasets may have algorithm errors and algorithms may also change the initial purpose of the data. Big social data can also be a tool of inclusion and exclusion, because of the digital divide and exclusion of human participants, who do not have access to the internet and social media. In addition, the engineers behind the creation of algorithms have their ideas about the purpose of the data, which means that technology is not neutral. Thus, when dealing with big social data, researchers must always be aware that the data may not reflect the entire truth; it only provides a snapshot or idea of the truth. Thus, staying respectful during the entire research process is not only essential but must also be guided by shared human values and universal principles such as human rights and justice. Hence, the following questions are important: Does this data reflect human reality as it is? Is this data based on a personalised search? Which algorithm errors could potentially be embedded in the data? Which humans were potentially excluded in the data? How can any bias about the dataset be reported and overcome?

6. DISCUSSION

The contribution of this paper is twofold. Firstly, in the absence of a universal agreement on this topic, the study opens opportunities for further debate and studies by extending the concept of ethical maturity to big social data research. Secondly, the findings of this study will help researchers with practical ethical directives, anchored in autonomous moral reasoning during all phases of the research process. Because it advocates for more reflection on the potential harm to human participants, these principles can act as a moral compass to guide researchers with decision-making when accessing, analysing, using and sharing big social data. The current study thus contributes to our knowledge by addressing both theoretical and practical issues pertaining to ethics around big social data research. Big social data is inherently not ethics friendly when it comes to the ideas put forward in ethics theory (Herschel & Moir, 2017) and generated from non-neutral technologies (Philbeck et al., 2018). How to address ethics when it comes to the sensitivity surrounding human behaviour and interactions embedded in the data, obtained without informed consent, have not only been a controversial topic, but also a grey area in big social data research (Richterich, 2018; Zook et al., 2017). It is therefore vital for researchers to not only become more knowledgeable about concerns about ethics surrounding big social data research (Marcus, 2015), but also to be ethically responsible when making ethical decisions concerning big social data, as proposed in this paper. By asking questions about ethical issues around the big social datasets, researchers have a greater awareness of the current and new context of big social data, can provide justifications for ethical decisions and be attentive to the fact that a big social dataset only provides a snapshot or idea of the reality of the phenomenon under investigation. By being vigilant, ethically sensitive, flexible, resilient, and by adopting a human-centred approach and staying respectful, researchers adhere to shared human values and universal principles such as human rights and justice. Moreover, ethics must be a conscious consideration whenever a new big social data research project commences. Table 2, below, depicts the proposed ethical directives for when researchers approach big social data research.

Table 2. Proposed ethical directives for moral reasoning when approaching big social data research

Directive	Proposed questions for studies using big social data
Directive 1: Appreciation of the current and new context of the bi social data	Where does the data come from? Will the data fit into the new context of the study? Is it lawful to obtain the data? What harm can the data inflict upon humans when used in a study? What new knowledge will the data generate that will improve society?
Directive 2: Justification of the reasons for ethical decision-making	How is ethics applicable to all the phases of the study? Are there any ethical issues that have emerged not previously being aware of? Are there any risks involved for the researcher when using the data? How can the researcher become more experienced in ethical decision-making? How can decisions about the ethical implications of using this data be justified to others?
Directive 3: Awareness of the tailored reality of the big social dataset	Does this data reflect human reality as it is? Is this data based on a personalised search? Which algorithm errors could potentially be embedded in the data? Which humans were potentially excluded in the data? How can any bias about the dataset be reported and overcome?

7. CONCLUSION

The paper concludes by arguing that the ethical directives proposed in this study could act as a contribution to the debate about ethics about big social data and be further developed through productive discussion. These directives are thus not proposed as final but must continue to evolve as part of lifelong learning. The complex nature of big social data continues to hamper ethical decision-making, while ethical concerns about big social data research, in the absence of informed consent, are well-documented. No doubt, harvesting and using big social data, when humans did not give their consent to use their data or are not aware of the research, have ethical implications in all spheres of life. The volume of big social data is also still mounting as new technologies become available, while researchers will continue to harvest and use large volumes of data for research. It is acknowledged that ethics in big social data research is highly specified and that there is no one-size-fits-all approach. Also, the results of this study can only be generalised to the sample of this study while documents could have been omitted during searches. The insights gained from the analysis, nevertheless, provide another angle to not only address but also to expand on ethics about big social data research. Despite the study's limitations, the results are valuable considering the idea that ethical maturity could be a novel way in which to deal with sensitivities around human activities embedded in large volumes of social data. When researchers are aware of the potential harm to human participants when making decisions about big social data, their actions could become more aligned with shared human values and human rights. This is very much the key component in future attempts to further develop the concept of ethical maturity through different methodologies within the context of big social data. It will be important for future studies to develop and add to the ethical directives proposed in this study. Equally important is to rethink the nature, importance and practice of research integrity when it comes to large scale social media datasets.

REFERENCES

Barnett, T. (2016). The Zettabyte Era Officially Begins (How Much is That?). Cisco Blogs. https://blogs.cisco.com/sp/the-zettabyte-era-officially-begins-how-much-is-that.

Bowen, GA. (2009). Document analysis as a qualitative research method. *Qualitative Research, 9*(2), 27–40.

Beninger, K., Fry, A., Jago, N., Lepps., H., Nass., L., & Silvester, H. (2014). Research using Social Media Users' Views. *NatCen Social Research*, 1–40.

boyd, D., & Crawford, K. (2012). Critical questions for big data. *Information, Communication and Society*, *15*(5), 662-679.

Braun, V., & Clarke, V. (2013). *Successful qualitative research: A practical guide for beginners*. SAGE.

Carroll, M. (2011). Ethical maturity: Compasses for life and work decisions-Part I. *Psychotherapy in Australia*, *17*(3), 12 – 23.

Carroll, M., & Shaw, E. (2013). *Ethical Maturity in the Helping Professions*. Jessica Kingsley Publishers.

Carroll, M. (2014). *Effective Supervision for the Helping Professions*. 2nd edition. SAGE.

Herschel, R., & Miori, VM. (2017). Ethics & Big Data. *Technology in Society, 49*, 31 – 36.

Fusch, P. I., & Ness, L.R. (2015). Are we there yet? Data saturation in qualitative research. *The Qualitative Report*, *20*(9), 1408-1416.

Floridi, L. (2014). *The Fourth Revolution: How the Infosphere is reshaping human reality*. Oxford University Press.

Just, N., & Latzer, M. (2017). Governance by Algorithms: Reality Construction by Algorithmic Selection on the Internet. *Culture & Society*, 39(2), 238–258.

Kitchin, R., & McArdle, G. (2016). What makes Big Data, Big Data? Exploring the ontological characteristics of 26 datasets. *Big Data & Society,* January–June, 1–10.

Kohlberg, L. (1984). *The Psychology of Moral Development: Nature and Validity of Moral Stages*. Harper.

Lategan, L.O.K., & Van Zyl, G J. (Eds). (2017). *Healthcare ethics: For healthcare practitioners*. Sun Media.

Marcus, A. (2015). Data and the fourth industrial revolution. World Economic Forum. https://www.weforum.org/agenda/2015/12/data-and-the-fourth-industrial-revolution/.

Metcalf, J., & Crawford, K. (2016). Where are human subjects in Big Data research? The emerging ethics divide. *Big Data & Society,* January–June, 1–14.

O'Leary, Z. (2014). *The Essential Guide to Doing Your Research Project.* 2nd ed. SAGE.

Olshannikova, E., Olsson, T., Huhtamaki, J., & Karkkainen, H. (2017). Conceptualizing Big Social Data. *Journal of Big Data*, *4*(3), Springer Open, https://doi.org/10.1186/s40537-017-0063-x.

Philbeck, T, Davi, N., & Larsen, A.E. (2018). *Values, Ethics and Innovation Rethinking Technological Development in the Fourth Industrial Revolution*. World Economic Forum.

Richterich, A. (2018). The Big Data Agenda: Data Ethics and Critical Data Studies in *Critical Digital and Social Media Studies Series.* University of Westminster Press, 1 -14.

Steven W., McCrary, P.E., & Godkin, L. (2017). An Organizational Construction Ethics Maturity Model: The Integration of Process and Normative Values [Paper Presentation]. *53rd ASC Annual International Conference Proceeding*, Seattle, WA (pp. 317 – 327), Associated Schools of Construction.

Tight, M. (2019). *Documentary Research in the Social Sciences*. SAGE.

Van Baalen, S. (2018). 'Google wants to know your location': The ethical challenges of fieldwork in the digital age. *Research Ethics*, *14*(4), 1–17.

Van den Hoven, J. (2017). Ethics for the Digital Age: Where are the Moral Specs? [Paper Presentation] In H. Werthner & F. van Harmelen (Eds). *Proceedings of the 11th European Computer Science Summit: Informatics in the Future,* Vienna (pp. 65–76), Springer.

Van Dijk, J. (2010). Search engines and the production of academic knowledge. *International Journal of Cultural Studies*, *13*(6), 574–592.

Vivian-Byrne, K.l., & Hunt J. (2014). Ethical Decision-Making – social metaphors towards ethical action. *Journal of Systemic Therapies, 33*(1), 1 – 15.

Wickham, M., & O' Donohue, W. (2012). Developing an ethical organization: exploring the role of ethical intelligence. *Organization Development Journal, 30*(2), 9 – 29.

Zook, M., Barocas, S., boyd, D., Crawford, K., Keller, E. & Gangadharan, S. P., et al. (2017). Ten simple rules for responsible big data research. *PLoS Comput Biol*, *13*(3), e1005399 https://doi.org/10.1371/journal.pcbi.1005399.

DESIGN THINKING AS AN APPROACH TO FOSTER RECIFE'S CREATIVE TOURISM

Ana Elisa L. Ribeiro and Renata S. Souza
Cesar School, Brazil

ABSTRACT

The contemporary traveller wishes, beyond the simple contemplation, to experience and get involved with a city as a local resident. On the other hand, the resident itself often does not know the city deeply and craves to explore this space, seeking for new experiences and the feeling of belonging. How to facilitate the connection between these people and the small entrepreneurs and artists of the city, who, on the flip side, need to offer their services, but suffer from the lack of visibility and incentive? Design emerges here as a tool to enable opportunities and solve problems. The methodology of this research follows an applicable cutout of the creative process of Design Thinking (divided into the phases of inspiration, ideation and implementation) having been worked only on the first phase. This approach encourages the researcher to make the right questions before thinking about giving answers and solutions to a given question. Thus, users are investigated in an empathetic way, in order to understand their real needs, making a critical analysis of the raised data to understand the problems and opportunities. This article reports the investigation of creative tourism in Recife (Brazil) and the application of design processes, aiming to alert to the tourism potential and to guide the development of future projects involving services, which allows a true cultural and affective immersion. The purpose is to bring the designer's performance to the issue, in order to promote memorable experiences for all involved, in addition to local economy development.

KEYWORDS

Experience Tourism, Creative Tourism, Design Thinking, Service Design

1. INTRODUCTION

Tourism, one of the most important sectors in a country's economy, grew above the global economy in 2018, as the World Travel & Tourism Council (WTTC) reported in 2019. In a globalized society, where it is possible to move easily and even virtually to other scenarios, the contemporary traveler is increasingly active, well-informed and autonomous when looking for new places to explore as a form of leisure. This individual wants to have experiences beyond the simple knowledge of history and culture, seeking to truly enjoy the destination, making connections and getting involved in the activities of the city as a local. As a reflection of a postmodern society's desire, comes the so-called Creative Tourism, which is not limited to offer tangible resources, such as museums, parks and facilities, and brings innovation through the promotion of original experiences that provide new sensations and emotions, whether tourist or resident.

In this context, we came across Recife's residents, known for being very "*bairrista*", a term that refers to those who are vigorously proud and defend their homeland, sometimes considering it the best place in the world. Nevertheless, the expectation that Recife's residents will get to know their city in depth is not always fulfilled. On the one hand, there is the population's desire to know and explore its hometown, seeking a sense of belonging and identity. On the other hand, there is great tourism potential, but it suffers from lack of visibility and encouragement.

The central question here is how to facilitate the connection between people who want to live an experience and the services offered by small entrepreneurs and artists in the city, to foster Creative Tourism practices in the city. To understand customers, besides investigating their real desires, needs and concerns, it is necessary to map their culture, context and personal experiences, acquiring a holistic view. From that, it is possible to generate alternatives, proposing strategic solutions, aligned with reality, and delivering more value to customers and business. At this point, we find the value of the design, which is seen as an activity used to drive the processes and systems that underpin experiences, from the strategies and philosophies of the project to the final details of the results. Due to the intangible and interactional nature of services, understanding consumer experience becomes essential (Freire, 2009). In the context of tourism, it is necessary to investigate the traveler's decision-making process in relation to their travel experience.

2. EXPERIENCE ECONOMY AND THE GROWTH OF CREATIVE TOURISM

By the end of the twentieth century, in a context of great social and cultural changes, catalyzed by technology and global mobility, the logic of industrial production is shaped by the needs of modern man (Pardo, 2011). In this Information Era, scholars observe new trends in consumer behavior, which moves from rational interest to emotional involvement.

Some new concepts such as Experience Economy (Pine; Gilmore, 1999) or Dream Society (Jensen, 2000) emerge from this new era. The essence of the terms is focused on offering experiences and emotions, providing individualized experiences, even if based on collaborative processes. In the Experience Economy, intangible aspects are highlighted as valuable, which is based on culture, diversity and originality.

According to the report by Euromonitor International (2019) on consumer trends, clients are looking for genuine products and experiences that allow them to express their individuality. This desire is also manifested in the travel industry. In this context, the consumer is the traveler, who becomes the protagonist of this travel experience that will attach affective value to his life through the experience of unforgettable moments. The economic value of this experience goes beyond building and maintaining customer loyalty, it is set on the appreciation of a significant service, and its ability to be eternal in the user's memory. Yet, according to the World Tourism Organization (1997) the desire of the millennium tourist is traveling to destinations where, more than visiting and contemplating, it is also possible to feel, live, be moved and be a character in your own journey.

From the investigation of this new tourist profile, the term Creative Tourism was coined, first called by Richards & Raymond (2000), who defended the idea that people today are eager for a deeper interaction with the culture of the place they visit, through experiences with the community, expressing their creative skills and feeling like a true local citizen. Richards (2011) further explains that the essence of Creative Tourism seems to be the experiences related to self-realization and self-expression through which tourists become co-interpreters and co-creators as they develop their creative skills. The authenticity of these experiences, as highlighted by the Creative Cities Network of the United Nations - Unesco in 2006, provides a connection between those who visit with those who live, creating spaces of alive culture.

In addition to digital technologies, creativity appears as a tool for identifying and promoting these factors. Reis (2008) calls "creative cities" those that are characterized by continuous innovation processes. These are based on a variety of connections and have in culture a great support for economic and urban changes. Reis defends as a development strategy the transformation of the cities into global creative hubs.

The city of Barcelona was a pioneer in the conception and commercialization of this new idea of tourism, its action plan, developed in 2006, became a model and spurred the creation of the international network for the promotion of creative tourism in 2010, the Creative Tourism Network. In Brazil, experience tourism started in 2006 as an initiative of the Ministry of Tourism and Sebrae (Brazilian Micro and Small Business Support Service) that implemented the experimental project in Rio Grande do Sul. The purpose was to publicize the wine region. The project was a success and then started to be replicated in other regions. Following this path, the National Creative Tourism Network - Recria was created in 2017, with the purpose of supporting the building of a different idea of tourism, capable of integrating people and creative segments in co-participation processes.

In the Northeast region of Brazil, the first city to organize a public policy aimed at creative tourism was Recife. The Creative Tourism Plan was created in late 2018, in an effort to provoke and provide experiences in which tourists and citizens from Recife feel the city as part of it. This document proposes several work fronts, in order to strengthen the system and make tourism an important economic and social asset for the city. The city of Recife is recognized for its cultural effervescence and richness of rhythms, in addition, in the last decade it started to emerge as an important hub of creative economy, having in Porto Digital, the largest technological park in the country in sales and number of companies. In its current tourist campaign, Recife calls itself the Capital of Creativity. It is in this scenario that we find the opportunity to explore local tourism from a creative perspective, using design as a tool to identify, spread and sell, priceless experiences to delight the public.

3. DESIGN THINKING AS AN APPROACH TO IDENTIFY INNOVATION

For this study, the Design Thinking methodology was used as the main process. According to Vianna (2012), it is an approach focused on the human being that uses multidisciplinary, collaboration and tangibility of thoughts and processes, to achieve business innovation.

Design Thinking is not a conventional methodology, but a set of methods, which has the characteristics of adaptation to different situations, without imposed rules or defined linearity, a reflection of the current world. The method makes it possible to generate business ideas and practices in a systematic and organized manner. Its efficiency lies in the user-centered approach. To understand customers, besides investigating their real desires, needs and concerns, it is necessary to map their culture, context and personal experiences, acquiring a holistic view. From that, it is possible to generate alternatives, proposing strategic solutions, aligned with reality, and delivering more value to customers and business. According to Brown (2008), Design Thinking is the junction among what is desirable for people, plus what is technologically possible and at the same time feasible for business.

The essence of the designer's role is to know how to balance a project on these three pillars. Feasibility concerns a financially sustainable business model. Viability considers the technical and technological practicability of developing what is being proposed. The differential of design thinking lies in the goal of desirability. According to Clatworthy (2009, apud Stickdorn and Shneider, 2014), desirable interactions generate trust and loyalty to the service, in addition to having a strong emotional appeal. To work with these intangible needs, it is essential to exercise empathy, which, according to Brown (2018), are the attempt to put ourselves in other people's shoes and connect with how they might be feeling.

In the innovation process guided by design, Brown (2018) identifies three spaces for innovation, namely: inspiration, idealization and implementation. The first phase is Immersion, where the problem is identified, taking an approach from different points of view. At that moment, hypotheses are formulated and data are collected to be analyzed and synthesized. After that, relevant information and insight patterns are obtained, which will help in understanding the problem, redefining the project's framework, scope, and limits.

The second phase is the ideation, when collective brainstorming sessions are conducted, among other tools, which contribute to generation of solutions. Brainstorming is a technique to stimulate the generation of a large number of ideas in a short period of time (Vianna et al, 2012). After defining and refining the best ideas, prototypes are created, which help to make these solutions tangible, bringing them from conceptual field to reality. From this, it is possible to run tests with prototypes, in order to validate the effectiveness of solutions, as well as their value for the final customer and business. For Vianna, in this step possibilities are explored so that to optimize concepts through the application of improved co-creation techniques, together with users. Finally, the Implementation phase is the effective operationalization of ideas qualified to be developed. After tests, solutions best suited to the reality of business and which best meet the user's needs are optimized for development.

4. TRIGGER QUESTION, OBJECTIVES AND METHODOLOGY

This article was built from the question about the difficulty of finding tourist experiences in Recife that are outside of the standard route. In other words, how to facilitate the connection between people interested in creative tourist experiences and entrepreneurs who offer these services in Recife. The methodology used and the defined objectives try to answer the question from the bias of Design and its user-oriented problem-solving processes.

The objectives of this study were divided into two parts. First: investigation of the potential of creative tourism of the city and stakeholders needs. Second: Identification of resident's pains when looking for and decision making about tours in the city; identifying the problems of small entrepreneurs who work with creative tourism in Recife; investigation of existing creative tourism initiatives in the city.

In order to achieve objectives, three stages were defined throughout the research. The first managed with the literature review on "creative tourism" and surrounding areas. Second one was an exploratory research on the market situation in the city of Recife, increasing significant data to reinforce and support the study's interpretations and analyzes. Finally, surveys were applied splitting into three groups: consumers of Recife's tourist experiences, local creative tourism entrepreneurs and managers of the Recife Department of Tourism.

Regarding the approach, a mixed quantitative-qualitative research was applied. The survey conducted with consumers of Recife's tourist experiences was carried out using structured questionnaires with 14 questions. The survey was sent online to more than 200 participants and reached a total of 152 completed forms. Among entrepreneurs and stakeholders from City Hall, a model of structured interviews with 6 questions was adopted, involving a total of 12 respondents. The goal was to investigate how creative tourism initiatives are being managed and its main obstacles, in addition to discovering how current management's positioning on this.

After the research phase, gathered data were evaluated and synthesized, based on the identification of patterns, using charts and statistical analysis, in addition to triangulation of information considered relevant to some questions. The results present theories formulated from the identified phenomena, which help in understanding the problem, redefining the framework, scope and limits of performance of a potential project.

5. RESULTS

The research involved 164 participants, of which 93% belong to the group that includes users of tourist experiences in the city and the rest belonging to the category of creative entrepreneurs and government officials. The latter group encompasses workers who work in management, planning, events, sports, quality, development and consultancy in the Department of Tourism, Sport and Leisure in Recife.

In the first group, focus was on city residents, who enjoy leisure and tourism services in the city. The total public was made up of people of legal age, 74% of whom were between 18 and 30 years old. Regarding gender, 75% of respondents identified themselves as being female.

The survey showed that for 70% of consumers, the Internet search engine, such as Google and Yahoo !, are the main source of information about different tourist activities, while 66% of respondents said they also look for referrals from people they know.

Only 18% of users consider themselves to be tourists in their own city. Most of them, 69% of respondents, stated that the frequency of going out to explore their city is low, being motivated by the desire to do something different or by invitations from friends or relatives. On the other hand, only 1 person out of 152 stated that he has no interest at all in getting to know the city better.

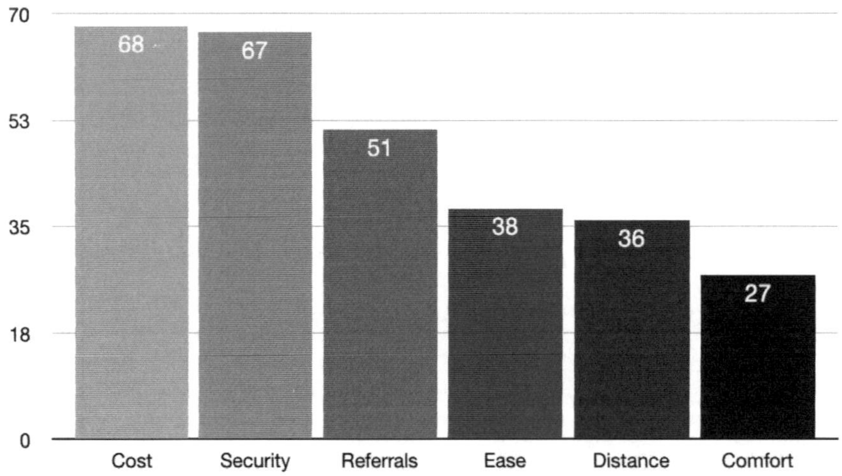

Figure 1. Decisive factors when making decisions about doing something new in the city

Respondents reported important factors to consider when deciding whether to do something for the first time in the city (Figure 1). The most important items were: Cost (68%), Security (67%) and Referrals from friends (51%). Among the respondents over 46 years old, 95% reported the importance of the Ease/practicality factor to use or book a service, thus being an essential item for older consumers. The Distance factor is taken into account by 36% and Comfort by 27% of the respondents. It is possible to notice that an important portion of people prefer to explore nearby places, where they are used to, whether it is their home or workplace, an evidence of why these people do not know the entire region of their city well, along with the problem of insecurity reported. Another point that may contribute to this issue is the lack of referrals given by acquaintances to visit these different and distant places, since this has been pointed out as an important factor for people to consider going to. This question arises not only in the motivation to go to an unknown place, but also in the moment of discovering the options available in the city, being therefore a significant point to take into account when publicizing and offering services.

In order to investigate familiarity with the use of online platforms for searching and booking tours, the research points out that AirBnb and Tripadvisor are the most popular services, used by 68% and 65% of people, respectively. The survey also found people's perception of the amount and diversity of tourist experiences in Recife. Revealing more than half of consumers said that there are not many options, confirming the hypothesis that there is a huge lack of knowledge about the alternatives that the city offers.

The poll also showed that most respondents consume the same types of tourist experience. When it came to choosing the coolest and unique option that was experienced, most common options are mentioned: Museums and Art Galleries (47%), Historic Center (40%), Beach (39.5%), Boat trips (36 %), Public Market (32%) and Gastronomic Experiences (29%). The survey revealed an interesting data, which is 22% of users chose Bicycle tours as the most pleasant leisure, showing a possible potential in the city. Only 4% of the answers mentioned walking tours, photographic tours and visits to the Technological Pole (Porto Digital) as the nicest experiences, revealing a probable unknowledge of these existent possibilities by the public. 54% of people indicated that Festivals (music, gastronomy, cinema, theater, etc.) were the most enjoyable experience, signaling a potential to be explored and at the same time a predilection for events, which bring variety to the routine programming of a city.

About the knowledge of Creative Tourism concept, more than 75% of respondents understand it as "Alternative tours outside standard tourist route". A portion of 42% stated that the concept involves "Learning/exercising some skill related to local culture and activities", an alternative that is seldom mentioned in the respondents' experience, when it comes to the memory of their best experiences.

Although aware of the concept, 75% of respondents have never heard of Creative Tourism in Recife. This result reflects a vast lack of knowledge of the city's potential by the residents themselves, consequently unexplored by visitors as well. It can be concluded that the city should work hard on this issue, considering that it recently received the international title of "City of Creative Tourism", recognized by the Creative Tourism Network.

The survey also showed that 81% of users have already used a social network to find out about leisure options in Recife, indicating a strong channel to be explored in publicity. About tips and recommendations to friends and acquaintances, 95% of users indicate what they already know. This trend can limit the spread of new and different options, which shows the importance of knowledge about your own city. Only 1% recommended searching for guides and official information at the Tourist Assistance Center. Finally, the research investigated the degree of interest in an online platform aimed at different tourist experiences in Recife, pointing to a positive result of more than 90% chance of use by users.

Analyzing the interviews with the agents of the Tourism Department of Recife, attention was drawn to the importance of creating a public policy focused on the creative tourism sector and the existence of governance working in the area together with the National Creative Tourism Network. This initiative contributed to the creation of the Municipal Creative Tourism Plan, elaborated in a co-creative way with participation of the local community. The result of it can be seen in conquest of the international title of Creative City, granted by the Creative Tourism Network. Among the basic criteria required for this recognition are the identification of at least ten creative tourism experiences in the city and a website that promotes it. Although internationally recognized, the research shows that the majority of local customers are still unaware of the work of Creative Tourism in Recife.

Eyes on the future, 71% of respondents highlighted the need to follow up on the actions proposed in Recife's Creative Tourism Plan is essential. Therefore, it is necessary to act to strengthen the governance created and guarantee execution of the plan. The publicity of ongoing actions also requires attention, in order to establish as a reference in the area, both at the level of local, national and international tourism.

Regarding the identification of the sector's demands, the answers display a pattern about the importance of giving voice to the population through promotion of actions which allows the meeting of these groups. Mobilizations contributed to different areas of the city, engaging public schools and local organizations. In other words, the public sector is open to demands of the community, attentive to what may become part of this chain and bringing the user to the center of the issue. In addition, there is also exploratory research mapping emerging creative tourism experiences.

The public sector is assisting those initiatives by raising awareness of Creative Tourism, investing in dissemination and promotion of the initiatives created. Besides, there is incentive and support for qualification, through mentoring, training and distance courses.

Although the number of interviews with local entrepreneurs was below the expectations, it was possible to identify patterns of responses that deserve attention and reflection. The converging points were: Difficulty in attracting the local public, which can offer permanent demand for products and services, in opposite of external tourism, which is seasonal and limited; reach specific public interested in their services, since access to foreign agencies is limited. Other essential actions are the investigation and understanding of its target audience and the creation of a network involving different actors in creative tourism, with the aim of identifying new demands. Finally, the analysis of user satisfaction is a measure taken by all respondents. Providing an open channel of communication with the customer is essential to understand them better and improve services.

6. CONCLUSION

The era of Experience Economy brought an important reflection on the role of designers, expanding their professional performance in the process of planning services focused on creative tourism. The designers must see beyond the object and bring discussions about the quality of consumers' use experience, whether in the use of a product or service. Thus, it is necessary to deepen the study about the user, to better understand their pains, needs and satisfactions. In the field of tourism, the user of the modern era becomes a demanding traveler, more explorer and in search of immersive and real experiences.

This work sought to contribute to the perception of Creative Tourism for the city of Recife. Through the designer perspective, the Recife tourism context and the actors involved in this process were investigated in order to raise opportunities for new business and improvements in the current scenario. It was possible to assess the relationship between the theory and the points raised in the research.

The research worked on three fronts of investigation in order to cross the views and facts of different audiences involved and get a better understanding of the creative tourism chain and its barriers. The residents and tourists of the city of Recife were interviewed, the so-called "experience consumers", also the agents of the public sector and finally the creative entrepreneurs. It was not possible to reach the expectations of the research regarding the results of the last group, due to the number of respondents reached.

The results show that Recife advanced in the area of Creative Tourism, articulated by public investments and the emergence of small local enterprises, yet, there is a long way to go. A good part of the public, especially the local tourists, are unaware of the opportunities and tourist activities in the city, in addition, they are not used to going out frequently and seeking new places. There is, however, interest and availability by a good part of the users.

Regardless, it is necessary to point out some aspects that have proved to be of great importance for the consumer of local tourism. The question of cost and safety are essential factors for more than two thirds of the interviewees. The holding of cultural and artistic festivals and events can greatly contribute to dissemination and growth of tourism in Recife. Beyond that, it is important to promote dissemination made by the users themselves, including bloggers and local influencers, since it was found that only 1% of people search for official information in the Tourist Assistance Centers.

From the point of view of creative tourism managers and entrepreneurs, it became evident the need for the actions proposed in the Municipal Plan for Creative Tourism to be implemented and improved over time.

The actions operate on several fronts; how to disseminate knowledge about the concept; professional qualification program; encouraging improvements in infrastructure; implementation of a marketing program; and the establishment of a management council to supervise and advise the plan. In addition, bearing the title of City of Creative Tourism, as part of the International Creative Tourism Network, the local government should be committed to maintaining the promotion as a destination for creative tourism, through a strong digital presence, international campaigns, organization of events, et cetera.

The moment is favorable to invest in a business in the area of creative tourism. It is necessary to awaken the resident's gaze to local experiences, either on the side of which they want to invest in the business, or from the perspective of the consumer of the experiences. For future work, the objective is to extend the research procedure with entrepreneurs, conducting interviews in person. Besides that, conduct collaborative brainstorming sessions uniting entrepreneurs and users. Thus, it is possible to collect more meaningful insights and go deeper in the identification of needs. Accessing more data, the next step to be taken would be the ideation phase, using design process tools such as creating personas, empathy map, user journey map etc, to guide the project design. The role of the designer is of great importance in the development of a project that integrates all this potential and strengthens the city as a recognized destination for creative tourism.

REFERENCES

Binkhorst, E, 2007. *Creativity in tourism experiences: the case of Sitges.*

Capital da Criatividade e do Turismo Criativo. VisitRecife, 2020. Available at https://visit.recife.br/artigo/capital-da-criatividade-e-do-turismo-criativo

Euromonitor International, 2019. *Top 10 Global Consumer Trends 2019.*

Fesenmaier, D. R., Xiang, Z., 2017. *Introduction to Tourism Design and Design Science in Tourism.*

Kageyama, P. (orgs), 2011. *Cidades criativas: perspectivas.* São Paulo.

Mitchell, T., 1993. *Redefining designing: From form to experience.* New York.

Moritz, S., 2005. *Service Design: pratical acess to an envolving field.* London.

Pardo, J., 2011. *Gestão e governança nas cidades criativas.*

Pezzi, E. et al, 2015. *A Experiência Turística e o Turismo de Experiência: um estudo sobre as dimensões da experiência memorável.* From Revista Turismo em Análise, v. 26, n. 1.

Pine, B. J. et al, 1999. *The experience economy: work is theatre & every business a stage.* Boston.

Reis, A.C.F (Org.), 2008. *Economia Criativa como Estratégia de Desenvolvimento.* São Paulo. Available at: https://garimpodesolucoes.com.br/downloads/ebook_br.pdf

Richards, G. & Raymond, C., 2000. *Creative tourism.* Atlas News, 23, 16-20.

Richards, G., 2011. *Creativity and tourism: the state of the art.* Annals of Tourism.

Stickdorn, M.; Schneider, J., 2014. *Isto é design thinking de serviços: Fundamentos, ferramentas, casos.*

Sun Tung, V. W.; Ritchie, J. R., 2011. *Exploring the essence of memorable tourism experiences.* Annals of Tourism Research, [s.l.], v. 38, n. 4.

Vianna, M., 2012. *Design thinking: inovação em negócios.*

PARENTS, SOCIAL MEDIA, AND ONLINE SUPPORT: A SYSTEMATIC REVIEW OF THE LITERATURE

Vanessa P. Dennen, Daeun Jung, Casey Cargill and Amber Hedquist
Florida State University
Tallahassee, FL USA

ABSTRACT

Much like every other aspect of contemporary life, parenting has been affected by the Internet. Parents use the Internet in a variety of ways while raising their children, including as a source of information and support. In addition to accessing static information, they engage with others in social media contexts. In this study, we present a systematic review of the research on social media use to support parenting activities, examining research trends and more substantively how parenting and social media intersect. A search of studies published between 2010-2019 yielded 70 relevant articles, classified as providing health-related support, school-related support, and general support. Findings suggest that research in this area is emergent and growing quickly, and most existing studies focus on specific instances of support. The field would benefit from underlying work to establish the prevalence, scope, and nature of parent social media support activities.

KEYWORDS

Health Information, Online Community, Parents, Scoping Review, Support, Social Media

1. INTRODUCTION

Parenting is a hands-on activity, but the Internet nonetheless plays a role in the contemporary parent-child relationship. Parents with questions unsurprisingly turn to search engines and their online networks for answers. For example, a study of an online community for parents, babycenter.com, found that it was frequented by parents looking for affirmation related to normative child development (Jang & Dworkin, 2012). That behavior quite naturally extends from search engines and private online communities to social media-based ones. A 2015 survey of American parents by the Pew Research Center found that among social media users (75% of the sample in 2015 and surely higher now), parents were likely to use social media within their friend networks to share and seek support, affirmation, and information (Duggan et al., 2015).

For parents, social media can provide online friendship, and it can also provide an outlet for being empowered by telling one's stories of parenting, as experienced by the fraught-titled mommy bloggers (Chen, 2013). An earlier review of literature found that for most parents, online engagement with other parents is a satisfying activity (Dworkin et al., 2013), although 'parents' most often means mothers in this context. Fathers have been less frequently studied and when studied less likely to express satisfaction (He & Dworkin, 2015/2016).

2. METHOD

2.1 Study Design and Research Questions

The purpose of this study is to systematically review the existing empirical research on how parents use social media to identify the current research trends and illuminate areas that would be appropriate for future research. The research questions guiding this review are:

1. What are the research trends related to social media use to support parenting activities?
2. How do people use social media to support parenting activities?

We draw upon Arksey and O'Malley (2005) scoping review framework to investigate this topic. They indicated that among the four reasons for conducting a scoping review, one might seek to map the range of research previously conducted on a topic and summarize that research while answering research questions of a general nature (Arksey & O'Malley, 2005). Although there is some disagreement in the literature as to whether or not scoping reviews are a form of systematic literature review (Morris et al., 2016), based in part on the wide range of methodological rigor apparent across published scoping reviews (Pham et al., 2014; Tricco et al., 2016), in this study we apply a systematic approach to the scoping review (Peters et al., 2015).

2.2 Sampling

The article sampling procedure followed the PRISMA 2020 guidance for systematic reviews (Page et al., 2021). Articles were sampled via a search using Web of Science, focusing on four major journal indices (Social Science Citation Index, Science Citation Index, Arts & Humanities Citation Index and Emerging Sources Citation Index). The Web of Science Database is frequently used as a data source for review articles (Li et al., 2018), including scoping reviews (e.g., Dennen et al., 2020). A topical search was used, based on the following parameters:

Topic = "parent*" AND "social media"
Years = 2010-2019
Language = English
Type = journal article

The initial search was conducted on October 3, 2019, with a secondary search conducted on March 20, 2020 focused solely on 2019 publications to identify additional articles published during late 2019.

As shown in Figure 1, after an initial 845 articles were identified, 582 were removed during a screening for relevance. Three team members independently screened each article, and when in doubt the full article was reviewed by the full team in a meeting. In some instances, the articles were about teenagers' use of social media, and mentioned parents somewhere within the articles. These articles contained adjacent research, but did not focus on the main phenomenon we were interested in. In others, the search terms merely appeared somewhere in the article but the overall topic was not relevant, or the focus was on using social media as a research recruitment or data collection method for studies of other phenomena.

The 263 relevant articles were retrieved and reviewed independently by two team members with the third and fourth team member weighing in where discrepancies arose. In this secondary screening process, 139 non-empirical articles were removed, along with 54 articles that were empirical studies at the intersection of parents and social media but looking at other topics (e.g., how parents monitor their children's social media use and how social media mediates the parent-child relationship). The remaining 70 empirical articles all focused on some aspect of how social media is used to support parenting. References for the full sample can be found at https://studentssocialmediaschools.files.wordpress.com/2021/07/wbc2021-reviewsamplereferences.pdf.

2.3 Coding and Analysis

The final sample of 70 studies were coded by year, country of study, data collection method(s), data sources (parents, children), and age of parents' children. Frequency distributions were created for each of these areas. Then each study was reviewed and classified into four categories:

(1) Parenting – health-related (physical, mental, and behavioral)
(2) Parenting – school-related
(3) Parenting – general support
(4) Parenting – other (articles that did not fit other categories)

Within each category, the articles were examined by research method and sub-topic to identify areas where most research is focused.

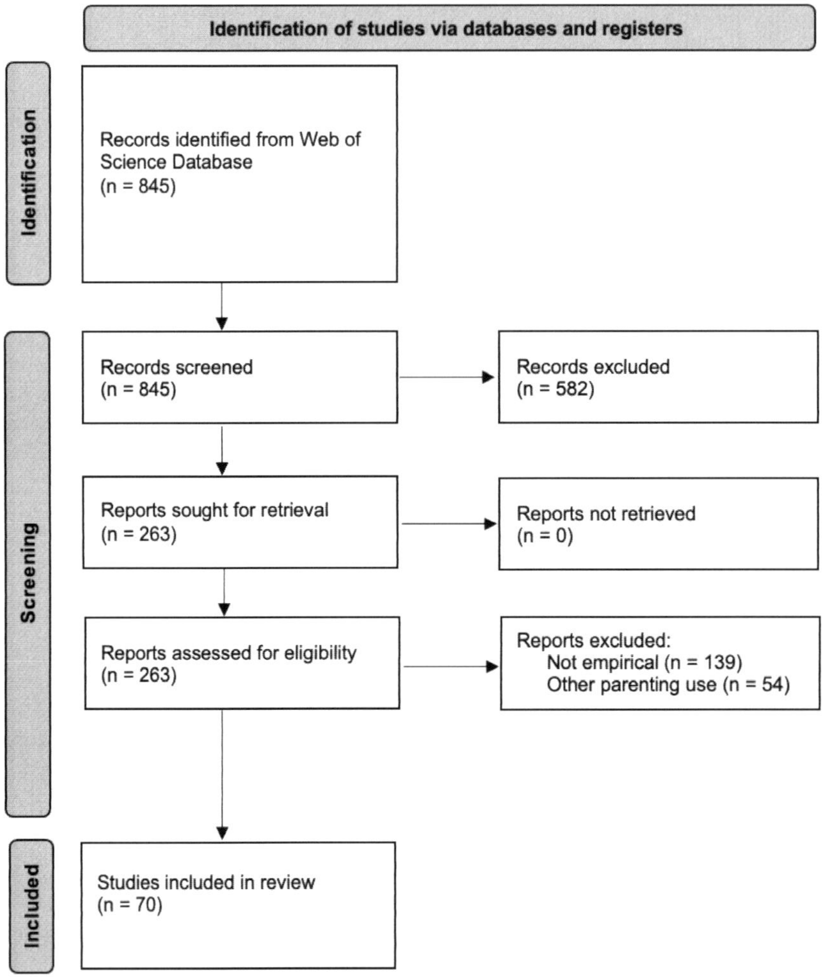

Figure 1. Overview of sampling procedure following PRISMA 2020 guidelines (Page et al., 2021)

3. FINDINGS

3.1 Overview of Research Trends

Findings show that publications about parent social media use have steadily risen since 2015 (see Figure 2), and that trajectory is expected to continue to increase. Of the 70 articles in the sample, 49 (70%) of the articles were situated in the United States. An additional 5 were situated in Canada, and the remaining 16 were from Australia (3), the UK (2), Israel (2), Germany, Italy, Lebanon, South Africa, Switzerland, Taiwan, and Turkey. Twelve of these articles from outside North America were from 2019, the last year included in this study, and two were from 2018. This shows how interest in this research area has increased globally.

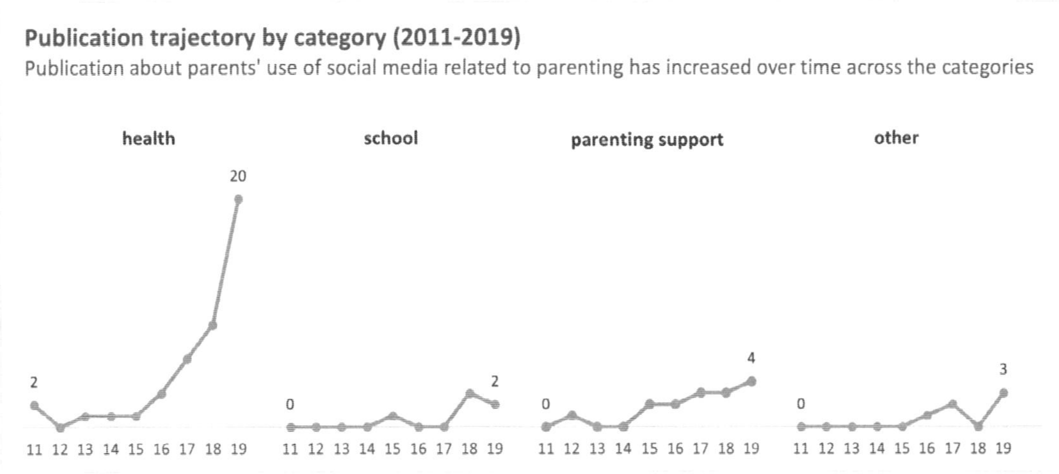

Figure 2. Publication trajectory by category across years

In terms of participants, all 70 studies had parents as research participants, and 4 studies (5.7%) also included children as participants. When specific child age groups were specified, parents of younger children (age 0-4) were the most common participants, with 32 (46%) of the studies focusing on them. None of the studies focused on parents of adult children.

Surveys were the most common form of data collection, followed by social media archives, and interviews (See Figure 3). Survey and interview methods were commonly used to collect data about parents' social media habits and attitudes (Barton et al., 2019), their interest in using new resources (Swindle et al., 2014) or their perceptions of existing social media resources (Külhaş Çelik et al., 2019), and their actions after encountering social media information resources (Hwang & Shah, 2019). In contrast, social media archives were used to conduct content analyses of parents' online conversations and the resources they use. Through these content analysis, researchers explored issues such as the quality and accuracy of parenting content online (Kallem et al., 2018; Turner et al., 2011) and the nature of support and interactions offered to parents online (Zhao et al., 2019).

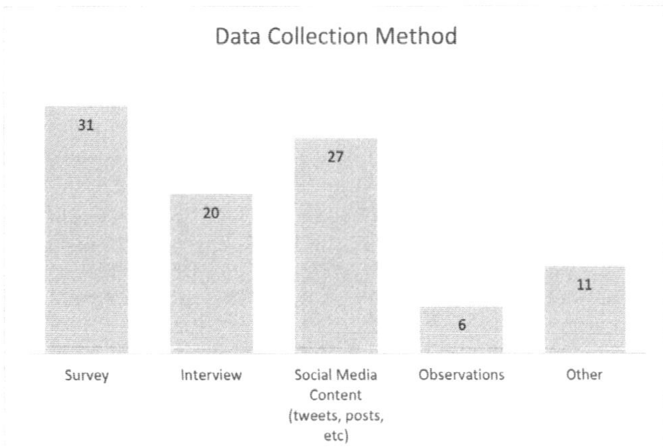

Figure 3. Data Collection Method

3.2 Social Media Use to Support Parenting

Three main categories of research were apparent among the studies. Most prominent was research on parenting in a health-related context (see Figure 2). This category represented 44 (62.9%) of the studies. More general parenting support research comprised 15 articles (21.4%), and finally six studies (8.6%) focused on school-related support. Five studies stood alone, not fitting in a category with other studies.

3.2.1 Health-related Uses

Parents use social media to access information about a diverse array of health-conditions, ranging from the general topics such as healthy behaviors (Laws et al., 2019) to specific health conditions like leukemia (Gage-Bouchard et al., 2017). These two articles investigate differences in who accesses health-related information online (Laws et al., 2019) and how social media spaces can unite parents with others who have similar parenting experiences for mutual information-sharing and support (Gage-Bouchard et al., 2017). Among the health-related parenting articles, one health topic stands out: vaccination. Vaccination rates are a public health concern, and social media has been a space where anti-vaccination groups have frequently spread misinformation. Articles in this area explored the nature and quality of information parents encounter in social media spaces along with how this information shapes their vaccination decisions for their children (Deas et al., 2019; Modanloo et al., 2019).

3.2.2 General Parenting Support

Most of the general parenting support articles focused on parenting of young children or parenting concerns prior to giving birth. They include studies about mommybloggers (Steiner & Bronstein, 2017) and parenting groups (Das, 2019), demonstrating the powerful influence of stories shared online. Many of these articles are closely related to the health-related articles, with the main difference being the locus of information. Whereas health-related parenting support involves accessing information about health conditions from medical professionals or crowdsourcing health information with parents who have shared experiences caring for children with medical conditions, the general parenting support articles are situated in spaces where parents gather for camaraderie and to find other parents with similar philosophies and life choices. These studies explore how parents use social media to share their stories and perform their personal choices about birthing and raising children. Topics raised in the general parenting support category may touch on issues like mental health, but in the sense that participation on parenting forums may affect a parent's mental health (McDaniel et al., 2012).

3.2.3 School-related Parenting Uses

The six articles related to parenting and schools included two Israeli studies and one American study of how parents used social media as a leveraging tool for protest (Addi-Raccah & Yemini, 2018; Avigur-Eshel & Berkovich, 2018; Schroeder et al., 2018). Two others looked at social media as a tool for facilitating parent-school communications (Fan & Yost, 2018; Vigo-Arrazola & Dieste-Gracia, 2018). The final article examined how social media was used to gather information during a school crisis (Mazer et al., 2015). Collectively these six articles show how parents find alternate between using social media to have a voice and to gather information about school events and topics.

4. DISCUSSION

The heavy emphasis on health-related parenting support in social media settings was not a surprising finding. A recent literature review about social media use by healthcare providers similarly identified health care promotion and education as important uses of the medium (Farsi, 2021). Based on this literature, it appears that both parties – parents and medical professionals – have a mutual interest in maintaining online forums with accurate information and support for children's healthcare needs. Vaccination-focused studies aside, most of these articles investigate health conditions and communities in isolation. Pooling their knowledge across conditions and communities, researchers could help health professionals better meet their patients' needs by fostering helpful, positive online support spaces and identifying appropriate levels of their presence and intervention in these environments. A key takeaway from this collection of studies is that it is important to find a balance between accurate information and peer interaction. Parents seek these online spaces because they provide alternate perspectives and often a broader view than their own healthcare providers. Social media cannot treat their children, and the risk of misinformation is always present, but at the same time parents are pooling knowledge and learning from each other, often yielding positive outcomes.

Through this pooling of knowledge and collective learning, whether discussing health topics or parenting more generally, a lot of personal sharing takes place in online forums. This sharing may be done in the interest of supporting parents or meeting children's health needs, but at the same time it potentially makes families vulnerable. Parenting online raises concerns about children's privacy and digital footprints, affecting them before they are born (Seko & Tiidenberg, 2016) or go on the Internet themselves (Dennen, 2016). This phenomenon of discussing one's children online has been dubbed *sharenting* and is often engaged in naively, with little consideration of the potential perils (Cino & Formenti, 2021). Although parents do it freely, they may object when others, like teachers and schools, post about their children online (Cino & Dalledonne Vandini, 2020). Given the personal nature of health information, more research on the risks within health-related parenting communities is warranted, including longitudinal studies to determine if any material or emotional harm has come to children through their parents' social media activities.

4.1 Limitation

A major limitation is the sampling approach used in this study. By focusing solely on the Web of Science database, the sample was not inclusive of international journals (Mongeon & Paul-Hus, 2015). To some degree, this limitation was mitigated by our focus on English language journals. Additionally, we make no claim to provide a comprehensive overview of journal articles on our topic, but instead use Web of Science indexed journals as a proxy for overall research and publishing trends. Additionally, although this paper summarizes research trends and describes the types of parenting support that can be supported by social media, these trends should not be considered exhaustive or fully representative of the ways parents use social media as a tool to connect to other parents and gain information and support.

5. CONCLUSION

Twenty-first century parents have a powerful tool at their fingertips 24 hours a day: the Internet. Although the Internet is a vast and easily searchable digital library, it also is a space where two-way communication can occur and relationships can be fostered. For parents who may find that they have questions about child health and development, or who feel isolated and alone, social media can be alluring. A clear advantage of social media over static information sources is the ability to interact with others. Parents can either use their social media profiles to reach out to their regular networks, or use social media to make new contacts and discover communal virtual spaces inhabited by other parents with similar interests, needs, and experiences. Across the articles sampled in this study were instances of professionals (e.g., in healthcare or education) using social media to push information to and develop connections with parents; more experienced parents sharing with less experienced parents; and parents more generally developing community and sharing their stories with each other. Each of these approaches helps unite people and share information in more dynamic and flexible ways and build relationships that would likely not be possible if parents were constrained to interactions with people encountered through their physical networks.

The studies found in this review focus most heavily on parents of younger children and parents seeking health-related support. This could represent a greater need for online support among these groups, or it could represent targeted areas of interest within specific disciplines. Both parents of young children and parents of children with medical conditions are likely to interact with medical professionals about their children's' development milestones or health needs on a regular basis, and healthcare professionals are concerned about how social media can be used to provide accurate information and how misinformation spreads online as well. However, these findings should not be taken to mean that parents are most likely to seek social media-based parenting support when their children are young or have healthcare needs. We do not currently have an empirically supported depiction of how widespread the practice of seeking parenting support via social media is, nor of the platforms that best support these activities and the topical areas around which parents are most likely to connect. These areas constitute a research gap.

As can be seen by the publishing trends over time, this area is just beginning to blossom. The field would benefit from studies that help establish a baseline for understanding parent use of social media, in which the more specific and context-based studies included in this sample might be situated. Future research might focus on how parents use social media across their child-rearing years, considering how their needs for different types of information and support change as their children age and they become more secure as parents. Additionally, such research might look for differences in parenting social media behaviors between first time parents and more experienced parents. With a stronger sense of when and how parents seek support and build networks on social media, the field will have greater direction for specific sub-topics that might be investigated.

ACKNOWLEDGEMENT

We would like to thank the rest of the Students, Social Media & Schools Research Team at Florida State University who helped as we began this project.

REFERENCES

Addi-Raccah, A., & Yemini, M. (2018). What is up? Parental Whatsapp discussion groups in diverse educational settings in Israel. *Multicultural Education Review, 10*(4), 310-326. https://doi.org/10.1080/2005615x.2018.1532224

Arksey, H., & O'Malley, L. (2005). Scoping studies: Towards a methodological framework. *International Journal of Social Research Methodology, 8*(1), 19-32. https://doi.org/10.1080/1364557032000119616

Avigur-Eshel, A., & Berkovich, I. (2018). Who "likes' public education: Social media activism, middle-class parents, and education policy in Israel. *British Journal of Sociology of Education, 39*(6), 844-859. https://doi.org/10.1080/01425692.2017.1418294

Barton, K. S., Wingerson, A., Barzilay, J. R., & Tabor, H. K. (2019). "Before Facebook and before social media...we did not know anybody else that had this": Parent perspectives on internet and social media use during the pediatric clinical genetic testing process. *J Community Genet, 10*(3), 375-383. https://doi.org/10.1007/s12687-018-0400-6

Chen, G. M. (2013). Don't call me that: A techno-feminist critique of the term mommy blogger. *Mass Communication and Society, 16*(4), 510-532. https://doi.org/10.1080/15205436.2012.737888

Cino, D., & Dalledonne Vandini, C. (2020). “Why does a teacher feel the need to post my kid?”: Parents and teachers constructing morally acceptable boundaries of children’s social media presence. *International Journal Of Communication, 14*. https://ijoc.org/index.php/ijoc/article/view/12493

Cino, D., & Formenti, L. (2021). To share or not to share? That is the (social media) dilemma. Expectant mothers questioning and making sense of performing pregnancy on social media. *Convergence: The International Journal of Research into New Media Technologies, 27*(2), 491-507. https://doi.org/10.1177/1354856521990299

Das, R. (2019). The mediation of childbirth: ‘Joyful’ birthing and strategies of silencing on a Facebook group. *European Journal of Cultural Studies, 22*(5-6), 495-510.

Deas, J., Bean, S. J., Sokolovska, I., & Fautin, C. (2019). Childhood vaccine attitudes and information sources among Oregon parents and guardians. *Health Promot Pract, 20*(4), 529-538. https://doi.org/10.1177/1524839918778830

Dennen, V. P. (2016). Digital by default: Growing into your digital footprint. In P. G. Nixon, R. Rawal, & A. Funk (Eds.), *Digital media usage across the life course* (pp. 67-83). Routledge.

Dennen, V. P., Choi, H., & Word, K. (2020). Social media, teenagers, and the school context: A scoping review of research in education and related fields. *Educational Technology Research and Development, 68*, 1635-1658. https://doi.org/10.1007/s11423-020-09796-z

Duggan, M., Lenhart, A., Lampe, C., & Ellison, N. B. (2015). *Parents and social media*. https://www.pewresearch.org/internet/2015/07/16/parents-and-social-media/

Dworkin, J., Connell, J., & Doty, J. (2013). A literature review of parents’ online behavior. *Cyberpsychology: Journal of Psychosocial Research on Cyberspace, 7*(2). https://doi.org/https://doi.org/10.5817/CP2013-2-2

Fan, S., & Yost, H. (2018). Keeping connected: Exploring the potential of social media as a new avenue for communication and collaboration in early childhood education. *International Journal of Early Years Education, 27*(2), 132-142. https://doi.org/10.1080/09669760.2018.1454301

Farsi, D. (2021). Social media and health care, part I: Literature review of social media use by health care providers. *J Med Internet Res, 23*(4), e23205. https://doi.org/10.2196/23205

Gage-Bouchard, E. A., LaValley, S., Mollica, M., & Beaupin, L. K. (2017). Communication and exchange of specialized health-related support among people with experiential similarity on Facebook. *Health Communication, 32*(10), 1233-1240. https://doi.org/10.1080/10410236.2016.1196518

He, Y., & Dworkin, J. (2015/2016). Cyber dads: What are fathers doing online? *Fathering, 13*(3), 219-230. https://doi.org/10.3149/fth.1303.219

Hwang, J., & Shah, D. V. (2019). Health information sources, perceived vaccination benefits, and maintenance of childhood vaccination schedules. *Health Communication, 34*(11), 1279-1288. https://doi.org/10.1080/10410236.2018.1481707

Jang, J., & Dworkin, J. (2012). Babycenter.com: New parent behavior in an online community. *The Forum for Family and Consumer Issues, 17*(2), 1-14.

Kallem, S., Gruver, R. S., Virudachalam, S., & Fiks, A. G. (2018). Mothers' Facebook posts about infant health: Findings from the Grow2Gether study. *BMC Pediatrics, 18*, 8, Article 341. https://doi.org/10.1186/s12887-018-1315-4

Külhaş Çelik, İ., Büyüktiryaki, B., Civelek, E., & Kocabaş, C. N. (2019). Internet use habits of parents with children suffering from food allergy. *Asthma Allergy Immunology, 17*(3), 134-139. https://doi.org/10.21911/aai.485

Laws, R., Walsh, A. D., Hesketh, K. D., Downing, K. L., Kuswara, K., & Campbell, K. J. (2019). Differences between mothers and fathers of young children in their use of the Internet to support healthy family lifestyle behaviors: Cross-sectional study. *J Med Internet Res, 21*(1), e11454. https://doi.org/10.2196/11454

Li, K., Rollins, J., & Yan, E. (2018). Web of Science use in published research and review papers 1997-2017: A selective, dynamic, cross-domain, content-based analysis. *Scientometrics, 115*(1), 1-20. https://doi.org/10.1007/s11192-017-2622-5

Mazer, J. P., Thompson, B., Cherry, J., Russell, M., Payne, H. J., Kirby, E. G., & Pfohl, W. (2015). Communication in the face of a school crisis: Examining the volume and content of social media mentions during active shooter incidents. *Computers in Human Behavior, 53*, 238-248. https://doi.org/10.1016/j.chb.2015.06.040

McDaniel, B. T., Coyne, S. M., & Holmes, E. K. (2012). New mothers and media use: Associations between blogging, social networking, and maternal well-being. *Maternal and Child Health Journal, 16*(7), 1509-1517. https://doi.org/10.1007/s10995-011-0918-2

Modanloo, S., Stacey, D., Dunn, S., Choueiry, J., & Harrison, D. (2019). Parent resources for early childhood vaccination: An online environmental scan. *Vaccine, 37*(51), 7493-7500. https://doi.org/10.1016/j.vaccine.2019.09.075

Mongeon, P., & Paul-Hus, A. (2015). The journal coverage of Web of Science and Scopus: A comparative analysis. *Scientometrics, 106*(1), 213-228. https://doi.org/10.1007/s11192-015-1765-5

Morris, M., Boruff, J. T., & Gore, G. C. (2016). Scoping reviews: Establishing the role of the librarian. *J Med Libr Assoc, 104*(4), 346-354. https://doi.org/10.3163/1536-5050.104.4.020

Page, M. J., Moher, D., Bossuyt, P. M., Boutron, I., Hoffmann, T. C., Mulrow, C. D., Shamseer, L., Tetzlaff, J. M., Akl, E. A., Brennan, S. E., Chou, R., Glanville, J., Grimshaw, J. M., Hrobjartsson, A., Lalu, M. M., Li, T., Loder, E. W., Mayo-Wilson, E., McDonald, S., McGuinness, L. A., Stewart, L. A., Thomas, J., Tricco, A. C., Welch, V. A., Whiting, P., & McKenzie, J. E. (2021). PRISMA 2020 explanation and elaboration: updated guidance and exemplars for reporting systematic reviews. *BMJ, 372*, n160. https://doi.org/10.1136/bmj.n160

Peters, M. D., Godfrey, C. M., Khalil, H., McInerney, P., Parker, D., & Soares, C. B. (2015). Guidance for conducting systematic scoping reviews. *Int J Evid Based Healthc, 13*(3), 141-146. https://doi.org/10.1097/XEB.0000000000000050

Pham, M. T., Rajic, A., Greig, J. D., Sargeant, J. M., Papadopoulos, A., & McEwen, S. A. (2014). A scoping review of scoping reviews: Advancing the approach and enhancing the consistency. *Res Synth Methods, 5*(4), 371-385. https://doi.org/10.1002/jrsm.1123

Schroeder, S., Currin, E., & McCardle, T. (2018). Mother tongues: The Opt Out movement's vocal response to patriarchal, neoliberal education reform. *Gender and Education, 30*(8), 1001-1018. https://doi.org/10.1080/09540253.2016.1270422

Seko, Y., & Tiidenberg, K. (2016). Birth through the digital womb. In P. G. Nixon, R. Rawal, & A. Funk (Eds.), *Digital media usage across the lifecourse* (pp. 50-66). Routledge.

Steiner, L., & Bronstein, C. (2017). Leave a comment: Mommyblogs and the everyday struggle to reclaim parenthood. *Feminist Media Studies, 17*(1), 59-76. https://doi.org/10.1080/14680777.2017.1261840

Swindle, T. M., Ward, W. L., Whiteside-Mansell, L., Bokony, P., & Pettit, D. (2014). Technology use and interest among low-income parents of young children: Differences by age group and ethnicity. *Journal of Nutrition Education and Behavior, 46*(6), 484-490. https://doi.org/10.1016/j.jneb.2014.06.004

Tricco, A. C., Lillie, E., Zarin, W., O'Brien, K., Colquhoun, H., Kastner, M., Levac, D., Ng, C., Sharpe, J. P., Wilson, K., Kenny, M., Warren, R., Wilson, C., Stelfox, H. T., & Straus, S. E. (2016). A scoping review on the conduct and reporting of scoping reviews. *BMC Med Res Methodol, 16*, 15. https://doi.org/10.1186/s12874-016-0116-4

Turner, A., Kabashi, A., Guthrie, H., Burket, R., & Turner, P. (2011). Use and value of information sources by parents of child psychiatric patients. *Health Information and Libraries Journal, 28*(2), 101-109. https://doi.org/10.1111/j.1471-1842.2011.00935.x

Vigo-Arrazola, B., & Dieste-Gracia, B. (2018). Building virtual interaction spaces between family and school. *Ethnography and Education, 14*(2), 206-222. https://doi.org/10.1080/17457823.2018.1431950

Zhao, Y., Zhang, J., & Wu, M. (2019). Finding users' voice on social media: An investigation of online support groups for autism-affected users on Facebook. *Int J Environ Res Public Health, 16*(23). https://doi.org/10.3390/ijerph16234804

UNDERSTANDING SMART LOCKER USER BEHAVIOR THROUGH TWITTER

Colette Malyack and Pius Egbelu
New Jersey Institute of Technology, USA

ABSTRACT

Understanding smart locker sentiment and use is an area of increasing interest for package delivery organizations. Applications of this data could result in cost savings through route optimization and increased placement of smart locker technology. However, there has been little effort applied to gathering information related to public sentiment on this topic. Therefore, we gather and analyze Twitter data related to smart lockers to determine if there is change in sentiment over time and if socialization is greater in certain regions or communities. This analysis is performed through multiple statistical analyses, linear regression, time series decomposition, and logistic regression. Some significant findings indicate that socialization of tweets related to smart lockers increased over time and socialization is greatest in the more densely population continent of Asia. Future studies are encouraged to continue analysis of data related to smart lockers based on population density, as this could provide marketing and delivery optimization improvements to decrease cost without decreasing customer sentiment or service.

KEYWORDS

Smart Locker, Microblogging Sites (MS), Statistical Analysis, Time Series Decomposition, Logistic Regression

1. INTRODUCTION

Movement of goods through package delivery services has become a requirement of modern life. With Amazon and other online retailers providing the ability to purchase goods and have those goods arrive at a customer's home within twenty-four hours, more people than ever have been shipping packages. From Thanksgiving 2019 to New Year's Day 2020, USPS is expecting to ship an average of 20.5 million packages per day (USPS, 2019). While customers do not usually think about the process behind package delivery, companies like UPS and USPS (United States Postal Service) prepare all year to ensure customers are satisfied with their package delivery experience, especially during the holiday season.

Smart lockers provide a new opportunity to ensure customers have a positive delivery experience while reducing the number of stops necessary for delivery of those packages. Adopting smart locker technology can assist companies in what is known as the "last mile delivery problem", where delivering a package from the hub to a pickup location could account for up to 53% of the total shipping cost (Dolan, 2018). Reducing this cost would benefit these companies and their customers, who could see a reduction in shipping costs or incentives to use smart lockers. These lockers also provide other benefits for customers such as avoiding the need for repeat delivery calls and protection from package theft.

However, getting customers to use smart lockers requires gaining an understanding of how they view this new delivery option. Understanding customers and their use of available services is a well-known aspect of all companies that provide a service or product, including package delivery. Customers have multiple options for package delivery ranging from requiring a signature on delivery to informing companies of a preferred location on their property to drop the package. The launching of Amazon's smart lockers in the early 2010s allowed a growing population access to shared and secure package storage, with lockers currently in over 900 cities and towns across the United States (CBS San Francisco, 2012; Holsenbeck, 2018). However, delivery optimization algorithms do not currently consider customer preference for shared pickup locations and lockers at this time.

Lack of customer sentiment incorporation in these models is likely due to lack of access to information relating to the topic. The gap could be closed through the use of microblogging sites (MS), such as Twitter, where customers publically share opinions and knowledge on a wide range of topics. These posts, known as "tweets" in the case of Twitter, can allow companies to gain real-world insights into how their products are being viewed and where to focus marketing strategies. In the case of package delivery, this could be used to optimize the use of smart locker locations to decrease driver stops and increase customer satisfaction.
As with all optimization and model development, it is first necessary to analyze the applicability of a data point prior to considering adding the attribute to a model. The intent of this research is to examine the potential role of MS in understanding customer sentiment for smart lockers.

2. LITERATURE REVIEW

To our knowledge, there has been no previous work done on the analysis of customer sentiment through MS relating to the use of smart lockers. However, there have been many previous accomplishments relating to the incorporation of customer sentiment through MS in other industries.

Several studies have focused on the effects of MS on marketing campaigns ranging from the stock market to product sales. In one study by Mittal and Goel, it was found that Twitter data allows for the collection of public sentiment through natural language processing, before showing a correlation between certain moods and stock values (Mittal & Goel, 2012). A finding that is further defended by Li et al, who reveal that stock markets are sensitive to public sentiment relating to online blogs and news postings (Li et al., 2014). These articles reveal the effect MS can have on financial markets and how public sentiment can result in changes to those values. Another area of interest for public sentiment is marketing products to consumers. One study, conducted by Gaikar and Marakarkandy, attempted to determine the effect of valance and volume in MS reviews on intention to purchase a product. Results indicated that "valence of the review, attitude towards the product and prior product knowledge was found to significantly predict purchase intention of the product" (Gaikar & Marakarkandy, 2015). Even purchasing an experience MS data can be applied to understand marketing campaign impacts. This is shown in the study by Philander and Zhong, where multiple presence of resorts on MS were compared to show the effect of promotions and campaigns showing positive associations (Philander & Zhong, 2016).

3. RESEARCH QUESTIONS

With the goal of attaining an understanding of public sentiment for smart lockers, we conducted an evaluation through the use of the microblogging site (MS) known as Twitter. Socialization involving smart lockers was applied for this analysis. For the purposes of this analysis socialization was defined as the conversation occurring on the MS, this was quantified by the number of retweets, favorites, mentions, and hashtags relating to smart lockers. Data based on this definition allowed us to obtain an understanding of the conversations occurring on the MS and the number of potential participants in those conversations.

To accomplish our goal of obtaining an understanding of socialization related to smart lockers through MS we aimed to look at the data historically and in real-time, with the additional application of sentiment analysis for tweet content, to analyze the following hypotheses.

- H1: Tweets (postings) related to smart lockers have increased in socialization over time (count, retweets, favorites, mention use, and hashtag use).
- H2: Tweets (postings) with positive sentiment related to smart lockers have increased in socialization over time (retweets, favorites, mention use, and hashtag use).
- H3: Tweets (postings) related to smart lockers have greater socialization (count, retweets, favorites, mention use, and hashtag use) in different continents.

4. SAMPLING

First it was necessary to choose the terms that would be applied to query the tweets. For the purposes of this study we queried for hashtags "#amazonhub", "#amazonhublocker", "#amazonlocker", "#deliverylocker", "#packagelocker", and "#smartlocker". The hashtags "#smarthub", "#packagehub", and "#deliveryhub" were purposefully excluded to avoid gathering tweets related to package sorting hubs or computer packages instead of smart lockers for package pickup.

For each term it was then necessary to access the historical data through Twitter using the GetOldTweets python package (Henrique, n.d.). This package uses queries to search Twitter through word search, username, hashtags, etc. In our case we used the query search and returned all tweets for each term for each month from June 2018 to November 2019. The given time period was chosen since smart lockers reached over 70 cities in June 2018 (Holsenbeck, 2018). For each term we searched for the full hashtag above in the text of the tweets, no spelling changes or abbreviations were applied to avoid potential bias.

More recent data containing location information was attained through the use of the Twitter API and rtweet package (Kearney et al., 2020). Since the Twitter API limits the historical period that can be queried, tweets from December 2nd, 2019 to January 6th, 2020 were collected, resulting in 1,616 tweets. This time period was intentionally chosen to include Cyber Monday and the following days since this time period marks an increase in online shopping, and therefore package deliveries, for the holiday season. Additionally, it includes twelve days after Christmas to allow for returns and late package delivery. This makes it more likely tweets relating to delivery and smart lockers will occur. We searched for the full hashtag above with no abbreviations.

Tweets with locations were also attained through the Twitter API. Since the Twitter API limits the historical time period that can be queried we were able to attain 143 unique tweets for the above time period. These tweets were analyzed by hand to determine location based on the location and language of the tweet text, where location is considered continent (Europe, North America, Asia, etc.). Since a majority of the tweets were found to be neutral and informative, sentiment was dropped.

5. METHODOLOGY

Raw tweets from Twitter were obtained historically for all tweets mentioning each hashtag and sentiment analysis was performed. This sentiment analysis was done through the use of the TextBlob python package (Loria et al., 2020). Output from the analysis was applied to categorize the text of the tweet as "Positive", "Neutral", or "Negative" based on natural language processing. Once this was accomplished the data was aggregated for analysis.

5.1 Statistical Analysis of Historical Twitter Data

In order to examine whether the data elements changed over time and test our first two hypotheses we initially applied a time series decomposition with a seasonality of six months. This time period was chosen since we did not have the minimum of two full years of data to make up the required two period for decomposition. Additionally, we fit a regression model to the data, where time was the predictor and the results from each term were considered separate observations. Once this was completed an F-Test was performed to determine if change over time was significant.

5.2 Statistical Analysis of Geographical Twitter Data

In testing our third hypothesis, we examined whether the location based data was normally distributed, we employed the Shapiro-Wilke Test and tests of skewness and kurtosis. Since the results of these tests indicated that none of the variables had strong probability of being normally distributed, we applied the non-parametric Mann Whitney U (Wilcoxon Ranked Sum) Test in order to make comparisons between locations. Finally, we also created a logistic regression model to determine which factors had the most significant relationship to location.

6. VARIABLE DEFINITION AND RESULTS

Data was aggregated to include aggregated variables with sentiment labels from historical Twitter data and geographical Twitter data. Here we present a breakdown of results for historical and geographical based Twitter data analysis. The importance of these results is discussed later in the Discussion section.

6.1 Time Series Decomposition

As part of evaluating trend over the given time period for our hypotheses an additive time series decomposition was completed on the historical Twitter attributes. For this decomposition a seasonality of tweet counts over six months was chosen to ensure a minimum of two periods would be available to provide the trend breakdown. Results show that for a majority of attributes (count of retweets, favorites, etc.) we see a spike and then a decrease, this can be seen in Figure 1. Interestingly, the trend for neutral related behaviors was shown to increase in the final months based on the decomposition in Figure 2.

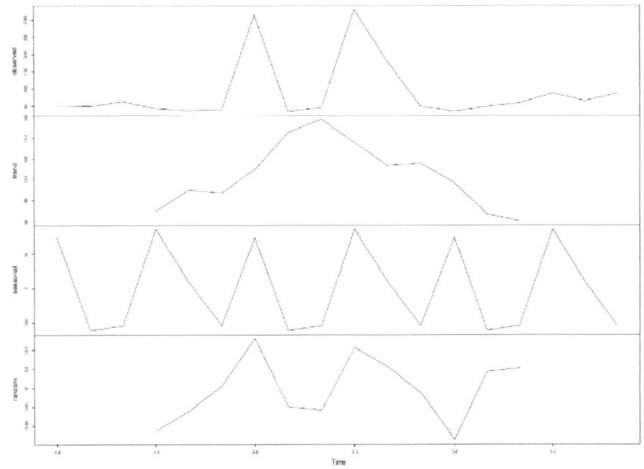

Figure 1. Time Series Decomposition for Number of Tweets per Month (shows time series similar to other attributes (retweets, favorites, etc.))

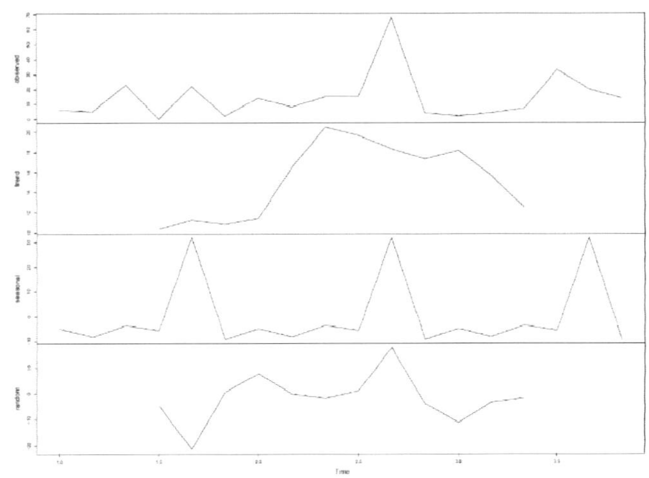

Figure 2. Time Series Decomposition for Number of Neutral Retweets per Month

6.2 Linear Model over Time

To confirm if the observed trends should be considered statistically significant and officially prove or disprove our first two hypotheses, we fit a regression model to the data. As can be seen in Figure 3, all attributes (count of retweets, favorites, etc.) were summed for the month and month was used as the predictor variable. This means for each attribute (count of retweets, favorites, etc.) 17 data points were used to fit a linear model to the data.

F-Tests to determine whether or not $\beta_1=0$ for each regression line were then performed. Only the slope for Neutral Hashtags regression line showed $\beta_1\neq0$ at the $\propto=0.1$ significance level, with a β_1 value of 12.663. The F-score of 3.086 was compared to the F-statistic of 3.048 to attain this conclusion.

6.3 Tests of Normality

The four independent variables counting retweets, mentions, favorites, and hashtags from geographical Twitter data were tested for normality. The results showed that none of the variables had a normal distribution, all were skewed to the right. This can be further illustrated in Figure 4, which shows a histogram of the values for number of hashtags in each tweet. Normality results can be found in Table 1.

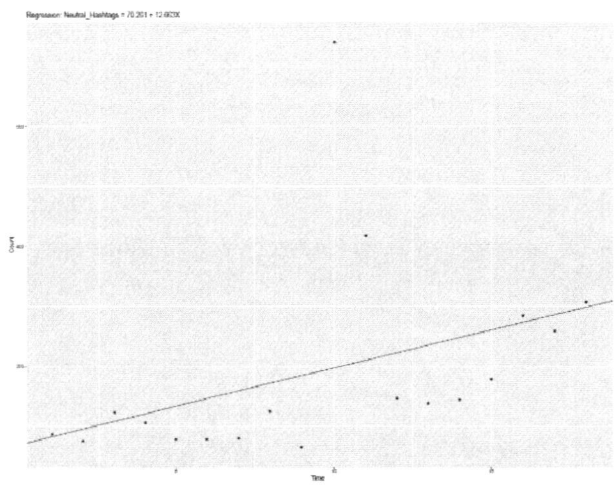

Figure 3. Regression Plot for Neutral Hashtags

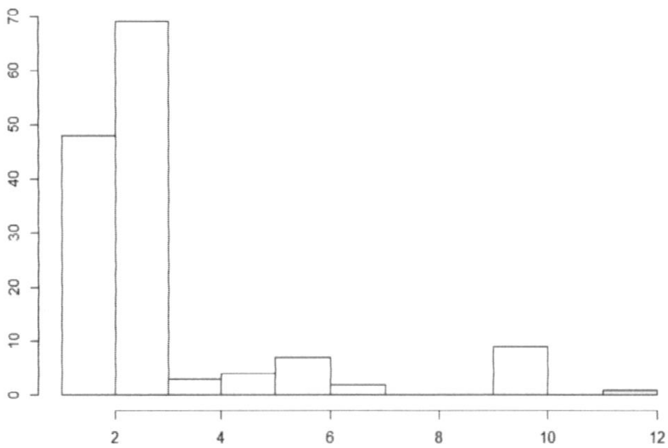

Figure 4. Count of Hashtags per Tweet

Table 1. Shapiro-Wilke, Skewness, and Kurtosis Test Results

Geography Twitter Data Test for Normality				
Attribute	Shapiro Wilke Test (P-Value)	Skewness	Kurtosis	Distribution
Retweet Count	<2.2e-16	4.465	24.839	Non-Normal
Favorite Count	<2.2e-16	4.130	20.272	Non-Normal
Mention Count	<2.2e-16	4.693	28.329	Non-Normal
Hashtag Count	<2.2e-15	1.966	6.646	Non-Normal

6.4 Univariate Analysis

In our third hypothesis, for the purposes of comparison we consider tweets created in different continents. Only results from Asia compares to tweets created outside of Asia were found to be significant. According to the Mann Whitney U (Wilcoxon Ranked Sum) Test two attributes showed a significant difference between the populations at the $\propto=0.01$ significance level. It is found that favorite count is greater and mention count is smaller for each tweet in Asia with p-values of 5.76e-4 and 9.065e-4, respectively. All univariate analysis results are in Table 2.

Table 2. Univariate Analysis

Geography Twitter Data Test for Difference in Distribution			
Attribute	Mean in Asia	Mean Outside Asia	P-Value
Retweet Count	0.388	0.270	0.962
Favorite Count	2.24	0.54	**5.76e-4 (Significant)**
Mention Count	0.025	0.302	**9.065e-4 (Significant)**
Hashtag Count	2.91	3.76	0.591

6.5 Logistic Regression Results

In order to complete logistic regression and prove or disprove our third hypothesis it was first necessary to gain an understanding of the variable distribution and covariance. During the course of this evaluation it was necessary to consider this for the geographical Twitter data. A correlation between the number of retweets and the number of favorites was seen in the results for Asia vs. other continents. However, this makes sense when considered that many Twitter users will favorite and then retweet a tweet so their followers can see it.

After controlling for covariant variables that are correlated the data was run through a series of 15 logistic regression models to determine which attributes could be considered significant. These results did show that hashtag and mention count is a significant variable in determining location when comparing tweets created in Asia vs. outside of Asia. Of the 15 models created, 6 of the models identified mention count as significant and 4 of the models identified hashtag count as significant, both at the $\propto=0.01$ level, with p-values ranging from 0.003 to 0.009. This showed that for every mention and hashtag count decrease there are greater odds that the tweet was created in Asia. Results for 1 the 6 models can be found in Tables 3 as an example.

Table 3. Logistic Regression Analysis. (Significant Model Example)

Geography Twitter Data Regression Analysis			
Attribute Included	P-Value	Adjusted Odds Ratio	Beta
Retweet Count	0.483	0.75	-0.293
Favorite Count	0.044	1.53	0.425
Hashtag Count	**0.009 (Significant)**	0.77	-0.259
Mention Count	**0.003 (Significant)**	0.09	-2.354

7. DISCUSSION

In the linear analysis over time performed on historical Twitter data our findings indicated that hashtags in neutral tweets relating to smart lockers had increased. This lends some weight to our first hypothesis that socialization amongst tweets related to this package storage option have increased. However, it should be noted that hashtags are often used as an attempt to increase the socialization of a tweet, similar to mentions. Retweets and favorites show socialization between individuals since they indicate that others are actually viewing the tweet. Therefore, the results of the time series and linear analysis provide limited support for our first hypothesis. Unfortunately, no support is provided for our second hypothesis since no significant change over time were found for positive tweets.

For our third hypothesis relating to socialization in countries in Asia there is support. Favorites and mentions are shown to increase in Asia through the Mann Whitney U Test, indicating that more individuals are directing tweets to others and reading tweets related to smart lockers in Asia. Retweets not showing a substantial change could be the result of individuals not wanting to share tweets to their followers, since tweets relating to this topic could differ drastically from the theme of a user's Twitter account and result in decreased follower count. It is interesting that in the linear regression models mentions and hashtags appear as significant at the $\propto=0.01$ level, while favorites do not. However, favorites do show significance at the $\propto=0.05$ level. This makes sense since it shows a connection between attempts to socialize a tweet (mentions and hashtags) and actual socialization of that tweet (favorites and retweets).

Additionally, it could reasonable that socialization of smart locker tweets would increase in Asia, since this correlates to population density. Currently Asia has the highest population density, with 257.8 people per square mile as of May 2019. This is significantly higher than the other continents, with the next runner up being Europe with 187.7 people per square mile (Rosenberg, 2019). Individuals living in densely populated areas would have more exposure and interest in smart lockers, since smart lockers offer an easily accessed pickup point with security measures in place. Additionally, there are more individuals within the given area that would participate in the conversation. Therefore, both attempts and actual socialization of tweets related to smart lockers would increase for the region.

8. LIMITATIONS

There is a lack of literature related to this topic, which limits the available information and best practices to be applied to the data. Previous research would allow for comparison of results and additional insights into the change over time and in continents. However, this also allows us to fill in a gap in the literature and provide information for future studies.

The main limitation of this study is the sample size. Due to the limits on querying historical data through the Twitter API there were limited results with location data available. Even for those available, location data had to be understood and categorized for continents by hand. However, this is a typical limitation for studies examining Twitter data. Since this data is based entirely on public conversations and topics that will attain the most socialization, the number of tweets is subject to popular discussions at the time.

9. CONCLUSION

Through this research we have provided a review of Twitter data related to smart lockers. Historically we reviewed data from June 2018 to November 2019, which did show a small increase in socialization overall providing some support to our first hypothesis. Unfortunately, the results did not support our second hypothesis that tweets identified to have positive sentiment would increase in socialization over time. Location based data was also considered for December 2nd, 2019 to January 6th, 2020, revealing an increase in socialization in the densely populated continent of Asia. This supported our third hypothesis that socialization would increase in this region.

Future studies in this area should continue to focus on the concept of popularity in regions. Increased socialization in densely populated regions is reasonable since those individuals would have more use for smart lockers, but that will require further investigation to prove. Additional applications for this research is in delivery optimization models, since knowledge of where smart lockers would be best utilized relies on individual sentiment towards the lockers and their use. Alternatively, marketing campaigns could apply the data to focus on areas with low sentiment and increase smart locker use. Either application could then be applied with the goal of saving delivery resources through the increased use of smart lockers.

REFERENCES

Beigi, G., Hu, X., Maciejewski, R., & Liu, H. (2016). An overview of sentiment analysis in social media and its applications in disaster relief. *Sentiment analysis and ontology engineering*, 313-340.

CBS San Francisco. (2012, August 07). Amazon Offering Lockers For Secure Product Delivery. Retrieved from https://sanfrancisco.cbslocal.com/2012/08/07/amazon-offering-lockers-for-secure-product-delivery/.

Cooper, P. (2019, December 17). 25 Twitter Statistics All Marketers Should Know in 2020. Retrieved from https://blog.hootsuite.com/twitter-statistics/.

Dolan, S. (2018, May 10). The challenges of last mile delivery logistics and the tech solutions cutting costs in the final mile. Retrieved from https://www.businessinsider.com/last-mile-delivery-shipping-explained.

Gaikar, D., & Marakarkandy, B. (2015). Product sales prediction based on sentiment analysis using twitter data. *International Journal of Computer Science and Information Technologies*, *6*(3), 2303-2313.

Henrique, J. (n.d.). GetOldTweets-python. Retrieved from https://github.com/Jefferson-Henrique/GetOldTweets-python

Holsenbeck, K. (2018, June 21). Everything you need to know about Amazon Hub Locker. Retrieved from https://www.amazon.com/primeinsider/tips/amazon-locker-qa.html.

Hughes, A. L., & Palen, L. (2009). Twitter adoption and use in mass convergence and emergency events. *International journal of emergency management*, *6*(3-4), 248-260.

Kearney, M., Heiss, A., & Briatte, F. (2020, January 9). Package 'rtweet'. Retrieved from https://cran.r-project.org/web/packages/rtweet/rtweet.pdf.

Leetaru, K. (2019, March 04). Visualizing Seven Years Of Twitter's Evolution: 2012-2018. Retrieved from https://www.forbes.com/sites/kalevleetaru/2019/03/04/visualizing-seven-years-of-twitters-evolution-2012-2018/#662569987ccf

Li, Q., Wang, T., Li, P., Liu, L., Gong, Q., & Chen, Y. (2014). The effect of news and public mood on stock movements. *Information Sciences*, *278*, 826-840.

Loria, S., Keen, P., Honnibal, M., Yankovsky, R., Karesh, D., Dempsey, E., ... Rachum, R. (2020). Simplified Text Processing. Retrieved from https://textblob.readthedocs.io/en/dev/.

Malyack, C. T., Hunter, K. M., & Hiltz, S. R. (2020). Twitter and the Prediction of Oscar Winners.

Mittal, A., & Goel, A. (2012). Stock prediction using twitter sentiment analysis. *Standford University, CS229 (2011 http://cs229. stanford. edu/proj2011/GoelMittal-StockMarketPredictionUsingTwitterSentimentAnalysis. pdf), 15.*

Neppalli, V. K., Caragea, C., Squicciarini, A., Tapia, A., & Stehle, S. (2017). Sentiment analysis during Hurricane Sandy in emergency response. *International journal of disaster risk reduction*, *21*, 213-222.

Philander, K., & Zhong, Y. (2016). Twitter sentiment analysis: Capturing sentiment from integrated resort tweets. *International Journal of Hospitality Management*, *55*(2016), 16-24.

Rosenberg, M. (2019). What Is Population Density and Where Is It Highest? Retrieved from https://www.thoughtco.com/population-density-overview-1435467

USPS. (2019, November 7). Hundreds of Millions of Holiday Packages Expected Between Thanksgiving and New Year's Day. Retrieved from https://about.usps.com/newsroom/national-releases/2019/1107-20-million-packages-to-be-delivered-daily-this-holiday-season.htm.

EVALUATION OF NEURAL NETWORK COMPRESSION METHODS ON THE RESPIRATORY SOUND DATASET

Tamás Pál[1], Bálint Molnár[1], Ádám Tarcsi[2] and Csongor László Martin[2]
[1] *Department of Information Systems, Faculty of Informatics, Eötvös Loránd University, Hungary*
[2] *Department of Data Science, Faculty of Informatics, Eötvös Loránd University, Hungary*

ABSTRACT

Recently, the use of smart medical solutions has experienced significant growth and the area of Internet of Medical Things (IoMT) has been established as an independent field. Artificial intelligence-based analysis of physiological signal data has resulted in promising results. This paper aims to assess neural network compression possibilities applied to a respiratory classification problem. The experiment is carried out on an Nvidia Jetson TX2 edge device and a personal computer. Respiratory sounds are classified into 8 classes of disease using two distinct deep learning networks. The trained models are compressed using half-precision and 8-bit integer quantization methods, and the inference results are compared and analyzed based on predictive powers, memory footprint, and inference time. Traditional, interpretable models (SVM, KNN) are also compared to the former deep models. The results are promising, the compression techniques manage to decrease memory usage 8 times while experiencing a negligible decrease in model accuracy.

KEYWORDS

Model Compression, Respiratory Classification, IoT, Deep Learning

1. INTRODUCTION

The gradual automation of healthcare has allowed the expansion of embedded and wearable devices in the field. These smart devices coupled with artificial intelligence software can potentially lead to reliable, clinically acceptable solutions.

In the last few years, neural networks have established themselves as models with high predictive power and great generalization capability. A number of models have been developed for complex problems in computer vision or natural language processing that despite their near-perfect performance, have a huge number of layers that make their deployment on under-powered devices impossible. Thus, their complex and computationally expensive nature have resulted in limited applications on smart devices and IoT. This motivates the use of model compression, in which recent advances (quantization, pruning, low-rank approximation, knowledge distillation, weight sharing, etc...) have opened the gate for more widespread use of deep learning in IoT.

Established methods in feature extraction and machine learning for signal and audio classification can be applied to IoT devices using model compression. In this experiment, two deep learning architectures are submitted to half-precision (16-bit float weights) and 8-bit quantization (8-bit integer weights) experiments on an Nvidia Jetson TX2 and a PC. The developed solutions are applied to a respiratory sound dataset in the hope of achieving more efficient, more computational-friendly method combinations.

The detection of respiratory diseases has been an important field of study, as such illnesses are responsible for millions of deaths yearly. The Respiratory Sound database (Rocha, et al., 2018) used in this experiment is detailed in Section 3.2.

The main contributions of this paper are the positive results on the compressed models that indicate the presence of potential in the use of lightweight models operating on smart devices that tackle medical problems, like respiratory classification.

Section 2 describes related research in neural network compression on edge devices. Sections 3.1, 3.3, 3.4 present the details of the experiment, the feature-extraction steps and the deep-learning models, respectively. The low-precision inference techniques are introduced in Section 3.5. The evaluation methodology and the results are presented in Sections 3.6 and 4, respectively.

2. RELATED WORK

Hadidi et al. (2019) evaluate the deployment possibilities of different deep learning frameworks on edge devices through the running/inference of different well-known models (ResNet, VGG, MobileNet, AlexNet) on a set of IoT/edge devices. The following frameworks were tested: TensorFlow, TensorFlow-Lite, Keras, Caffe/2, Movidius NCSDK Toolkit, PyTorch, TensorRT, DarkNet, FPGA Framework. The devices were the following: Raspberry Pi 3B, Nvidia Jetson TX2, and Nvidia Jetson Nano. The paper discusses the quantization and other model optimization capabilities of the frameworks in question.

Jain et al. (2020) propose a new dialect called QNN (Quantized Neural Network) which can be built into the deep learning compilers to support quantization operations across multiple platforms. They hope to fill the void caused by the lack of quantization support in some frameworks and also hardware configurations. The proposed solution is then tested on multiple devices of different architecture: Intel Xeon Cascade Lake CPUs, Nvidia Tesla T4 GPUs, ARM Cortex-A CPUs, and Raspberry Pi3 and Pi4. Acharya & Basu (2020) consider the ICBHI challenge by downsampling to 4 kHz, extracting Mel-spectrograms, and using a hybrid CNN-RNN (Convolutional Neural Network – Recurrent Neural Network) model that can handle variable-sized input. The Int. Conf. on Biomedical Health Informatics (ICBHI) challenge consists of the task of classifying respiratory sounds into crackles and wheezes. The authors discuss the applicability of models in mobile systems and consider weight quantization as a tool for reducing the model complexity.

Yang et al. (2018) experiment with complex quantized convolutional neural networks on an Intel Edison IoT board. They propose a new, local-based quantization scheme. They compare the 32-bit floating-point inference with the 8-bit fixed point, 6-bit, 4-bit, and 2-bit fixed-point quantizations on two CNNs: AlexNet and VGG-16. The quantized networks' inference times were reduced to half of the 32-bit float network's time. Moreover, there was no significant drop in accuracy for the 8, 6, and 4-bit quantization, while the 2-bit network produced results half as poor.

3. METHODS

3.1 Experimental Design

The experiment was designed in the following way: the models were constructed, trained, compressed and tested on the respective device. A detailed platform taxonomy of the experiment is presented in Table 1.

Table 1. Detailed Platform Taxonomy

Information system: PC + Nvidia Jetson TX2 model training and compression experiment			
Platform service category	Subcategory	Required	Supporting technology
Data Interchange Services	Audio Processing	yes	Librosa (resampling, splitting, MFCC conversion)

	Electronic Data Interchange	yes	Google Drive
Data Management Services	Data Dictionary/Repository	yes	Numpy (encode dataset into binary format, .npy files)
			Joblib (sklearn model persistence), PyTorch (pickle-based model serialization, .pt files), ONNX
Location and Directory Services	Filtering	yes	Imbalanced-learn (undersampling of majority class)
Network Services	Data Communications	yes	http, ftp
	Distributed Data	yes	Google Drive
System and Network Management Services	Software Installation	yes	pip (Python package manager system)
			Nvidia SDK Manager
Operating System Services	Command Interpreter and Utility	yes	psutil (for memory queries. Python library)
			time (Python library)
Software Engineering Services	Programming Language	yes	Python (3.6.9)
	Computer-Aided Software Engineering (CASE) Environment and Tools	yes	Geany (IDE)
	Software library	yes	PyTorch (1.6.0), Scikit-learn, TensorRT (7.2.3.4), Neural Network Distiller

The neural network models were constructed using the PyTorch (Paszke, et al., 2019) deep learning framework. The dataset was saved to Numpy binaries and then transferred to the Jetson for the inference task.

The Nvidia Jetson TX2 module is a high-performance computing device, that is created to handle intensive AI tasks despite its small size. The device is comprised of a 256-core Nvidia Pascal GPU, a dual-core NVIDIA Denver2, and a Quad-Core ARM Cortex-A57 CPU, 8GB of memory, and 32 GB of storage space. The Jetson TX2's Pascal GPU architecture doesn't support 8-bit integer inference on the GPU but supports 16-bit float inference. The ARMv8-A architecture CPUs on the device support 8-bit integer quantization operations. The Jetson device has been supplied with the required drivers and libraries (CUDA, cuDNN, TensorRT) using the Nvidia SDK Manager software.

The installation of PyTorch on the Jetson is necessary to run the inference and quantization experiments. The framework currently only supports CPU-based quantization. Quantization operations are implemented using two back-end libraries: FBGEMM (for x86 systems) and QNNPACK (for ARM architectures). QNNPACK (Quantized Neural Network Package) provides implementations of common operations/layers in neural networks on quantized 8-bit tensors. Layers like 2D convolution, 2D max pooling, fully connected layer, activations are all supported. Unfortunately, the pre-built PyTorch wheels offered by Nvidia for the Jetson TX2 are built using the USE_QNNPACK=0 flag, thus QNNPACK will not be present in the installation. As the quantization operations of the library rely on QNNPACK, it is necessary to build PyTorch from the source with the proper build options.

The PC environment used for the other half of the experiments is equipped with an Intel(R) Core (TM) i5-10300H 2.50GHz CPU and an Nvidia GeForce GTX 1650 Mobile GPU. The same version of PyTorch and TensorRT is present with enabled quantization.

3.2 Dataset

The Respiratory Sound Database (Rocha, et al., 2018) was created by a Portuguese and Greek research group. It is a set of 920 annotated breathing sounds containing 8 classes of recordings: 7 classes that indicate the presence of a specific disease and the class of healthy breathings. The data is collected from 126 patients that span all age groups: children, adults, elderly. Each recording is a collection of multiple consecutive breathing cycles, 6898 in total for the whole dataset. The dataset contains both clean and noisy recordings.

The recordings are from 7 locations on the upper body: trachea, left and right side of the anterior, posterior and lateral side of the chest. Single- and multi-channel acquisition mode is used.

The dataset has an imbalanced nature in terms of label distribution: the majority class (COPD - chronic obstructive pulmonary disease) contains 793 recordings, while Asthma has only one associated audio file. The lengths of the breathing cycles are also varied.

The recordings were captured by 3 different devices, therefore multiple sampling rates are present in the data: 4000 Hz, 10000 Hz, 44100 Hz.

3.3 Preprocessing and Feature Extraction

Firstly, all recordings have been resampled to the common sampling frequency of 16000 Hz. No filtering was applied. Then, the breathing cycles were extracted from the audio files. These recordings have been split into segments of 0.5 seconds with 0.125 second overlap. This resulted in an increase in the model performance. The final preprocessing step was to apply random undersampling, which reduced the imbalanced nature of the dataset.

The feature extraction step consists of extracting MFCC (Mel Frequency Cepstral Coefficients) (Mermelstein, 1976) spectrograms. MFCCs are intensively used in audio classification tasks since their introduction by Paul Mermelstein in 1976.

Algorithm:

1. Take the Short-time Fourier transform of the signal.
2. Apply the Mel filterbank to the power spectra of each frame, summing the energies in each frequency band. The Mel filterbank is a set of overlapping triangular filters.
3. Take the logarithm of the calculated energies.
4. Take the Discrete Cosine Transform (DCT) of the log filterbank energies, resulting in a so-called cepstrum. Intuitively, the cepstrum captures information on the rate of change in frequency bands.
5. The MFCC coefficients are the resulting DCT coefficients.

40 MFCC coefficients were used. Moreover, each coefficient was extended with its delta value (change in coefficient).

3.4 Models

3.4.1 Dense Neural Network (DNN)

This procedure involves the extraction of MFCC coefficients, reshaping of feature set through aggregation along the time axis, and finally feeding these to a dense neural network (DNN) classifier.

The peculiarity of this method lies in the reshaping step, which is described more clearly below. By calculating some statistical features across all frames, the spectrogram can be reduced to one feature vector, where statistical values (e.g.: mean + standard deviation) calculated for each frequency band are stacked vertically in a continuous fashion. Using this method, a feature set of shape (k, n) will take the $(2 \times k, 1)$ form after the reshaping operation (Pál, Molnár, & Tarcsi, 2020). This operation is illustrated in Equation 1 (μ_X - mean of random variable, σ_X - standard deviation of random variable). The reshaped dataset is then normalized with standard scaling.

$$\begin{bmatrix} f_{11} & f_{12} & f_{13} & \cdots \\ f_{21} & f_{22} & f_{23} & \cdots \\ \vdots & & & \ddots \end{bmatrix} \Rightarrow \begin{bmatrix} \mu_{f1} \\ \sigma_{f1} \\ \mu_{f2} \\ \sigma_{f2} \\ \vdots \end{bmatrix}$$

Equation 1

The DNN classifier contains two hidden layers. The size of the first hidden layer is $1/2 \times (I + C)$, where I is the size of the input and C is the number of classes, thus having several nodes corresponding to the arithmetical mean of the input and output dimensionality. The second layer has $1/4 \times (I + 3 \times C)$ nodes, which is the mean of the first hidden and output layer sizes. ReLU activations are used in the hidden layers, while Softmax activation is used in the output layer. This design is the result of testing multiple network sizes and topologies.

The DNN model has a very low number of trainable parameters, just 17,810. The relatively low number of parameters is an advantage for use in IoT devices. For comparison, the CNN model presented below has 368,684 trainable parameters.

3.4.2 2D Convolutional Neural Network (CNN)

This is the most widely used method for such tasks, it is used by feeding the MFCC spectrograms directly into a convolutional neural network (CNN).

In terms of normalization, "per-image" normalization achieved the best results. The following transformation is applied to each spectrogram:

$$X = \frac{X - \mu(X)}{\sigma(X)}$$

where X marks a spectrogram matrix, and $\mu(X)$, $\sigma(X)$ are the mean and standard deviation of the values in X.

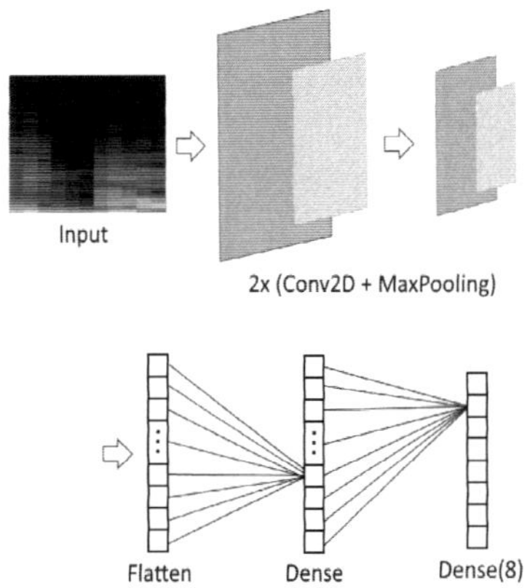

Figure 1. 2D CNN architecture.

The model architecture is described in the followings:

- 2D Convolution (16 filters, 5x5 kernel size, ReLU activation)
- Max Pooling (stride=2) + Dropout (0.5 probability)
- 2D Convolution (16 filters, 5x5 kernel size, ReLU activation)
- Max Pooling (stride=2) + Dropout (0.5 probability)
- Flattening
- Dense layer (size corresponds to the mean of the flattened layer and output layer sizes)
- Dense (Output) layer (size corresponds to the number of classes)

Figure 1 illustrates the details of this architecture.

3.4.3 SVM

Some traditional and explainable methods are used for comparison against the deep learning models.

The first such method is the Support Vector Machine. SVM constructs a hyperplane that separates the classes by maximizing the margin between the outermost points of the classes.

Since the linear separation of data is easier in higher dimensions, SVM can potentially achieve better results with higher dimensional data. A popular solution called the *kernel trick* is used to project the data into a higher-dimensional space. Any transformation can be used as a kernel function, some popular variants exist, such as the polynomial function or the Gaussian radial basis function. A few of these kernels were compared on both devices to find the optimal configuration.

3.4.4 KNN

The second traditional method is the K-nearest Neighbors (KNN) model. KNN effectively works without the necessity of a training phase: the points are classified using the k nearest elements of the training set and based on a majority vote. A few of these k-values were compared on both devices to find the optimal value.

The implementation of the SVM, KNN models are taken from the *Scikit-learn* machine learning library. Both algorithms run on the respective machine's CPU.

3.5 Low-Precision Calculations

3.5.1 Half-Precision Inference

A popular method for lower bit-width weight representation is the use of 16-bit float weights. The memory representation of a 16-bit floating-point number can be seen in Figure 2. There is a higher risk of overflows and underflows with the use of 16-bits, as the represented range of numbers is significantly smaller. In practice, the use of half-precision networks with the appropriate architectural constructions has resulted in decreased memory usage with a negligible loss of accuracy (Courbariaux, Bengio, & David, 2015).

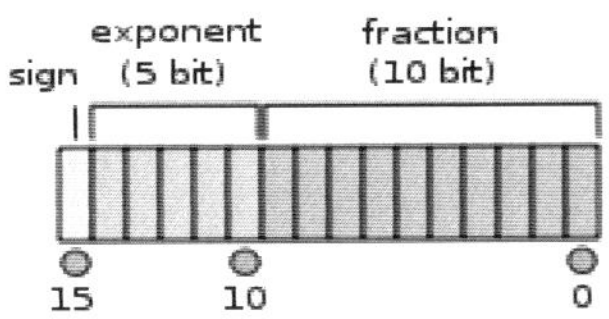

Figure 2. 16-bit float representation

There is precedent for the use of 16-bit float weights in the training phase too, but in this experiment, their use will be restricted only to the inference step. The recent *bfloat16* representation is not discussed in this paper.

Nvidia TensorRT is a library for deep learning inference and model optimization, compression. There are reports of 10-fold speedup for deep models after being optimized using the available TensorRT methods: mixed-precision conversion (16-bit float, 8-bit integer), layer fusion, parallelization, dynamic batching. The library supports the use of ONNX exported networks, thus models created in third-party deep learning frameworks such as Tensorflow and PyTorch can be imported into a TensorRT experiment.

3.5.2 8-Bit Weight Quantization

Weight quantization is the process of converting the weights of the neural network from 32-bit float representation to integer representation. The integer bit-width can vary, while the most popular bit-width is 8 bits, there are promising results with more aggressive 4-bit (Zhou, et al., 2018), 2-bit, or even 1-bit (binarized neural networks (Courbariaux, Hubara, Soudry, El-Yaniv, & Bengio, 2016)) representations.

Quantized networks are predominantly used at inference, i.e.: training is performed using traditional 32-bit float weights. This experiment implements a per-tensor, symmetric quantization solution. In the case of symmetric quantization, the procedure follows the following formula:

$$x_q = round\left(x_f \cdot \frac{2^n - 1}{max_{x_f} - min_{x_f}}\right)$$

where x_q, x_f, n are the quantized value, the original floating-point value and the number of bits used (here 8), respectively. The floating-point values are mapped to the $[-128,127] \cap \mathbb{Z}$ range. Per-tensor (also called per-layer) quantization means that all weights in a layer are scaled the same way, while in the case of per-channel quantization each channel (e.g.: convolutional kernel) has a different scale and offset.

The Neural Network Distiller (Zmora, Jacob, Zlotnik, Elharar, & Novik, 2019) is a vast library of implemented model compression methods from scientific papers. The library is based on PyTorch. In the subfield of quantization, there is a variety of algorithms implemented.

From the PyTorch API, 3 different quantization approaches were compared:

- Post-training static quantization: The algorithm feeds batches of data through the network to learn the weight and activation distributions. This data is then used to quantize the layers.
- Dynamic quantization: It involves not just the conversion of the weights to int8 - as it happens in all quantization variants - but also converting the activations to int8 on the fly.
- Quantization-Aware Training: Weights and activations are "fake quantized" during training: float values are rounded to mimic int8 values, but the computations still involve floating point numbers.

The Neural Network Distiller and TensorRT solutions both implement some variant of the post-training static quantization.

4. EVALUATION

The dataset is randomly split into training and testing sets with a train-test ratio of 90 – 10%.

The models are evaluated and compared based on the following metrics:

- Classification metric - Accuracy:

Accuracy is the proportion of samples correctly classified as positive and correctly classified as negative over the whole population. Mathematically:

$$Acc = \frac{TP + TN}{TP + FP + TN + FN}$$

- Classification metric - Precision:

Precision is the proportion of predicted positives that are truly positive.

$$Prec = \frac{TP}{TP + FP}$$

- Classification metric - Recall:

Recall is the proportion of true positives that are classified correctly as positive.

$$Rec = \frac{TP}{TP + FN}$$

- Memory footprint:

The memory usage of a program at a specific point in time is queried by the *psutil* Python library.

- Inference time:

Inference time is measured using Python's *time* library.

5. RESULTS

The overall results are summarized in Tables 2, 3, 4, 5. Inference time is measured in seconds. Graphical comparisons of the model accuracies can be seen in Figures 3, 4 while memory footprint comparisons are shown in Figure 5.

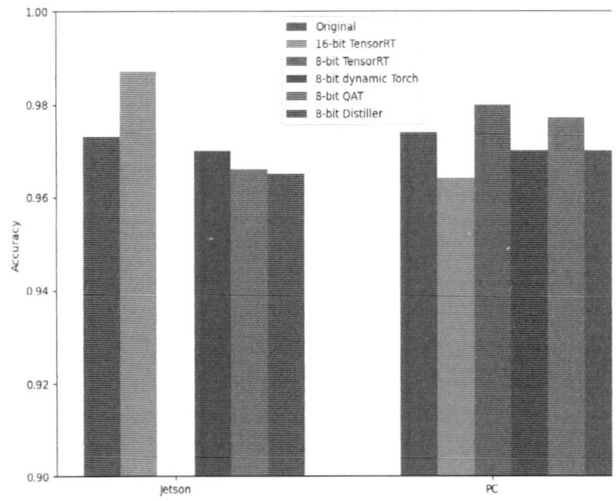

Figure 3. Accuracy of the DNN model on the PC and the Jetson

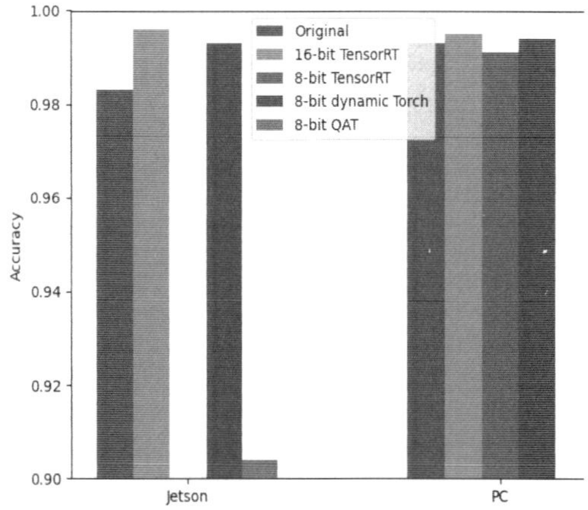

Figure 4. Accuracy of the CNN model on the PC and the Jetson

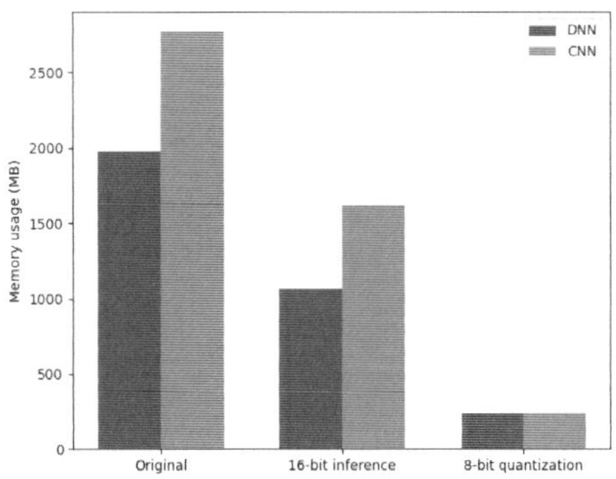

Figure 5. Comparison of model memory footprints on the Jetson

Table 2. DNN model results on the PC

Method	Acc.	Prec.	Recall	Time
Original	0.974	0.974	0.974	0.006
16-bit TensoRT	0.964	0.964	0.964	-
8-bit post-t. Torch	0.974	0.974	0.974	0.004
8-bit dyn. Torch	0.970	0.971	0.970	0.004
8-bit QAT Torch	0.977	0.977	0.977	0.004
8-bit post-t. Distiller	0.970	0.971	0.970	0.008
4-bit post-t. Distiller	0.417	0.838	0.417	0.009
2-bit post-t. Distiller	<0.1	<0.1	<0.1	0.009
8-bit TensorRT	0.980	0.981	0.980	-

Table 3. CNN model results on the PC

Method	Acc.	Prec.	Recall	Time
Original	0.993	0.993	0.993	0.067
16-bit float	0.995	0.995	0.995	-
8-bit post-t.Torch	0.595	0.838	0.595	0.334
8-bit dyn. Torch	0.994	0.994	0.994	0.129
8-bit QAT Torch	0.886	0.896	0.886	0.309
8-bit TensorRT	0.991	0.991	0.991	-

Table 4. DNN model results on the Jetson device

Method	Acc.	Prec.	Recall	Time
Original	0.973	0.973	0.973	1.54
16-bit float	0.987	0.987	0.987	-
8-bit post-t. Torch	0.968	0.968	0.968	0.269
8-bit dyn. Torch	0.970	0.971	0.970	0.144
8-bit QAT Torch	0.966	0.967	0.966	0.156
8-bit post-t. Distiller	0.965	0.966	0.965	0.066
4-bit post-t. Distiller	0.596	0.866	0.596	0.064
2-bit post-t. Distiller	<0.1	<0.1	<0.1	0.060

Table 5. CNN model results on the Jetson device

Method	Acc.	Prec.	Recall	Time
Original	0.983	0.983	0.983	3.23
16-bit float	0.996	0.996	0.996	-
8-bit post-t. Torch	0.980	0.981	0.980	2.966
8-bit dyn Torch	0.993	0.994	0.993	96.559
8-bit QAT Torch	0.904	0.910	0.904	2.741

6. DISCUSSION

The results contain some promising and interesting information. Most importantly, both the 8-bit integer quantization and the 16-bit float half-precision calculations achieve similar values in terms of the 3 classification metrics.

The methods of PyTorch are easy to use, as they are accessible through a high-level API. From the 3 presented quantization approaches, the dynamic quantization seems to be the most stable one on both the Jetson and the PC. It is even outperforming the original CNN (Convolutional Neural Network) model on the Jetson machine. To be noted, that the dynamic quantization had a significantly higher inference time on the Jetson / CNN model, for unknown reasons.

The Neural Network Distiller library is a highly useful collection of algorithms for researchers, as it contains the implementations of methods presented in a number of important papers. As it also offers the possibility to use fewer bits than 8 to represent the weights, 4- and 2-bit representations were compared as well. Although the 8-bit quantization has promising results, the smaller bit sizes produce significantly weaker and unusable models.

Considering the TensorRT methods, the results are consistently positive. However, in terms of the inference time, the amount of time that the inference needs is ambiguous, as the library performs a number of preliminary and model optimization tasks, that in total take a longer time (around 2 minutes for the Jetson, in the case of the CNN model). The configuration of the library is also cumbersome, and errors can frequently occur.

An important result lies in the difference in the memory footprints. The 8-bit quantized DNN model has a memory footprint of around 8.5 times smaller compared to the original model when using the PyTorch quantization. Similarly, for the CNN, the memory usage is around 11.4 times less.

The SVM seems to be unfit for this dataset, as it produces weaker results, poor predictions (Table 7). The model size is also considerably larger, 13.2 MB and the memory usage is high, 1977 MB. From the available kernels, the radial basis function (rbf) achieves the best results. The KNN model produces good quality predictions (Table 6) and has reasonable memory usage (281 MB). The running time however is higher and the model size inconveniently high (47.7 MB), resulting in the biggest model size by far. The optimal value for k proves to be 3.

Table 6. KNN Results

Platform	k	Acc.	Prec.	Recall	Time
PC	3	0.881	0.865	0.881	0.010
PC	5	0.854	0.870	0.854	0.011
PC	7	0.828	0.847	0.828	0.011
PC	10	0.762	0.798	0.762	0.011
Jetson	3	0.881	0.865	0.881	0.331
Jetson	5	0.854	0.870	0.854	0.332
Jetson	7	0.828	0.847	0.828	0.332
Jetson	10	0.762	0.798	0.762	0.332

Table 7. SVM Results

Platform	kernel	Acc.	Prec.	Recall	Time
PC	linear	0.762	0.775	0.762	0.014
PC	poly	0.589	0.812	0.589	0.020
PC	rbf	0.828	0.844	0.828	0.046
PC	sigmoid	0.609	0.630	0.609	0.019
Jetson	linear	0.762	0.775	0.762	0.165
Jetson	poly	0.589	0.812	0.589	0.161
Jetson	rbf	0.828	0.844	0.828	0.179
Jetson	sigmoid	0.609	0.630	0.609	0.175

In conclusion, the favorable results indicate that the use of model compression techniques could further advance the field of IoMT (Internet of Medical Things) and allow the implementation of medical classification problems on IoT devices. As future work, the analysis of further model compression methods like structured pruning is planned. The goal is to find compressed models that achieve both a significant decrease in memory usage and inference time.

REFERENCES

Acharya, J., & Basu, A. (2020, 4). *Deep Neural Network for Respiratory Sound Classification in Wearable Devices Enabled by Patient Specific Model Tuning.* IEEE Transactions on Biomedical Circuits and Systems (TBioCAS. doi:10.1109/tbcas.2020.2981172

Courbariaux, M., Bengio, Y., & David, J.-P. (2015, 12). *Training Deep Neural Networks with Low Precision Multiplications.* Accepted as a workshop contribution to ICLR 2015.

Courbariaux, M., Hubara, I., Soudry, D., El-Yaniv, R., & Bengio, Y. (2016, 2). *Binarized Neural Networks: Training Deep Neural Networks with Weights and Activations Constrained to +1 or -1.* Advances in Neural Information Processing Systems 29 (NIPS 2016).

Hadidi, R., Cao, J., Xie, Y., Asgari, B., Krishna, T., & Kim, H. (2019, 11). Characterizing the Deployment of Deep Neural Networks on Commercial Edge Devices. *2019 IEEE International Symposium on Workload Characterization (IISWC)* (pp. 35–48). IEEE. doi:10.1109/iiswc47752.2019.9041955

Jain, A., Bhattacharya, S., Masuda, M., Sharma, V., & Wang, Y. (2020, 6). *Efficient Execution of Quantized Deep Learning Models: A Compiler Approach.* Retrieved from https://arxiv.org/abs/2006.10226.

Mermelstein, P. (1976). Distance Measures for Speech Recognition, Psychological and Instrumental. *Pattern recognition and artificial intelligence, 116*, 374–388.

Pál, T., Molnár, B., & Tarcsi, Á. (2020, 10). Lightweight, Length Invariant Models and Dimensionality Reduction in Respiratory Disease Detection. *Annales Universitatis Scientiarum Budapestinensis de Rolando Eötvös Nominatae. Sectio Computatorica*. Submitted, unpublished.

Paszke, A., Gross, S., Massa, F., Lerer, A., Bradbury, J., Chanan, G., . . . Chintala, S. (2019). Pytorch: An Imperative Style, High-performance Deep Learning Library. In H. M. Wallach, H. Larochelle, A. Beygelzimer, F. d'Alché-Buc, E. B. Fox, & R. Garnett (Ed.), *Advances in Neural Information Processing Systems 32: Annual Conference on Neural Information Processing Systems 2019, NeurIPS 2019, December 8-14, 2019, Vancouver, BC, Canada*, (pp. 8024–8035).

Quantized Neural Network Package. (n.d.). *Quantized Neural Network Package*. Retrieved from https://github.com/pytorch/QNNPACK

Rocha, B. M., Filos, D., Mendes, L., Vogiatzis, I., Perantoni, E., Kaimakamis, E., . . . Maglaveras, N. (2018). A Respiratory Sound Database for the Development of Automated Classification. In N. Maglaveras, I. Chouvarda, & de Carvalho P. (Eds.), *Precision Medicine Powered by pHealth and Connected Health. ICBHI 2017. IFMBE Proceedings* (Vol. 66, pp. 33–37). Springer, Singapore. doi:10.1007/978-981-10-7419-6_6

Yang, Y., Chen, A., Chen, X., Ji, J., Chen, Z., & Dai, Y. (2018, 5). *Deploy Large-scale Deep Neural Networks in Resource Constrained Iot Devices with Local Quantization Region.* Retrieved from https://arxiv.org/abs/1805.09473.

Zhou, S., Wu, Y., Ni, Z., Zhou, X., Wen, H., & Zou, Y. (2018, 6). *Dorefa-net: Training Low Bitwidth Convolutional Neural Networks with Low Bitwidth Gradients.* Retrieved from https://arxiv.org/abs/1606.06160.

Zmora, N., Jacob, G., Zlotnik, L., Elharar, B., & Novik, G. (2019, 10). Neural Network Distiller: A Python Package For DNN Compression Research. Retrieved from https://arxiv.org/abs/1910.12232

SOCIAL INFORMATION SYSTEMS IN PUBLIC HEALTH: EMPIRICAL EVIDENCE IN BRAZIL

Jeferson Gonçalves de Oliveira[1], Cristiana Fernandes De Muylder[1], Fernando Hadad Zaidan[2], Ana Maria Pereira Cardoso[1] and José Nelio Januário[3]

[1]*Fumec University, 200 Cobre St, Belo Horizonte, MG, 30.310-190, Brazil*
[2]*Technological Education Institute, 1061 Tomé de Souza St, Belo Horizonte, MG, 30.140-131, Brazil*
[3]*Federal University of Minas Gerais, 6627 Antônio Carlos Ave, Belo Horizonte, MG, 31.370-901, Brazil*

ABSTRACT

Public health systems have been cited as complex in several recent studies. At the same time, information systems are discussed from a strictly technological perspective to separate from a social context in which they are inseparable. In addition, there is a lack of studies in the literature about the implementation of these systems in environments that aim at social innovation. To study these relationships, this study aims to answer the following question: What are the relationships / influences between the Social Information System, Public Health and Social Innovation? Thus, the purpose of this research is to develop an analysis model of the relationship between the studied constructs and apply it to the reality of the Neonatal Screening Program of the State of Minas Gerais (PTN-MG). For this, the study was applied within the SUS, in Minas Gerais State, using the 15-year database of the program. To test the relationships between the model constructs, the statistical techniques of multivariate data analysis were used. As main results, it is confirmed that health care networks are configured as complex systems that require information systems with characteristics that adhere to this concept. In addition, it is noted that the information system is a fundamental pillar in social innovation in health, as it has shown a significant relationship with the reduction of health problems and with the PTN-MG quality indicators. From this model tested new, others will emerge indicating the scientific and social contribution of this research, organized in papers.

KEYWORDS

Social Information Systems, Complexity Theory, Public Health, Social Innovation

1. INTRODUCTION

Health care is described in the literature as complex adaptive systems, where there is interdependence between the actors involved promoted by interconnectivity, that is, the action of an actor can broadly influence the other connected actors (Begun et al., 2003). Therefore, a system can be understood as "complex" when the interdependencies that define it also makes it highly dynamic, alternating between periods of stability and chaos.

Adhering to this complexity, the principle of integrality of the SUS makes it necessary to aggregate actions - including health promotion, disease prevention, treatment and rehabilitation - to allow an integration between the different areas that influence the health of the individual (Brasil, 2018). Thus, the health system has multidimensional characteristics due to its interaction with other sectors of society, which has a direct or indirect impact on the health-disease process, suffering and causing transformations in the context of the ethical, ecological, epidemiological, strategic, educational, transcendental, economic, political and psycho-socio-cultural dimensions of the health sector (Chaves, 1998).

At the same time, health care has also been the focus of research by the *Centre de Recherche sur les Innovations Sociales* (CRISES) 1 from the point of view of Social Innovation. Martinelli et al. (2003) show that social innovation, in its product and process dimensions, is characterized by at least three forms of

---

[1] Canadian interuniversity and multidisciplinary organization founded in 1986 and a pioneer in the studies of social innovation. It is formed by the Universities of Québec, Laval, Concordia, School of High Commercial Studies of Montreal and the National Institute of Scientific Research - Urbanization, Culture and Society.

achievement, alone or combined, carried out through some form of collective action: a) contributes to meeting human needs not considered/satisfied; b) increases access rights; c) increases human capabilities.

Recently, several studies on social innovation have been carried out, however, the literature shows the complexity about this concept (Edwards-Schachter and Wallace, 2015). There are difficulties in the elaboration of indicators that allow to explain empirical phenomena related to the theme (Castro-Spila and Unceta, 2015; Unceta et al., 2016).

In the health context, social innovation is understood to be necessary to promote the development of new medicines, vaccines, and essential diagnoses, in addition to helping in public and private efforts to maintain essential services and promote health at the individual and community level (Gardner et al., 2007).

Considering this scenario of complexity to provide social innovation, Information Technology (IT) should be discussed and used to satisfy the conditions of this environment. Thus, the scope of Social Information Systems (SISs) is broader, as it should support and foster the development of social and collaborative skills over time. In addition, they should facilitate the provision of services (e.g., patient in the health system) and develop social skills inherent to these systems (Kuziemsky et al., 2016).

The aim of this study is to empirically test a model that evidences the role of the social information system in the process of social innovation in the health area.

2. METHODOLOGY

The research field of this study is the state of Minas Gerais, located in the southeast of the country and with an estimated population of more than 21,000,000 inhabitants (IBGE, 2017), where we sought to focus on the Neonatal Screening Program of Minas Gerais.

The database used to verify the proposed model was analyzed from 01/2004 to 04/2019, corresponding to approximately 15 years (equivalent to approximately 3,700,000 children screened). The source of these data will be the Center for Actions and Research in Diagnostic Support of the Faculty of Medicine of UFMG (Nupad), which is the reference center of PTN-MG in the state of Minas Gerais.

The model proposed in this article can be classified as exploratory and, from the literature review, Figure 1 is observed that illustrates the proposed research problem: **What are the relationships/influences between the Health Information System (Social Information System), PTN-MG and health problems?**

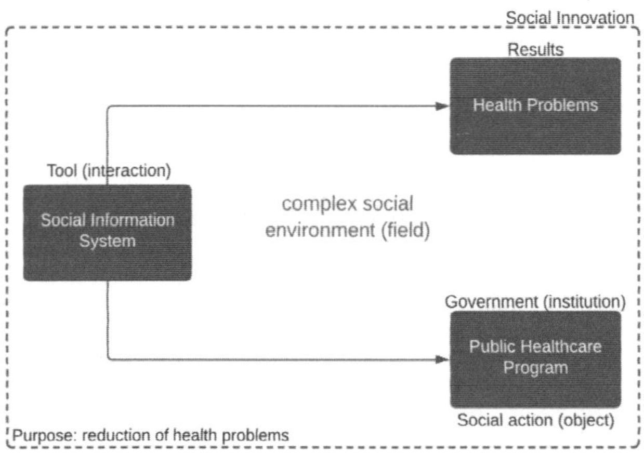

Figure 1. SISs impact assessment model on SI and Health Problems (Source: Prepared by the authors)

Thus, it is intended to quantitatively measure the result of Social Innovation in Health (Health Problems), during the challenges of complexity (Public Health), and to investigate the role of the SIS in this relationship. The factors investigated in this model are based on the literature as highlighted in Table 1.

Table 1. List of authors who affirm the factors of the model

Variable	Factors of the Social Information System	References
SIS1	Number of users or nodes of SI access (systemic and hologram principles of complexity)	Casti (1994); Bar-Yam (1997); Baranger (2000), Cilliers (2000), Aritua et al. (2008)
SIS2	Amount recorded daily interactions (systemic and hologram principles of complexity)	Casti (1994); Bar-Yam (1997); Baranger (2000), Cilliers (2000), Aritua et al. (2008)
SIS3	Number of feedback functions (retroactive, recursive principles and autonomy/dependence on complexity)	Wiener (1950); Luhmann (1999); Aritua et al. (2008)
SIS4	Number of feedback actions observed in the IS (retroactive, recursive principles and autonomy/dependence on complexity)	Wiener, 1950; Luhmann (1999); Aritua et al. (2008);
SIS5	Number of self-regulation adjustments in IS resulting from feedback actions (retroactive, recursive principles and autonomy/dependence on complexity)	Wiener, 1950; Luhmann (1999); Aritua et al. (2008)
PTN1	Percentage of test collection on the optimal date	
PTN2	Age of newborn at first visit – hypothyroidism	
PTN3	Age of newborn at first visit – phenylketonuria	
PTN4	Age of newborn at first fibrosis consultation - cystic	Brazil (2018b)
PTN5	Newborn age at first visit - sickle cell disease	
AS1	Overall death rate (mortality rate)	Nuño-Solinís (2014); Hean et al. (2015);
AS2	Hypothyroidism death rate (mortality rate)	Grindell et al (2018); Vechakul et al. (2015);
AS3	Phenylketonuria death rate (mortality rate)	Schiavo et al. (2016)
AS4	Sickle cell disease death rate (mortality rate)	
AS5	Cystic fibrosis death rate (mortality rate)	

Source: Prepared by the authors

The factors of the social information system were based on the principles of complexity theory, considering the social information system as part of a complex social system. For this, variables were thought that could indicate adherence to the principles: systemic, hologramic, recursive, autonomy/dependence and retroactive.

The variables SIS3, SIS4 and SIS5 were obtained from the PTN-MG database and accounted for all the actions or feedback functions that the information system had in the period. Self-regulation was considered when the feedback action resulted in an adjustment in the PTN-MG - identified some need and generated automatic correction actions that were successful.

Regarding the factors of the Neonatal Screening Program of the State of Minas Gerais, this study uses variables recommended by the Ministry of Health: coverage of the program, percentage of collections performed at the age considered ideal (up to the 5th day of life), the age of the newborn at the time of the first consultation (for those who presented altered tests in the screening) and the number of collection points for the test in the State. Thus, this construct does not measure the PTN-MG itself, but rather the variables considered fundamental by the Ministry of Health to evaluate the quality and efficiency of the Program.

On the other hand, the factors of Health Problems of the model are based on the metrics found in the literature, specifically for measuring the results of social innovation in health (Nuño-Solinís, 2014; Hean et al., 2015; Grindell et al., 2018; Vechakul et al., 2015; Schiavo et al., 2016; Currie and Seddon, 2014; Bazzano et al., 2017; Mummah et al., 2016; Singh, 2017). In addition, for the application of these concepts in PTN-MG, indicators were pointed out based on the final objective of neonatal screening: "early diagnosis, in a timely manner, so that the necessary interventions allow the reduction of mortality and morbidity for congenital and hereditary diseases of the newborn" (Januário, 2015, p.7).

The death rates used were related to children who had early outpatient follow-up in PTN-MG. Monthly accumulated rates were used since the beginning of the tests for each disease in order to analyze a longer period for the calculation (above 1 year). Thus, the accumulated monthly rate was calculated as follows for each of the diseases: (number of children who died/number of children under follow-up) x 100. All other variables were also calculated or accounted for month by month from January 2004 to April 2019.

Thus, this study considered program variables that could translate the impact and social transformation, in addition to clear results through the reduction of health problems in the children of the program. From the proposed model, we intend to test the following hypotheses (Figure 2):

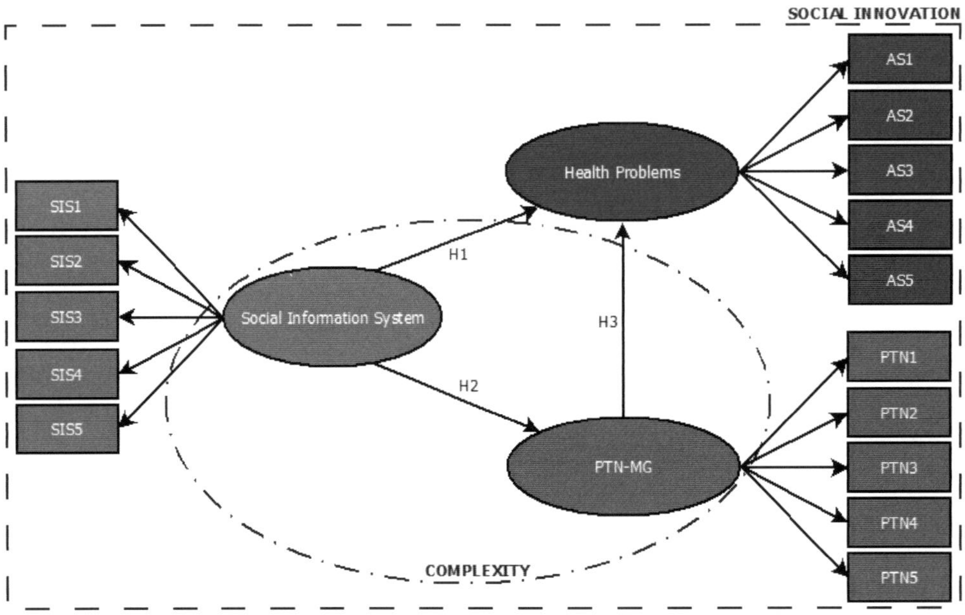

Figure 2. Hypotheses to be worked
Source: Prepared by the authors

Thus, the hypotheses are described below:

- Hypothesis 1 (H1): The social information system influences health problems.
- Hypothesis 2 (H2): The social information system influences PTN-MG.
- Hypothesis 3 (H3): The social information system and the PTN-MG influence health problems.

In the proposed model, it is observed that social innovation (territory type) comprises all constructs. This is because they present themselves as an integral part of IS. For this, this work was based on the dimensions of analysis of The SI of Cloutier (2003) that considers the following items: object (PTN-MG), field (State of Minas Gerais), target (individuals), objective (reduction of health problems), process (multisectoral and interdisciplinary) and result (health problems metrics).

In addition, the Tardif and Harrison (2005) thesaurus represented by social transformation (Table 2) are also considered:

Table 2. Social innovation concepts used

Social Transformatioı	Social Action	Proposal	Institution	Restriction
Reconstruction	Neonatal Screening Program (Policies and Programs)	Reduction of Health Problems (Common Good, General interest)	Government	Complexity presented by Public Health

Source: Prepared by the Author

Although the SIS is an integral part of the PTN-MG, we opted for separation to better understand its role in both the Program and health problems. In addition, it has been pointed out as one of the main characteristics of IS in health (Wass and Vimarlund, 2015; De Rosa, 2017; Warnecke, 2017; Sliwa et al., 2017). It is therefore intended to confirm this finding.

Thus, the suggested model aims to measure relationships between constructs of the model and the possible influences exerted between them. For illustration purposes, the variables of each construct were represented by its abbreviated name and a sequence number (construct variable 01 "social information system" was named SIS1, and so on).

3. RESULTS

This work made an analysis of the outliers, which are observations that present a different response pattern from the other ones. The univariate outliers were diagnosed by standardizing the results, so that the mean of the variable was 0 and the standard deviation 1. Thus, observations with standardized scores outside the range of [-3.29; 3.29] were considered outliers (Hair, et al., 2009). Based on this criterion, only 9 (0.33%) observations considered atypical in a univariate way. Multivariate outliers were diagnosed based on mahalanobis d^2 measurement. According to this criterion, no multivariate atypical observations were found.

The measurement and regression models were performed using the PLS method. This has been referred to as a soft modeling technique with minimal demand, when considering the scales of measurements, sample size and residual distributions (Monecke, et al., 2012). Table 3 presents the structural model.

Table 3. Structural Model

Endogenous	Exogenous	β	E.P. (β)[1]	I.C. - 95%[2]	Valor-p	R^2
Neonatal Newborn Screening Program	Social Information System	-0,57	0,06	[-0,64; -0,51]	0,00	32,23%
Health Problem	Social Information System	-0,77	0,04	[-0,82; -0,71]	0,00	82,08%
	Neonatal Screening Program	0,20	0,04	[0,15; 0,27]	0,00	

[1] Standard Error; [2] Bootstrap range; GoF = 65.01%.

Source: Prepared by the Author

Thus, it is possible to:

- There was a significant influence (p-value=0.00) and negative (β= - 0.57 [-0.64; -0.51]) of social information system on the Neonatal Screening Program, so the higher the Social Information System, the smaller the indicator of Neonatal Screening Program will tend to be.
- There was a significant influence (p-value=0.00) and negative (β= - 0.77 [-0.82; -0.71]) of social information system on health problems, so the higher the Social Information System, the smaller health problems will tend to be.
- There was a significant influence (p-value=0.00) and positive (β=0.20 [0.15; 0.27]) of the Neonatal Screening Program on Health Problems, so the higher the Neonatal Screening Program, the greater the health problems will tend to be.
- The Construct of Social Information System was able to explain 32.23% of the variability of the Neonatal Screening Program and both were able to explain 82.08% of the variability of Health Problems. In addition, it is worth mentioning that the model presented a GoF of 65.01% (Figure 3).

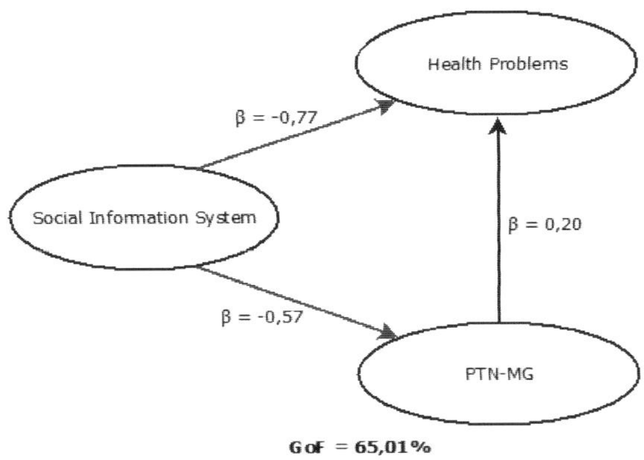

Figure 3. Structural Model Illustration
Source: Prepared by the Author

It is important to point out that the value β shows the strength of relationships. This means that the closer to 1, the greater the influence. The Social Information System had a β = -0.77 on health problems and was the largest β the model. Thus, it represents an influence 3.85 times greater than the indicators of PTN-MG (β = 0.20) on health problems.

Therefore, of the 82.08% observed in R2 of the model, it can be affirmed that the Social Information System represents approximately 65.16% of the total variability of health problems. PTN-MG represents 16.92% since it has a 3.85 times lower influence.

4. CONCLUSION

This study tries to explain the influence of the information system in a large public health program and, specifically, in the results that this program as a social innovation must achieve.

The results show that PTN-MG is a public health program that is configured as a social innovation, as it managed to solve the problems it proposes, that is, it reduced the mortality rate of the patients involved. The model showed that the reduction in the program's indicators has a significant relationship with the reduction of health problems over 15 years. In addition, considering that the SISO is part of the PTN-MG, 82% of the reduction observed in health problems can be explained by the program.

It is also noticed that the indicators recommended by the Ministry of Health to assess the quality of programs in the country may be insufficient. This is due to the strength of the indicators' relationship to health problems below the strength observed by the information system (3.5 times less). It is concluded, therefore, that the management of the program is a primary factor to be considered by federal policies regarding neonatal screening. The indicators pointed out by the government represent only part of the measurement.

Another important detail was the significant and negative relationship of the information system with both PTN-MG and health problems, that is, the higher the SISO, the lower the indicators and mortality. This is a valuable contribution, given the weight observed in the relationships between the constructs, as it reinforces that the complex characteristics must be considered when implementing a SISO.

Therefore, as a contribution, it can be emphasized that the results indicate that some factors must be considered in the planning and implementation of health information systems. These data are important so that initiatives, especially social innovation, can have indicators or clear metrics to demonstrate their effectiveness, especially in public policy actions.

As work limitations, it is understood that this study had its research carried out based on a specific health information system in operation in a Brazilian state. As a proposal for future research, the following can be indicated: application of the model in other realities and in other information systems to confirm the relationships identified.

REFERENCES

Aritua, B. et al., 2008. *Construction client multi-projects: A complex adaptive systems perspective*. International Journal of Project Management, Vol. 27, No. 1, pp. 72-79.

Baranger, M., 2000. *Chaos, complexity, and entropy*. New England Complex Systems Institute, Cambridge.

Bar-Yam, Y., 1997. *Dynamics of complex systems*, Vol. 213, Addison-Wesley, Reading, MA.

Bazzano, A. N. et al, 2017. *Human-centred design in global health: A scoping review of applications and contexts*. PloS one, Vol. 12, No. 11, pp. e0186744.

Begun, J. W et al, 2003. *Health Care Organizations as complex adaptive systems*. In: S. S. Mick, & M. E. Wyttenbach (Eds.), Advances in Health Care Organization Theory, Jossey-Bass, San Francisco, California, USA.

Brasil., 2018. Ministry of Health. The Unified Health System. Available in: <http://portalms.saude.gov.br/sistema-unico-de-saude> .

Casti, J. L., 1994. *Complexification: Explaining a paradoxical world through the science of surprise*. New York: Harper Collins.

Castro-Spila, J. and Unceta, A., 2015. *Modes d'innovation sociale et gouvernance*. La Transformation Sociale par L'innovation Sociale Quebec, CRISES.

Chaves, M., 1998. *Complexidade e transdisciplinaridade: uma abordagem multidimensional do setor saúde*. Revista Brasileira de Educação Médica, Vol. 22, No. 1, pp. 7-18.

Cilliers, P. (2000). What can we learn from a theory of complexity?. Emergence, 2(1), 23-33. https://doi.org/10.1207/S15327000EM0201_03.

Cloutier, J., 2003. *Qu'est-ce que l'innovation sociale?*, Crises, Montréal.

Currie, W. L. and Seddon, J. J., 2014. *Social innovation in public health: can mobile technology make a difference?* Information Systems Management, Vol. 31, No. 3, pp. 187-199.

De Rosa, E., 2017. *Social innovation and ICT in social services: European experiences compared.* Innovation: The European Journal of Social Science Research, Vol. 30, No. 4, pp. 421-432.

Edwards-Schachter, M. and Wallace, M. L., 2017. *Shaken, but not stirred: Sixty years of defining social innovation.* Technological Forecasting and Social Change, Vol. 119, pp. 64-79.

Grindell, C. et al, 2018. *Exploring the acceptability and usability of a novel social innovation to encourage physical activity: The iStep prototype*. Health & social care in the community. Vol. 27. No. 2, pp. 383-391

Hair, Joseph F., et al, 2009. *Multivariate Data Analysis: A Global Perspective*. Upper Saddle River: Prentice Hall.

Hean, S. et al, 2015. *Using social innovation as a theoretical framework to guide future thinking on facilitating collaboration between mental health and criminal justice services*. International Journal of Forensic Mental Health, Vol. 14, No. 4, pp. 280-289.

IBGE, D. D. P. (2017) Coordenação de População e Indicadores Sociais. *Estimativas da população residente no Brasil e unidades da federação com data de referência em 1º de julho de 2017.* Available in: ftp://ftp.ibge.gov.br/Estimativas_de_Populacao/Estimativas_2017/estimativa_dou_2017.pdf.

Januário, J. N., 2015. *Triagem neonatal em Minas Gerais: análise do contexto histórico e político-institucional com enfoque nas estratégias empregadas e resultados alcançados.*

Kuziemsky et al, 2016. *A connectivity framework for social information systems design in healthcare.* AMIA Annual Symposium Proceedings, Vol. 2016, pp. 734. American Medical Informatics Association.

Luhmann, N., 1999. *Zweckbegriff und Systemrationalität*. Suhrkamp, Frankfurt am Main.

Martinelli et al, 2003. *Social innovation, governance and community building*. Singocom-Scientific Periodic Progress Report Month, 18.

Monecke, A. and Leisch, F., 2012. *semPLS: structural equation modeling using partial least squares.*

Mummah, S. A. et al, 2016. *IDEAS (Integrate, Design, Assess, and Share): a framework and toolkit of strategies for the development of more effective digital interventions to change health behavior*. Journal of medical Internet research, Vol. 18, No. 12, pp. 317.

Nunnally, J. C., & Bernstein, I. H. (1994). Psychometric Theory (3rd ed.). New York, N.Y.: McGraw-Hill.

Nuño-Solinís, R., 2014. *Social and organizational innovation to tackle the challenge of integrated care of the chronically ill*. Enfermeria clinica, Vol. 24, No. 1, pp. 18-22.

Schiavo, R. et al, 2016. *Building community-campus partnerships to prevent infant mortality: Lessons learned from building capacity in four US cities*. Journal of Health Disparities Research and Practice, Vol. 9, No. 3, pp. 5.

Singh, S., 2017. *Gendered Bop Hygiene Markets in Rural India: A Case Study of Social Entrepreneurship and Social Innovation*. The Hong Kong Journal of Social Work, Vol. 51, No. 01n02, pp. 51-72.

Sliwa, S. I. et al, 2017. *E-health, health systems and social innovation: a cross-national study of telecare diffusion.* International Journal of Foresight and Innovation Policy, Vol. 12, No. 4, pp. 171-197.

Tardif, C. and Harrisson, D., 2005. *Complémentarité, convergence et transversalité: la conceptualisation de l'innovation sociale au CRISES* (No. 513). Crises.

Warnecke, T., 2017. *Social innovation, gender, and technology: Bridging the resource gap*. Journal of Economic Issues, Vol. 51, No. 2, pp. 305-314.

Wass, S. and Vimarlund, V., 2015. *Challenges of Stimulating a Market for Social Innovation: Provision of a National Health Account*. In MIE 2015, Vol. 210, pp. 546-550. IOS Press.

Wiener, N., 1950. *Cybernetics. Bulletin of the American Academy of Arts and Sciences*, Vol. 3, No. 7), pp. 2-4.

Unceta, A. et al, 2016. *Social innovation indicators. Innovation:* The European Journal of Social Science Research, Vol. 29, No. 2, pp. 192-204.

Vechakul, J. et al, 2015. *Human-centered design as an approach for place-based innovation in public health: a case study from Oakland, California*. Maternal and child health journal, Vol. 19, No. 12, pp. 2552-2559.

DESIGNING AND EVALUATING A WEARABLE SEMG DEVICE FOR THE ELDERLY

Pin-Jun Chen, Chien-Hsiang Chang, Yu-Liang Kuo and Yang-Cheng Lin
Department of Industrial Design, National Cheng Kung University
No.1, University Road, Tainan, Taiwan

ABSTRACT

As muscle and strength decline with age, the risks of falling down and becoming disabled increase for the elderly. However, rehabilitation for patients through long-term treatments and assessments in medical institutions take a long time. It reduces the elderly people's quality of life and causes a burden on their living and financial on their family. Therefore, the goal of this study is to design the wearable sEMG device based on wireless sensing technology for muscle rehabilitation. We aim to help the elderly train their lower limbs at home and simultaneously collect physiological signals though training for remote medical diagnosis. In this study, the design direction is established through focus group interviews. The rehabilitation actions were observed, and the position of muscle movement was measured to establish design parameters and procedures. The designed wearable device was evaluated through a pilot study and semi-structured interview to understand its usability and feasibility. Finally, experts evaluated the usability of the device. From the results, it was found that rehabilitation at home using the designed wearable sEMG device was accepted by most of the elderly respondents. They think that it is very convenient to receive medical feedback at home. Furthermore, medical staff can also use the physiological data to understand the patient's condition and provide diagnosis and treatment. We hope that the product can be widely used to receive signals of the rehabilitation of elderly's lower limb muscles at home in the future. Further discussions on the design implications of the development process can be a reference for future related product development.

KEYWORDS

sEMG, Wearable Device, Lower Limbs, Elderly, Usability

1. INTRODUCTION

Many studies have confirmed that weakness is highly correlated with loss of muscle strength and is more likely to result in falls and disability (Cruz-Jentoft *et al.* 2018). Daily strength training and rehabilitation therapy are effective ways to prevent or improve muscle weakness (Ouellette *et al.* 2004). In the current medical form, patients need to go to medical institutions for regular rehabilitation treatment and muscle recovery tracking. This reduces the elderly's quality of life and causes a living and financial burden on their families. Moreover, as the elderly population grows, medical resources are becoming insufficient, which is inevitably making the development of smart medical care a trend nowadays.

In the medical rehabilitation industry, the application of smart wearable devices has risen with the development of wireless sensing technology. The goal of telemedicine is to upload the surface electromyography (sEMG) signal to the cloud for medical staff through a sensor for diagnosis and treatment. Among them, wireless sEMG signal sensing wearable devices are an important element of development.

The lower limbs of the human body include the hips, knees, and ankles, which account for about 70% of the body. It supports normal walking, running, jumping, and other sports. Furthermore, the interaction of lower limb muscles and joints is very important for the balance and stability of the human body (Kuruganti *et al.* 2006). Elderly people have a 15% to 40% chance of falling each year, and the chance of injuries to upper and lower limbs is about 70% (Hartholt *et al.* 2011). A number of studies have shown that the forward impulse causes the elderly to fall, which is the most common type of fall among this demographic (O'neill *et al.* 1994). It usually causes serious damage to the head and limbs (DeGoede et al. 2003). Moreover, injuries to the lower limbs restrict the movement of the elderly, who could feel inferior due to disability. The elderly experience a sense of inferiority when they cannot live on their own (Pizzigalli *et al.* 2011).

The goal of this study is to design a wearable sEMG device for the rehabilitation of the lower limbs of the elderly at home. The design focuses on the following four points: (1) the surface EMG patch must be placed in the correct muscle position; (2) the needs of rehabilitation and medical treatment must be met; (3) the principles of human factors engineering must be complied with; and (4) the process flow must be smooth.

Our study contributes to the literature in three ways: (1) We design a wearable sEMG device which can be used for the muscle rehabilitation of the lower limbs of the elderly to obtain specific muscle's sEMG signals. (2) We establish design requirements through wearing behavior research. (3) We attempt to understand the elderly's acceptance of designed wearable sEMG devices.

2. RELATED LITERATURE

The goal of this study is to design a wearable sEMG device for the rehabilitation of the lower limbs of elderly people at home. We focus on the usability of wearable devices for the elderly and the application of sEMG in the market in the literature review.

2.1 Technology and Interfaces for the Elderly

Physiological monitoring and disease prevention are the main applications of wearable devices for the elderly (Kekade *et al.* 2018). Previous studies are mostly related to technology development. After the sensing technology becomes mature, we then pay attention to improving the feasibility of the practical applications of the technology. It is necessary to consider that more problems may be encountered when operating wearable devices due to a decline in cognition and various physical functions (Li & Luximon 2016; Rodríguez *et al.* 2017). Many studies have pointed out that elderly people can accept health tracking by wearing devices (Batsis *et al.* 2016; Mercer *et al.* 2016). Elderly people's willingness to use wearable devices is affected by their usefulness and comfort of use (Bodine & Gemperle 2003; Keogh *et al.* 2020). The design should avoid multiple tasks at the same time (Verhaeghen *et al.* 2003). In addition, the elderly have their own special subjective consciousness (Abbate *et al.* 2014). Therefore, the design of a wearable device for the elderly not only needs to meet technical feasibility, but also consider the physical and psychological factors of their elderly users.

2.2 sEMG Signal Application

Surface electromyography (sEMG) is a bioelectric signal generated by the nervous system during muscle contraction. It is usually recorded in pairs or multiple potentials, and the difference between the two potentials is amplified and recorded. The sEMG signal can track the exercise frequency and intensity of the elderly, and the activity state of their muscles during rehabilitation (Chen *et al.* 2019). It has been proven by clinical research as an effective evaluation of coordinated exercise and treatment effect (Rainoldi *et al.* 2004). Although a large number of studies have confirmed the feasibility of its clinical application, the technology has problems it needs to address in its medical applications. For example, the part of the skin touching the sensors must be cleaned before being tested and action posture must be corrected during the test (Falla *et al.* 2002). The sensor structure must comply with the following basic regulations: (1) the myoelectric sensor direction should be parallel to the muscle fiber; (2) the ground terminal should be perpendicular to the myoelectric sensor; and (3) the distance between the centers of the two electrodes should be about 20mm. In order to ensure the stability of the signal, a gel-type Ag/AgCl electrode should be used to contact the skin's surface, and a light-weight material should be used to fix the sensor to avoid artifacts when receiving the signal (Hermens *et al.* 2000).

The MYO gesture recognition armband was developed by Canada's Thalmic Labs in 2013. It uses a myoelectric sensor and nine-axis detector to detect more than 20 hand movements for controlling computer games, robots, a mouse, and more (Benatti *et al.* 2014). In addition, the smart fitness clothing developed by Athos has a total of 26 sEMG and heart rate sensors to monitor muscle fatigue as a judgment for sports injury prevention. According to the above two examples, the combination of surface myoelectric signals with wearable devices does have potential for development. However, there is still a big gap in the precision of receiving signals in medical applications. With the gradual rise of telemedicine, it is estimated that wearable devices combined with surface myoelectric signal sensing will be widely used in medical treatment in the future. Therefore, the goal of this study is to design a wearable sEMG device for muscle rehabilitation that helps the elderly to train their lower limbs, and simultaneously collects physiological signals though training for medical diagnosis.

3. METHOD

In this section, we thoroughly explain how to determine the design criteria and describe the overall design process of the wearable device. Finally, the appropriate methods of designing the wearable device are detailed.

3.1 Focus Group Interview

In this study, a focus group interview was conducted with three professionals from the fields of medicine and industrial design, and three elder people. We discuss the content of rehabilitation medical care, human factors engineering design and physical psychology of the elderly, then determine the goal of the wearable design. Some statements are given followed by four conclusions: (1) Common training muscle groups required for complete lower extremity rehabilitation include quadriceps, tibial anterior, gastrocnemius, soleus. It effectively improves muscle endurance and reduces degenerative-related nervous system pain. (2) For patients with degenerative neuritis, the four major muscle groups are usually trained with knee extension, dorsiflexion, and plantar flexion. (3) Since the position of the muscles of the lower limbs differs depending on the individual's height, weight, subcutaneous fat, and other factors, an adjustable design should be considered to increase the accuracy of physiological signal detection. (4) It is necessary to use a sEMG patch to receive the accurate sEMG signal.

3.2 Implementation

This section divides the wearable device design process into two parts: (1) establishing design criteria and (2) wearable device design process. The following is a detailed description based on the design steps:

(1) Design Criteria

Based on the focus group interviews and related works, three design criteria were summarized:

A. The myoelectric sensor should be attachable to the best sensing position of the target muscle group.

B. The wearable device should be fixed on the body for it to function smoothly during rehabilitation.

C. The sensor is designed to be easy to remove and clean since the wearable device needs to be cleaned regularly.

(2) Circuit Components-Muscle Sensor

The circuit components for sensing myoelectric signals were made by the ready-made MyoWare muscle sensor modules. We used the potential difference to judge the position of muscle movement and the degree of force, combined with the nine-axis accelerometer to judge the direction of movement. Then, with Arduino software for programming, we used the surface electrode patches to measure sEMG signals. They were processed by the amplifying unit, using Wifi to connect the ready-made Unity software to transfer the potential values.

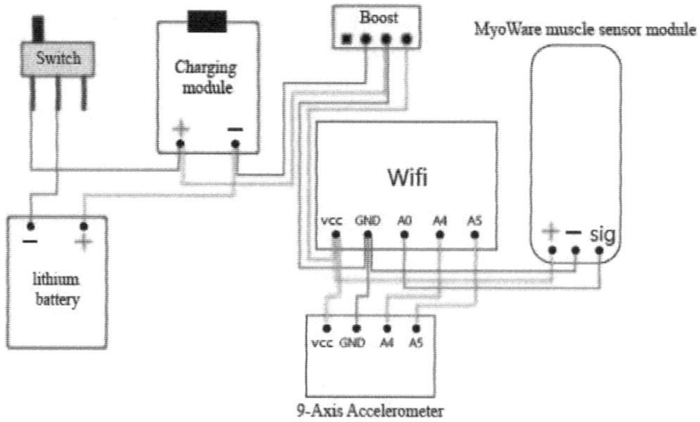

Figure 1. Schematic diagram of the hardware circuit

(3) Wearable Device Design Process

Conceptual development. At this stage, two design plans are proposed according to the design criteria: (1) the first type of design is that the sensor is embedded in the wearable device; and (2) the second type is the detachable sensor design.

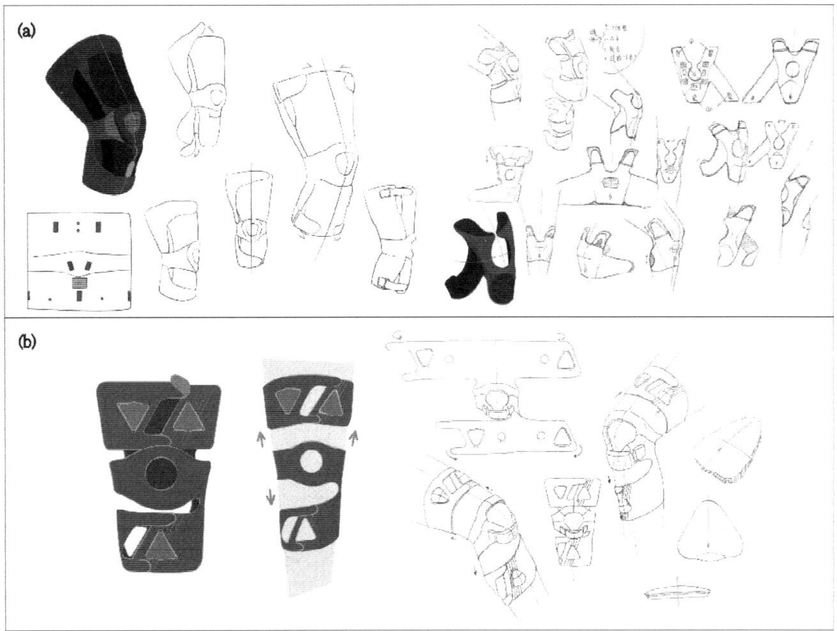

Figure. 2. Sketch description. (a) The first type of design is that the sensor is embedded in the wearable device. (b) The second type is the detachable sensor design

Design decision. Iterative design was carried out according to the evaluation results of the prototype. The detailed design description of the wearable device is as follows:

A. Wearable device design: The wearable device was designed to be composed of the upper and lower parts (Figure 2.). In addition to easily adjusting the position, each rehabilitation may only train one muscle group, so the unused parts can be removed. The part of the wearable device that is in contact with the skin needs to be cleaned regularly; thus, cloth material is used, and the sensor is designed to be detachable. The middle round hole is used as a calibration point for the user's knee (Figure 2. (a)). The black circles on two parts of the wearable device are where the quadriceps, tibial anterior, and gastrocnemius sensors are positioned (Figure 2. (b)-(d)).

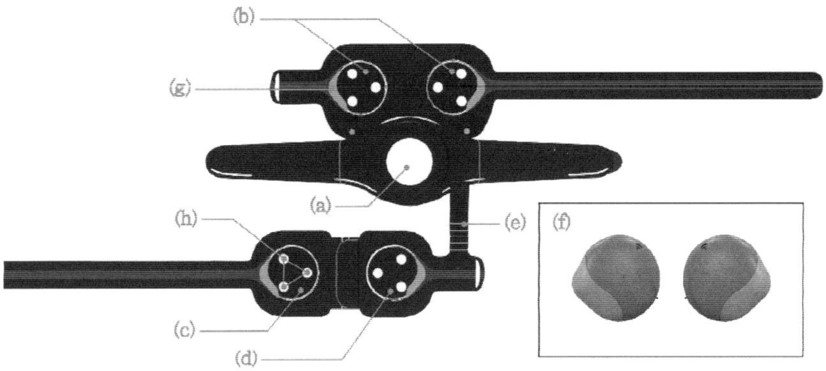

Figure 3. Wearable device design

B. Size adjustment design: The quadriceps position is found to the left and right sides about three fingers above the knee; the tibial anterior is in the front part of the middle lower leg; and gastrocnemius muscles is in the back part of the lower leg. The wearable device is adjusted by the belt to control the size and position of the sensors. Moreover, a tick mark on the wearable device records the position for finding the correct location faster when users wear it next time.

C. Sensor design and instruction recognition: The sensor was designed in the shape of a water drop, and the its sharp corners are used to indicate direction (see Figure 2. (f)). When the sensors are attached to the corresponding orange color block, the three buttons below them can be aligned with the three small round holes of the EMG patch on the wearable device. The devil felt can be used to attach the sensor to the wearable device(see Figure 2. (f)-(g)). This fool-proof design allows users to operate the device more smoothly.

4. PILOT STUDY DESIGN

As the basis for future product development, we aimed to understand the usability of the wearable device through a pilot study. The designed wearable device was evaluated through a wearing behavior test and user study to understand the using situation. The detailed descriptions of the experiments are as follows:

4.1 Wearing Behavior Test

The wearing behavior test confirms the expected effect, understanding the problems that may occur during the experiment, and establishes the purpose of observation. Therefore, three males and females who have never used the wearable device are recruited for the test. First, the researchers explained and demonstrated how to wear it. Second, it was operated by the test subject. Third, the subject was required to perform lifting, tipping, and hooking three lower limb rehabilitation actions. Finally, a semi-structured interview was conducted to understand the subjective thoughts, willingness to use, and problems encountered by the elderly in the process of wearing the wearable device. Each subject took about 15 minutes for the experiment.

Three key points of design adjustment were observed from the wearing behavior test: (1) the direction of the combination of sensors, wearable device, and EMG patch should be clearly marked; (2) the operation steps should be appropriately marked on the wearable device; and (3) instructions and assistance are required when conducting user study for the elderly.

4.2 User Study

Participants

Eight participants with an average age of 70.5 were recruited in the community center. All participants have the ability to perform simple movements with their lower limbs, have normal cognitive ability, and are able to clearly express their thoughts. In order to ensure the smoothness of the experiment, a social worker from the institution and two researchers were present to assist.

Procedure

First, the researchers explained and demonstrated how to wear it. Second, the device was operated by the test subject. Third, the subject was required to perform lifting, tipping, and hooking three lower limb rehabilitation actions. Finally, a semi-structured interview was conducted to understand the subjective thoughts, willingness to use, and problems encountered by the elderly in the process of wearing the wearable device. Each subject took about 15 minutes for the experiment.

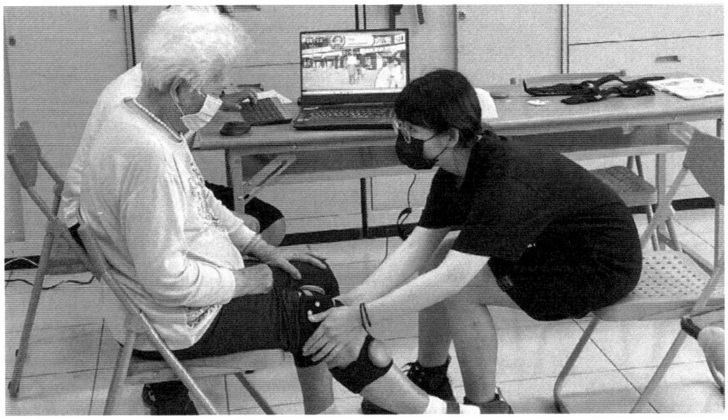

Figure 4. Field test situation

5. RESULT AND DISCUSSION

Based on the results of the thematic analysis of the interview, this chapter is divided into two parts: (1) wearable device usability and (2) expert feedback for discussion. The following are detailed explanations:

5.1 Wearable Device Usability

The usability of this wearable device is discussed in three parts: (1) wearable device operation; (2) rehabilitation with the wearable device; and (3) the willingness of the elderly to use the wearable device. As for the operation of the wearable device, the design with two detachable parts has a higher degree of freedom when being operated. However, too much adjustment will make the user feel confused while wearing it. To allow users to operate the device themselves, we designed different shapes, colors, and other fool-proof mechanisms on the wearable device for their ease of use. According to the current design, young people can easily wear them by following the instructions. On the other hand, while a single step can be successfully completed by the elderly, they still need assistance on the overall process of wearing the device because of the integration steps. We will reduce adjustable places and simplify operational steps in future works. In terms of rehabilitation with the designed wearable device, majority of the subjects showed positive reactions in wearing comfort. One subject is an extreme case in size. He feels the device is too small to wear and can bring discomfort when performing an action. Therefore, the size adjustment step needs to be enlarged. There was another subject who caused the positioning point to shift due to wearing errors. In terms of willingness to use, three elderly people expressed their willingness to use this product, and the other three indicated that they would use the products if the steps for wearing can be simplified. The six test subjects thought it was very helpful to save time for rehabilitation in a medical institution, and the other two subjects thought that they could perform well without this wearable device.

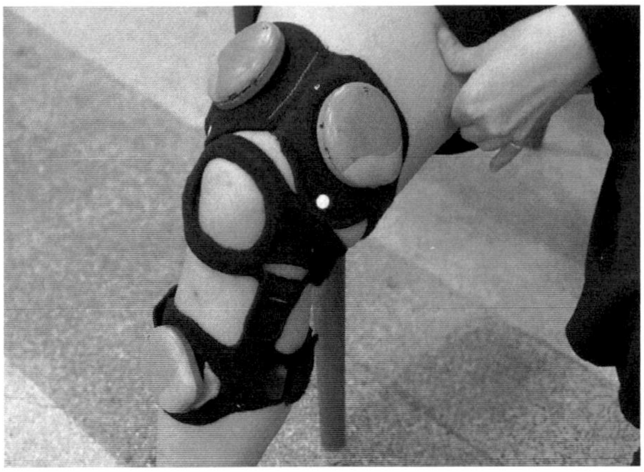

Figure 5. The lower limbs wearable sEMG device featured in this study

5.2 Expert Feedback

We invited the attending physicians of the Rehabilitation Department of the National Cheng Kung University Hospital in Taiwan to conduct expert interviews and give suggestions on the designed wearable device. Dr. Lian gave a positive response to the design concept of this product. In terms of the human-related design of wearable devices, although the medical staff can easily adjust according to different patient conditions, elderly people with severe decline in cognitive and physical functions may increase operational errors due to the multiple steps. Therefore, we should increase the fool-proof mechanisms to avoid errors in wearing the device. In terms of human body measurement, as muscle and strength decline with age, the measurement position and muscle size of the elderly vary more than those of young adults. It is recommended to recruit more elderly people for the measurement. Besides, this wearable device is mainly used for long-term muscle rehabilitation. It is necessary to increase the strength of the mutual combination of each part.

6. CONCLUSION

The study aims to design the wearable sEMG device of muscle rehabilitation, which helps the elderly to train their lower limbs, and simultaneously collect physiological signals though training for medical diagnosis. It can not only save patients time spent in visiting medical institutions for rehabilitation, but also solve the shortage of medical resources. To collect clinical pain points, focus group interviews were conducted to determine the value of development and design requirements. The design is based on medical restrictions and human factors engineering. Since the wearable device needs to be cleaned regularly, the sensor was designed to be detachable from the wearable device. To increase the degree of freedom of position adjustment, the sensor is composed of two parts; the upper part of the wearable device is used to sense the electromyographic signals of the quadriceps, and the other part is used to sense the electromyographic signals of the tibial anterior and gastrocnemius. In addition, considering the decline of the cognitive ability of the elderly, we designed different shapes, colors, and other fool-proof mechanisms on the wearable device as reminders. After designing the wearable device, we conducted a two-stage pilot study to evaluate the usability of the designed wearable device by the target group. In the future, we will improve the current wearable devices based on the results. The three noteworthy points regarding the design of the device are as follows: (1) elastic structures must be added at specific locations of the wearable device to increase strength; (2) visual recognition must be increased to reduce the wearing error rate of the elderly; and (3) adjustable places must be reduced and the sticking direction of the devil felt must be unified to improve the integrity of the wearable device.

ACKNOWLEDGEMENT

This work was supported by Guan Shengli community activity center in Tainan.

REFERENCES

Abbate, S. et al, 2014. Usability study of a wireless monitoring system among Alzheimer's disease elderly population. *International journal of telemedicine and applications*, Vol. 2014.

Batsis, J. A. et al, 2016. Use of a wearable activity device in rural older obese adults: A pilot study. *Gerontology and geriatric medicine*, Vol. 2.

Benatti, S. et al, 2014. Towards EMG control interface for smart garments. *Proceedings of the 2014 ACM International Symposium on Wearable Computers: Adjunct Program*. New York, United States, pp. 163-170.

Bodine, K. and Gemperle, F., 2003. Effects of functionality on perceived comfort of wearables. *Seventh IEEE International Symposium on Wearable Computers*. New York, United States, pp. 57-57.

Chen, P. et al, 2019. Exploring Adoption Intention of Interactive Somatosensory Game for Elders' Lower Limb Rehabilitation. *Basic & Clinical Pharmacology & Toxicology*, Vol. 124, pp. 206-207.

Cruz-Jentoft, A. J. et al, 2019. Sarcopenia: revised European consensus on definition and diagnosis. *Age and ageing*, Vol. 48, pp. 16-31.

Degoede, K. et al, 2003. Fall-related upper body injuries in the older adult: a review of the biomechanical issues. *Journal of biomechanics*, Vol. 36, pp. 1043-1053.

Falla, D., et al, 2002. Location of innervation zones of sternocleidomastoid and scalene muscles–a basis for clinical and research electromyography applications. *Clinical Neurophysiology*, Vol. 113, pp. 57-63.

Hartholt, K. A. et al, 2011. Societal consequences of falls in the older population: injuries, healthcare costs, and long-term reduced quality of life. *Journal of Trauma and Acute Care Surgery*, Vol. 71, pp. 748-753.

Hermens, H. J. et al, 2000. Development of recommendations for SEMG sensors and sensor placement procedures. *Journal of electromyography and Kinesiology*, Vol. 10, pp. 361-374.

Kekade, S. et al, 2018. The usefulness and actual use of wearable devices among the elderly population. *Computer methods and programs in biomedicine*, Vol. 153, pp. 137-159.

Keogh, A. et al, 2020. Comparing the Usability and Acceptability of Wearable Sensors Among Older Irish Adults in a Real-World Context: Observational Study. JMIR mHealth and uHealth, Vol. 8(4).

Kuruganti, U. et al, 2006. Strength and muscle coactivation in older adults after lower limb strength training. *International journal of industrial ergonomics*, Vol, 36, pp. 761-766.

Li, Q. and Luximon, Y., 2016. Older adults and digital technology: A study of user perception and usage behavior. Advances in physical ergonomics and human factors. *Springer*, Vol. 489. pp 155-163.

Mercer, K. et al, 2016. Acceptance of commercially available wearable activity trackers among adults aged over 50 and with chronic illness: a mixed-methods evaluation. *JMIR mHealth and uHealth*, Vol. 4.

O'neill, T. et al, 1994. Age and sex influences on fall characteristics. *Annals of the rheumatic diseases*, Vol. 53, pp. 773-775.

Ouellette, M. M., 2004. High-intensity resistance training improves muscle strength, self-reported function, and disability in long-term stroke survivors. *Stroke*, Vol. 35, pp. 1404-1409.

Pizzigalli, L. et al, 2011. Prevention of Falling Risk in Elderly People: The Relevance of Muscular Strength and Symmetry of Lower Limbs in Postural Stability. *The Journal of Strength & Conditioning Research*, Vol. 25, pp. 567-574.

Rainoldi, A. et al, 2004. A method for positioning electrodes during surface EMG recordings in lower limb muscles. *Journal of neuroscience methods*, Vol. 134, pp. 37-43.

Rodrýguez, I. et al, 2017. Helping elderly users report pain levels: A study of user experience with mobile and wearable interfaces. *Mobile Information Systems*, Vol. 2017.

Verhaeghen, P. et al, 2003. Aging and dual-task performance: a meta-analysis. *Psychology and aging*, Vol. 18, pp. 443.

HELPING PARAMEDICS IN ASSESSING A PATIENT'S CONDITION BASED ON ECG BY MEANS OF MOBILE PHONE

Aleksandra Vatian[1], Dmitrii Peredreev[1], Konstantin Rodiontsev[1], Anastasia Murzina[1], Elizaveta Klevtsova[1], Anna Tatarinova[2], Tatiana Treshkur[2], Anatoly Shalyto[1] and Natalia Gusarova[1]

[1]*ITMO University, Saint Petersburg 197101, Russia*

[2]*Almazov National Medical Research Centre, Saint Petersburg 197341, Russia*

ABSTRACT

One of the most common cardiovascular diagnostic test is the electrocardiogram (ECG). However, physicians' skills in ECG interpretation are far from always satisfactory. There is a problem of rendering assistance to a primary care physician in making an operative decision on the tactics of managing a patient with a cardiovascular accident, which is especially relevant in regions where specialized medical equipment has not received mass distribution. The article addresses the issue of rendering assistance to a primary care physician in making an operative decision on the tactics of managing a patient with a cardiovascular accident, if the physician has only the simplest electrocardiograph. We discuss possibility of using mobile phones for this purpose. It is proposed to use them in two ways: for the automated assessment of ECG parameters, which are promptly reported to the paramedic, as well as for transmitting the ECG image to a qualified cardiologist in order to obtain a second (advisory) opinion remotely. We have built and implemented an algorithm for assessing the main morphological parameters of the ECG on a physician's mobile phone when taking photos of 12 leads-ECG on a phone camera. We have shown experimentally that the accuracy of evaluating the morphological parameters of the ECG when working on an image captured with a phone camera is not worse than when working on a digital signal. Using the example of typical emergency medical service scenarios, we have shown that for a consultant cardiologist to obtain an image of the patient's cardiogram with a quality no worse than that of the original cardiograph, it is enough of the phone that does not go beyond the cheap price segment. Thus, the proposed solution is quite applicable in developing countries and in provincial regions, i.e. outside big cities.

KEYWORDS

Electrocardiogram, Second Opinion, Mobile Phones, Automated ECG Processing

1. INTRODUCTION

Cardiovascular diseases rank first in the world as a cause of death [Cardiovascular]. Unlike slowly developing diseases such as oncology, cardiovascular diseases often manifest themselves as disasters, requiring the fastest possible medical intervention and, accordingly, immediate and correct decision-making.

One of the most common cardiovascular diagnostic test is the electrocardiogram (ECG). However, physicians' skills in ECG interpretation are far from always satisfactory. According to the review [Cook], the accuracy of ECG interpretation varies depending on the qualifications of the interpreter and is 48.1–63.6% for lower-level physicians, 57.6–79.5% for medical practitioners, and 63.2–86.7% for cardiologists.

This problem is especially acute in developing countries and in provincial regions, i.e. outside big cities. Here, primary care for a patient with suspected cardiovascular catastrophe is most often provided by paramedics (when calling an ambulance) or by the staff of a paramedic center who does not have professional knowledge in the field of cardiology. It is their decision that determines the choice of tactics for the further management of the patient (including such an expensive procedure as transportation to a specialized clinic) and, ultimately, his life. Thus, the significance of accuracy and reliability of urgent ECG parameter interpretation is obvious.

In recent years, methods of automated determination of ECG parameters have been actively developed [Kligfield, Kligfield, Atti]. Their accuracy varies for different monitored ECG parameters [Xie]. For example, an automated assessment of deviations from sinus rhythm can be performed with an accuracy of 99% [Sangaiah], but, while finding the sophisticated features in ECG using the standard 10 s ECG an accuracy of 79.2% is achieved [Attia]. In general, automated methods, firstly, require specialized equipment, which, as a rule, are absent in primary health care in developing countries, and, secondly, they are consultative, i.e. do not remove the need for an integral ECG assessment by a qualified cardiologist.

Thus, there is a problem of rendering assistance to a primary care physician in making an operative decision on the tactics of managing a patient with a cardiovascular accident, which is especially relevant in regions where specialized medical equipment has not received mass distribution.

The article discusses the possibility of using mobile phones for this purpose. It is proposed to use them in two ways: for the automated assessment of ECG parameters, which are promptly reported to the paramedic, as well as for transmitting the ECG image to a qualified cardiologist in order to obtain a second (advisory) opinion remotely.

2. BACKGROUND AND RELATED WORKS

An ECG (Figure 1a) is a recording of a sequence of electrical impulses corresponding to a heartbeat. Recording can be performed in several leads (from 1 to 12) and have different lengths (from 6-7 heartbeats to continuous monitoring).

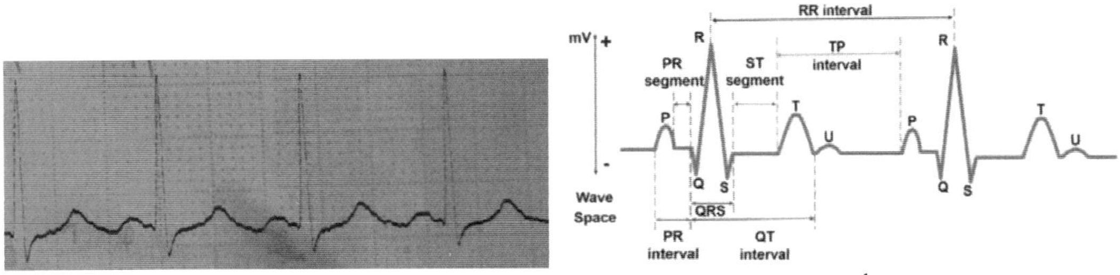

a b

Figure 1. Fragment of ECG (a) and its characteristic intervals (b)

Various assessment techniques are used for analysis and interpretation of the ECG [Xie]. In recent years, more and more methods based on machine learning have been proposed, but methods based on the assessment of ECG features, such as wavelet and statistical features, are much more widespread. However, the basic ones are morphological features (intervals) that can be directly observed on the ECG (Figure 1b). There are routine methods for their assessment, as well as tables of their normal and abnormal values. For example, going beyond the normative limits of the PR interval may be a sign of stroke [Montalvo], of the ST segment - a sign of myocardial ischemia or infarction [Hausenloy] etc.

Traditionally, obtaining an ECG is fulfilled by trained medical personnel using a special device - a cardiograph. As a rule, cardiographs record the ECG on paper. More advanced models also have a linear output for digital recording of the electrical signal from the sensors. In clinical practice, there are already models of cardiographs equipped with means of automated calculation of morphological indicators, however, as the practice of Russia shows, their distribution in developing countries is limited by large medical centers. As for the automated analysis of the ECG in general by means of machine learning, as well as wavelet and statistical features, such methods have not yet gone beyond the scope of experimental investigations.

The widespread use of mobile phones among the population has given rise to such a direction of mobile health applications as smartphone ECG monitoring [Walker, Gropler, Bansal]. Most all smartphone ECG technologies involve the use of a special device that the patient installs on the body by himself. The device communicates with a smartphone on which specialized software is installed that processes the collected data. Such implementations are widely represented on the market (see reviews [Walker, Gropler, Bansal]). For example, the Kardia Mobile device (AliveCor®, Mountain View, CA, USA) is widely popular in the United States. The device is based on the principle of plethysmography and includes a detector pad and specialized software. The signal generated by the device is most similar to lead I on a conventional 12-lead ECG. The signal is sent to a physician through the application installed on the smartphone, and within 24 h, user receives an interpretation of the reading. On subsequent uses, the device classifies the ECG into categories: normal, interference, atrial fibrillation or undetermined, and, according to the manufacturer, a reading of AF is not diagnostic.

Another example is the D-Heart device (D-Heart®, Genova, Italy) is positioned as a means of self-monitoring of ECG for regions with insufficient medical care. The kit includes the cardiograph itself, the electrodes of which the patient independently installs on the body, and software for the smartphone. The recorded ECG (from 8 to 12 leads) is transmitted via the application to the phone and from there is sent to the cardiologist, who forms a conclusion. Directly on the device (without the participation of a cardiologist), the patient is informed only of the suspicion of the presence of atrial fibrillation.

Problem-oriented analysis of the smartphone ECG technologies presented on the market shows: ECG recording in them is made using specialized devices, the signal from which is transmitted to mobile phones in digital form; the scenario of their work provides for a delayed (up to 24 hours) decoding of the ECG and the formation of a conclusion by a cardiologist; a very limited set of morphological indicators is calculated directly on the mobile phone, and the accuracy of the estimate is not indicated. Such scenarios are not actual in the provision of primary or emergency medical care in non-advanced regions (for example, in Russia - outside large cities). Here, a doctor or a paramedic most often has at his disposal only a conventional 12-lead ECG cardiograph, which records on paper and is not equipped with automated analysis or at least calculation of indicators. He must make a decision about the patient's condition based only on his own assessment of morphological features and taking into account the integral assessment of the EEG as a whole.

The article discusses the possibilities of supporting the actions of a primary care physician in the specified scenario via a mobile phone. The authors set themselves the following tasks:

- to build and implement an algorithm for assessing the main morphological parameters of the ECG on a physician's mobile phone when taking photos of 12 leads-ECG on a phone camera;
- to evaluate the accuracy of the constructed algorithm;
- to evaluate the possibilities of prompt transmission of the ECG image via the phone for a remote consultation of a qualified cardiologist on-line.

3. METHOD AND MATERIALS

The proposed pipeline for ECG processing using a mobile phone is shown in Figure 2. As a basic algorithm for calculating the morphological characteristics of the ECG, the MTEO algorithm [Sedghamiz] was used. This choice was due to the fact that the MTEO algorithm allows you to find the peaks of all ECG waves necessary for diagnostics (P, Q, R, S, T). For comparison, algorithms such as Pan-Tompkins [Sedghamiz2014], Nonlinear Phase Space Reconstruction [Lee], and Filter Bank [Afonso] find only the QRS complex, while the State-Machine algorithm [Sedghamiz2014a] finds only the peaks R, S, and T (see Figure 1b). Compared to other solutions that allow finding peaks of all ECG waves (for example, algorithms from the ECG-kit package [ECG-kit]), the used MTEO implementation compares favorably with a higher stability of processing ECG "edge cases". This is important both for testing the algorithm using a digital ECG base, and for use with photographs of real ECGs, since a distortion of the signal amplitude or a rotation of the ECG relative to the horizontal position may be observed in the photograph.

The proposed pipeline for ECG processing includes the following sequence of steps. First, the signal is filtered to reduce noise. To do this, the signal is passed through a narrow notch filter, normalized, de-trend is performed, and a pass through the Butterworth filter (5-1200 Hz) is made. Then MTEO (Multiresolution Teager Energy Operator) is calculated as follows:

$$Y_k(nT) = x^2(nT) - x(nT - kT)x(nT + kT),$$

$$t(nT) = \max\left\{\hat{Y}_1(nT), \hat{Y}_2(nT), ..., \hat{Y}_k(nT)\right\}.$$

Here $x(n\text{T})$ is the raw ECG signal for n= 1, 2, ...N, N is the number of signal sample, $\hat{Y}_k(nT)$ is $Y_k(nT)$ after it is smoothed with a Hamming window of size $4k$+1 and normalized by the squared variance at scale k. For a more accurate selection of the R peaks against a noisy background, binary hypotheses are tested at the points of the MTEO graph:

$$H_0 : t(nT) = G(nT) \quad vs \quad H_1 : t(nT) = s(nT) + G(nT) .$$

Peaks P, Q, S, T are found on the basis of the peaks R found at the previous stage by an algorithmic method. For this, certain distances are plotted from the R peaks, which differ depending on the type of the sought peak (see Figure 1b). Then, in the obtained intervals, local minima and maxima are found and the necessary ones are selected depending on the type of peak.

In the filtered signal, a characteristic segment of length RR with a center in one of the peaks R is highlighted. For each type of teeth, in a certain interval from the corresponding peak, there are points of intersection of the tangent to the point of steepest increase / decrease with the isoline (see the fragment Start / END Points in Figure 2). Then the distance between the obtained points is determined in accordance with the ECG interval diagram.

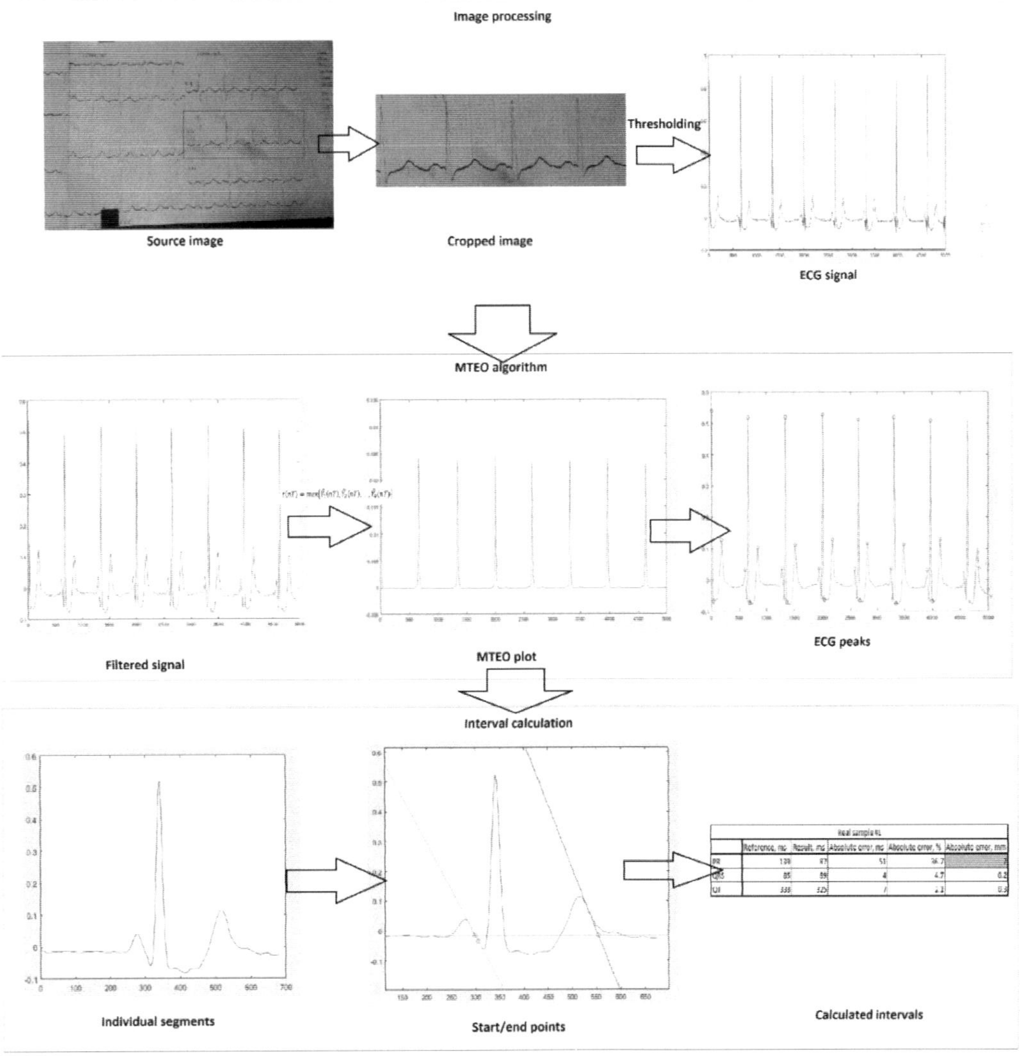

Figure 2. Pipeline for ECG processing

The developed algorithm for translating an ECG image into a graph is implemented in the java programming language using the openimaj library. The algorithm for finding peaks and calculating intervals is implemented in the MatLab language and is integrated into the final android application using the Simulink

Support Package for Android Devices. The current version is available at: https://github.com/Pmvop19/ECG_Mobile.

Our development is focused on equipment and technologies available in Russia (see table 1). Table 1, built according to YandexMarket data as of 03/27/21, shows examples of popular phone models in the price range up to $ 50, available in Russia and satisfying the necessary characteristics for using the application.

Table 1. Characteristics of mobile phones sufficient for using the application

	Rear (main) camera resolution	Used data transmission technologies	Android version
INOI 2 Lite	5 Мп	2G 3G	7.0
ZTE Blade L8 1	8 Мп	2G 3G	9.0
Alcatel 1A (2020) 5002F	5 Мп	2G 3G 4G	10.0
Alcatel 1 (5033D)	5 Мп	2G 3G 4G	8.0
ZTE Blade A3	8 Мп	2G 3G 4G	9.0

Real cardiograms contain noise and interference, which makes it difficult to isolate characteristic peaks by algorithmic means. In this regard, the question arises about the reliability of calculating morphological intervals from an ECG image taken with a smartphone camera. To answer this question, a comparative assessment was made of the efficiency of calculating intervals basing on digital ECGs and on ECG images.

A dataset of Lobachevsky University [Kalyakulina] containing digital ECGs was used as a data source. From the dataset, 150 ECGs were selected with varying degrees of noise. To obtain ECG images for comparative evaluation, in the MATLAB environment, graphs of signals from the dataset were built, from which the coordinate axes and other marks were removed. The plotted graphs were photographed with a smartphone camera with the above parameters (see Table 1). Thus, we get an imitation of a high-quality image taken with a phone camera.

For a comparative assessment of the accuracy, the MAE (mean absolute error) metrics were used in milliseconds (the initial unit of measurement of ECG intervals) and as a percentage of the right border of the characteristic reference intervals ([Xie], table 1). As the analysis of cardiograms from the dataset [Kalyakulina] shows and is confirmed by real medical practice [Goldenberg], preliminary filtering of the ECG signal from noise and interference can affect the result of calculating morphological intervals, especially when finding the end of the S peak. In this regard, for a more accurate imitation of real scenarios, the MAE metric was calculated in two options: when evaluating intervals without pre-filtering and with pre-filtering. For this, appropriate changes were made to the calculation algorithm at the "Calculation of intervals" stage.

To assess the possibilities of prompt transmission of an ECG image by telephone for a remote consultation of a qualified cardiologist on-line, we considered two typical scenarios:

Scenario 1 - taking an ECG, processing and sending the results for obtaining an advisory opinion is static - for example, at the patient's home or in the premises of a primary medical institution. In this case, the transmission speed is taken as the maximum possible using a specific transmission technology.

Scenario 2 - taking an ECG, processing and sending the results for obtaining an advisory opinion occurs in motion at a speed of up to 120 km / h (for example, an ambulance team is next to the patient while driving to the hospital). In this case, the transmission rate is taken as a tenth of the maximum using a specific transmission technology.

4. RESULTS AND DISCUSSION

The results of the comparative assessment of the efficiency of calculating intervals basing on digital ECGs and on ECG images are presented in Tables 2 and 3.

Comparison of the results of both tables shows that the use of ECG images instead of digital data at least does not impair the accuracy of ECG interval calculations.

Table 4 shows the typical values of the image transmission time in the implementation of the above scenarios. For the calculation, an ECG image of 200 Kb (0.195 Mb) in .jpg format was used, which is typical for the parameters of equipment and technologies presented in Table 1.

The data in Table 4 show that the image transmission time in any case does not exceed 1.5 minutes, which is quite reasonable and does not go beyond the realizable scenario.

Table 2. The accuracy of calculating morphological intervals based on digital ECG

	Reference interval, ms		MAE, ms	MAE, %
P	600	1200	24	2,0
PR	80	110	26	23,6
QRS	120	200	95	47,5
ST	60	100	103	103,0
T	50	155	59	38,1
QT	350	440	49	11,1

Table 3. The accuracy of calculating morphological intervals based on image ECG

	Reference interval, ms		MAE, ms	MAE, %
P	600	1200	17	1,4
PR	80	110	23	20,9
QRS	120	200	75	37,5
ST	60	100	84	84,0
T	50	155	37	23,9
QT	350	440	33	7,5

Table 4. The accuracy of calculating morphological intervals based on image ECG

Data transmission technology	Maximum transfer rate, Mb / s	Transfer time for Scenario 1, s	Transfer time for Scenario 2, s
2.5G	0.019	10	100
2.75G	0.058	3.3	33
3G	0.25	0.8	8
3.5G	0.72	0.3	3
4.G	2.5	0.1	1
2.5G	0.019	10	100

Thus, in order for the physician or paramedic providing primary care to be able to quickly obtain data on the morphological parameters of the patient, and the consultant cardiologist to obtain an image of the patient's cardiogram with a quality no worse than that of the original cardiograph, in addition to the conventional cardiograph, it is sufficient to have a mobile phone with the following parameters:

• camera with a resolution of at least 5MP;

• operational system v. Android 6.0 and higher.

Let us emphasize that the proposed solution is highly accessible both for Russia and for other developing countries, since the required characteristics of the phone for using the application do not go beyond the cheap price segment. A big plus of the solution is the fact that no additional devices are needed to use it, except for a suitable telephone and a simple cardiograph.

5. CONCLUSION

The article addressed the issue of rendering assistance to a primary care physician in making an operative decision on the tactics of managing a patient with a cardiovascular accident, if the physician has only the simplest electrocardiograph. The article discusses the possibility of using mobile phones for this purpose. It is proposed to use them in two ways: for the automated assessment of ECG parameters, which are promptly reported to the paramedic, as well as for transmitting the ECG image to a qualified cardiologist in order to obtain a second (advisory) opinion remotely.

The tasks set by the authors of the article have been successfully fulfilled. We have built and implemented an algorithm for assessing the main morphological parameters of the ECG on a physician's mobile phone when taking photos of 12 leads-ECG on a phone camera. We have shown experimentally that the accuracy of evaluating the morphological parameters of the ECG when working on an image captured with a phone camera is not worse than when working on a digital signal. Using the example of typical emergency medical service scenarios, we have shown that for a consultant cardiologist to obtain an image of the patient's cardiogram with a quality no worse than that of the original cardiograph, it is enough of the phone that does not go beyond the cheap price segment. Thus, the proposed solution is quite applicable in developing countries and in provincial regions, i.e. outside big cities.

ACKNOWLEDGEMENT

This work was financially supported by Russian Science Foundation, Grant 19-19-00696 and Ministry of Science and Higher Education of the Russian Federation, Grant MK-5723.2021.1.6.

REFERENCES

[Afonso] Afonso V.X., Tompkins W.J., Nguyen T.Q. and Shen LuoECG beat detection using filter banks. IEEE Transactions on Biomedical Engineering, vol. 46, no. 2, pp. 192-202, Feb. 1999, doi: 10.1109/10.740882.

[Attia] Attia Z.I., Noseworthy P.A., Lopez-Jimenez F., Asirvatham S.J., Deshmukh A.J., Gersh B.J., Carter R.E., Yao X., Rabinstein A.A., Erickson B.J. et al. An artificial intelligence-enabled ECG algorithm for the identification of patients with atrial fibrillation during sinus rhythm: A retrospective analysis of outcome prediction. Lancet 2019, 394, 861–867.

[Bansal] Bansal A., Joshi R. Portable out-of-hospital electrocardiography: A review of current technologies. J Arrhythm. 2018 Apr; 34(2): 129–138. doi: 10.1002/joa3.1203.

[Cardiovascular] Cardiovascular diseases. World Health Organization. https://www.who.int/health-topics/cardiovascular-diseases#tab=tab_1

[Cook] Cook DA, Oh S, Pusic MV. Accuracy of Physicians' Electrocardiogram Interpretations: A Systematic Review and Meta-analysis. JAMA Intern Med. 2020; 180(11): 1461–1471. doi:10.1001/jamainternmed.2020.3989

[ECG-kit] Goldberger AL, Amaral LAN, Glass L, Hausdorff JM, Ivanov PCh, Mark RG, Mietus JE, Moody GB, Peng C-K, Stanley HE. PhysioBank, PhysioToolkit, and PhysioNet: Components of a New Research Resource for Complex Physiologic Signals. Circulation 101(23):e215-e220 2000 (June 13). https://archive.physionet.org/physiotools/ecg-kit/

[Goldenberg] Goldenberg I., Moss A.J., Zareba W. QT Interval: How to Measure It and What Is "Normal". J Cardiovasc Electrophysiol, Vol. 17, pp. 333-336, March 2006. doi: 10.1111/j.1540-8167.2006.00408.x

[Gropler] Gropler M.R.F., Dalal A.S., Van Hare G.F., Avari Silva J.N. Can smartphone wireless ECGs be used to accurately assess ECG intervals in pediatrics? A comparison of mobile health monitoring to standard 12-lead ECG. PLOS One. Published: September 27, 2018https://doi.org/10.1371/journal.pone.0204403

[Hausenloy] Hausenloy D.J., Botker H.E., Engstrom T., Erlinge D., Heusch G., Ibanez B., Kloner R.A., Ovize M., Yellon D.M., Garcia-Dorado D. Targeting reperfusion injury in patients with ST-segment elevation myocardial infarction: Trials and tribulations. Eur. Heart J. 2016, 38, 935–941.

[Kalyakulina] Kalyakulina A., Yusipov I., Moskalenko V., Nikolskiy A., Kozlov A., Kosonogov K., Zolotykh N., Ivanchenko M. Lobachevsky University Electrocardiography Database. Published: June 4, 2020. Version: 1.0.0. https://www.physionet.org/content/ludb/1.0.0/

[Kligfield] Kligfield P., Badilini F., Rowlandson I., Xue J., Clark E., Devine B., Macfarlane P., de Bie J., Mortara D., Babaeizadeh S., Gregg R., Helfenbein E. D., Green C.L. Comparison of automated measurements of electrocardiographic intervals and durations by computer-based algorithms of digital electrocardiographs. American Heart Journal, V. 167, No.2, pp. 150-159.

[Lee] Lee JW., Kim KS., Lee B. et al. A Real Time QRS Detection Using Delay-Coordinate Mapping for the Microcontroller Implementation. Annals of Biomedical Engineering 30, 1140–1151 (2002). https://doi.org/10.1114/1.1523030

[Montalvo] Montalvo M., Tadi P., Merkler A., Gialdini G., Martin-Schild S., Navalkele D., Samai A., Nouh A, Hussain M., Goldblatt S; et al. PR Interval Prolongation and Cryptogenic Stroke: A Multicenter Retrospective Study. J. Stroke Cerebrovasc. Dis. 2017, 26, 2416–2420.

[Sangaiah] Sangaiah A.K., Arumugam M., Bian G. An intelligent learning approach for improving ECG signal classification and arrhythmia analysis. Artif. Intell. Med. 2020, 103, 101788.

[Sedghamiz] Sedghamiz H., Santonocito D. Unsupervised detection and classification of motor unit action potentials in intramuscular electromyography signals," 2015 E-Health and Bioengineering Conference (EHB), Iasi, Romania, 2015, pp. 1-6, doi: 10.1109/EHB.2015.7391510.

[Sedghamiz2014] Sedghamiz H. Matlab Implementation of Pan Tompkins ECG QRS detector. March 2014. DOI: 10.13140/RG.2.2.14202.59841. https://www.researchgate.net/publication/313673153_Matlab_Implementation_of_Pan_Tompkins_ECG_QRS_detector/

[Sedghamiz2014a] Sedghamiz H. An online algorithm for R, S and T wave detection. September 2014. DOI: 10.13140/RG.2.2.23774.64328. https://www.researchgate.net/publication/316960619_An_online_algorithm_for_R_S_and_T_wave_detection

[Tison] Tison G.H., Zhang J., Delling F.N., Deo R.C. Automated and Interpretable Patient ECG Profiles for Disease Detection, Tracking, and Discovery. Circulation: Cardiovascular Quality and Outcomes. 2019;12:e005289. Sep 2019 https://doi.org/10.1161/CIRCOUTCOMES.118.005289.

[Walker] Walker A.L, Muhlestein J.B. Smartphone electrocardiogram monitoring: current perspectives. Advanced Health Care Technologies. 8 June 2018 Volume 2018:4 Pp.15—24

[Xie] Xie L., Li Z., Zhou Y., He Y. and Zhu J. Computational Diagnostic Techniques for Electrocardiogram Signal Analysis. Sensors 2020, 20, 6318; doi:10.3390/s20216318

ENABLING TIME-CRITICAL COMMUNICATIONS IN MEDICAL IoT APPLICATIONS

Dino Mustefa[1,2], Hossein Fotouhi[2], Sasikumar Punnekkat[2] and Detlef Scholle[1]
[1]*Embedded Systems, ALTEN Sweden AB, Stockholm, Sweden*
[2]*Mälardalen University, Västerås, Sweden*
https://www.alten.se, https://www.mdh.se

ABSTRACT

Efficient communication is paramount for time-critical applications. Emerging time-critical healthcare applications will require extremely low latency, high reliability, and security guarantees. There are existing and emerging network technologies such as 5G that could enable efficient communications for these time-critical applications. However, it requires detailed identification of the required Quality of Service (QoS) of the applications and careful selection of the appropriate connectivity technology or combination of technologies to fully realize these time-critical healthcare applications. Network slicing is known as a proposed backbone of 5G technology that aggregates logical network functions and configurations of parameters to support a particular service. In this paper, we address the QoS requirements of medical IoT applications, with a particular focus on their time-critical nature and show how network slicing could be a key technology for meeting such requirements.

KEYWORDS

Medical IoT, Time-Critical Applications, Cybersecurity, Reliability, Wireless Communication, Software-Defined Networking, Network Function Virtualization, Network Slicing

1. INTRODUCTION

As life expectancy continues to rise worldwide, the increase in the elderly population places greater demands on the health care system (Rees et al., 2012). Infectious diseases such as COVID -19 are emerging and leaving greater impacts not only on the health sector and people's lives, but also on the global economy. Among other things, this clearly indicates that more effort and investment is required in the realization of novel and complex healthcare solutions, especially for remote monitoring and treatment applications.

One or more sensors and smart medical devices can communicate with each other to achieve a specific medical application. This interaction between the smart sensors and devices using connectivity technologies forms a Medical Internet of Things (MIoT) (Dimitrov, 2016). There are several emerging MIoT applications due to advanced wearable sensors, smart devices and advanced communication technologies such as emerging 5G mobile technology. This will bring many benefits in the field of healthcare. It will enable location-based monitoring and treatment of patients, which will minimize the time required to diagnose and treat diseases and the need for hospitalization and emergency room visits. Moreover, these applications will minimize the transmission of infectious diseases through ubiquitous MIoT infrastructure (Haghi et al., 2020). In general, it will be possible to improve survival rates, especially for patients living in rural areas, and reduce healthcare costs for both patients and healthcare organizations.

By definition, *"time-critical applications are those applications whose failure could result in loss of life, significant property damage, or damage to the environment"* (Knight, 2002). Data processing and storage on a remote server may be sufficient for certain non-time critical MIoT use cases where unreliable and slow response time does not harm the system (Campolo et al., 2018). However, for time-critical MIoT applications, reliability and fast response as well as cybersecurity are of paramount importance. Therefore, time-critical MIoT applications require the use of novel technologies to provide a reliable and secure service.

Due to the advancements in data communications, by providing ultra-high data rate and high throughput and very low latency technologies, it is possible to develop 5G-powered time-critical MIoT applications that will revolutionize the healthcare sector. Remote surgery is an example of a future MIoT application powered by 5G technologies that is also considered a time-critical application (Lacy et al., 2019). 5G is envisioned to be a network that supports multiple services in different application domains, taking into account different performance and service requirements, e.g., data transmission rate and latency (Foukas et al., 2017).

Network slicing technique is considered as the backbone of 5G technology and is an important enabler for time-critical applications equipped with wireless technologies (Campolo et al., 2017, 2018). It has been proposed to provide tailored and reliable services with limited network resources. Network slicing is able to efficiently deal with multiple tenants, some of which may have specific infrastructure requirements. For example, the use case of remote surgery within the healthcare application requires extremely low latency, which can be provided by assigning a specific network slice with such a guarantee.

Contribution. There are a variety of MIoT applications that are considered time critical. These applications have different Quality of Service (QoS) requirements. In this paper, we elaborate time-critical MIoT applications in terms of QoS requirements, addressing the technique of network slicing as a potential solution and important enabler.

Structure of the Paper. Section 2 presents the background on communication technologies. Section 3 describes the performance and security challenges in time-critical MIoT applications. Network slicing to address requirements for time-critical MIoT applications is presented in Section 4. Section 5 describes a use case for remote operations supported by 5G network slicing. Finally, Section 6 concludes the paper.

2. COMMUNICATION TECHNOLOGIES

There are a variety of existing and emerging communication technologies. These technologies can be divided into wired and wireless communication technologies. Wired communication technologies have an advantage in terms of security and can be used in combination with wireless technologies to connect sensors and end devices at the IoT level. Wireless communication technologies offer an unprecedented level of flexibility for system design and legacy updates (Johnston et al., 2018). By adopting wireless technologies and wireless sensor networks, there are significant benefits in reducing cables and connectors, lowering system costs, reducing system size and mass, reducing maintenance associated with inspection, reducing pin failures, improving system resilience to hazards, incorporating additional functionality, and increasing system flexibility for dynamic operations in the system.

IoT Technologies. Wireless radio technologies such as Bluetooth Low Energy (BLE), Zigbee, WiFi are widely used in healthcare applications today to connect sensors and end devices at IoT level (home or hospital). They are optimal in power consumption and favor mobility within a certain radius. With careful design, these wireless communication technologies can provide reliable and fast connectivity and can be used for time-critical MIoT applications in the field.

Cellular Technologies. Cellular technologies have evolved over the past 3 decades from 2G (second generation) to 5G (fifth generation). The functionalities of these generations have changed from audio-only communications to fluid video streaming. The network evolution from 2G to 5G is shown in Figure 1. The 5G New Radio Evolution (NR) is being driven by a variety of key stakeholders from the traditional commercial wireless industry, a wide range of industries, and the non-terrestrial access ecosystem. It will be a key enabler for time-critical IoT applications in the industrial, transportation and medical sectors. The 5G NR technology promises to provide a common platform for radio access networks (RAN) to address the challenges of current and future time-critical IoT use cases and services, not only those we can imagine today, but also those we cannot yet imagine. This technology is expected to be a network that supports various performance and service requirements, such as data transfer rate (up to 10 GB/s), latency (theoretical latency of 1 ms), multiple increases in base station capacity, and higher capacity to handle more connections simultaneously (Foukas et al., 2017).

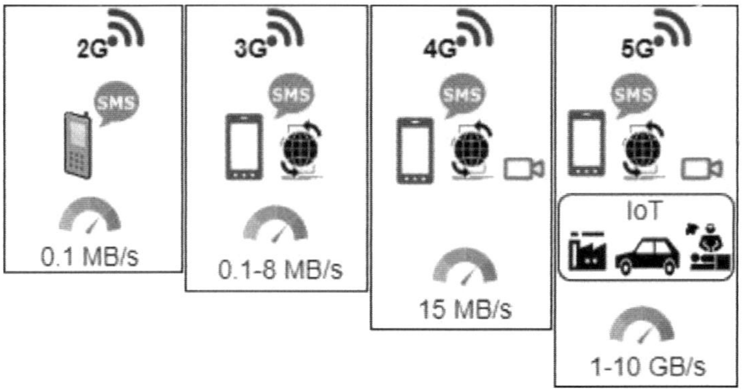

Figure 1. Overview of the evolved topology for cellular network technologies functionalities

MIoT applications can use both wired and wireless technologies, creating a heterogeneous network with different radio and software technologies. This brings challenges in the form of different requirements and constraints. There are also several critical challenges in considering wireless technologies in system design. Some examples of common challenges are unpredictable communication behavior, unreliable wireless channels, interference and collisions. Such challenges are also common in wired systems where there are cases where the medium is shared with different users. Network slicing provides the ability to efficiently manage resources while ensuring QoS of the application. The technique of network slicing is an important requirement for providing guarantees to support time-critical applications equipped with wireless technologies (Campolo et al., 2017, 2018).

3. MIoT APPLICATIONS

There are several performance and security challenges related to connectivity when considering time-critical MIoT applications. It requires careful design considerations and selection of connectivity technologies that can enable reliable and secure communication between a patient and a healthcare provider.

3.1 Performance Challenges

Reliability and fast response are paramount in case of remote surgery. Table 1 lists some of the QoS requirements for remote surgery. A packet is considered lost if it is not received by the destination application within the maximum tolerable end-to-end latency for that application. For example, 10^{-3} means that, on average, the application will tolerate at most 1 in 1000 packets that are not successfully received within the maximum tolerable latency. Providing ultra-high reliability close to 10^{-3} is defined as the maximum tolerable packet loss rate at the application layer. The 5G Ultra-Reliable Low-Latency Communications (URLLCs) service is one way to meet such a high reliability requirement.

Another challenge to enabling remote surgery is coping with resource management in data communications, although it is very possible that this could be supported by a cellular network. Traditional resource management schemes for radio access networks (typical cellular networks) consist of distributing the same radio access to all devices. This scheme may not meet the latency requirements in a remote surgery (e.g., $<10ms$ in the case of haptic feedback). The provision of end-to-end latency under $<10ms$ is defined as the contribution of the wireless network to the time between the sending of a packet by the source and the reception of the packet by the destination. Knowing the urgency of some services within an application, intelligent resource management is required to meet time-critical demands. For example, it is necessary to allocate more resources with dedicated channel bandwidth for such critical applications. Large delays in the network have a significant impact on the quality of surgery. It is naive to allocate the same resources to different applications, similar to traditional resource management methods. An intelligent network slicing is able to detect the requirements and constraints of the applications to allocate the resources dynamically. Therefore, it is important to develop end-to-end network slicing to manage and control the network and ensure sufficient quality of service for time-critical applications such as remote surgery.

Table 1. QoS requirements for a remote surgery application (Perez et al., 2016; Eid et al., 2010; Cizmeci et al., 2017),(Patel & Wang, 2010),(Hachisu & Kajimoto, 2016)

	Data Type	Latency	Jitter	Packet Loss Rate	Data Rate
Real-time multimedia stream	2D camera flow	<150 ms	3–30 ms	$<10^{-3}$	<10 Mbps
	3D camera flow	<150 ms	3–30 ms	$<10^{-3}$	137 Mbps-1.6 Gbps
	Audio flow	<150 ms	<30 ms	$<10^{-3}$	22–200 Kbps
Physical vital signs	Temperature	<250 ms	-	$<10^{-3}$	<10 kbps
	Blood pressure	<250 ms	-	$<10^{-3}$	<10 kbps
	Heart rate	<250 ms	-	$<10^{-3}$	<10 kbps
	Respiration rate	<250 ms	-	$<10^{-3}$	<10 Kbps
	ECG	<250 ms	-	$<10^{-3}$	72 kbps
	EEG	<250 ms	-	$<10^{-3}$	86.4 kbps
	EMG	<250 ms	-	$<10^{-3}$	1.536 Mbps
Haptic feedback	Force	3–10 ms	<2 ms	$<10^{-3}$	128–400 Kbps
	Vibration	<5.5 ms	<2 ms	$<10^{-3}$	128–400 Kbps

3.2 Security Challenges

In general, the integration of IoT devices and cloud services enabled by cellular technologies leads to a more complicated and dynamic threat landscape (Ahmad et al., 2017). The security threat vectors in 5G will be even greater than in previous generations (Madhusanka et al., 2018), even though the security of 5G mobile technology is better than that of previous ones. Therefore, attackers will have a higher chance to perform malicious activities on time-critical MIoT applications (Ahmad et al., 2017). For example, when performing a remote surgery, attackers can perform a denial of service (DoS) attack to disrupt the operation, compromising patient safety.

Therefore, it is of utmost importance to mitigate such security concerns in time-critical MIoT applications, and there are a few options to choose when a customer intends to deploy a 5G network, each of which has security adaptation implications. The first option is to deploy a private 5G network on premises and apply security measures to the private 5G network, but this requires investment in a separate network infrastructure. The second option is to extend the macro 5G service using Distributed Antenna Systems (DAS) (Kim et al., 2020) or alternatively small cells[1], but with this option it is difficult to implement custom security solutions for a particular application. The third option is to purchase a network slice from an operator and then apply customized security solutions for a specific application. Network slicing can reduce the threat vector through isolation and enable the implementation of specific security solutions for a particular time-critical application.

4. NETWORK SLICING

This section highlights the idea of network slicing, which is defined within the 5G architecture. The term network slicing stands for "*a logical network built on a common physical infrastructure that includes RAN, core networks (CNs), edge and cloud computing nodes*" (Khan et al., 2020). To provide tailored and reliable services using limited network resources, Network Slicing has been proposed by the mobile industry as the key to convergence of network services (Rost et al., 2016), (Jiang et al., 2016). Network slicing can offer radio, cloud and network resources to application providers or different vertical segments without physical network infrastructure, enabling service differentiation by customizing network operations.

1 https://en.wikipedia.org/wiki/Small cell

4.1 Network Slicing Enablers

Software-defined networking (SDN) and network function virtualization (NFV) are important components for implementing network slicing. These two are the software and hardware enablers respectively in the context of 5G.

SDN approach brings intelligence and flexibility to the network by enabling orchestration and centralized management (Kreutz et al., 2014). SDN has been defined as the physical separation of the network control plane from the forwarding plane[2]. This separation of the data plane from the control plane gives the SDN controller a global view of the network and provides the ability to make rapid changes to the network. More specifically, SDN creates a virtual control plane that makes intelligent decisions. In addition, the SDN controller brings increased processing power and provides the ability to run complex deep learning and machine learning algorithms to improve network performance. This is where the communication network and artificial intelligence techniques meet to improve network performance.

NFV is the virtualization of network functions traditionally executed on proprietary hardware, i.e., NFV allows network functions to be executed on standard hardware instead of dedicated hardware. It provides for instantiation of virtual network functions on hardware (Yi et al., 2018). Changes to the functions are made at the Internet Service Provider (ISP) level, as opposed to the traditional process of configuration at the customer premises. NFV can ensure that resource provisioning is optimized while meeting quality of service.

4.2 Network Slicing Services

According to International Telecommunication Union Radiocommunication Sector (ITU-R), which manages radio-frequency spectrum, the main objective is to support three generic services with vastly heterogeneous requirements: (i) Enhanced Mobile Broadband (eMBB), (ii) Massive Machine Type Communications (mMTC), and (iii) Ultra-Reliable Low-Latency Communications (URLLC) (Popovski et al., 2018). eMBB supports stable connections with very high peak data rates as well as moderate rates for cell edge users. mMTC supports massive numbers of IoT devices that are sporadically active and send small data payloads. URLLC supports low latency transmissions of small payload data with very high reliability. MIoT applications may require any of the above 5G services depending on system-level and use case-level requirements, but time-critical MIoT applications such as remote surgery require URLLC to meet their high reliability and ultra-low latency requirements.

4.3 Network Slicing Layers

A generic framework for network slicing (see Figure 2) considers a 3-layer model divided into (1) infrastructure, (2) control (network function), and (3) business (service) layers (Soenen et al., 2017; Foukas et al., 2017). The infrastructure layer contains all the physical components of an operator. Under this layer we can find RAN, computational and storage resources and wired connections. The control layer is a library of virtual network functions. These functions are used to control the infrastructure to establish logical networks that meet the requirements of the slice. virtual network functions are required to reserve segments of spectrum from RAN to prioritize traffic. This layer also manages and orchestrates virtual network functions. The business layer contains services and use cases, such as healthcare and intelligent transportation systems. One of the important issues in the service layer is how to map the components to the different layers of the architecture to meet the end-to-end requirements. Two types of mapping are (1) mapping service requirements to network functions and (2) mapping network functions to vendor implementations (Zhou et al., 2016).

---

[2] https://www.opennetworking.org/

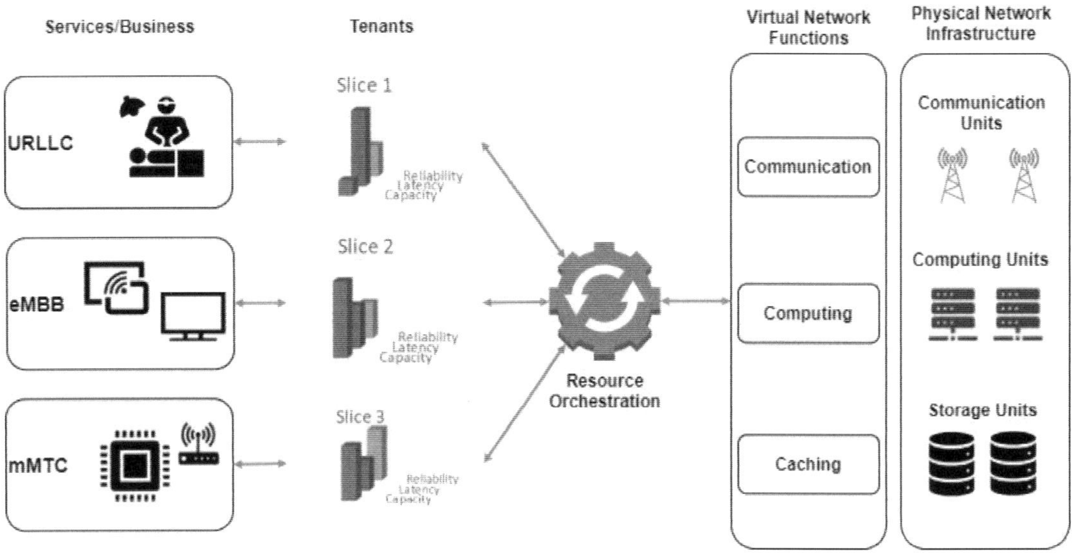

Figure 2. Generic 5G network slicing framework (Shen et al., 2020)

4.4 Performance in Network Slicing

Mobile network operators (MNOs) are actively working with the medical domain[3] and they will be able to deploy multiple slices on their network infrastructure by splitting a physical network into multiple logical networks, where these logical networks can support customised on-demand services for different applications with different requirements and specifications. In other words, if a customer in the medical field requires 5G network infrastructure for an ultra-low latency application, an operator can provision a segment of spectrum on the RANs and a segment of bandwidth on the links in the CN connecting those RANs that can meet the demand of the customer traffic. This makes it possible to reduce network congestion that would have resulted from a shared network infrastructure. This means that the ultra-low latency ($<10ms$) required by the remote surgery can be provided by assigning a dedicated network slice with such a guarantee. Moreover, resource management schemes in typical cellular networks are supposed to distribute RAN resources across all services. This potentially leads to increased and fluctuating delays, which is an undesirable property in time-critical applications. Intelligent network slicing can identify the QoS requirements of an application and can guarantee the latency requirements by dynamically and efficiently allocating dedicated resources for a time-critical application using intelligent resource management (Zhang et al., 2017).

4.5 Cybersecurity in Network Slicing

Network slicing can operate with different security functionality, such as firewall configurations, access policies, packet inspection, and can provide authentication schemes. In another word, a network slice enables applying a customized security mechanisms and policies for time-critical applications such as remote surgery contrary to using a private 5G network or extended macro 5G service using DAS. But most importantly, network slicing provides isolation between the slices[4], both in terms of traffic and resources which plays an important role in protecting time-critical applications, e.g. from DoS attack. The more network slices introduced for a use case application the better the resources can be isolated which in turn improves security guard of the use case application against cyber attacks.

[3]https://www.groundalerts.com/5g-infrastructure-in-healthcare-market-to-witness-robust-expansionthroughout-the-forecast-period-2020-2025
[4] https://www.ericsson.com/en/blog/2019/9/future-network-slicing-security-iot

5. REMOTE SURGERY

Remote surgery is a surgery where a surgeon performs surgery on a patient that is physically in a different location as shown in Figure 3. The telesurgical system in remote surgery is a close-loop communication system consisting of forward link and feedback link. Forward link transports real-time commands in order to control the motions and rotation of robotic arms at the teleoperator, along with voice stream from the surgeon to communicate with the surgical team remotely. Feedback link transports real-time multi-modal sensory feedback from the teleoperator, including 3D video stream, force feedback e.g., pressure, and tactile feedback e.g. tissue mechanical properties, and patient's physiological data e.g. blood pressure and heart rate, along with voice stream from assistant nurses, anaesthetist and other collaborating surgeons at the patient's side.

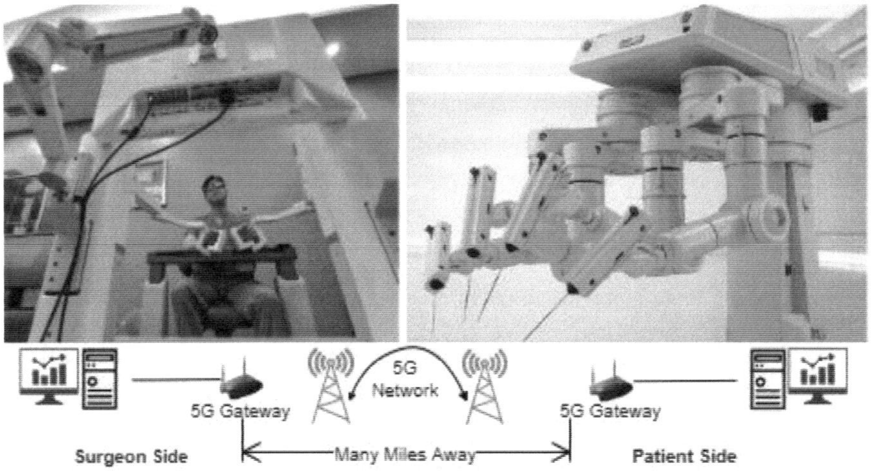

Figure 3. Remote surgery setup scenario[9,8,7]

The first remote surgery test via a 5G network was conducted by Ericsson and its partners[5]. This surgery combined haptic sensing and a transluminal surgical system, network slicing, edge computing, low latency and large bandwidth for intelligent sensing and human-machine interaction. The demonstration of remote surgery leveraged end-to-end network slicing to ensure quality of service. In this demonstration, a probe is a robotic representation of a biological finger that gives sense of touch in an invasive surgery. It can send accurate real-time localization of hard nodules in soft tissue. With 5G connectivity, intelligent network slicing separates and prioritizes time-critical functions, such as machine communication, which is required for a remote surgery.

In March 2019, People's Liberation Army General Hospital (PLAGH) carried out a real surgery on the brain of a Parkinson's disease patient in Beijing from the PLAGH Hainan Hospital 3,000*km* away[6]. 5G technologies have provided the basis and infrastructure to perform remote surgery, while achieving application requirements. Edge computing architecture has enabled local processing of big data in an edge server, and network slicing has assigned dedicated channel bandwidth to gain high throughput.

In Milan, around mid of 2020, Italian healthcare professionals were able to perform a remote surgery on the vocal cords of an adult human cadaver via a 5G powered surgical robotic system located at nine miles away[7] [8]. This was possible due to the fast and reliable network connections provided by 5G (Acemoglu et al., 2020). In Sept 2020, a similar remote surgery was conducted in East China's Shandong province using the reliable and low latency connection provided by 5G technology. In this procedure a patient underwent the urological surgery located in different location, Southwest China's Guizhou province [9]. These recent developments are clear evidence that 5G and its enablers are the future communication infrastructure to enable time-critical MIoT applications.

---

[5] King's College London, Tianjin University, China Mobile Research Institute, Industrial Research Institute and CMCC Tianjin.
[6] https://www.medicaldevice-network.com/features/5g-remote-surgery/
[7] https://www.courthousenews.com/socially-distant-surgery-doctor-uses-5g-to-perform-remote-operation/
[8] https://mytechdecisions.com/it-infrastructure/research-5g-could-usher-in-telesurgery-and-remote-surgicalprocedures/
[9] https://www.chinadaily.com.cn/a/202009/25/WS5f6d6286a31024ad0ba7bd6e.html

6. CONCLUDING REMARKS

This paper has addressed possible solutions and evolution towards enabling time-critical MIoT applications powered by 5G technology, namely network slicing. The e2e latency and reliability required by time-critical MIoT applications can be provided by employing 5G network slicing. However, to date reported prototypes are lacking a practical implementation of an intelligent slicing across administrative domains. Static over-provisioning of latency and bandwidth is not enough to guarantee network characteristics. The dynamic slicing of the network needs to be supported with artificial intelligence-based management system for a large network.

Network slicing minimize DoS attack by providing an isolated network and creates possibility to apply specific security solutions targeting certain time-critical application. However, the challenges of providing reliable and protected slices will grow due to the increasing threat vector as well as due to enablers like SDN and NFV (Cunha et al., 2019). The challenges will be even more if resources are allowed to be shared by multiple tenants. Therefore, network slicing shall address such challenges, e.g. compromise of a NFVs, side-channels attacks, or dealing with end-devices vulnerabilities[10].

ACKNOWLEDGEMENT

This work was supported by the Swedish Knowledge Foundation (KKS) through the ARRAY project and the FlexiHealth Prospekt, and the EU Celtic Next/Vinnova project, Health5G (Future eHealth powered by 5G).

REFERENCES

Acemoglu, A., Peretti, G., Trimarchi, M., Hysenbelli, J., Krieglstein, J., Geraldes, A., ... Mattos, L. (2020, 07). Operating from a distance: Robotic vocal cord 5g telesurgery on a cadaver. *Annals of Internal Medicine*, *173*.

Ahmad, I., Kumar, T., Liyanage, M., Okwuibe, J., Ylianttila, M., & Gurtov, A. (2017). 5g security: Analysis of threats and solutions. In *2017 ieee conference on standards for communications and networking (cscn)* (p. 193-199).

Campolo, C., Molinaro, A., Iera, A., Fontes, R. R., & Rothenberg, C. E. (2018). Towards 5g network slicing for the v2x ecosystem. In *2018 4th ieee conference on network softwarization and workshops (netsoft)* (pp. 400–405).

Campolo, C., Molinaro, A., Iera, A., & Menichella, F. (2017). 5g network slicing for vehicle-toeverything services. *IEEE Wireless Communications*, *24*(6), 38–45.

Cizmeci, B., Xu, X., Chaudhari, R., Bachhuber, C., Alt, N., & Steinbach, E. (2017). A multiplexing scheme for multimodal teleoperation. *ACM Transactions on Multimedia Computing, Communications, and Applications (TOMM)*, *13*(2), 1–28.

Cunha, V. A., da Silva, E., de Carvalho, M. B., Corujo, D., Barraca, J. P., Gomes, D., ... Aguiar, R. L. (2019). Network slicing security: Challenges and directions. *Internet Technology Letters*, *2*(5), e125. Retrieved from https://onlinelibrary.wiley.com/doi/abs/10.1002/itl2.125

Dimitrov, D. V. (2016). Medical internet of things and big data in healthcare. *Healthcare informatics research*, *22*(3), 156-163.

Eid, M., Cha, J., & El Saddik, A. (2010). Admux: An adaptive multiplexer for haptic–audio–visual data communication. *IEEE Transactions on Instrumentation and Measurement*, *60*(1), 21–31.

Foukas, X., Patounas, G., Elmokashfi, A., & Marina, M. K. (2017). Network slicing in 5g: Survey and challenges. *IEEE Communications Magazine*, *55*(5), 94–100.

Hachisu, T., & Kajimoto, H. (2016). Vibration feedback latency affects material perception during rod tapping interactions. *IEEE transactions on haptics*, *10*(2), 288–295.

Haghi, M., Neubert, S., Geissler, A., Fleischer, H., Stoll, N., Stoll, R., & Thurow, K. (2020). A flexible and pervasive iot-based healthcare platform for physiological and environmental parameters monitoring. *IEEE Internet of Things Journal*, *7*(6), 5628-5647.

Jiang, M., Condoluci, M., & Mahmoodi, T. (2016). Network slicing management & prioritization in 5g mobile systems. In *European wireless 2016; 22th european wireless conference* (pp. 1–6).

[10] https://www.ngmn.org/publications/5g-security-recommendations-package-2-network-slicing.html

Johnston, A. B., Schiffers, W., & Kharaz, A. H. (2018, aug). Towards wireless technology for safety critical systems. *Journal of Physics: Conference Series*, *1065*, 072032.

Khan, L. U., Yaqoob, I., Tran, N. H., Han, Z., & Hong, C. S. (2020). Network slicing: Recent advances, taxonomy, requirements, and open research challenges. *IEEE Access*, *8*, 36009–36028.

Kim, J., Sung, M., Cho, S., Won, Y., Lim, B., Pyun, S., ... Lee, J. H. (2020). Mimo-supporting radio-over-fiber system and its application in mmwave-based indoor 5g mobile network. *Journal of Lightwave Technology*, *38*(1), 101-111.

Knight, J. C. (2002). Safety critical systems: challenges and directions. In *Proceedings of the 24th international conference on software engineering* (pp. 547–550).

Kreutz, D., Ramos, F. M., Verissimo, P. E., Rothenberg, C. E., Azodolmolky, S., & Uhlig, S. (2014). Software-defined networking: A comprehensive survey. *Proceedings of the IEEE*, *103*(1), 14–76.

Lacy, A., Bravo, R., Otero-Pin˜eiro, A., Pena, R., De Lacy, F., Menchaca, R., & Balibrea, J. (2019). 5g-assisted telementored surgery. *British Journal of Surgery*.

Madhusanka, L., Ijaz, A., Bux, A. A., Andrei, G., & Mika, Y. (2018). *A comprehensive guide to 5g security*. https://doi.org/10.1002/9781119293071: John Wiley & Sons, Incorporated.

Patel, M., & Wang, J. (2010). Applications, challenges, and prospective in emerging body area networking technologies. *IEEE Wireless communications*, *17*(1), 80–88.

Perez, M., Xu, S., Chauhan, S., Tanaka, A., Simpson, K., Abdul-Muhsin, H., & Smith, R. (2016). Impact of delay on telesurgical performance: study on the robotic simulator dv-trainer. *International journal of computer assisted radiology and surgery*, *11*(4), 581–587.

Popovski, P., Trillingsgaard, K. F., Simeone, O., & Durisi, G. (2018). 5g wireless network slicing for embb, urllc, and mmtc: A communication-theoretic view. *IEEE Access*, *6*, 55765–55779.

Rees, P., van der Gaag, N., de Beer, J., & Heins, F. (2012). European regional populations: Current trends, future pathways, and policy options. *European Journal of Population / Revue europ´eenne de D´emographie*, *28*.

Rost, P., Banchs, A., Berberana, I., Breitbach, M., Doll, M., Droste, H., ... Sayadi, B. (2016). Mobile network architecture evolution toward 5g. *IEEE Communications Magazine*, *54*(5), 84–91.

Shen, X., Gao, J., Wu, W., Lyu, K., Li, M., Zhuang, W., ... Rao, J. (2020). Ai-assisted networkslicing based next-generation wireless networks. *IEEE Open Journal of Vehicular Technology*, *1*, 45-66.

Soenen, T., Banerjee, R., Tavernier, W., Colle, D., & Pickavet, M. (2017). Demystifying network slicing: From theory to practice. In *2017 ifip/ieee symposium on integrated network and service management (im)* (pp. 1115–1120).

Yi, B., Wang, X., Li, K., Huang, M., et al. (2018). A comprehensive survey of network function virtualization. *Computer Networks*, *133*, 212–262.

Zhang, H., Liu, N., Chu, X., Long, K., Aghvami, A.-H., & Leung, V. C. (2017). Network slicing based 5g and future mobile networks: mobility, resource management, and challenges. *IEEE communications magazine*, *55*(8), 138–145.

Zhou, X., Li, R., Chen, T., & Zhang, H. (2016). Network slicing as a service: enabling enterprises' own software-defined cellular networks. *IEEE Communications Magazine*, *54*(7), 146–153.

AN INNOVATIVE APPLICATION ARCHITECTURE TO REDUCE CONTACT IN WORK ENVIRONMENTS

Aycan Vargün, Emin Tolgahan Polat, Özgür Macit and Uğur Serkan Taşkın
Research and Development Department
Koçtaş Construction Market Incorporated Company
İstanbul, Turkey

ABSTRACT

COVID-19 has caused changes in working conditions and environments as well as in living conditions all over the world. The e-Health approach, on the other hand, can help employees to work in healthier environments with the appropriate use of information and communication technologies. In this paper, a solution architecture is presented to reduce the number of physical contacts that cause risk in work environments and to monitor the health status of employees. This architecture has been realized as a mobile application that employees can download on their phones. Usage results among employees have been included in the paper.

KEYWORDS

E-Health, COVID-19, Mobile Application, Java, Rest

1. INTRODUCTION

E-Health is a concept that aims to perform health transactions such as the realization of diagnosis and treatment procedures, clinical services, health data storage, patient registration and information tracking in electronic environment. It is getting more important day by day. Within the scope of E-Health, applications that provide decision support and reminders for users, electronic clinical management and communication tools, telemedicine applications for patient-doctor communication or communication between experts and applications that provide online training for healthcare personnel are acquiring significance every day (Toygar 2018).

There are many examples of e-health applications that touch on many different issues. The scope is expanding, from monitoring mother health by providing health questionnaires for postpartum depression (Jiménez-Serrano et al. 2015), to a variety of applications that offer blood glucose measurement and education for diabetic patients (Veazie et al. 2018). In addition, it is also possible to monitor health information with smart applications which use wearable sensor technology for various measurements such as heart rate, blood pressure, body temperature etc. It is also important that healthcare personnel and managers contribute with their time to design and develop new technologies (Royal Society 2006).

E-Health technologies can play an important role in COVID-19 test and indoor quarantine processes for COVID-19 positive patients with mild symptoms and can help for early intervention before these symptoms become severe (Adans-Dester et al. 2020).

Since COVID-19 affected working environments, monitoring the health of employees have become a very important issue to be addressed. For this purpose, this paper introduces a mobile application with its architecture in order to reduce contact caused by tools in common use. In addition, it controls the entries and exits of employees with the risk of COVID-19, by tracking contact records among employees and by monitoring their health status in the same environment.

The paper continues as follows: In section II, the problem definition is detailed, and a solution proposal is presented. In section III, the architectural infrastructure of the solution proposal is described with the necessary services and the technologies used. In section IV, the results of the application and future studies are presented.

2. PROBLEM DEFINITION AND SOLUTION PROPOSAL

2.1 Problem Description and Requirements

The problem can be grouped under three headings. The first topic is that employees are using tools in common use at the starts and ends of their shifts in the working environment. A solution is required to eliminate these tools and to reduce contact. Secondly, monitoring health of employees is required. With the information obtained from this monitoring, it is necessary to prevent unhealthy employees from entering to the working area. Thirdly, all employees in contact with unhealthy employees should be determined. After the employees in health risk are identified, necessary steps should be taken by the responsible persons.

2.2 Proposed Solution

In Figure 1, A thorough application has been developed as a solution for the problem under three headings in Section 2.1. The key components of the application are four services at the backend, a mobile client and a web client using these services.

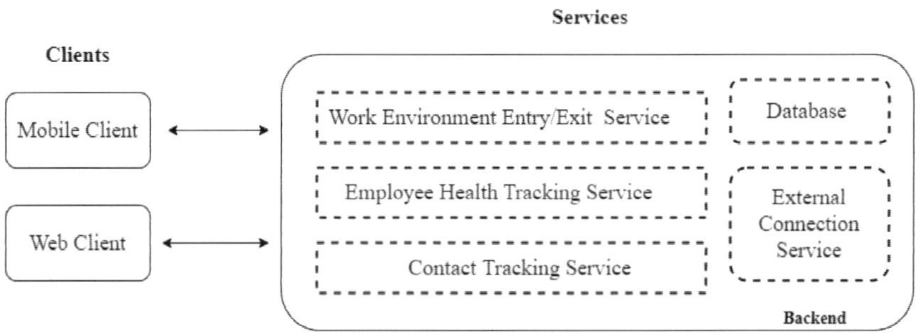

Figure 1. Key Architectural Components

2.3 Solution Implementation and Results

Java Spring Boot Framework has been used for the creation of Rest based APIs (Application Programming Interface) in the Backend. Spring Boot Framework is a stand-alone open-source framework produced by Pivotal Team, to develop microservices (Tutorialspoint 2021). An SQL server for database and the Hibernate/JPA (Java Persistence API) implementation for Java object mapping with tables in database are used. An SQL server is used since the data structure requires a relational database. A relational model is a model in which the data can be associated with each other (Codd 1970). JPA is a standard for associating Java objects with tables in a database. Hibernate is an implementation of this standard that performs object mapping (Javatpoint 2021).

Flutter SDK (Software Development Kit) has been used for the mobile client. Flutter SDK is a mobile software development environment developed by Google, which includes the Dart SDK that allows cross-platform application development and has a rich tool library (Flutter 2021). Html, CSS and JavaScript Fetch API for the web client is used to send requests to the backend services. Fetch API is a JavaScript interface that transmits Http/Https requests to the relevant server through the browser and transmits the returned responses to client (Mozilla 2021). The application backend is deployed on the Azure platform as an App Service and made available to employee users. Azure Web service is an HTTP-based Azure service that allows hosting web applications, REST APIs and mobile application backends by providing security, load balancing, and automatic scaling (Microsoft 2021).

2.3.1 Preparation of Backend Services

- *Employee Health Tracking Service*: The purpose of this service is to obtain the daily health information of each employee and to convey this to other services. Employees are presented with a questionnaire containing pre-formed health questions by the institution doctor through the mobile interface. These survey questions can be delivered to the mobile client by creating and using the /getHealthQuestions API in Figure 2. The mobile client presents the questions to the users through the survey interface in its content. Employees' responses to the questionnaire are recorded daily in the database with the /postEmployeeAnswers API. The blocking information about the employees with health risk is added to the database by using BlockEmployeeIfUnhealty() function. This blocking information states that they cannot work that day.

The web client can receive blocking information on a list with /getBlockedEmployees or on an employee-based schema including health survey answers with /getBlockedEmployeeAnswers. The institution doctor can access the web client via browser and can obtain daily health information for the employees' health.

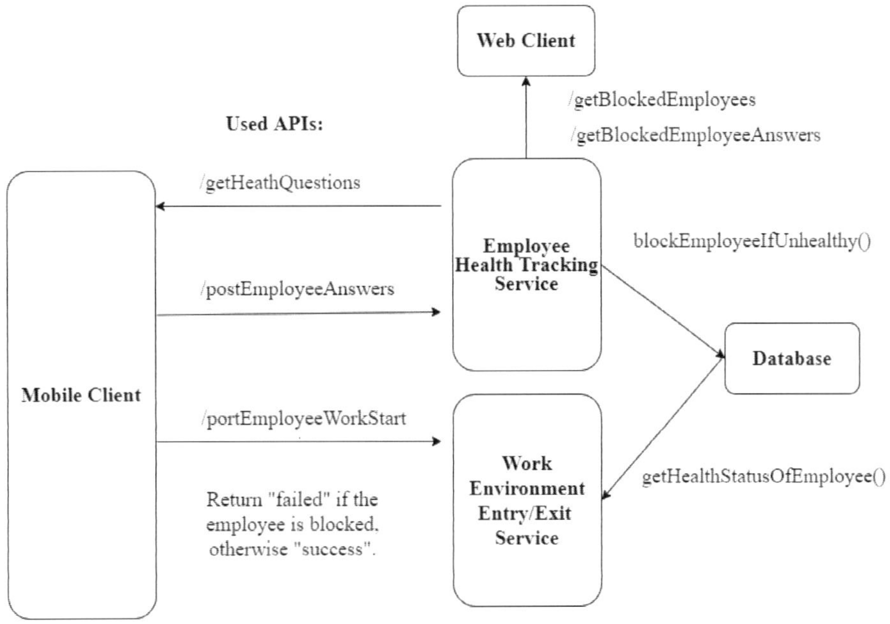

Figure 2. Working Environment Entry/Exit Service and Employee Health Monitoring Service

- *Working Environment Entry/Exit Service*: The main purpose of this service is to eliminate the contact by ensuring that the tools in common use while entering to the working environment are no longer needed. For this reason, special buttons are shown to the employees in the mobile interface so that they can report the start and the end of their shifts. There are two conditions that employees must meet to be able to make a report with these special buttons. The first is the GPS control that verifies that the employee is near the working environment. The second is whether he/she has a health risk. Mobile client receives GPS information on the phone and sends it to the backend via the /postEmployeeWorkStart API. This GPS information is compared with the actual GPS information of the working environment in the database. If the GPS information from the mobile client is closer than 100 meters to the actual GPS information of the working environment, the first verification has been achieved. Then, the database is checked with the getHealthStatusOfEmployee() function for employee health verification. If the employee has answered the health questionnaire of that day and no block has been added to the database for that employee in line with the answers, the second verification has also been achieved. The employee's shift report is logged, and "success" returns to the mobile client. If one of these verifications fails, "failed" is returned to the mobile client.
- *Contact Tracking Service:* The purpose of this service is to record the points where employees touch at the working area during the day, to identify all employees who touch the same point in case of a possible illness and to communicate with them with the approval of the institution doctor.

A unique QR code was generated for each contact point and placed in the work area. Building, floor and room information are embedded to these QR codes. After that, employees who stand at a QR code point for more than a certain time must read this QR code from the mobile client and state that they are at that point. The mobile client sends the QR code to the backend with /postNewTouch API. This QR code is searched in the database and the point it belongs to is determined. Then, this record of reading QR code is saved to the database for that employee with the function addNewTouch(Employee, Checkpoint, TimeofContact).

The web client helps the institution doctor to identify the unhealthy employees and find the employees who have contacted the same points with these unhealthy employees. The filter on the web client interface requests employees at health risk using the /getEmployeesInRisk API. First, the employees who are blocked by giving risky answers to the health questionnaire are found by using the getUnhealtyEmployees() function. Second, QR code reading points that these employees come into contact with are obtained with the getRiskPoints(employees) function. These points are also used by the getEmployeesInRisk(riskPoints) function to find employees at risk who have touched the same points. The result is returned to the web client. In this way, the institution doctor obtains the list of employees at risk in Figure 3.

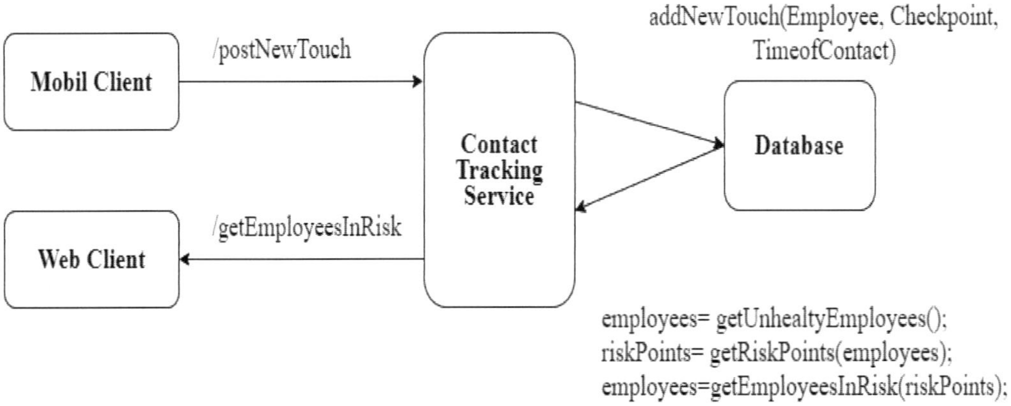

Figure 3. Contact Tracking Service

- *Database and External Connection Services:* This service is created to establish connection between the backend services and the external identity verification service for employees. This service speaks to the external authentication server for login.

2.3.2 Preparing Clients

- *Mobile Client*: First of all, screens are designed for each scenario. Second, a Flutter project is created by using the Flutter SDK. Next, models in line with APIs are created for requests of the Backend services. The functions to send requests and receive their responses have been added to Flutter project. Then the mobile application is uploaded to the Google Play Store and the IOS APP Store.
- *Web Client:* Web client is created by using Html, CSS and JavaScript. Through web client, the institution doctor can filter the employees according to their health status and can view the employees' responses to the health questionnaire with a time-based filtering. Web client requests are sent to the APIs in the backend by using the JavaScript Fetch API.

2.3.3 Deployment Process

A Resource Group has been created to put all application-related objects before the application backend is uploaded to Azure as an App service. An SQL database and SQL server have been created in this Resource Group. An App Insight has been created for logging and monitoring the application. Then, the backend is uploaded to the Resource Group as an App Service. After the deployment process has been completed successfully, the application backend has been serving the mobile and the web clients.

3. CONCLUSION

3.1 Usage Results

The application has been used among employees since July 2020. The total number of users has reached to 1000 after January 2021. After the users login the application with their e-mail addresses, they answer the health questionnaire ever day to report their shifts. Employees who respond to the questions by stating that they don't pose any health risks can enter to the working environment. Those whose health status is at risk are blocked and cannot enter to the area.

On the left of the Figure 4, the health survey is shown on the mobile interface screen. The questions are health related like "Do you cough?", "Do you lose smell?" etc. When employees give a risky answer to the questionnaire, they are informed on a red screen (in the middle of the Figure 4) that they cannot make a report of shift. In addition, when they try to make a report of shift on the work reporting page (on the right of the Figure 4.), a warning is issued that they will not be able to report because their health might not be good.

Figure 4. Working Environment Enter/Exit Report Scenario for Employees with Health Risks

Each QR reading transaction is recorded in the database. Employees can view the contact points they have read from the application. Since the contact points of the risky employees are recorded in the database, employees who touch the same points on the same day can also be determined. In Figure 5, there are two mobile client pages which belong to the Contact Tracking Service. On the left, the popup message which says "The reading operation is successful" is shown after a QR Code has been read by an employee. On the right, the employee's QR code history is listed. Three reads are listed.

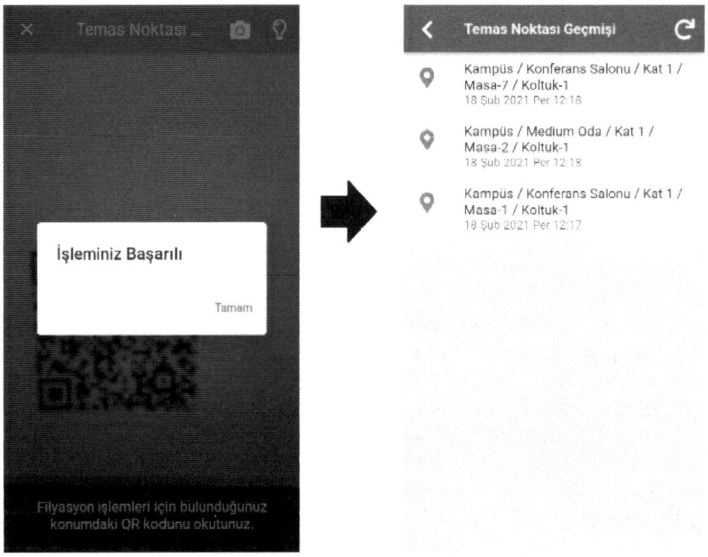

Figure 5. Touch Point QR Reading Process

The application has begun to run in July 2020. As seen in Table 1, the number of Entry/Exit reporting of employees by mobile application has increased in line with the increase in the number of employee users. The number of blocked people has reached its peak in October and November 2020. In the table, the row of "Blocked Employees Who Have Read Qrcodes" shows the number of blocked employees who have also read qrcodes within the same month in the working environment. As an example, if an employee is blocked in September 2020, and has read Qrcode in the same working environment in September 2020, he is added to the number in 9/20. The row "Number of People in Contact with The Blocked Persons" shows the number of the employees who have contacted within a month with the employees in the row "Blocked Employees Who Have Read Qrcodes". The number of blocked and contacted persons has reached its peak in November and December 2020. Thanks to the application, employees who have had risky contacts are identified and the opportunity to take action is provided.

Table 1. Working Environment Enter/Exit Report and Total UsageEnter/Exit Report and Total Usage

Months:	7/20	8/20	9/20	10/20	11/20	12/20	1/21	2/21	3/21
Total Number of Users	63	212	718	889	944	975	1144	1594	1967
Number of Entry/Exit Reporting of Employees	29	317	1303	7660	7304	5104	11564	13936	19406
Number of Blocked Employees	15	8	103	109	116	38	17	9	17
Blocked Employees Who Have Read Qrcodes	4	8	9	16	9	4	7	3	5
Number of People in Contact with The Blocked Persons	22	19	31	55	28	9	18	16	26

In Figure 6, the graph shows the daily positive and negative questionnaires. The negative questionaries means that the employee health is risky per their answers to the health questions while the positives means that they are healthy. By the end of 2020, there is an increase in the number of positive questionnaires since the total users of the mobile application has increased as seen in Table 1. The number of negative questionnaires changes 1-10 each day.

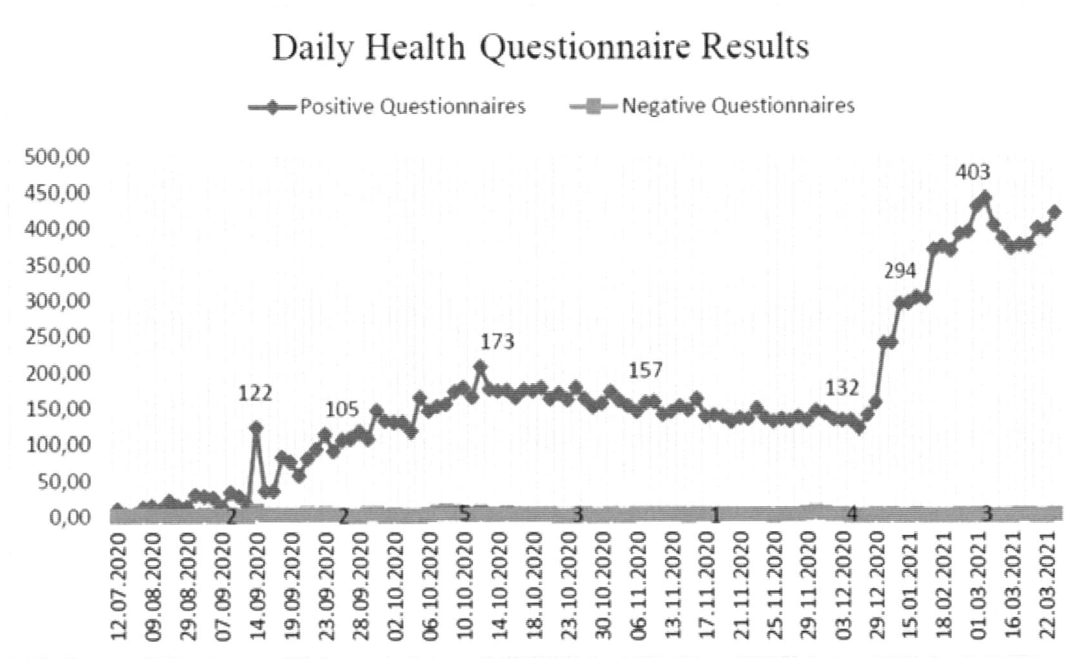

Figure 6. Daily Positive and Negative Questionnaires

3.2 Future Developments

Health monitoring of vaccinated employees, health training for employees and direct access to the institution doctor via the application as a telemedicine application are considered and planned for future developments.

ACKNOWLEDGEMENT

This work has been realized in the context of research and development works at Koçtaş Construction Market Incorporated Company.

REFERENCES

Adans-Dester, C.,P. et al., 2020. Can mHealth Technology Help Mitigate the Effects of the COVID-19 Pandemic?, *In IEEE Open Journal of Engineering in Medicine and Biology*, Vol. 1, pp. 243-248.

App service overview, Microsoft, viewed 27 March 2021, <https://docs.microsoft.com/en-us/azure/app-service/overview/>.

Codd, E., F., 1970. A Relational Model of Data for Large Shared Data Banks, *In Communications of the ACM*, Vol. 13, No. 6, pp. 377–387.

Fetch API, Mozilla, viewed 27 March 2021, <https://developer.mozilla.org/en-US/docs/Web/API/Fetch_API>.

Jiménez-Serrano, S. et al, 2015. A Mobile Health Application to Predict Postpartum Depression Based on Machine Learning, *In Telemedicine and e-Health*, Vol. 21, No. 7, pp. 567-574.

JPA vs. Hibernate, Javatpoint, viewed 27 March 2021, <https://www.javatpoint.com/jpa-vs-hibernate>.

Royal Society 2006. *Digital Healthcare: The impact of information and communication technologies on health and healthcare*, Royal Society, viewed 27 March 2021, <https://royalsociety.org/-/media/Royal_Society_Content/policy/publications/2006/8218.pdf >.

Spring Boot - Introduction, Tutorialspoint, viewed 27 March 2021, <https://www.tutorialspoint.com/spring_boot/spring_boot_introduction.htm>.

Toygar, Ş., A., 2018. E-Sağlık Uygulamaları, *In Yasama Dergisi*, Vol. 37, pp. 101-123.

Veazie, S. et al, 2018. Rapid Evidence Review of Mobile Applications for Self-management of Diabetes, *In Journal of General Internal Medicine*, Vol. 33, pp. 1167–1176.

What is Flutter?, Flutter, viewed 27 March 2021, <https://flutter.dev/docs/resources/faq#what-is-flutter>.

A CANCER PATIENT RECOMMENDER SYSTEM FOR MANAGING END-OF-LIFE DECISION MAKING

Raghav Pavan Karumur
University of Minnesota, Twin Cities, MN, USA 55455

ABSTRACT

Cancer is the leading cause of death across the world. Most cancer patients get diagnosed in advanced stages, and in most cases, there is no full cure. Once diagnosed, cancer patients suffer from a variety of disorders that can lead to physical, mental, and emotional trauma. In most cases, the patient symptoms are not adequately addressed. Moreover, today's technology does not allow oncologists and clinicians to accurately estimate the patient survival time. In most countries, the end-of-life care expenditure can also be significantly high. However, research shows that palliative care and hospice services offered early in the disease trajectory can significantly bring down end-of-life care expenditures and improve the quality of care. This paper presents the design of a Cancer patient end-of-life care recommender system and primarily focuses on its various components. Using the lens of one of my studies performed in the context of Ovarian Cancer patients, in this paper, I try to establish the usefulness of such a recommender system's various components in light of other contemporary studies that have shown success using these individual tools.

KEYWORDS

Decision-Support, Recommender System, Web Intervention, Cancer

1. INTRODUCTION

Prior research and the World Health Organization (WHO) statistics from 2019 show Cancer as the first or second leading cause of death among people, and an important barrier in improving the life expectancy of people across the world. A GLOBOCAN report for 36 different types of cancers in 185 countries worldwide estimates 10 million cancer deaths worldwide and 19.3 million new cases in 2020 (Bray, 2020). Assuming the national rates estimated remain constant for the various countries, by 2040, the number of cancer-related deaths is expected to rise to 16.4 million, and the number of new cases is expected to rise to 29.5 million (National Cancer Institute, 2020). And cancer equally affects people of all genders. For most types of cancers, the precise causes are currently unknown and often, their symptoms are vague. Most get diagnosed at an advanced stage. There is a high risk for recurrence and in most cases of recurrence, the patients cannot be completely cured.

In the United States alone, the number of cancer-related deaths is estimated to be at 0.6 million people and the number of new diagnoses is expected to be at 1.8 million for 2020. The number of cancer survivors was estimated to be around 16.9 million by the end of 2018. The number is projected to be at 22.2 million by 2030.

End-of-life care is 10-12% of all national annual healthcare expenditures and about 25-27% of Medicare expenditures are spent on patients during the last two months of their life (Emanuel, 1996; Riley, 1993; Lubitz, 1993). In 2018, these national expenditures associated with cancer treatment and end-of-life care were estimated to be at $150.8 billion (National Cancer Institute, 2020). In addition, significant psychological burden and emotional distress are associated with cancer diagnosis (Arriba, 2010) and these are known to persist beyond diagnosis and treatment with anywhere between 35% to 60% of the patients experiencing distress after diagnosis (Mitchell et al, 2011).

Some studies have shown that palliative care and hospice services offered early in the disease trajectory can improve the quality of care and significantly bring down the end-of-life care expenditures. Some researchers found a significant cost difference between cancer patients treated aggressively and those that sought supportive care such as hospice. The mean cost savings per physician per patient ranged from $34,677 to $112,707 (the range being a result of differences in individual practice patterns). Additionally, some researchers found that patients not enrolled in hospice were more likely to undergo an invasive procedure within a month of their closing moments. Although there are benefits associated with supportive care, most patients are not aware of such services until the fag end of their life. For instance, for 2008, the National Hospice and Palliative Care Organization (NHPCO, 2010) estimates that the median length of service was only three weeks, which means that half of the hospice patients received end-of-life care only for about three weeks!

Palliative care involves addressing physical, intellectual, emotional, social, and spiritual needs related to an illness. It also facilitates patient autonomy, access to information, and choice thereby improving the quality of life. This kind of care is provided by a multidisciplinary team made up of medical practitioners, nurses, social workers, and spiritual counselors, and is, often, offered in conjunction with all other appropriate forms of medical treatment. Cancer patients have significant physical, psychosocial, and spiritual needs for holistic care at a manageable expense from diagnosis through survivorship and end-of-life care. (CMS, 2008; WHO, 2002) This being the case, palliative care is well-positioned to address most of the symptoms that cancer patients experience throughout their disease and supports them in their journey. However, because few physicians have the adequate communication skills needed to discuss palliative care and end of life issues, expert palliative care is not currently a standard of care in treatment protocol and is not used early enough. While there is anecdotal and growing research support for the value of palliative care, evidence demonstrating sound methodology and definitive results is scarce (Petzel et al., 2009).

Thus, there are gaps in the current health care system regarding the available information and supportive resources throughout the cancer disease trajectory. The net effect of a diagnosis of cancer is that in most patients this disease has drastically poor outcomes and will result in death. For patients and family, ultimately decisions will be made surrounding end-of-life care. Despite the goal of palliative care and hospice to provide compassionate, holistic care for patients, and their families and to maximize their quality of life, most patients do not receive palliative care or hospice information until they are close to death. This approach to the end of life and the important decisions that surround this time is inadequate often making patients and their family members feel abandoned, frightened or unsure about the decisions they have to make.

This paper is based on a study that was conducted to improve end-of-life cancer management through technology. Patients and caregivers were provided with an interactive, innovative health aware recommender system (Schäfer et al., 2017) that allows access to information and decision support earlier in the disease trajectory. They were presented with information on palliative care and hospice at the time of diagnosis and at the time of their first recurrence, much earlier than this information is usually presented to them. This approach differs from the status quo in that it promotes interdisciplinary, holistic, less-expensive care for cancer patients and involves them and their caregivers much earlier in the clinical decision-making process surrounding end of life issues. This research is aimed at advancing the field of palliative care and oncology as the greater understanding of options will improve outcomes and reduce costs and thereby drastically reduce the burden of cancer on patients, families and society.

To control and tease out the effects, the study was limited to one population of Cancer patients suffering from Ovarian Cancer. The current paper primarily focuses on the design aspects of the cancer-related recommender system for making end-of-life decision making in Ovarian cancer patients. While there is already prior published work related to this stream of research (McClellan et al 2016), this paper primarily focuses on the design and the various components of the recommender system for the benefit of researchers.

2. BACKGROUND

Ovarian Cancer is the second most common cause of death from cancer in women in the United States (Center for Disease Control, 2021). It is one of the most pernicious forms of cancer with the highest incidence in Africa, Europe, and North America. About 70% get diagnosed at an advanced stage (Stage III-IV). The estimated five-year survival is 45% for all stages of disease, and this becomes as low as 18% for Stage IV (American Cancer Society, 2008). There is a 60-70% risk for recurrence and women who recur currently cannot be cured.

Symptoms such as abnormal menstrual cycles, and digestive symptoms such as constipation, increased bloating, indigestion, lack of appetite, nausea and vomiting, unexplained back pain that worsens over time, vaginal bleeding between periods, unusual weight gain or loss, excessive hair growth that is coarse and dark, sudden urge to urinate, and needing to urinate more often than usual may be indications of ovarian cancer. Because these symptoms are also common in women who do not have ovarian cancer, the majority of cases are diagnosed late. By the time the cancer is diagnosed, the tumor often spreads beyond the ovaries.

Also, no lab or imaging test has ever been shown to be able to screen for or diagnose ovarian cancer in its early stages. A physical examination or surgery such as a pelvic laparoscopy or exploratory laparotomy, ultrasound, X-rays, the CA-125 blood test may be done to evaluate symptoms and perform a biopsy to help make the diagnosis and determine staging. Only about 20% of the women are diagnosed early, when the disease may be curable.

Patients with ovarian cancer are commonly impacted by symptom clusters including but not limited to fatigue, anxiety, pain, bloating, bowel disturbances, nausea and vomiting, anorexia, and depression (Bankhead et al. 2005). Long time effects of survivors include surgical menopause, gender and role identity disturbances, peripheral neuropathy, cognitive dysfunction, and decreased quality of life related to fears of recurrence, sexual dysfunction, depression, and employability and symptoms are undertreated in 16-49% of survivors (Koldjeski, 2007; Le, 2003, 2005; Lockwood-Rayermann, 2006). In a study by Stone et al. (2000), more than half of the participants ranked cancer-related fatigue worse than anxiety, pain, and nausea/vomiting. However, in 59% of them, cancer-related fatigue goes unreported to oncologists, while 53% never receive counseling from oncologists on how to treat fatigue (Donovan and Ward, 2005). This calls for the necessity of access to a multidisciplinary palliative care team.

Critical questions persist concerning the decision-making processes involved. For example, how women approach palliative care and hospice at different times during their disease trajectory and what might be done to assist women with ovarian cancer in making decisions surrounding palliative care and the end-of-life. This confirms the need for rigorous study of how women with ovarian cancer use palliative care and hospice information and support at different times from diagnosis through end-of-life care.

Research studies have shown that about 80% of adult web users have searched online for health information and seniors on the internet are the fastest growing internet population. Most Ovarian cancer patients want to be aware, informed and are in need of constant social support. In general, they suffer from loss of memory, difficulty in remembering, anxiety. They look for similar people to connect and share their thoughts. So, an online forum serves this purpose the best.

Also, most existing websites either present heavy text-based information, or information that is not timed to the patient's stage of disease or emotional state at the time they access the information, and lack proper discussion forums, or existing forums are not well-maintained. Many questions never get answered, and some of them present conflicting information because of lack of moderators.

Given these constraints, an online portal was designed for Cancer patients that provides holistic care and supports the end-of-life decision-making in collaboration with oncologists from Fairview Masonic Cancer Clinic, psychologists, decision support system experts, and usability experts. The portal was designed with interactive controls and resources tailored to the phase of the disease. The portal comprised of multiple modules such as a content management system, a social networking platform, a scheduling system, and distress monitoring system. This paper is primarily focused on describing the various components of this portal.

The objective was to design and pilot-test a technology-based approach for recurrent ovarian cancer patients, families, and their providers to assist in and study the decision-making process that surrounds end-of-life decisions, specifically things such as entry into hospice care. The central scientific hypothesis is that an interactive web-based system designed with and for patients, families, and providers that can provide support and tailor information to women's needs at the end-of-life will increase the number of patients electing to use hospice care and at a time point earlier in the course of their disease and will result in improved outcomes for patients and their families in terms of better quality of life.

Women with advanced stage ovarian cancer at the time of diagnosis and at recurrence were planned to be recruited and a pilot evaluation study was designed using a longitudinal, before, during, and after, experimental design with two arms – a control group and an intervention group. All subjects were to complete a battery of demographic, psychosocial, health status and outcomes, health information, and decision-making measures at baseline and 30-day post-baseline. Primary patient data was planned to be complemented with continuous data automatically collected by the system as well as clinical data from medical records. In order to develop useful guidelines for these discussions, reliable data about the prognostic indicators and an understanding of the psychological factors surrounding patient preferences and decisions are necessary.

The intervention group was to be presented with a wide gamut of resources and tools in a customized way while the control group will have access to all the documents presented to the intervention group, but with no customization. The study was aimed primarily at understanding how the behavior of patients exposed to controlled and customized content varies from those that are presented with random content. Therefore, I have developed two different portals – one for the control group patients with the least amount of customization, and the other for the intervention group patients with maximum amount of customization. Along with these, I have developed two other portals – one for the patient's caregiver and one for the clinician whom the patient visits. While the caregiver has a portal similar to that of the intervention group patient whom they are caregiving, both the caregiver as well as the clinician are presented with a summary view of how the patient's end-of-life behavior is changing as is being intervened by the currently designed portal.

3. IMPLEMENTATION

3.1 Key Elements of the Recommender System

The system was originally envisioned to have a look and feel similar to popular social networking websites and blogs. This would mean including features that allow users to create and modify their own profile, connect with peers, and post to discussion forms. Profile fields were seeded to encourage participants to address specific issues of living with ovarian cancer. In addition to social networking features, core intervention components such as medication, appointment, and symptom monitoring would be made available, providing tailored feedback on disease and psychological health.

Our aim was to design a creative user interface that is intuitive and optimized for patients at every level/stage of illness. During the design events, we have learned that the patients needed an all-the-time access to their families, caregivers and healthcare team during their end-of-life. This motivated us to bring the three categories of people together, having three subdivisions within our portal – one for patients, one for their caregivers and one for the physicians. While each of them has space for their own journaling and participation in forum discussions, they also can mutually interact with one another.

Many patients have indicated that they wanted a way to easily keep track of past appointment dates with summaries, current and upcoming appointments. This has motivated us to provide access to a calendar, that they can use to quickly browse through their appointments.

Studies on cancer patients found that 62.5% preferred participating in clinical decisions (Cassileth BR, et al., 1980) and that younger patients were significantly more likely to desire participation that were patients over age 60. Other studies however found that in the context of cancer, a majority of patients preferred their physician to make treatment decisions on their behalf (Degner and Sloan, 1992; Sutherland, 1989). Still another study of breast cancer patients found that two thirds preferred autonomous or collaborative treatment decision making (Degner, 1997). In order to make the decision-making process easier, we have provided a section called "Action Plan" which facilitates the users to maintain a quick list of items they need to make decisions on.

Critical questions persist concerning the decision-making processes involved. For example, how women actually approach palliative care and hospice at different times during their disease trajectory and what might be done to assist women with ovarian cancer in making decisions surrounding palliative care and the end-of-life. Therefore, we believe that the data collected from these action plan items could help us better understand the decision-making process surrounding palliative care and the end-of-life.

According to Zimmermann et al., (2008), cancer patients have significant physical, psychosocial, and spiritual needs for palliative care from "diagnosis through survivorship and end-of-life care". To address this, we have provided access to a rich library of topics and resources called "Learning Library" categorized into eight major families – (1) Palliative Care, (2) Decision Making (3) Understanding Ovarian Cancer, (4) Practical Considerations, (5) Emotional Well-being, (6) Physical Well-being, (7) Social Support, and (8) Communication.

Furthermore, a selected list of topics relevant to the patient based on their stage of disease is presented in the "Recommended topics" section. We have basically identified four categories of patients, namely – newly diagnosed, recurrent, multiply recurrent and remission. Each is presented with their own set of recommended topics.

Often times cancer patients are unable to speak for themselves due to sudden medical crisis. Hence, they often choose to nominate a person to make healthcare decisions on their behalf in case they become unable to make or communicate their decisions. These nominations are usually done using a form called "Advance Healthcare directive". We have included this along with the instructions to fill this out in our website.

A distress thermometer is a validated tool used to monitor one's psychological distress level. Use of this tool is important in cancer related distress as often this is not recognized by cancer care providers, although it is present in the patients. The drawback of this is that when it is not recognized, it is likely that interventions known to reduce their distress will not occur. And increased distress is related to several negative outcomes for patients, including poorer satisfaction with care, lower follow through with treatment recommendations and poorer quality of life. Therefore, we have provided a distress thermometer for the patients to periodically record their distress levels along with the factors contributing to the distress. There is also a provision for the patients to let their providers and caregivers view their distress levels and factors using a stress graph.

Also provided in this portal are sections for patients to vent their feelings and thoughts through social networking. Journaling is an expressive way of writing very personally about emotional and/or stressful experiences and research demonstrates that it can have beneficial effects on emotional well-being and physical wealth. Writing about an upsetting event such as cancer can limit its impact in several ways by (a) providing a new understanding of cancer experience to the patients. (b) helping them limit possible threatening thoughts or images (c) encouraging positive expectations (d) improving sleep and increasing functioning during the day in case of some advance-disease cancer patients and so on. It is often times helpful to write about one's positive responses to illness, such as finding benefit in their cancer experience. Hence, we have provided active ways for patients to journal and communicate with their caregivers.

Ovarian cancer patients (cancer patients in general) look for solace in the form of support groups and forums to exchange ideas with similar women or those that have similar experiences. Research shows that based on common experiences, women who discuss may help others understand their illness differently and how to combat against it. It also helps them understand in ways that friends, family and providers haven't provided. Hence, we have provided discussion forums that represent using social media to share, interact and communicate with similar groups of women having similar experiences.

Clinical trials are research studies focused on finding ways to improve health and cancer care. Each study tries to answer scientific questions relating to the prevention, diagnosis, or treatment cancer. We have also included a section on clinical trials along with suitable decision aids regarding clinical trials.

Some of the key components are listed below

Calendar A calendar has been provided to the patients for easily keep track of past appointment dates with summaries, current and upcoming appointments. They can enter their medical appointments as well as other important appointments.

Action Plan It is a place for the patients to have their own to-do items which can be added from within various topics by clicking on one or more of the suggested action plan items as shown below:

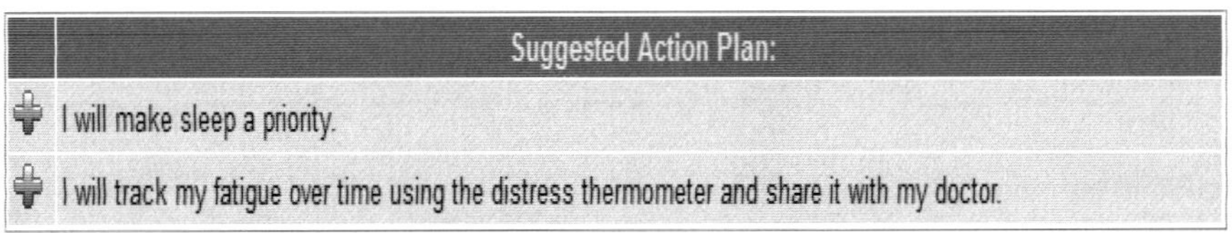

Figure 1. A snapshot of the Patient's Suggested Action Plan

Learning Library A place where the patients have a list of recommended readings for them based on their stage of disease, followed by the full library of educational topics. A quick list of this is also provided on the patient home page as shown below:

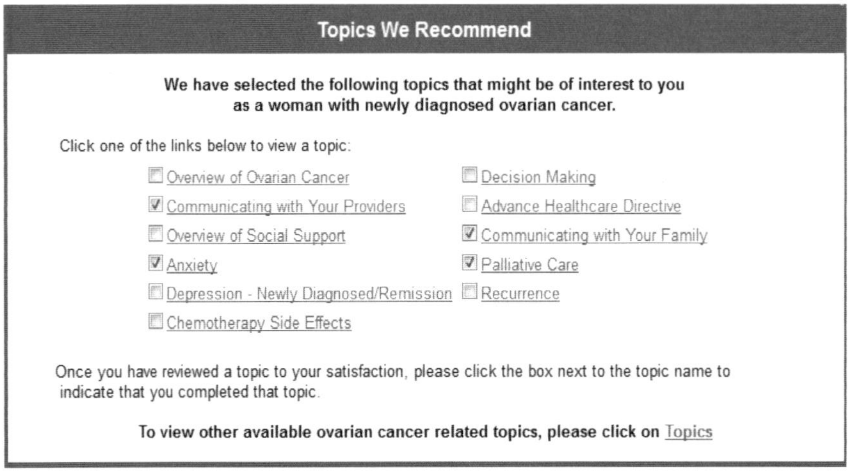

Figure 2. A snapshot of the recommended topics to the patients

Distress Thermometer This is a place where the patients can use a thermometer to enter and track their levels of distress over time. Along with the thermometer, the patients are presented with a list of factors they can choose from, that have contributed to their distress in the past week including that day. They also have an option to view a summarized list of factors that contributed to distress, along with a graph depicting their distress levels during the course of the study. On the other hand, both the caregiver and the clinician are presented with a summary view of how the patient's end-of-life behavior is changing as is being intervened by our portal.

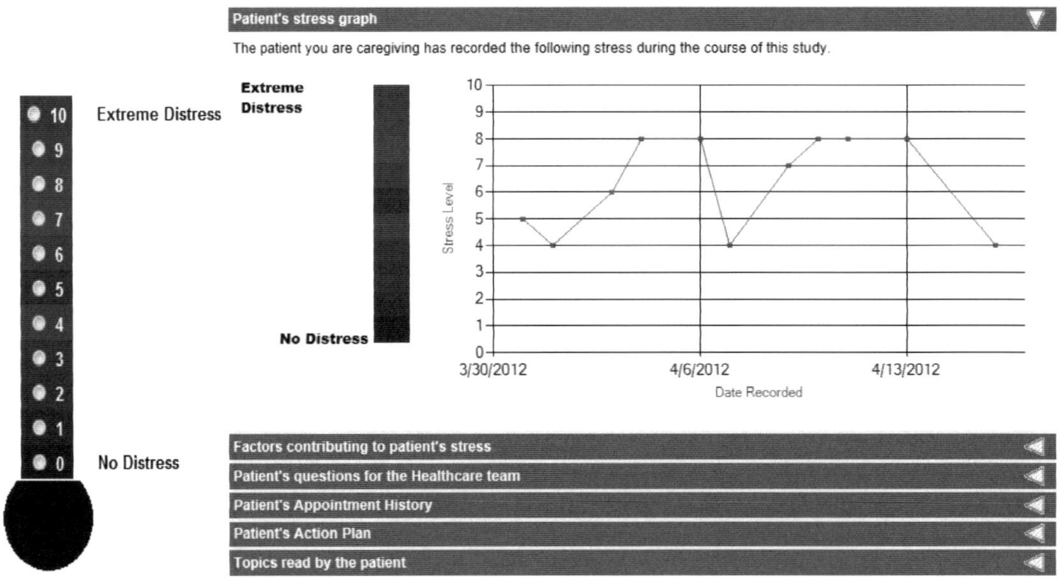

Figure 3. Snapshots of the Patient's Distress Thermometer and the Distress Graph

Journal and Discussion Forum The journal is a place where the patients can write about how they are feeling. They have an option to keep it private or share it with their caregiver. The Discussion Forum is a public avenue to post questions and share thoughts with other woman having ovarian cancer.

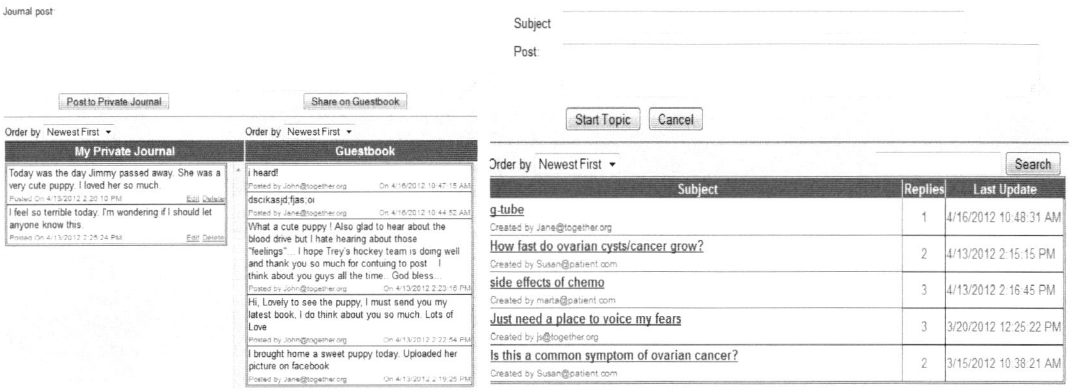

Figure 4. Snapshots of the Patient's Journal and Discussion Forum

Glossary This is an index of terms and definitions found in this website

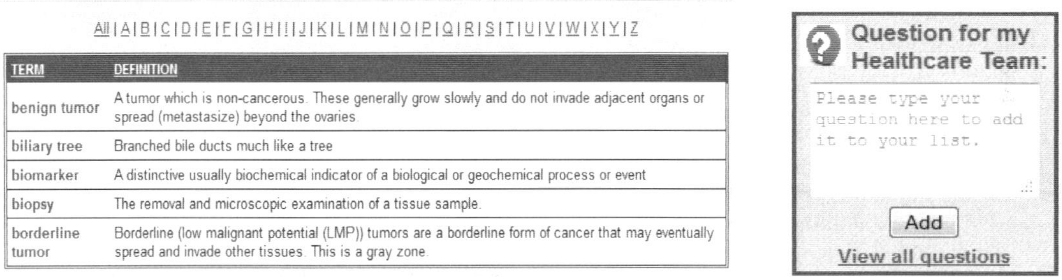

Figure 5. A snapshot of the Patient's Glossary list

3.1.1 Healthcare Team and Questions for the Healthcare Team

This contains access to the multidisciplinary palliative care team made up of medical practitioners, nurses, social workers, spiritual counselors. The Questions section can be used by the patients to write down questions they always wanted to ask their providers.

4. CONCLUSION

To address the challenges associated with end-of-life care such as insufficiently addressed symptoms, lack of supportive care for a significant portion, and substantially high expenditures, an end-of-life cancer recommender system was designed to support patients through their cancer journey. This paper is part of a stream of research publications which focuses only on the elements of the design of the recommender system. For the details related to the usability testing of this tool, the readers of this work are requested to refer to McClellan, M.A (2016).

ACKNOWLEDGEMENT

I would like to acknowledge the gynecological oncology team at the University of Minnesota that assisted me with my development of this portal and funded my research through a grant from the Academic Health Center.

REFERENCES

American Cancer Society. Cancer Facts and Figures 2008. Atlanta: American Cancer Society; 2008.

Arriba, L.N., 2010. A review of issues surrounding quality of life among women with ovarian cancer. Gynecologic oncology, 119(2), pp.390-396.

Bankhead et al. 2005. Symptoms associated with diagnosis of ovarian cancer: a systematic review. BJOG, 112; 857-865.

Bray, F., 2020. Erratum: Global cancer statistics 2018: GLOBOCAN estimates of incidence and mortality worldwide for 36 cancers in 185 countries. CA Cancer J Clin, 70(4), p.313.

Cassileth BR, et al. 1980. Information and participation preferences among cancer patients. Ann Intern Med. 1980; 92: 832-836.

Center for Disease Control, 2021. https://www.cdc.gov/cancer/ovarian/statistics/index.htm

Centers for Medicare & Medicaid Services (CMS) 2008, p.2204. Center to Advance Palliative Care. Defining palliative care. Retrieved Dec 23, 2008, from http://www.capc.org/building-a-hospital-based-palliative-care-program/case/definingpc/

Degner LF and J Sloan. 1992. Decision making during serious illness: What role do patients want to play?. J Clin Epidemiol 45, pp. 941–950.

Degner LF, et al. 1997. Information needs and decisional preferences in women with breast cancer. JAMA; 277(18): 1485-1492.

Donovan, H.S., & Ward, S. 2005. Representations of fatigue in women receiving chemotherapy for gynecologic cancers. Oncology Nursing Forum, 32, 113-116. doi: 10.1188/05.ONF.113-116

Emanuel EJ. 1996. Cost savings at the end of life. What do the data show? Jama ;275: 1907-14.

Koldjeski, D et al. 2007. Families coping with cancer. Cancer Nursing,

Le, T et al. 2005. Quality of life assessments in epithelial ovarian cancer patients during and after chemotherapy. International Journal of Gynecological Cancer, 15, 811-816.

Le, T et al. 2003. Quality-of-life issues in patients with ovarian cancer and their caregivers: A review. Obstetrical and Gynecological Survey, 58(11), 749-758.

Lockwood-Rayermann, S. 2006. Survivorship issues in ovarian cancer: A review. Oncology Nursing Forum, 33(3), 553-562.

Lubitz JD, Riley GF. 1993. Trends in Medicare payments in the last year of life. N Engl J Med;328: 1092-6.

Stone, P., et al. 2000. Cancer- related fatigue: inevitable, unimportant and untreatable? Results of a multi-center patient survey. Cancer Fatigue Forum Annals of Oncology 11: 8, 971-975.

McClellan, M.A., et al. 2016. Designing an educational website to improve quality of supportive oncology care for women with ovarian cancer: an expert usability review and analysis. International journal of human-computer interaction, 32(4), pp.297-307.

Mitchell, A. J., et al. 2011. Prevalence of depression, anxiety, and adjustment disorder in oncological, hematological, and palliative-care settings: a meta-analysis of 94 interview-based studies. The lancet oncology, 12(2), 160-174.

National Cancer Institute. Cancer Statistics 2020. https://www.cancer.gov/about-cancer/understanding/statistics

NHPCO, www.nhpco.org/nds, accessed online on March 9, 2010.

Ovarian Cancer, A.D.A.M Medical Encyclopedia, U.S. National Library of Medicine

Petzel S et al. Learning about cancer: Pros and cons. Psychosomatic Medicine. 2009;71(3): A30.

Schäfer, H., et al. 2017. Towards health (aware) recommender systems. In Proceedings of the 2017 international conference on digital health (pp. 157-161).

World Health Organization 2002. WHO definition of palliative care. Retrieved April 13, 2008 from http://www.who.int/cancer/palliative/definition/en/

Zimmermann, C, et al. Effectiveness of specialized palliative care: A systematic review. Journal of the American Medical Association. 2008;299(14):1698-1709.

HARNESSING TECHNOLOGY TO RESPOND TO THE GLOBAL DEMAND FOR LEARNING DURING THE COVID-19 PANDEMIC

Richelle George[1], Heini Utunen[1], Christian Willems[2], Ngouille Ndiaye[1], Stefanie Schweiger[2], Thomas Staubitz[2], Anna Tokar[1], Melissa Attias[1], Oliver Stucke[1] and Gaya Gamhewage[1]
[1]World Health Organization, Avenue Appia 20, 1202 Genève, Switzerland
[2]Hasso-Plattner-Institut für Digital Engineering gGmbH, Prof.-Dr.-Helmert-Str. 2-3, D-14482 Potsdam, Germany

ABSTRACT

The COVID-19 pandemic generated an unprecedented global demand for learning about the disease and how to manage it. This paper draws on the World Health Organization (WHO)'s experience of COVID-19 knowledge-transfer to a worldwide audience of millions of learners registered on OpenWHO, WHO's massive open online course platform. It aims to illustrate the technological solutions that WHO, in collaboration with the Hasso Plattner Institute (HPI), OpenWHO's platform provider, employed in response to the unique challenges this surge in demand for learning engendered. Data on OpenWHO use, including geographic patterns and certificate attainment, were extracted from OpenWHO's internal and external reporting systems. Descriptive analysis was employed to identify trends and compare OpenWHO use with COVID-19 caseload in each WHO region. Data on the OpenWHO system load were obtained from the OpenWHO load balancer (HAProxy). The OpenWHO team responded to the need for trustworthy, evidence-based knowledge on COVID-19 via three main avenues: increased scale, targeting the needs of affected and underserved communities, and prioritising multilingualism. Each approach brought novel problems, which WHO and HPI leveraged their collaboration to meet by employing technology. This included increasing server bandwidth, expanding support teams, adding new language capabilities, and deploying functions to streamline workflows and boost learner experience. In doing so, the ability to effectively and efficiently harness technology became a critical step towards empowering learning's life-saving potential during the COVID-19 pandemic.

KEYWORDS

MOOC, e-Learning, World Health Organization, Hasso Plattner Institute, COVID-19, Technology-Enhanced Learning

1. INTRODUCTION

The World Health Organization Health Emergencies Programme Learning and Capacity Development (LCD) team launched the OpenWHO platform in 2017 to facilitate the transfer of public health knowledge for emergencies on a massive scale, anticipating the next pandemic. Grounded in open access and equity principles, the LCD team offered free, self-paced courses, accessible in low-bandwidth and offline formats, and available in national and local languages. While the platform served front-line responders in previous outbreaks from Ebola to plague, 2020 marked its first pandemic test.

In 2012, the year of the massive open online course (MOOC) (Pappano, 2012), the Hasso Plattner Institute (HPI), a privately financed university institute focusing on the engineering of complex information technology (IT) systems, launched openHPI, the first European platform for MOOCs. Since then, it has offered free access to current university knowledge from the rapidly changing IT and innovation fields. In that time, openHPI has registered more than 900,000 course enrolments. More than 260,000 people from 180 countries belong to the platform's permanent user base. The scalable platform infrastructure of openHPI was the basis for the cooperation with partners such as SAP (for the first Enterprise MOOC platform, openSAP) and the World Health Organization (WHO).

The LCD team began collaborating with HPI in 2016 to develop and run the online learning platform that would become OpenWHO. WHO had three requirements of the platform HPI would provide: it had to be accessible to all, have a global reach, and the ability to upscale, withstanding the traffic of millions of learners in the event of a worldwide health emergency such as a pandemic. An open tender process determined that HPI's technology would meet these needs, offering a highly scalable infrastructure accessible via desktop and mobile browsers (and a mobile app) and suitable to use in areas with reduced internet connectivity. HPI's approach had already proven to be successful in running MOOC platforms such as openSAP and openHPI.

The COVID-19 pandemic has altered how people conduct their lives, and the extent to which may only be apparent in years to come. There has been a shift towards e-learning and an urgent need to educate and engage health care professionals, communities and the general public (Aldohyan et al., 2019; Fernández-Díaz et al., 2020; Chick et al., 2020; Zitzmann et al., 2020). Digital learning has effectively increased public health professionals' knowledge (Brown et al., 2020; Martinengo et al., 2019; Tudor Car et al., 2019; Vaona et al., 2018), rivalling the efficacy of traditional learning methods (Tudor Car et al., 2019).

Digital approaches to learning are more intuitive and interactive, facilitating students' continuous participation (Zitzmann et al., 2020) and contributing to lifelong learning, helping learners achieve better practical outcomes due to their context-specific nature (Regmi and Jones, 2020). By allowing students to work at their own pace, digital learning is more flexible, self-directive, and inclusive. As a result, digital learning can be a means to educate the adult population that is less likely to force them to choose between their professional or familial lives and a return to education (Zitzmann et al., 2020; Martinengo et al., 2019; Regmi and Jones, 2020; Carapeto and Barros, 2019).

This paper aims to examine how technological solutions deployed by HPI enabled the OpenWHO team to meet the immense global demand for evidence-based learning on COVID-19.

2. METHODS

Data on historical patterns in OpenWHO use, including enrolment trends, certificate attainment and the number of COVID-19 courses and languages, were obtained from OpenWHO's in-built reporting system. A descriptive statistical analysis was conducted in Microsoft Excel to identify trends. The data reflects OpenWHO use between January 2020 and January 2021 to provide insight into the first year of pandemic response on OpenWHO.

Data on geographic trends in learner activity were retrieved from Google Analytics and consist of the cumulative number of web sessions on OpenWHO by country. As measured by Google Analytics, a web session refers to the period a user actively engages with the OpenWHO platform. The data spans from December 2019 to December 2020. The data were aggregated according to the six WHO regions (African, Americas, Eastern Mediterranean, European, South-East Asian and Western Pacific). This data was subsequently merged with a dataset covering the same period extracted from the WHO COVID-19 Dashboard (World Health Organization, 2020), which records the cumulative number of confirmed COVID-19 cases worldwide.

System load data were extracted from the OpenWHO load balancer (HAProxy). It reflects the non-negative derivation of the request counter from the load balancer. The load balancer counted all requests, and the information was collected from the counter every 10 seconds. The data were used to visualise the request rate, covering 25 February to 23 March 2020. For every pixel (longer than 60 seconds), the most significant requests per minute (rpm) was displayed.

3. RESULTS

The OpenWHO team responded to the significant global demand for learning about COVID-19 in three ways:

1. By rapidly scaling up the production and dissemination of COVID-19 learning materials, drawing crowds of new users to the platform
2. By serving vulnerable populations
3. By widening access to learning through offering courses in the national and local languages of communities affected by COVID-19

The technological innovation and advancements executed by the Hasso Plattner Institute were critical in enabling all three aspects.

3.1 Upscaling OpenWHO Platform Capacity

OpenWHO built on the collaborative systems already in place within WHO to quickly scale up course production for the pandemic, making life-saving information from WHO experts available online at a time when lockdowns and social distancing limited the ability to unite for face-to-face learning. The first COVID-19 course launched on 26 January 2020, even before the outbreak was declared a public health emergency of international concern.

Since late January 2020, the OpenWHO team has worked with more than 50 WHO experts to produce 25 COVID-19 courses – covering everything from infection prevention and control to risk assessment for mass gatherings – which are updated as new guidance and tools become available. As working from home increased during the pandemic, the OpenWHO team devised new protocols for remote audio-visual production, allowing courses to be launched in real-time, even as the pandemic evolved.

Mainly fuelled by the COVID-19 courses, traffic to OpenWHO grew exponentially (+2900%) in one year of responding to the pandemic. Total enrolments increased from 160,000 in January 2020 to 4.8 million in January 2021 (Figure 1). Such a massive surge in users was also uncharted territory for the HPI team.

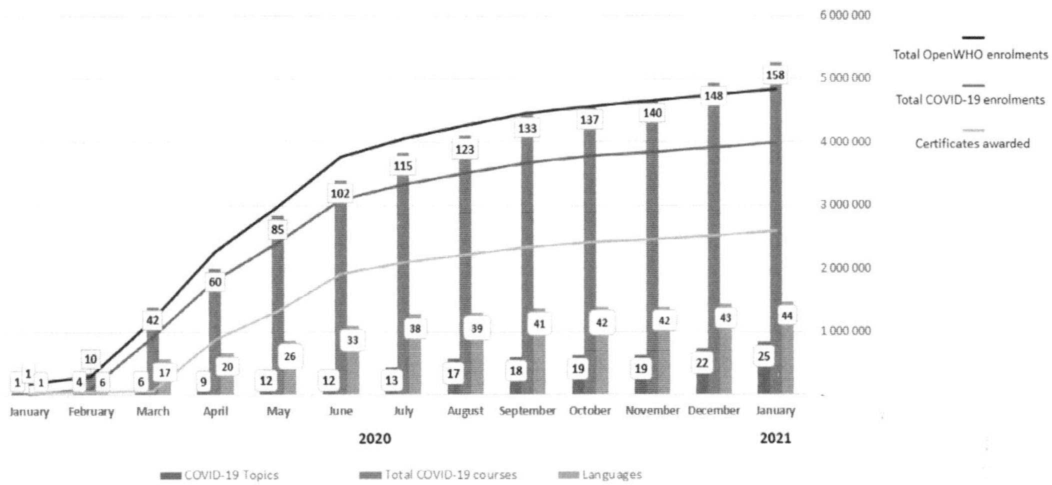

Figure 1. Growth in total OpenWHO enrolments, COVID-19 course enrolments and certificates awarded by the platform, alongside the growth in COVID-19 course and language offerings

Before it launched its first COVID-19 course, the OpenWHO platform saw a baseline load from 300 to 1,000 rpm. Between 24 January (two days before the first COVID-19 course launched) and 25 February 2020, this increased to approximately 1,000 rpm with peaks at 2,500 rpm. 25 February was a turning point, as the number of attempts to access the platform doubled. The baseline load now lay between 2,000 and 2,500 rpm with peaks between 4,000 to 5,000 rpm. The requests increased exponentially from 15 March onwards, coming in at a minimum of 5,000 rpm, up to 15,000 and at times 20,000 rpm. Since then, the platform has witnessed peaks of well over 30,000 rpm, and 15,000 rpm during relatively idle phases, constituting a total increase in the range of 30 times the number of requests to the OpenWHO servers (Figure 2).

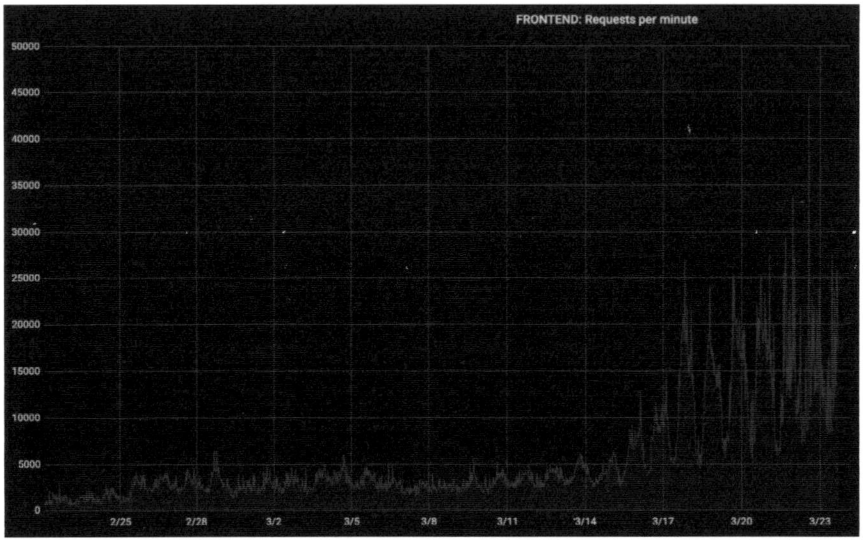

Figure 2. Requests per minute on the OpenWHO server between 25 February and 23 March 2020

The increased load led to HPI implementing several emergency measures to keep the system running stably and smoothly. The existing bandwidth of the servers' Internet connection had to be swiftly increased from 100 to 1,000 Mbit/s. Due to the urgency of the situation and the pandemic's fast-evolving seriousness, HPI sidestepped the lengthy processes that would typically be involved in scheduling an appointment with a technician who would implement the bandwidth increase.

The scalable infrastructure of the OpenWHO platform was also critical in withstanding the massive change in load. Since HPI runs the OpenWHO platform in an OpenStack-based private cloud infrastructure, new virtual servers could easily be added (Figure 3).

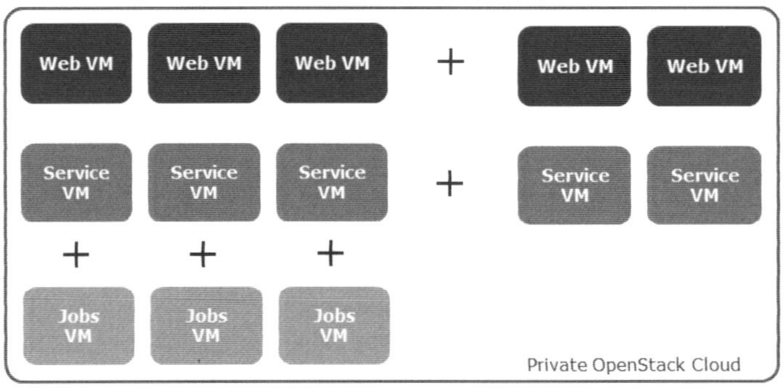

Figure 3. Scaling the OpenWHO infrastructure

Given that OpenWHO's load baseline rarely drops below 10,000 rpm, it would be safe to assume a very international audience, geographically dispersed across all time zones. This differs from other HPI-run MOOC platforms, where peak traffic times coincide with the European daytime.

3.2 Serving the Vulnerable

When examining OpenWHO activity in the six WHO regions, compared with the burden of COVID-19 in these regions, it is evident that OpenWHO platform use correlates with COVID-19 caseload (Figure 4).

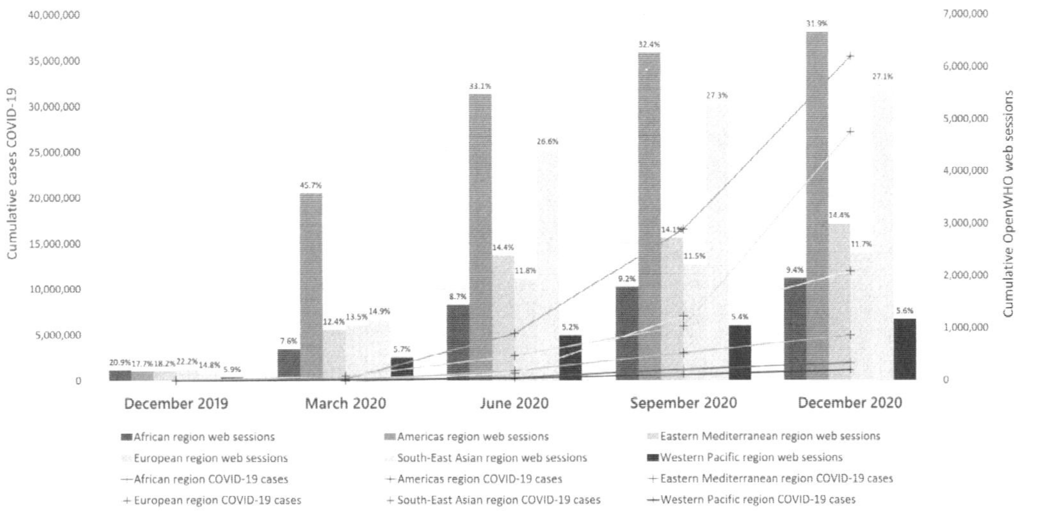

Figure 4. COVID-19 case burden and OpenWHO use by WHO region for each trimester between December 2019 and December 2020

In December 2019, the WHO African Region accounted for 20.9% of global OpenWHO web sessions and was second only to the European Region, which made up 22.2%. As the pandemic took hold in March 2020, the African Region's proportion fell to 7.6%, while the Americas Region increased to 45.7% from 17.7% in the previous quarter. The Americas Region has continued to see the highest levels of OpenWHO use throughout 2020, while also being the WHO region with the highest number of COVID-19 cases in the same period. Likewise, the WHO regions of Africa and the Western-Pacific had the lowest COVID-19 caseload and were also the two regions with the least OpenWHO activity in 2020. The three other WHO regions, the Eastern Mediterranean, European and South-East Asian regions, were sandwiched in the middle, both in COVID-19 caseload and OpenWHO usage. In the final half of 2020, the break-down of OpenWHO activity among the WHO regions remained roughly static in terms of the proportion of one area to another, despite continued overall growth in the platform's use.

As the pandemic took hold, OpenWHO drew learners from an increasingly wide range of professional backgrounds and age-groups seeking knowledge about the outbreak, reflecting the far-reaching impact of COVID-19 throughout affected communities (Utunen et al., 2020). This influx of new target groups brought novel questions and problems to the platform Helpdesk, for example, regarding the anticipated availability of specific courses in new languages. The workforce required to manage the OpenWHO Helpdesk, therefore, had to increase exponentially. HPI quickly enlisted international students taking the Institute's digital health master's course to the Helpdesk support team, ensuring the team could command several languages.

HPI found a more sustainable approach to tackling the flood of requests for support via enhanced automation. They introduced the first version of a chatbot that could answer platform-specific frequently asked questions on 5 May 2020, thereby guaranteeing a 24/7 customer support source. The result was that many of the most commonly asked questions were addressed by version one of the chatbot, leading to reduced manual effort on the part of the support team and, thereby, diminished cost to HPI. On average, 40% of the users who received a chatbot suggestion did not create a Helpdesk ticket (Zobel et al., 2020).

Another feature that HPI created specifically for OpenWHO users during this time was the Certificates tab. The Certificates tab acted as a dedicated space where learners could download their course certificates. The creation of the Certificates tab not only benefited learners by making certificates easier to find and download but, in doing so, substantially reduced the certificate-related tickets submitted to the Helpdesk. Some learners contacting the Helpdesk for certificate-related support relayed that their employers and academic institutions had requested the course certificates, indicating the increasing recognition of OpenWHO courses among these groups.

3.3 Addressing Equity in Access to Learning through Multilingualism

OpenWHO's COVID-19 courses are to date available in 44 languages, including the 15 most-spoken languages worldwide and languages selected specifically to reach vulnerable populations and those who lack access to trusted information about the pandemic. In support of this aim, HPI added the ability for courses to be published on the platform in 35 new languages. OpenWHO and HPI also worked together to oversee the translation and language localisation of the entire platform into the UN official languages of Chinese, French, Spanish and Russian, with Arabic under development and Portuguese also available.

The OpenWHO team has worked with translators around the world to translate roughly 7.2 million words as of January 2021. The translation process has involved harnessing the power of crowdsourcing, as the OpenWHO team partnered with WHO country and regional offices, volunteers and institutions to translate and ensure quality control. One such collaboration has been with WHO's Pan American Health Organization (PAHO). PAHO voluntarily translated OpenWHO's COVID-19 courses into Spanish and Portuguese and re-posted the courses on their learning platform, the Virtual Campus for Public Health. The re-posted courses have amassed 605,856 enrolments on PAHO's Virtual Campus for Public Health as of January 2021. In pursuit of broader linguistic representation, the OpenWHO team also initiated machine translation in 15 languages spoken by vulnerable populations.

The transcription of the audio from course videos (speech-to-text) and the subsequent translation of these transcripts remains a labour-intensive task for the OpenWHO team but ensures greater access for those with limited bandwidth and caters to learner preference. The automated transcripts sometimes require significant amounts of time to be reviewed for errors in the machine transcription. The resulting subtitles files must also be in "WebVTT" format and UTF-8 encoded, thus increasing the likelihood of human error in sharing and editing them. Translators, such as those the OpenWHO team partners with, sometimes on an ad hoc basis, are often unfamiliar with this process and its particularities. In response, HPI set out to design and develop a tool that would streamline the process by creating a single interface embedded within the OpenWHO platform. Audio from course videos would be transcribed using an automated transcription process. The resulting transcripts could be translated using automated translation and reviewed and edited by multiple administrators and translators, all within a single interface on OpenWHO. HPI students conducted an in-depth requirements analysis with HPI's main platform partners and developed a prototype. A first version of the tool will be available on OpenWHO in the coming months.

4. DISCUSSION

January 2021 marked one year since the launch of WHO's first online learning course on COVID-19. In that time, the OpenWHO team has significantly scaled up the production and distribution of learning on COVID-19, resulting in nearly 5 million learner registrations on the platform, concentrated mostly on the 25 COVID-19 courses it offers in 44 languages. While HPI could easily amplify the private cloud-based server infrastructure running OpenWHO to meet this massive increase in demand for learning, the server bandwidth turned out to be a bottleneck. It ultimately required a tenfold increase in the Internet connection to run smoothly.

As the pandemic progressed, the world's hardest-hit regions drew heavily on OpenWHO resources. The correlation found between OpenWHO use and COVID-19 caseload by WHO region between December 2019 and December 2020 is consistent with previous findings which illustrated that, in most cases, levels of OpenWHO use and COVID-19 caseload were similar in magnitude in the countries with the highest number of COVID-19 cases between March and May 2020 (Utunen et al., 2020). The influx of these new users increased the platform's cultural, linguistic and professional diversity and coincided with a flood of Helpdesk tickets requesting support with various platform features. To respond, HPI expanded the Helpdesk support team and initiated a chatbot that could promptly answer the most frequently asked questions. Through feedback from the Helpdesk and OpenWHO team, HPI also identified causes of suboptimal user experience and engineered tailor-made enhancements to the user interface, such as the Certificates tab.

The WHO South-East Asian Region is somewhat of an exception to the correlation witnessed between OpenWHO use and COVID-19 caseload. However, India, which makes up 78.5% of OpenWHO learner activity in the South-East Asian Region, already dominated global MOOC enrolment numbers outside of OpenWHO before the pandemic, second only to the United States of America (Chauhan, 2017). The popularity of MOOCs in India might explain, in part, the way that the country has fuelled OpenWHO use in the WHO region of South-East Asia, to which it belongs. Additionally, the popularity of OpenWHO's courses in the South-East Asian and Americas regions may be somewhat explained by the availability of all OpenWHO's COVID-19 courses in English, a language widely spoken in both regions. In contrast, COVID-19 courses have been most commonly translated into Spanish, Portuguese and French — 10, 9 and 8 out of OpenWHO's 25 COVID-19 courses have been translated into these languages, respectively. OpenWHO courses are also almost always available in English before being followed by translations, giving additional time for enrolments to accumulate on English courses compared with translated ones.

The OpenWHO team sought to bolster multilingualism on the platform and partnered with translators worldwide to widen access to learning. The partnership forged between PAHO's Virtual Campus for Public Health and OpenWHO helped broaden the audience reached by the courses, particularly in the Americas Region, and illustrated the powerful potential of joint efforts between existing learning platforms during health emergency response. To support the multilingualism efforts, HPI added the functionality for 35 new course languages on the platform and began creating an automated transcript and translation tool for integration directly onto OpenWHO.

As the pandemic has evidenced, correctly and swiftly utilising technology in response to public health challenges ensures that the following critical components of online learning delivery can be satisfied:

1. **Equity**: OpenWHO's MOOCs are available to all at no cost, democratising knowledge and learning. Providing equitable access to health emergency knowledge in affected populations' mother tongues must remain a core value of online learning for public health emergencies.
2. **Accessibility**: Low-bandwidth compatible online learning (with the ability for offline-modes) can enable participants with limited technology or internet connectivity to access learning. Online learning can be cost-effective and time and resource efficient. Self-paced, low-bandwidth-adjusted, downloadable, and portable learning (available on any device and offline) can also increase knowledge accessibility.
3. **Flexibility**: Self-paced learning can enable individuals to progress according to their preferred speed, time, and place, catering to the learner's needs and availability.
4. **Learner-centricity**: User-friendly options allow individuals to choose formats specific to their learning needs and provide the basis for a more customised learning experience. In this vein, they can attract repeat learners and encourage continuous, lifelong learning.
5. **Quality**: Courses based on reliable and trustworthy technical guidance and adult learning techniques can produce the highest quality of content and enhance learning.

5. CONCLUSIONS

By quickly employing innovative and novel solutions to technological limitations, and firmly rooted in the value of equity of access, HPI and the OpenWHO team were able to work together to meet the unprecedented global demand for learning during the COVID-19 pandemic. In doing so, they were able to contribute towards the WHO's goal of reducing transmission, saving lives and protecting the vulnerable. Despite the challenges involved, the COVID-19 pandemic has given rise to the first time in its history that WHO launched fast, high-quality, accessible learning on a massive scale, with an emphasis on multilingualism.

Our study is limited by the descriptive nature of the analysis performed; further research should employ statistical tests to ascertain measures of association and statistical significance. However, our study is strengthened by the fact that it uses the complete datasets available (which record all OpenWHO web sessions and COVID-19 cases that occurred during the study period) to conduct the analysis, instead of relying on an extracted sample from the data which may be unrepresentative. Our study illustrates the challenges faced in conducting a global, multilingual, "just-in-time" online learning response to a pandemic and exemplifies technological solutions that can be rapidly and effectively leveraged to address them.

The COVID-19 pandemic has proven online learning's power to ensure equitable access to knowledge for all learners. Online learning can no longer be considered a temporary solution when in-person gatherings are impossible. Instead, it demands to be seriously considered a modern approach to efficient and impactful public health work, requiring skilful and creative use of technological solutions. It is a fundamental part of the ecosystem needed to create a culture of lifelong learning in health.

REFERENCES

Aldohyan M., et al., 2019. The perceived effectiveness of MERS-CoV educational programs and knowledge transfer among primary healthcare workers: a cross-sectional survey. *BMC Infectious Diseases*, 19, 1, p. 273.

Brown A., et al., 2020. Effectiveness of technology-enabled knowledge translation strategies in improving the use of research in public health: Systematic review. *Journal of Medical Internet Research,* 22, 7, p.e17274.

Carapeto, C. and Barros, D.M.V., 2019. Nutrition and health as virtual class at Open University (Portugal): pedagogical strategies for higher education. *International Journal of Educational Technology in Higher Education*, 16, 1, p. 19.

Chauhan, J., 2017. An Overview of MOOC in India. *International Journal of Computer Trends and Technology*, 49, 2, pp. 111–120.

Chick C.R., et al., 2020. Using Technology to Maintain the Education of Residents During the COVID-19 Pandemic. *Journal of Surgical Education*, 77, *4,* pp. 729–732.

Fernández-Díaz, E., et al., 2020. Exploring WHO communication during the COVID-19 pandemic through the WHO website based on W3C guidelines: Accessible for all? *International Journal of Environmental Research and Public Health*, 17, 16, p. 5663.

Martinengo, L., et al., 2019. Digital health professions education on chronic wound management: A systematic review. *International Journal of Nursing Studies,* 104, p. 103512.

Pappano, L., 2012. The Year of the MOOC, in New York Times. Accessible at <https://www.nytimes.com/2012/11/04/education/edlife/massive-open-online-courses-are-multiplying-at-a-rapid-pace.html>.

Regmi, K. and Jones, L., 2020. A systematic review of the factors - enablers and barriers - affecting e-learning in health sciences education. *BMC Medical Education,* 20, 1, p. 91.

Tudor Car L., et al., 2019. Health professions digital education on clinical practice guidelines: A systematic review by Digital Health Education collaboration. *BMC Medicine,* 17, 1, pp. 139-16

Utunen H., et al., 2020. Global Reach of an Online COVID-19 Course in Multiple Languages on OpenWHO in the First Quarter of 2020: Analysis of Platform Use Data. *Journal of Medical Internet Research*, 22, 4, p.e19076.

Utunen H., et al., 2020. Responding to Global Learning Needs during a Pandemic: An Analysis of the Trends in Platform Use and Incidence of COVID-19. *Education Sciences,* 10, 11, p. 345.

Vaona A., et al., 2018. E-learning for health professionals. *Cochrane Database of Systematic Reviews*, 1, 1, CD011736.

World Health Organization, 2020. *WHO Coronavirus Disease (COVID-19) Dashboard.* Accessible at <https://covid19.who.int/>.

Zitzmann N.U., et al., 2020. Digital undergraduate education in dentistry: A systematic review. *International Journal of Environmental Research and Public Health,* 17, 9, p. 3269.

Zobel T., et al., 2020. Improving the Scalability of MOOC Platforms with Automated, Dialogue-based Systems. *IEEE Learning With MOOCs.* Antigua, Guatemala, pp. 42–46.

TOWARDS AN ETHICS-AUDIT BOT

Siani Pearson[1], Martin Lloyd[1] and Vivek Nallur[2]
[1]*Just Algorithms Action Group (JAAG), UK*
[2]*School of Computer Science, University College Dublin, Ireland*

ABSTRACT

In this paper we focus on artificial intelligence (AI) for governance, not governance for AI, and on just one aspect of governance, namely ethics audit. Different kinds of ethical audit bots are possible, but who makes the choices and what are the implications? In this paper, we do not provide ethical/philosophical solutions, but rather focus on the technical aspects of what an AI-based solution for validating the ethical soundness of a target system would be like. We propose a system that is able to conduct *an ethical audit* of a target system, given certain socio-technical conditions. To be more specific, we propose the creation of a bot that is able to support organisations in ensuring that their software development lifecycles contain processes that meet certain ethical standards.

KEYWORDS

Ethics Audit, Ethics Assurance, Corporate Social Responsibility, Audit Bot, Artificial Intelligence

1. INTRODUCTION

There is a complex relationship between AI, ethics and audit. AI refers "to any technology that performs tasks that might be considered intelligent – while recognising that our beliefs about what counts as 'intelligent' may change over time" (Nuffield, 2019). Recently, AI has come to refer just to machine learning (ML), but it can also encompass other techniques, including rules-based reasoning. It brings new opportunities but can also heighten ethical problems (IEEE, 2019; Munoko, 2020). Most ethical guidelines, principles for AI etc. seem to be focused on people building AI systems. In contrast, building AI systems that are themselves ethical has not received as much attention. There have been some attempts at adding ethical reasoning (rule-based, constraint-satisfaction, etc.) (Nallur, 2020), but not enough at testing systems for possible ethical violations. The main contribution of the paper addresses this issue by means of the proposal of an 'audit bot' solution. In the following sections we consider current usage of AI for audit, and then the need to define what ethics audit requires from AI to function properly, followed by the proposal of the ethics Audit Bot that we are designing and concluding remarks.

2. AI FOR AUDIT

AI can potentially increase efficiency of audit, provide greater evidence and insight into operational processes and create competitive advantages. Many of the larger auditing companies are already using AI and it already has a vital role in forensic accounting (for example, the 2016-20 investigation into corrupt payments made by some Airbus staff[1]). Condition monitoring, statistical analysis and business intelligence are embodied in a variety of computer-assisted audit tools and techniques that form a growing field within the IT audit profession. The term 'audit bot' is already being used within the audit realm[2], but typically just to validate system data, determine conclusions through logical checks, address problems such as poor password management, generate documents and information requests, and input received data into systems.

[1] https://www.bbc.co.uk/news/business-55306139
[2] https://auditbots.com/about-us/

In the security domain, security information and event management provide real-time analysis of security alerts, log security data and generate compliance reports. It is standard practice to integrate abnormality detectors in security tools, using ML techniques, but due to the use of these techniques the system will tend to replicate bias and historical undesirable features.

3. ETHICS AUDIT

Organisations undergo or use many different types of audit. An *ethics audit* is "the systematic, independent, and objective examination and evaluation of the ethical content of the object of the audit" (Kaptein, 2020). Thus, it is carried out in a way that provides essential conditions for the users of an ethics audit to trust the conclusions of the audit, and this includes a trusted entity (usually a suitably qualified professional) conducting the audit; by implication, all tools used in the audit shall be trustworthy as well.

Ethics audit is designed to dig deep into the practices of a business, to see how closely an organisation follows its rules, and conforms to or exceeds the ethical standards of its industry and society. An ethics audit (with clear definition of its scope and a committee established to oversee it) is increasingly seen as part of corporate social responsibility and governance; complementary aspects include incorporation of ethical values into organisational policies, high level support from top managers and the board of directors, and more proactive measures such as ongoing ethical impact assessment and design across the organisation's activities, and good security. Limited information exists about ethical audits carried out in practice (Kaptein, 2020).

3.1 Different Types of Ethics Audit

An ethics audit is necessarily more qualitative and subjective in nature than compliance checking, which considers adherence to legal requirements in given contexts. Auditing against high level, general principles such as those espoused in ethical guidelines (Hagendorff, 2020) is difficult to do, and especially if this activity involves trying to drill down into low level events occurring within the system. Therefore, we recommend "domain specific ethics", such as for bioethics (Beauchamp and Childress, 1991). Not only are these typically tailored to the social milieu but also easier to map to lower-level activities/events in the domain. Different approaches using technology in auditing ethical aspects are possible, including:

- Providing a tool that assists users in thinking about ethical issues and capturing their responses in a secure way that can be reviewed later. For example, based on an "Ethics Canvas" (ODI, 2020).
- Mapping high level ethical values to lower-level incidents that can be checked by software: this is extremely challenging and often of limited value (Pearson and Allison, 2009).
- Conversion of legal or other requirements into modal logic and using automated reasoning, with forms of conflict resolution, to contextually recommend actions. In practice, though, these have proven difficult to populate with encoded rules, keep up to date as legislation changes, and train and motivate users.
- Encoding organisational policies that already embed ethical values and legal requirements appropriate to the organisation, and using these policies within semi-automated enforcement and compliance checking.
- Multiple software agents, each with their own goals and values, perhaps representing different persons.
- Using a ML system trained to recognise anomalies to detect high risk activity and flag this up at an appropriate time for human users to consider.
- Broadly speaking, permitted exceptions audit may be achieved via anomaly detection techniques, obligations audit via model checking, and access legitimacy audit via query based reasoning and pattern matching (Reuben, 2016).

3.2 Ethical Audit Bots

A bot is an application that performs an automated task. Correspondingly, different kinds of *ethical audit bots* are possible, including one or more of the following potentially acting together:

(a) audit bot(s) running in the background within an organisation's systems, producing a secured repository of evidence that supports a human ethical auditor, highlighting events that might be considered unethical by monitoring (non)compliance with rules in which ethical values have been encoded

(b) audit bots that focus on detecting breaking of the rules and considering whether or not that is justified (for example, in an emergency or because of safety)

(c) a recommender bot, flagging up anything likely to have ethical repercussions and/or future recommendations about change of behaviour to a human based on analysis of logs: for example, it might detect that offensive language was being regularly used by an employee. This itself may cause privacy concerns and hence it should be clear to all employees what data is accessible to the bot.

The object of an ethics audit can differ, according to the judgment of the entity setting the scope. It may be set in terms of intentions, behaviour or consequences, following the main distinction of ethical theories in terms of virtue ethics, deontology and utilitarianism respectively (Harris, 2008). Choices have to be made, but by whom (DuQuenoy, 2005)? The answer is contextual, but in general it is better to have a more flexible and transparent system where: individual stakeholders can reflect their ethical values into the system; ethical encoding is robust and understandable to other parties; stakeholders or their representatives are involved within the ethical decision-making process, with potential harm flagged up to users to consider (IEEE, 2019).

4. EXAMPLE OF AI FOR ETHICAL AUDIT: 'AUDIT BOT'

We propose the introduction of Ethical Audit Bots to perform automated audit supporting analysis of the extent to which protection and social justice is being achieved during the design and/or operational support phases.

During development, one or more Audit Bots would be introduced into the processes of specifying, programming, verification, validation, and release of decision-making systems. Audit Bots will be used throughout the software life cycle and therefore applied during the operational support phase when the system is live and requires maintenance and or modification. An ethical Audit Bot needs to be assessed at all stages of its life cycle – just like the systems it is intended to monitor; for example, any proposed monitoring of employees by the audit bot needs to be assessed to ensure that this would be ethical.

This high-level vision may be addressed in different ways. The Ethical Audit Bot may gather and aggregate evidence in a form that is useful for a human auditor, potentially as part of an audit process mapping to new protection standards. Or it may, for example, be able to flag up harms itself, with a justification for the final outputs. With regard to risk, there are already several approaches that could be used. For example, ALARP (as low as reasonably practicable) categorises risks into intolerable; so small as to be acceptable; and those which lie in between, which must be reduced to the lowest practicable level (UK HSE, 2020). Mitigating the risks in the ALARP category concerns the balance between the cost of the risk and the cost of mitigation. This brings in the deep issues of the cost of harm. Some of the audit is likely to be very context specific; analogously in the field of sustainability accounting standards, new reporting metrics are currently being developed by the World Economic Forum (Tysiac, 2020).

What rules do we need to achieve ethical operations at all stages of the lifecycle? During the drafting of the system development part of the system lifecycle, both the questions to be investigated and the range of expected answers need to be defined, as part of a safety, ethics and quality plan. Once defined, at the next part of the system lifecycle an Audit Bot is built to automate this, in the sense of answering the questions for itself and building a log of the answers that can be shown to a human. These can be designed not only to drill down into the details, but also helping to flag up where there are particular concerns. It might be designed to flag up high harm events immediately and/or to produce reports periodically and/or on demand. An automatic auditor could run in the background.

If an organisation publicly commits to these rules, then it should also specify how the internal processes of the organisation will change to accommodate this. Once this is done, job descriptions will change and the bot can monitor whether the employee performed the activity that was expected of them.

Here are some diverse examples of what the Audit Bot could be doing:

- (*pre-operational*): Checking whether any data set used for training a ML system was assessed for bias.
- Checking that at least one person on each project team must have ethics training and there is a recorded process about resolving ethical issues; integration with an ethical issue tracking system, whereby ethical issues can be flagged up, a record kept, and appropriate responsibilities clearly assigned. Tracking this over time, ascertaining whether a software build happened before these issues were addressed.

- Auditing the due diligence that actors perform in order to make more informed decisions about ethical actions as part of their role, e.g., ML practitioners selecting from standardised datasheets listing the properties of different training data sets (Gebru et al, 2018).
- (*operational*): Every time a document is reviewed and checked into the document management system, checking that the review's author appears in the competence register that every entity participating in the project has to keep up-to-date (as for the safety domain), and so is qualified to perform that review; also checking in an independence register to determine whether the reviewer is sufficiently independent for this level of severity or safety of this system.
- Monitoring employees' online activity to detect excessive working hours.
- Preventing gender biased job descriptions going out.
- Using measures that check whether systems have changed significantly since a previous point, e.g., when they were initially trained; based on this, recommending if there is cause for alarm and the ML model might need to be changed.

This illustrates the various different types of checks that could be made. This approach allows greater accuracy, with the bot building the evidence of good practice in real time in a sealed repository which can then form the basis of building a case usable in court, to help justify why, for example, the systems used to build systems are ethical. It is intended to handle the lower-level routine tasks of pattern matching and recording, rather like the way static analysis of code picks up the more easily detected errors prior to review, although advances in technology have shown that some specialised analysers such as KLEE (Cadar et el, 2008) outperform humans in their bug detection capability.

5. CONCLUSION

We are working to develop an Audit Bot as a novel mechanism for ethical audit, in a way that takes tedious work away from humans, as well as being able to drill down and provide levels of evidence that might not be readily obtainable by workers. The authors' experience of auditing in the safety domain suggests the proposed approach would have benefit in the ethical domain by getting humans to think about their answers and actions, providing integrated and customised help, logging evidence about decisions made, and storing evidence securely.

If an organisation publicly commits to some principles (such as reducing bias to a low level), then it must also be possible to ask what processes it has put in place to ensure that these principles will be upheld. Using the proposed approach, once processes are defined, they can be traced back into job descriptions all the way down the employee chain. So, the Ethical Audit Bot should be able to pick up from employee-activity logs, where in the chain of command, the process failed (or was not followed); this helps real people to be held accountable in the case of an audit failure, and effort directed to avoid similar problems arising in future.

The Ethical Audit Bot is targeted at testing *any* kind of system (not necessarily limited to those employing AI techniques) for possible ethical violations. As with development of many other complex AI techniques, steps towards full automation are being done in an incremental way. In the short term, the parts that can be automated by the Ethical Audit Bot are much narrower in scope than a human-based ethics audit; these should therefore be considered supplementary to a human auditor. Automated checking to increase evidence is closely allied to checking the organisation's behaviour, corresponding to a deontological ethical approach, but other ethical perspectives apply too, notably the virtue ethics approach, whereby individuals' education is a key factor.

REFERENCES

Beauchamp, T.L. and Childress, J.F., 1991. Principles of Biomedical Ethics. *In Annals of Internal Medicine*, Vol. 114, No. 9, p. 827.

Cadar, C. et al, 2008. KLEE: Unassisted and Automatic Generation of High-Coverage Tests for Complex Systems Programs. *In 8th USENIX Symposium on Operating Systems Design and Implementation*, pp. 209-224.

Duquenoy P., 2005. *Ethics of Computing. In Perspectives and Policies on ICT in Society*, IFIP International Federation for Information Processing, Springer, Boston, MA, Vol. 179, pp. 159-170.

Gebru, T. et al, 2018. Datasheets for Datasets. In arXiv, pp. 1–17.

Hagendorff, T., 2020. The Ethics of AI Ethics. *In Minds and Machines*, Vol. 30, No 1, pp. 99-120.

Harris, I., 2008. Commercial Ethics: Process or Outcome? Gresham Lecture, London, 6 Nov. Commercial ethics: Process or Outcome? (gresham.ac.uk)

IEEE Global Initiative on Ethics of Autonomous and Intelligent Systems, 2019. *Ethically Aligned Design*, v2. ead_v2.pdf (ieee.org)

Kaptein, M., 2020. Ethics Audit. *In Encyclopedia of Business and Professional Ethics*. Springer, Cham.

Munoko, I. et al, 2020. The Ethical Implications of Using Artificial Intelligence in Auditing. *In Journal of Business Ethics*, Vol. 167, No. 2, pp. 209-234.

Nallur, V., 2020. Landscape of Machine Implemented Ethics. *In Science and Engineering Ethics*, Vol. 26, pp. 2381–2399.

Nuffield Foundation, 2019. *Ethical and Societal Implications of Algorithms, Data, and Artificial Intelligence.* Ethical-and-Societal-Implications-of-Data-and-AI-report-Nuffield-Foundat.pdf (nuffieldfoundation.org)

Open Data Institute (ODI), 2020. *Ethics Canvas*. https://theodi.org/article/data-ethics-canvas/

Pearson, S. and Allison, D., 2009. A Model-Based Privacy Compliance Checker. *In International Journal of E-Business Research*, Vol. 5, pp. 63-83.

Reuben, J. et al, 2016. Automated Log Audits for Privacy Compliance Validation: A Literature Survey. *In Privacy and Identity Management, Time for a Revolution?* Vol. 476, Springer, pp. 312-326.

Tysiac, K., 2020. Consistency sought in sustainability, corporate reporting through global effort. *In Journal of Accountancy*, 11th September.

UK HSE (Health and Safety Executive), 2020. *ALARP Guidance*. https://www.hse.gov.uk/managing/theory/index.htm

SINGLE NATIONAL NUMBER, A SOLUTION FOR AN OPTIMAL MANAGEMENT OF INSURANCE IN THE DEMOCRATIC REPUBLIC OF CONGO

Efrem Mbaki Luzayisu
Department of Mathematics and Computer Science, Faculty of Sciences
University of Kinshasa, Democratic Republic of Congo

ABSTRACT

The liberalisation of the insurance market offers new economic opportunities in the Democratic Republic of Congo (DRC). Indeed, it marks the end of the monopoly of the national state company and opens the door to competition by implementing the process of transformation of an economic sector whose purpose is to allow the exercise of an economic activity to different entities, private or public. Admittedly, the approvals of the new insurers bring a lot of money into the country, but beyond everything, the legitimate questions that everyone has the right to ask is whether this transaction leads to a decrease in prices, an increase in the number of subscriptions, improved quality of service and/or expanded choice for consumers. Only, taking advantage of our expertise in Information and Communication Technologies (ICT) with a long professional experience in the development of banking software and actuaries, we try to go into depth in our questions in order to bring our little stone to the edifice. As a matter of fact, when we look at the current situation, we point out some of the dysfunctions before we make proposals to improve the system. In other words, through this document, we ask ourselves about the current information system and propose solutions for taking into account all the components of a good insurance system and for implementing the conceptual and/or technical links that unite them. Basically, we define the conditions for the implementation of an insurance information system in DR Congo that can satisfy both technical, business, political and citizen needs. This paper focuses on one of these solutions with the implementation of a single national number.

KEYWORDS

Liberalisation, Insurance, Insurer, Monitoring Authority, DRC

1. INTRODUCTION

We are pleased to see market liberalisation in the field of insurance in the Democratic Republic of Congo (DRC). Everyone will recall that on 23 November 1966, via Ordinance Law N°66/0622a, the National Insurance Company (NIC) [la Société Nationale d'Assurances (SONAS)] came into existence with, as its primary mission, the unification of insurance activities formerly carried out by foreign private companies (Yav J.., 2021).

This development put an end to economic liberalism in this sector of economic activity in the Congo by entrusting the new company with the monopoly of all these activities. Thus, NIC became the only insurance company covering the entirety of the national insurance market (Liripa S., 2007; Wellmann A., 2004).

However, after 50 years, the Congolese government promulgated Law N°15/005 of 17 March 2015 relating to the Insurance Code, followed by Decree No°16/001 of 26 January 2016 relating to the creation, organisation and functioning of the Insurance Regulatory and Monitoring Authority (IRMA) [l'Autorité de Régulation et de Contrôle des Assurances (ARCA)] in order to animate this newly-liberalised market (Michael K., 2012).

This development is accompanied by a growth in competition and the arrival of new insurance products. Therefore, it represents a strong call to investors who, by their financial contributions, offer the country new employment possibilities (Ferdinand A., 2010). Furthermore, thanks to the competition, a significant decrease is hoped for in premiums for insurance contracts for all types of risk – Life or Non-Life – covered by the insurers. This document aims to analyse the insurance business-model in the RDC so as to reveal three points able to improve the effectiveness of good governance in this new market for insurance in the heart of Africa. With this in mind, the following is divided into four sections. Point 2, the problematic, describes our preoccupation with the insurance business-model in the RDC. Point 3 provides a succinct explanation of the current functioning of the insurance market. And point 4 describes the way in which we envisage establishing the link between IRMA and the client, so as to improve the new insurance market in the RDC by giving new powers to IRMA, thanks to underwriting data. We will finish with a brief conclusion before the bibliography.

2. PROBLEMATIC

Today, the insurance business-model in the RDC revolves around the Insurance Regulatory and Monitoring Authority (IRMA). This body carries out its role marvelously, wearing simultaneously three hats so as to accomplish its missions: monitoring - to identify and sanction possible abuses; advisory - to inform and steer governmental policy in insurance matters, and popularisation - to raise the awareness of the population and business regarding insurance products. From our analysis, this management model poses three problems which are presented in Figure1 below:

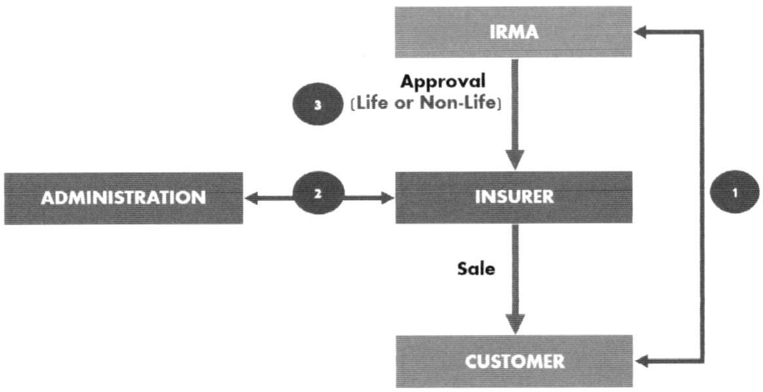

Figure 1. Business-Model and three points

Indeed, although IRMA works in harmony with business (insurers and insurance brokers), we regret that:

1. It has no contact with insurance policy-holders. In this way, it is deprived of critical information to enable it to fulfil the afore-mentioned three missions correctly ;
2. The licences are too broad : Life or Non-Life. Insurers alone define the conditions and terms for cover of one kind of risk or another. The main conern is that the insurance is in accordance with the licence obtained (Life or Non-Life) ;
3. The administrations are not closely involved in the acceptance of a request for insurance: in the majority of cases, the insurers alone study the clients' files, without prior verification with the administrations to validate or reject the declarations received.

The rest of this document attempts to shed more light on the first point concerning contact between IRMA and the policy-holder with a view to registering each client and the type of insurance being taken out. In so doing, follow-up can be organised and attempts made to propose IT solutions to overcome these shortcomings.

3. CURRENT FUNTIONING

To date, companies wishing to work in the new insurance market in the RDC apply to the competent authority, IRMA, for a licence. As Figure 2 below shows, by payment of the underwriter amount, which today stands at US$10 million for one branch (Life or Non-Life), and submission of a complete file, they obtain the right to sell insurance products on the Congolese market.

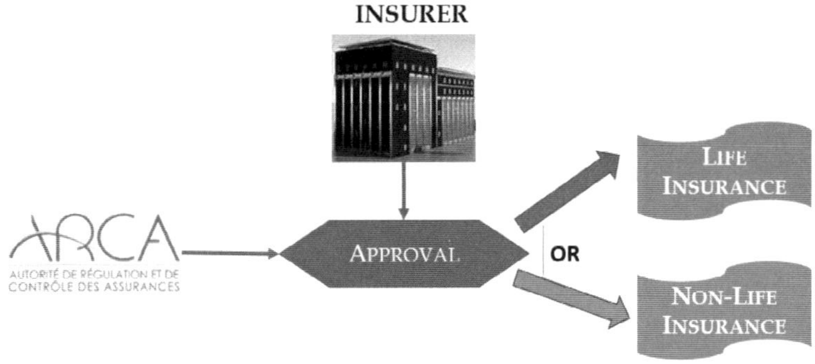

Figure 2. Underwriting an insurance company

It should be recalled that the concept of insurance implies a contractual arrangement whereby one party, the insurance company or insurer, commits to compensating loss or damages suffered by another party, the insured, by the payment of a determined amount, in exchange for an adequate consideration called a premium. As a general rule, an insurance is financial cover for an event that may occur in the future (Couilbault, and al., 2019).

Unless otherwise stated, Life insurance is a personal insurance. Payment of the premiums may be made all at once or periodically in line with the frequency determined in the contract (ARCA, 2010). Life insurance enables a person to insure for a capital sum in the event of death or life. As a general rule, life insurance concerns at least three players (Esbjörn O. and Björn J., 2014; Froment M. and Petauton P., 2017):

1. the policy-holder (the client): this is the person who takes out the life insurance with a company. This person pays the premiums for the life insurance and is the person who concludes a contract with the insurer ;
2. the insured: this is the person insured. Payment will be made in the event of death or life, in accordance with the terms of the contract;
3. the beneficiary: this is the person who receives the insured capital.

On the other hand, Non-Life insurance groups together all types of insurance with the exception of Life insurance contracts. In other words, it concerns all prudential agreements which are not connected to or directly conditional upon the life of the insured person (Esbjörn O. and Björn J., 2014). In this sense, Non-Life insurance groups together those insurance operations which do not concern the life of the insured person. In all probability, Non-Life insurance groups together all conctracts of type FADR (abbreviation for Fire, Accident and Diverse Risks) [Incendie, Accidents et Risques Divers IARD)] (Suru A., 2020). It is therefore principally made up of insurance of things or belongings, insurance for responsibility or debt and insurance of persons.

In simple terms, the main difference between Non-Life insurance and Life insurance is the occurrence of the loss or damage, which is more often certain in the case of Life insurance, whereas only probable (with a probability between 0 and 1) for Non-Life insurance. Moreover, for Non-Life insurance, the cost of the loss or damage is rarely known, another specific feature (Planchet F., 2004).

Furthermore, we are not aware that IRMA imposes on insurers any list of risks to be covered. It only limits the field of activity to Life or Non-Life, according to the licence obtained. Certain companies have been able to acquire two authorisations, to sell Life and Non-Life insurance.

4. ESTABLISH CONTACT WITH THE POLICY-HOLDERS

As described above, under the current functioning of the insurance market in the RDC, IRMA has no contact with the policy-holders. It is therefore incapable of drawing up a table indicating for each policy-holder the kind of insurance he/she has taken out. The insurers define the conditions and operating methods for the insurance products that they market, respecting, of course, the country's laws and regulations.

In these conditions, the insurer has sole responsibility for the monitoring and processing of the various events that may occur during the life-cycle of an insurance policy. This greatly reduces IRMA's role in its capacity to regulate the market and to intervene effectively in the event a client is mistreated.

Moreover, with this way of working, IRMA deprives itself of a significant basket of (sizeable) data able to allow it to recover its due from the insurers. Indeed, it is agreed that the insurer retrocedes to IRMA a percentage of each premium received from a client concerning an insurance policy. Without this data, it is virtually impossible for IRMA to anticipate expected revenue rationally. It is therefore dependent on the good-will of the insurers who themselves communicate the amount to be paid to the Authority.

More serious, without this data, IRMA has no control over evolution of the insurance market in order to compile statistics and draw up tables of key indicators. It cannot claim, therefore, to carry out correctly its advisory role towards the political instances who need rational information to be able to determine useful trends in the insurance market.

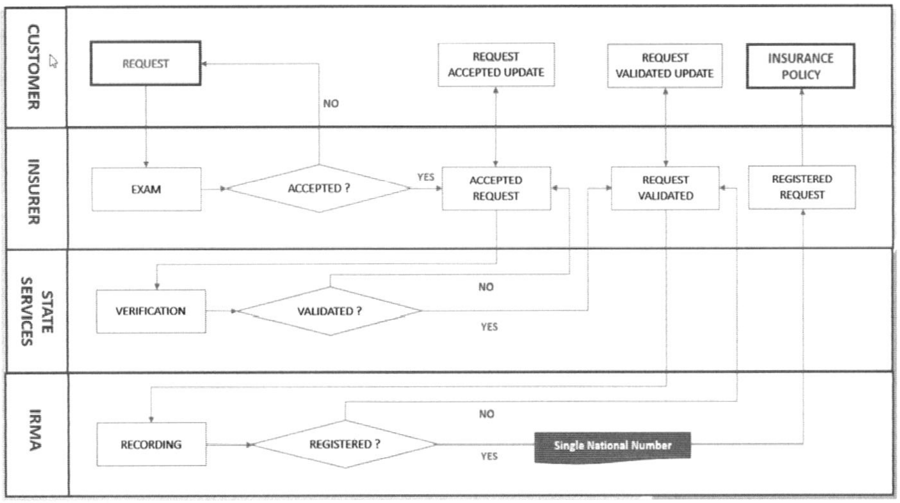

Figure 3. Flow Diagram

To overcome this inadequacy, we propose implementation of an IT system that would attribute a Single National Number (SNN) to each insurance policy. The SNN should accompany all procedures (administrative, legal and other) connected to the policy. To achieve this, the ideal solution would be to utilise an IT system able to support the flow chart shown in Figure 3 above. The client's request is in effect handled sequentially by the insurer, the administration and IRMA which validates the procedure by registering the insurance policy and providing it with an SNN. With difficulties due to the DRC context where the Internet and communication networks are problematic, we implemented and tested this system using two techniques: web services and FTP exchanges. We will take the time to explain the details of these two solutions in a separate document. In order to improve and optimise the current situation, we suggest implementation of an IT system able to support the flow-chart described above, a process resulting in the registration of every insurance policy by IRMA and the generation of a Single National Number as shown in Figure 4 above.

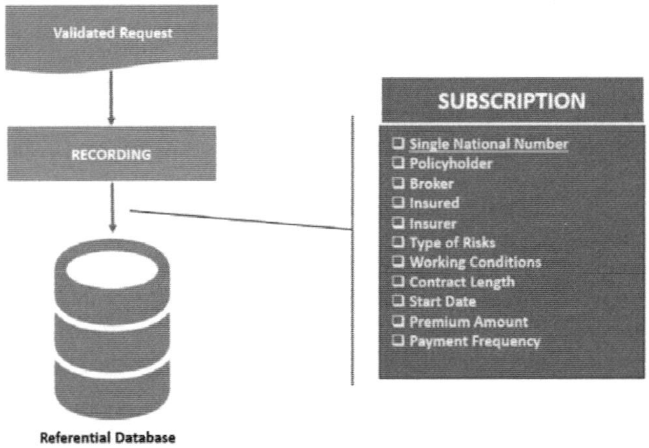

Figure 4. Registration of an insurance subscription

The subscription table that we implemented with SQL Sever is a gold mine. Indeed, its content would allow the authorities to make statistics, calculate indicators or draw up scoreboards. Similarly, actuaries would have useful data to make simulations and build models.

5. CONCLUSION

The foregoing clearly reveals the three shortcomings that characterise the insurance market in the RDC. Moreover, it shows the difficulties facing the competent Authority in monitoring the data which would allow it to play its role of regulator and advisor to the political instances.

Despite the concerns of the Internet and communication networks, we succeeded in implementing a solution that could allow a positive evolution of the insurance market in DR Congo. Indeed, with the registration of each insurance policy, the authorities will be able to monitor in real time the evolution of this newly reconstructed sector.

REFERENCES

ARCA, 2010. *Aperçu historique des Assurances en RDC*, https://arca.cd/apercu-historique-des-assurances-en-rdc/

Couilbault F. and al., 2019. *Les grands principes de l'assurance*, L'Argus de l'assurance, 14e édition

Esbjörn O. and Björn J., 2014. *Non-Life Insurance Pricing with Generalized Linear Models*, Springer; 1st ed.

Ferdinand A., 2010. *Financial liberalisation and performance in the insurance industry: evidence from ghana*, LAP Lambert Academic Publishing

Froment M. and Petauton P., 2017. *Théorie et pratique de l'assurance-vie* - 5e éd. - Cours complet et synthétique, exercices corrigés, Dunod; 5e édition

Liripa S., 2007. *Rapport de stageeport of traineeship effectué à la Société Nationale d'Assurances*, Université de Kisangani, Licence en Sciences économiques.

Michael K., 2012. *Stochastic Models in Life Insurance*, Springer; 2nd edition

Planchet F., 2004. *Assurance Non-Vie (Le modèle collectif)*, Support de cours 2003-2004, ISFA

Suru A., 2020. *Assurance Iard*, Economica

Wellmann A., 2004. *Liberalisation of Trade and reduction of protectionism*,GRIN Verlagµ

Yav J.., 2021. *Liberalization of Insurance Sector in Democratic Republic of Congo*,https://www.hg.org/legal-articles/liberalization-of-insurance-sector-in-democratic-republic-of-congo-35637, consulted on 02/19/2021

CLUBHOUSE: DETERMINING THE MOST TALKED ABOUT TOPICS AND THEIR EFFECT ON THE PLATFORM'S POPULARITY

Luka Skeledzija and Eva Skeledzija
University of Ljubljana, Slovenia

ABSTRACT

In early 2021, a new mobile app called "Clubhouse: drop-in audio" became extremely popular among internet users. This paper aims to give some insight into what topics are discussed on Clubhouse, what makes Clubhouse (and potentially other drop-in audio platforms) so appealing and what helped it acquire millions of users in a matter of weeks despite an invite-only registration system. It was determined through research that the 3 most popular topics on Clubhouse are all business related and that Clubhouse users tend to offer free high-value business advice to other entrepreneurs. Clubhouse's new media format was reported to be very authentic, which people from other industries are starting to take notice of.

KEYWORDS

Clubhouse, Business, Entrepreneurship, Mobile App, Drop-In Audio

1. INTRODUCTION

In early 2021, a new mobile app called "Clubhouse: drop-in audio" became extremely popular among internet users. In fact, it grew from 1.500 users in March 2020 (mainly from Silicon Valley) to more than 10.000.000 users as of February 2021 (Statista, 2021). The app offers the ability to create, listen and participate in the so-called drop-in audio rooms, where debates and interviews on different topics are taking place every day. This new kind of social media network became so interesting, that as of May 2021 there are more than 6 Clubhouse clones in the works by big technology companies (Instagram Audio Rooms, Telegram Voice Chat 2.0, LinkedIn Live Audio Rooms, Twitter Spaces, Spotify's Locker Room Talk, Discord Stage Channels, Facebook Audio Rooms) (Awa-Abuon, 2021). Similarly, Clubhouse's parent0020company, Alpha Exploration Co., is currently valued at over 1 billion USD (Culliford, 2021).

This paper aims to give some insight into what topics are discussed on Clubhouse, what makes Clubhouse (and potentially other drop-in audio platforms) so appealing and what helped it acquire millions of users in a matter of weeks despite an invite-only registration system.

2. RESEARCH QUESTION & METHODOLOGY

Since Clubhouse uses an invite-only registration system (e.g. a person has to be invited to the platform by another user), the platform must clearly provide *some* value to the users, that they want to tell their friends about. We looked at a few different factors: type & value of the discussed topics, interestingness of the speakers, an interesting media format and COVID-19 effect on the format.

As part of this research paper, different Clubhouse discussion topics were evaluated statistically. This was achieved using a reverse-engineered Clubhouse Application Programming Interface (API) provided by Harold Kim on Github (https://github.com/stypr/clubhouse-py).

To assess internet trends, Google Trends tools was used in combination with other social media websites (mainly Twitter and Reddit). Lastly, we used the app quite extensively ourselves to better understand how the platform operates.

3. DETERMINING THE MOST POPULAR TOPICS ON CLUBHOUSE

Clubhouse allows users to follow or become members of so-called “Clubs”, which are an interest-based collections of drop-in audio rooms. As followers, users can join and participate in the Club’s rooms while Club members can also create a room within the Club. Using the reverse-engineered Clubhouse Application Programming Interface (API) provided by Harold Kim (https://github.com/stypr/clubhouse-py) the number of followers and members for all Clubhouse Clubs was programmatically counted and organized by Club’s topic/subtopic. The twelve most popular subtopics on Clubhouse are presented in Table 1, followed by all 14 Clubhouse’s topics in Table 2.

Table 1. Twelve most popular subtopics (out of 145) on Clubhouse by number of followers as of May 1st 2021 (full list accessible at https://clubhouse-topics.netlify.app/)

Topic	Number of followers	Number of members
Entrepreneurship	**3.241.371**	776.603
Startups	**2.970.047**	512.547
The Future	**2.719.825**	508.450
Education	**2.128.504**	529.823
Networking	**2.088.713**	717.343
Mindfulness	**2.002.077**	377.709
Marketing	**1.586.286**	280.110
Meet People	**1.550.756**	584.051
Health	**1.408.662**	400.105
Advice	**1.125.091**	375.497
Crypto	**1.068.940**	216.701
Economics	**1.055.106**	145.059

Table 2. All topics on Clubhouse by number of followers as of May 1st 2021

Topic	Number of followers	Number of members
Hustle	**9.617.836**	2.595.789
Tech	**9.188.251**	2.006.251
Knowledge	**7.170.932**	1.804.038
Entertainment	**6.107.312**	2.956.458
Wellness	**5.653.833**	1.443.407
Arts	**4.157.663**	1.539.498
World Affairs	**3.674.111**	1.282.113
Hanging Out	**3.161.930**	1.326.444
Life	**2.893.659**	1.012.527
Identity	**2.239.496**	1.138.843
Faith	**1.378.905**	571.498
Languages	**1.257.470**	315.748
Sports	**531.386**	254.585
Places	**453.515**	532.355

As visible from Table 2, the three most popular topics on Clubhouse are all business oriented. This aligns with our personal experience in the app. There are many clubs focused on helping entrepreneurs from all kinds of industries, discussing different business, and marketing strategies. In our experience, speakers were usually real domain experts who were giving out free high-value advice to people who were just starting out. There were many instances of people taking notes of the speakers for the entire duration of the rooms. We also observed many people marketing their personal brands and offering services, using Clubhouse to create revenue.

Clubhouse community highly values the so-called "Bio" (Biography) section of a user's profile. By providing some information about themselves, their interests and their Twitter / Instagram profile links, Clubhouse becomes a powerful networking tool. By our own observation, many people agreed to connect offline to continue talking about their mutual (professional) interests, many silent networking rooms (with no active speakers, only Bio readers) were also observed on Clubhouse.

4. EFFECT OF CELEBRITIES ON CLUBHOUSE POPULARITY

Influencer marketing is a well-proven marketing strategy (Jahnke, 2018). On Clubhouse, there were multiple occasions of high-profile executive (Elon Musk, Bill Gates, Mark Zuckerberg, etc.) and celebrity (Oprah, Drake, Jared Leto, Kevin Hart, MC Hammer, etc.) appearances. It is believed they joined on their own initiative (not paid for) to be interviewed by the moderators (normal users) and/or to answer questions from the public (Dee, 2021). Some consider Clubhouse a new way to interact with fans while the COVID-19 pandemic lasts. They consider the platform's media format to feel very authentic (Ali, 2021).

According to Google Trends, Google's Web Search trend analysis tool, Clubhouse's popularity on the Google Web Search peaked between 31st of January and 6th of February (Figure 1). However, 31st of January is also the day Elon Musk, whose Tweets have proven to have effect on the stock market in the past (Pyeong Kang Kim, 2021), tweeted about speaking on Clubhouse later that evening.

While it is difficult to prove the exact cause and effect in this case, we will, however, conclude that it is very plausible that celebrity appearances made a significant impact on the platform's popularity.

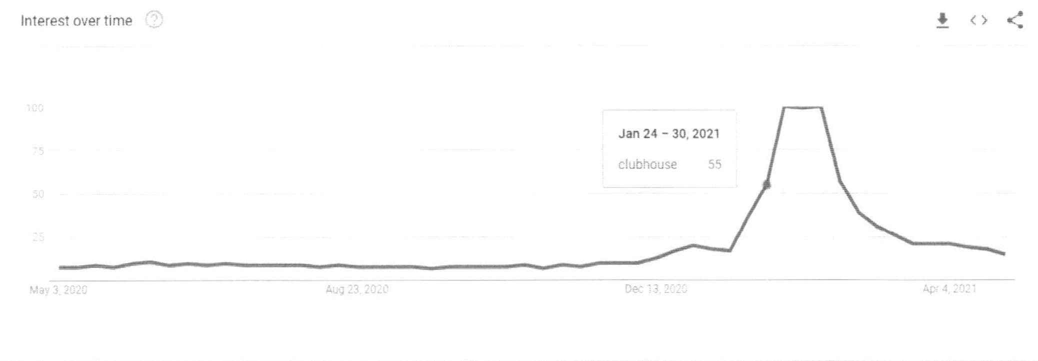

Figure 1. Google Search interest worldwide for term "clubhouse" for the past 12 months, % of max search volume

5. OTHER UNICORN PLATFORMS

To try and somewhat predict what Clubhouse's future will look like, we looked at another social media app that presented a new media format and saw incredible user growth - Snapchat. Snapchat acquired over 10 million users every 3 months in 2014 (Wagner, 2018). In 2016 Facebook introduced Instagram Stories that very closely resemble Snapchat's "Stories" media format, followed by stories on Facebook and WhatsApp. In the following years, Snapchat's growth almost stopped and maxed out at around 190 million daily active users in 2019. For Facebook, the introduction of Instagram Stories proved to be a big success with over 500 million daily active users in 2019 (Figure 2). Over a period of 3 years from '16 to '19, the two platforms coexisted. The same could happen to Clubhouse.

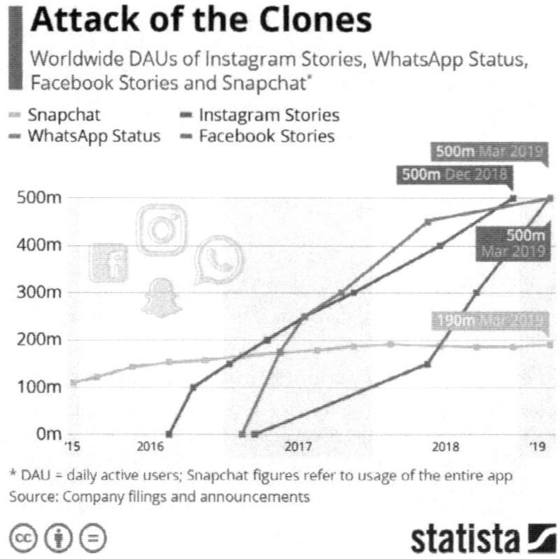

Figure 2. Number of daily active users on Snapchat, Instagram Stories, Facebook Stories and WhatsApp Status, 2015 – 2019, acquired from (Richter, 2020)

6. CONCLUSIONS

Using the data acquired through the Clubhouse API, we were able to conclude that most discussions and people's interests on Clubhouse are business oriented. By our own experience on the platform, we were able to confirm this as well. We can also conclude that some people are/were using Clubhouse as a learning platform, much like a webinar, where they can acquire high-value domain knowledge by listening in on expert discussions about a subject entirely free of charge. The popularity of "Networking" and "Meet new people" subtopics also signifies that Clubhouse is a (business) networking platform. People creating revenue with their personal brand on Clubhouse were also observed.

Many celebrities and high-profile executives also appeared on Clubhouse. We concluded that it is very plausible that their appearances had a significant impact on the platform's popularity. By reading the interviews, we were able to conclude that for celebrities, Clubhouse presents an interesting new media format and a new way to interact with fans. They find this new media format to be very authentic. This stands true in our own experience as well.

In conclusion, current Clubhouse's most popular topics are mainly business-oriented. However, that could quickly change, because the platform's format feels very authentic. This has already been noticed by the entertainment industry and might be noticed by even more people when the same core features are brought over to platforms such as Instagram, Twitter and Facebook. Recently, Clubhouse has been criticized for the lack of privacy options, especially because all user's contacts have to be uploaded to the app's servers in order to even use the app (Morrison, 2021). It remains to be seen whether Clubhouse will remain as popular once the COVID-19 pandemic ends and the competition catches up.

REFERENCES

Ali, R. (2021, February 22). *'Unfiltered access': Why Kevin Hart, Elon Musk, more celebs are connecting with fans on Clubhouse*. Retrieved from usatoday: https://eu.usatoday.com/story/entertainment/celebrities/2021/02/22/clubhouse-app-explainer-celebrities-how-to-get-unfiltered-access/6780989002/

Culliford, E. (2021, April 18). *Clubhouse closes new round of funding that would value app at $4 billion -source*. Retrieved from Clubhouse closes new round of funding that would value app at $4 billion -source: https://www.reuters.com/technology/clubhouse-closes-new-round-funding-that-would-value-app-4-billion-source-2021-04-18/

Daniel Pyeong Kang Kim, J. L. (2021). Elon Musk's Twitter and Its Correlation with Tesla's Stock. *International Journal of Data Science and Analysis, 7*(1), 13-19.

Dee, J. (2021). *Screenrant*. Retrieved from https://screenrant.com/celebrities-entertainers-comedians-follow-on-clubhouse-apple-social-media/

Jahnke, M. (2018). *Influencer Marketing* (1 ed.). Wiesbaden: Springer Gabler. doi:https://doi.org/10.1007/978-3-658-20854-7

John, A.-A. (2021, April 8). *Which Clubhouse Clone Is Most Likely to Succeed?* Retrieved from Make Use Of: https://www.makeuseof.com/which-clubhouse-clone-is-most-likely-to-succeed/

Morrison, S. (2021, February 22). *Vox Recode*. Retrieved from You've been invited to Clubhouse. Your privacy hasn't.: https://www.vox.com/recode/22278601/clubhouse-invite-privacy-contacts-app

Richter, F. (2020, August 7). *Statista.com*. Retrieved from Snapchat vs Facebook: Attack of the Clones: https://www.statista.com/chart/10558/daus-instagram-stories-whatsapp-status-snapchat/

Statista. (2021, April 30). *Number of weekly active Clubhouse users from April 2020 to February 2021*. Retrieved from Statista: https://www.statista.com/statistics/1199871/number-of-clubhouse-users/

Wagner, K. (2018, August 8). *'Stories' was Instagram's smartest move yet*. Retrieved from Vox Recode: https://www.vox.com/2018/8/8/17641256/instagram-stories-kevin-systrom-facebook-snapchat

FACTORS MOTIVATING WOMEN TO STUDY TECHNOLOGY: A QUANTITATIVE SURVEY AMONG YOUNG WOMEN IN NORWAY

Hilde G. Corneliussen, Gilda Seddighi, Anna Maria Urbaniak-Brekke and Morten Simonsen
Western Norway Research Institute, Norway

ABSTRACT

Women's underrepresentation in fields of information and communication technology (ICT) appears as a paradox in the context of Norway, a country that scores high on international gender equality indicators. Earlier research has argued that women's underrepresentation in ICT education might be a result of their lack of interest in ICT. In this paper we ask what motivates young women in Norway to enter technology studies. The analysis is based on a quantitative survey with 689 young women responding to questions about what had made them choose technology in high school or at university level. The results show that leading factors motivating the women are job opportunities, high salary and using technology for solving challenges. Interestingly, factors that are associated with boys' and men's interest in ICT such as computer games and leisure activities, are marginal as motivation for the women. The study thus confirms that young women are highly interested in fields of technology, however, their interests differ from what is often associated with young men. Based on the findings we suggest that measures recognising a wider image of technology are needed for motivating women to enter fields of technology.

KEYWORDS

Technology Studies, ICT Education, Motivational Factors, Young Women, Quantitative Data

1. INTRODUCTION

What motivates girls and women to study technology? This is an important question in today's society where technology has become ubiquitous across spheres and sectors. Digitalization has increased the need for technological experts and skills, suggesting a need for recruiting widely among young people, including women (Barbieri et al., 2020). However, women's underrepresentation in technology education and work has been persistent in many countries across the Western world. Currently, about 18% of information and communication technology (ICT) specialists in EU are women (EUROSTAT, 2019). In this paper we explore what motivates young women in Norway to study technology. Even though Norway scores high on international gender equality indicators, it has a strongly gender-segregated education and labour market. This is among other things visible in the fact that girls make up only one in four applicants to higher technology education in Norway (Samordna opptak, 2020).

Studies show that girls who are facing educational choices assume that boys have a higher interest in ICT than girls, and therefore also assume that boys are more skilled than girls in ICT subjects (Corneliussen, 2021). Although it has been suggested that women's lower participation in technology subjects is a result of lower career ambitious than men (Stoet & Geary, 2018), this is not supported by women's high participation in education and the labour force in Norway (Statistics Norway, 2018).

Both Norwegian and international research show that gender stereotypes identifying technology with boys and men make it particularly challenging for girls and women to establish professional self-confidence in technology and science (Cheryan et al., 2009; Jethwani et al., 2016; Margolis & Fisher, 2002; OECD, 2016). Such stereotypes also make it difficult for girls to identify female role models in technology professions (Corneliussen et al., 2019). While insight into higher technology education is a scarce commodity among both girls and boys (Grover et al., 2014), lack of such insight is more problematic for girls than for boys. Studies of girls' paths to technology education show that girls more than boys need support in order to make non-traditional educational choices (Corneliussen, 2021). This suggests that family and school are important supporters for girls' non-traditional educational choices (Eccles, 2015; Wang et al., 2015).

However, both parents and teachers have low expectations towards girls' interest in technology subjects (The Think Tank DEA, 2019), and girls are to a lesser degree than boys encouraged to engage in technology-related activities, both in education and leisure time (Corneliussen & Prøitz, 2016; Microsoft Corporation, 2017). Drawing from this literature, we explore what motivates young women to consider technology education as a relevant choice. Below we describe the quantitative method and the data gathered, before we present the analysis of how the women responded to the potential motivational factors we tested in this study.

2. METHOD

This paper is based on data gathered through a quantitative, online survey, with the title: "What motivates young women to choose technical vocational subjects, science subjects and technology subjects?" The questionnaire was distributed among young women to map a number of motivational factors. Attitudes were measured on a Likert scale with 5 values (e.g., strongly disagree, disagree, neutral, agree, strongly agree).

The survey was disseminated via random schools from all over Norway and through a majority of higher education institutions and vocational colleges. A total of 689 respondents completed the survey. Out of these, 61% were university and college students, 22% were students at upper secondary schools, and 9% at technical vocational schools. The survey includes young women from all parts of the country and respondents are distributed by city and village approximately in accordance with the general distribution of inhabitants in Norway. 7.7% of respondents were born in other countries than Norway, while the number of inhabitants with an immigrant background in Norway today is nearly 15%.

It is important to mention that in the question about factors influencing their motivation to study technology, respondents had the opportunity to choose more than one answer, and that is why the total number of answers (responses) is higher than the number of respondents. In order to avoid misunderstandings between number of respondents and number of responses, we present the results below in percentage (%).

3. FACTORS THAT INFLUENCE GIRLS' INTEREST IN TECHNOLOGY

We asked the women about a number of potential motivational factors identified in previous research, including motivational factors often associated with boys' "advantages" in technology (Corneliussen, 2021). This includes importance of support from family and school (Eccles, 2015; Ikonen et al., 2018), attitudes to technology originating in leisure activities and experiences from school (Master et al., 2017), and expectations for future profession and career (Vainionpää et al., 2019). The figure below (figure 1) provides an overview of how the girls responded "agree" (including "strongly agree"), "neutral" or "disagree" (including "strongly disagree") on the question of whether these factors have influenced them to choose or considering choosing science or technology subjects at high school or at university. In this part of the paper, we present the factors that prove to be most important for the respondents.

3.1 Working Life

As figure 1 shows, ambitions associated with working life dominate among the motivating factors for choosing science and technology subjects among the women, and all these factors have received more than 50% support. "Exciting job opportunities in technology professions" reigns supremely with over 93% agreement. More than 80% of the women agree that "job opportunities", the importance of "technology knowledge", and opportunities for a "good salary" are important motivating factors. In contrast to an often-repeated scepticism towards women's interest in technology, more than 3 out of 4 women in our study want to work with technology. More than 70% of the women are motivated by technology as a means of working practically and more than 80% are encouraged by using technology for solving societal challenges. A lower proportion, but still more than half, is motivated by the fact that "girls are wanted in technology professions", suggesting that a majority of the young women feel welcome in technology. About 3 in 4 applicants to health care are women in Norway (Samordna opptak, 2020). Therefore, we also wanted to learn whether the link between health care and technology was of interest for young women. Nearly 3 in 5 women agreed that "technology as important in the health sector" was motivating for choosing technology.

3.2 Schools and Education

"Technology as an elective in upper secondary school" is the most important motivating factor associated with schools and education, with 53% women agreeing that this has had the greatest impact on the choice of studying technology. On the other hand, only 26% agree that "technology as an elective in secondary school" has been important. This may reflect that the young women had not perceived technology at secondary school as very motivating, but it may also reflect that technology has not been a widespread elective at lower secondary levels in Norway.

Teachers' encouragement is the second most important motivating factor associated with schools, with 40% identifying this as important, with information received at an Education Fair (an annual event) (38%), and information from supervisors, teachers, and others at school (35.6%) following close behind. "Events that make girls familiar with technology" and "visits by technology companies" are among the factors that score the lowest with 25.5% and 24%.

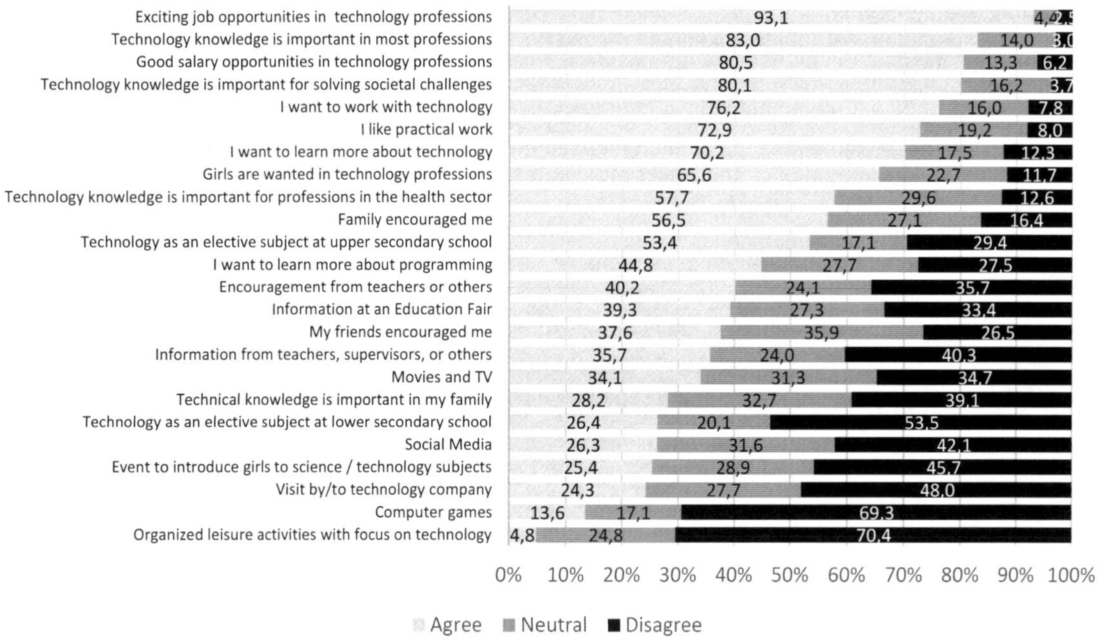

Figure 1. What has had the greatest impact on your choice of technical vocational subjects, science subjects, engineering, and technology subjects?

3.3 Family, Friends, and Leisure Activities

The family is important as a source of encouragement (56%). This is relatively independent of the family's relationship to technology, since only 28% of the women agree that technology is important in their family. Social media plays a role as a motivating factor for about one in four women, while traditional media such as film and TV scores slightly higher. Encouragement from friends scores 19 percentage points lower than encouragement from family and suggests that family influences the choice of field of study more than friends.

Contrary to what is often expected in surveys of boys' study choices (DiSalvo & Bruckman, 2009), we find that "computer games" (13.5%) and "leisure activities with focus on technology" (5%) are among the motivating factors that received the least support among the women. It is particularly interesting to note that some of the motivating factors that are most associated with boys and men (McKinsey & Company and Pivotal Ventures, 2018) have the least significance for the women in our study.

4. DISCUSSION

Gendered perceptions related to educations and professions influence young people who are in the process of choosing a career path. Gender stereotypes are shown to limit young people's "opportunities" – i.e., which professions and educations they can imagine themselves to enter (NOU, 2019: 19). For instance, subject areas related to ICT are often associated with boys' and men's interest in ICT such as gaming, and programming as a leisure time activity (McKinsey & Company and Pivotal Ventures, 2018). The same types of activities got a low score by the women in our survey and are thus less important for motivating young women to enter technology programs. Many of the highest rated motivational factors by women rather emphasise the importance of technology and technology knowledge in a future career perspective. More specifically, using technology for solving societal challenges was identified as an important motivation by 4 out of 5 women. Thus, different from earlier research claiming that girls are less ambitious in technology education and career than boys (Stoet & Geary, 2018), we find that the factors which have the greatest meaning for women considering studying technology are connected mainly to future career opportunities. Exciting jobs, good salary, and technology knowledge as important were the main motivational factors for our respondents.

Other studies show that parental support and encouragement is important for young people's educational choices, and especially for girls' and young women's choice to enter male dominated educational fields (Eccles, 2015; Think Tank DEA, 2019; Wang et al., 2015). Our study, however, supports earlier research finding that girls' and young women find less support and encouragement than boys and men from family and school for choosing technology. Our study shows that influence from family and school means less, and particularly at lower secondary school, few respondents felt that they had been motivated to think about choosing technology in their future education. Thus, we find that school, one of the main arenas for preparing students for future career ambitions, seem to play a minor role in motivating girls and young women for choosing technology. Furthermore, lower secondary school play a less important role for motivating young women than upper secondary school. This indicates that the young women have received support and encouragement for choosing technology late in the process of identifying the field of their future career.

5. CONCLUSION

To sum up, our survey documents that activities and interests that have been perceived as a door opener to ICT education for boys and men, in particular activities associated with leisurely relations to computers, have not had the same importance for young women. This should, however, not be misunderstood as women's lack of interest for technology, as the survey also documents young women's motivation to study technology. However, the most important motivational factors are associated with career prospects, solving societal challenges, and a desire to learn and to work with technology. The conclusion we draw from this study is thus that young women have high ambitions for choosing to study and work with technology, but also that they experience limited support from schools and family – arenas representing important influence on educational choices.

It has been suggested that measures are needed for supporting girls and young women to choose male dominated studies such as technology (Corneliussen, 2021; Margolis & Fisher, 2002). The actions should, however, involve schools to a greater extent than the survey documents, and the involvement should be at an earlier stage than upper secondary school. Furthermore, the study suggests that presenting technology as vital for solving societal challenges makes technology more attractive for young women.

Rather than emphasising technology in the image of boys' and men's interests in technology as a leisure activity (Corneliussen & Seddighi, 2020), the perspective of technology as important for solving societal challenges involves alternative images of technology, for instance associated with environmental issues. More importantly, a wider notion of what technology can be will also challenge gender stereotypes of who fits to work with technology.

ACKNOWLEDGMENT

The project was assigned and funded by the Norwegian Directorate for Children, Youth, and Family Affairs.

REFERENCES

Barbieri, D., Caisl, J., Karu, M., Lanfredi, G., Mollard, B., Peciukonis, V., . . . Salanauskaitė, L. (2020). *Gender Equality Index 2020: Digitalisation and the future of work*. Luxembourg: EIGE: European Institute for Gender Equality.

Cheryan, S., Plaut, V. C., Davies, P. G., & Steele, C. M. (2009). Ambient Belonging: How Stereotypical Cues Impact Gender Participation in Computer Science. *Journal of Personality and Social Psychology,* 97(6), 1045-1060.

Corneliussen, H. G. (2021). Women empowering themselves to fit in ICT. In E. Lechman (Ed.), *Technology and Women's Empowerment*. London: Routledge.

Corneliussen, H. G., & Prøitz, L. (2016). Kids Code in a rural village in Norway: could code clubs be a new arena for increasing girls' digital interest and competence? *Information, Communication & Society,* 19(1), 95-110.

Corneliussen, H. G., & Seddighi, G. (2020). Employers' Mixed Signals to Women in IT: Uncovering how Gender Equality Ideals are Challenged by Organizational Context. In P. Kommers & G. C. Peng (Eds.), *Proceedings for the International Conference ICT, Society, and Human Beings 2020* (41-48). IADIS: IADIS Press.

Corneliussen, H. G., Seddighi, G., & Dralega, C. A. (2019). Women's Experience of Role Models in IT: Landmark women, substitutes, and supporters. In Ø. Helgesen, E. Nesset, G. Mustafa, P. Rice, & R. Glavee-Geo (Eds.), *Modeller: Fjordantologien 2019* (375-395). Oslo: Universitetsforlaget.

DiSalvo, B. J., & Bruckman, A. (2009). Questioning video games' influence on CS interest *Proceedings of the 4th International Conference on Foundations of Digital Games* (272-278): ACM.

Eccles, J. S. (2015). Gendered Socialization of STEM Interests in the Family. *Journal of Gender, Science and Technology,* 7(2), 116-132. Retrieved from http://genderandset.open.ac.uk/index.php/genderandset/article/view/419/692

EUROSTAT. (2019). *ICT specialists in employment: statistics explained.* https://ec.europa.eu/eurostat/statistics-explained/index.php/ICT_specialists_in_employment [Accessed 10 May 2021].

Grover, S., Pea, R., & Cooper, S. (2014). Remedying misperceptions of computer science among middle school students *Proceedings of the 45th ACM technical symposium on Computer science education* (343-348): ACM.

Ikonen, K., Leinonen, R., Asikainen, M. A., & Hirvonen, P. E. (2018). The influence of parents, teachers, and friends on ninth graders' educational and career choices. *2018,* 9(3), 316-338. Retrieved from http://genderandset.open.ac.uk/index.php/genderandset/article/view/526/876

Jethwani, M. M., Memon, N., Seo, W., & Richer, A. (2016). "I Can Actually Be a Super Sleuth": Promising Practices for Engaging Adolescent Girls in Cybersecurity Education. *Journal of Educational Computing Research,* 55(1), 3-25.

Margolis, J., & Fisher, A. (2002). *Unlocking the clubhouse. Women in computing*. Cambridge, Mass.: MIT Press.

Master, A., Cheryan, S., Moscatelli, A., & Meltzoff, A. N. (2017). Programming experience promotes higher STEM motivation among first-grade girls. *Journal of Experimental Child Psychology,* 160, 92-106.

McKinsey & Company and Pivotal Ventures. (2018). *Rebooting representation: Using CSR and philanthropy to close the gender gap in tech*. https://www.rebootrepresentation.org/report-highlights/ [Accessed 10 May 2021].

Microsoft Corporation. (2017). *Why Europe's Girls Aren't Studying STEM.* https://bit.ly/2Q3Ba6q White paper, Microsoft Philanthropies [Accessed 10 May 2021].

NOU. (2019: 19). *Jenterom, gutterom og mulighetsrom— Likestillingsutfordringer blant barn og unge*. Oslo:KUD.

OECD. (2016). *PISA 2015 results (Volume I). Excellence and equity in education*. Paris: OECD Publishing.

Samordna opptak. (2020). *The Norwegian Universities and Colleges Admission*. https://www.samordnaopptak.no.

Statistics Norway. (2018). *Women and men in Norway*. Oslo: Statistics Norway.

Stoet, G., & Geary, D. C. (2018). The Gender-Equality Paradox in Science, Technology, Engineering, and Mathematics Education. *Psychological Science,* 29(4), 581-593. doi:10.1177/0956797617741719

The Think Tank DEA. (2019). *Putting the spotlight on STEM possibilities for youths in Denmark: Does gender play a role in developing youths' interest in STEM?* https://bit.ly/3q6I0po [Accessed 16 June 2021].

Vainionpää, F., Kinnula, M. et al. (2019). Gendering and Segregation in Girls' Perceptions of IT as a Career Choice: A Nexus Analytic Inquiry. In A. Siarheyeva, C. Barry et al. (Eds.), *Information Systems Development: Information Systems Beyond 2020 (ISD 2019 Proceedings)* (1-12). Toulon, France: ISEN Yncréa Méditerranée.

Wang, J., Hong, H., Ravitz, J., & Ivory, M. (2015). *Gender differences in factors influencing pursuit of computer science and related fields.* Proceedings of the 2015 ACM Conference on Innovation and Technology in CS Education.

TECHNOLOGICAL IMPERATIVES OF YOUNG PEOPLE IN FINLAND – COMPETENCES AND OPPORTUNITIES NEEDED FOR DIGITAL AGENCY

Sari Tuuva-Hongisto[1], Kristiina Korjonen-Kuusipuro[1] and Päivi Armila[2]
[1]South-Eastern Finland University of Applied Sciences (XAMK), Patteristonkatu 3 D, 50100 Mikkeli, Finland
[2]University of Eastern Finland, Yliopistokatu 2, 80100 Joensuu, Finland

ABSTRACT

This short paper investigates preconditions of digital agency of young people in Finland. Finland represents a society developed on digi-technological imperatives, and with young people who are considered as "digi-natives" with competences and opportunities to benefit digitalization in their everyday lives and life-courses. However, statistics still show "digital divide" and unequal sociomaterial stratification among them. To understand digital citizenship in the broadest possible sense and to empower youth as digital citizens, we need to make the inequalities visible, both at the societal, structural and life-course level.

KEYWORDS

Digital Agency, Digital Divide, Digital Natives, Finland, Youth

1. INTRODUCTION

The digital reality is a fundamental part of youth's everyday life: studies, work, leisure time, and activism – from personal and collective identity formations to different forms of participation (McMillan & Morrison 2006). Young people are active producers of digital youth cultures and digital contents and they actively participate in digital cultures in terms of their personal development, identity expression, and participation. Despite of all this, all socio-technical imaginaries and equality-based political promises of digitalization have not been realized among youth. Contemporary statistics in Finland inevitably prove that, in fact, there has been an increase in the number and complexity in, for example, youth's learning difficulties, even illiteracy, as well as growing inequality in welfare conditions and experiences. It is obvious that some users benefit digitalization over others (Hargittai 2008). In our paper, we argue that moving towards truly participatory digital agency requires analytic explorations of how digital information and communication technologies are implicated in social inequalities (Halford & Savage 2010) and in digital gaps and divides. Multidisciplinary research of digital divide has brought to the fore how digital skills, digital literacy, and benefits of using digital technologies vary greatly among people. Bridging these "new" digital divides calls for understanding of "digital literacy crusaders" (Meinrath et al. 2013), as well as critical multidisciplinary analysis of inequalities created by digitalization (van Dijk 2018).

In this paper we present the conceptual background and methodological choices of our ongoing research (2020-2024) where we explore structural inequalities as lived realities by asking: What kind of differences in gender, social class, (dis)ability, religion, and ethnicity produce and maintain in young people's use of digital opportunity structures - and what kind of a "loopback" their use has to their socio-economic and socio-cultural positions, in terms of pre-existing social inequalities connected with, e.g., education and homeplace. Methodologically we stress that ethnographic approach offers a possibility to study the dynamics of digital everyday, and thus enables self-reflection of the meanings of digital possibilities as well as accumulation with other opportunities and capacities, and thereby a modern understanding of how digital agency of young people evolve.

2. CONCEPTUAL BACKGROUND

Finland represents a crystallized idea of a digital society that has been developed around the ideology of technological imperatives (Talsi & Tuuva-Hongisto 2009) and socio-technical imaginaries (Jasanoff & Kim 2009). Technologies have been kept apart from social structures and processes, and digital ICTs are positioned as a neutral good (Halford & Savage 2010). These logics have been seen in, e.g., a non-questioning political push towards digitalization of significant services, education, and political participation; to transform life-chances and a way to equal opportunities for social/societal participation in every corner of the society, especially among youth as "digital natives" and "cyber-children" (Prensky 2001; Tapscott 2008; Holloway & Valentine 2003). In fact, youth seem to consider the benefits of new technology, and often they themselves are also directing the development of digitalization. They are seen as a generation who finds and adopts digital services first, and the youth-cultural meaning of digitalization is huge (Ito et al. 2010).

While youth with socio-culturally "proper" backgrounds cope well within the requirements and offerings of digitalization, the statistics show intensification of deprivation, disadvantage, and political withdrawal among those who lack the demanded socio-cultural and material resources (Statistics Finland 2016a; 2016b; 2018). In addition, digi-technological imperatives have not washed away the dividing significance of concrete homeplace spatiality in youth's life-choice possibilities concerning education, labor, leisure, and societal participation (Armila et al. 2018). Overall, today we witness a strengthening of structure-based, intersectional inequalities among youth: complex processes of socio-cultural stratification that is intertwined with material opportunities as well.

Digital agency as a methodological concept can clarify the dynamics of various connections between young people, their self and others, and the socio-cultural practices around them (Guo & Dalli 2016). This also means that attempts to support agency must always be embedded in situations where needs and desires of young people are influenced by their learning resources, which also include places and people around them. Thus, the 'self' dimension of agency can be seen closely connected to one's socio-cultural environment. Digital agency can also be seen as a situated and contextualized dynamic process where several modalities of agency (e.g. knowing how to, being able to, having to, having the opportunity to, wanting to and feeling) needs to be possessed (Jyrkämä 2008).

Place as a significant material and socio-cultural landscape to grow up towards early adulthood is considered far too seldom in social-scientific and cultural analyses of meanings, lifestyles and life-courses (Armila et al. 2016; Armila et al. 2018). Here, we understand youth's home-places as environments with asymmetrical material, socio-cultural and youth-cultural opportunity structures. To reveal the meaning of place and regionality, three fundamentally different Finnish localities are studied in our project: remote and emptying agricultural municipality in a regional "periphery", a small working-classed and industrial town that continuously seems to lose its young population, and a growing, "youthful" city that has an image of a tempting region especially for young adults. While in 2005 there were 2500 new inhabitants born in the youthful city, the remote municipality received only 20. In addition, the youthful city receives amounts of young movers every year, while youth of remote places often leave their homes at the age of 16, to seek educational possibilities that do not exist near them. The small town, then, appears as a place from where the young ones just want to move away, even though there are possibilities of schooling and at least low-paid working. As research sites, these three localities are chosen as cases that represent digital society differently and offer different socio-cultural, material, and physical environments for youth to grow up. In all this, the project makes use of the critical neo-materialistic perspective and brings it strongly into empirical analyses of digitalization and virtualization.

3. METHODOLOGICAL CHOICES

Previous research has called for more analyses on how everyday interactions and relationships influence how we see our digital selves, and research on how individual characters and structural factors shaping disadvantages come together (Helsper 2021). To answer these questions a special methodology is needed. One way to reach this in our project is to combine 'associational sociology' (Halford & Savage 2010) and multi-sited (digital) ethnographies (Marcus 1995; Hine 2015). This combination allows a unique investigation of digi-natives' realities, lived youth-cultures, and divides combined with digital materialism. The critical sociological scrutiny traces the systematic and structural divisions and socio-cultural mechanisms that produce and maintain disadvantages in how digital possibility structures are and can be "capitalized" among young people.

Our approach combines qualitative and quantitative data in its analyses of digi-cultural structures, opportunities, practices, and meanings. **Digital upstairs, downstairs** as a sub-project drives its inspiration from a need of understanding processes that link Internet and the web to social inequality (Halford & Savage 2010). The analytical aim is, first, to trace the unequal socio-cultural factors of the digital divide among youth, and second, to analyze the mechanisms within which they, in turn, become lived realities in young people's life-worlds and life-choices in the three different living areas. This look leans on views from critical sociology and utilizes the concept of digital opportunity structures. These contain, e.g., digital infra and access to it, but also the practice: individual, cultural, classed, and localized knowhow, and the contents, services, and preferences of digitality from the evaluative and choosy view of young informants. Concretely, a questionnaire for young participants has been developed and delivered.

The second sub-project, **lived digital practices,** defines young people not only as victims of unequal structures but also active agents within their social and youth-cultural environments. Their digi-cultural practices are made visible with a media ethnographic approach which enables to analyze different youth-cultural and territorialized forms in the ways young people themselves actively produce material into digital agendas and how these can be explained through the lenses of critical conceptualizations of new materialism. The aim is to understand different ways of how places traverse online/offline contexts and are collaborative, participatory, open and public (Postill & Pink 2012). It enables to make visible connections and intra-actions between online and locality-based realities (Tuuva-Hongisto 2012). Concretely, we have made individual interviews and focus group interviews with young people to discuss what young people think about digitalization and what kind of role it has in their lives. We have also used digital ethnographic approaches to look more closely what kind of practices these young people have in digital environments.

4. CONCLUSION

The ethical, youth political and science political basis of youth research can be traced back to a classical theory of the German sociologists of education, Karl Mannheim (1928), who celebrated young people as a generation with a fresh contact to society and its changes. Following this, it could be reasoned that youth as a generation have no problems in dealing with today's digital opportunity structures. However, the reality seems not to be so univocal. It is obvious that we cannot separate social inequalities from spatial and technical developments.

Inequalities in a digital society have usually been studied by looking at old people as incapable to adopt the digital ways to "come along" and take care of pressing matters. In our project, we bring youth as a special target for the scrutiny of inequalities in the digital society. Young people who were born in the year 2005 can be seen as a "digital generation" and are chosen to represent the target population of this project. During the four years of this research, they will go through fundamental transitions of their life-courses concerning education, employment, moving away from their childhood families, and becoming full-aged: growing up towards emerging adulthood in economically and socio-culturally different environments, and become mature citizens of a digital society. Our study also widens the analytical discussions of digital society by taking place as a concretely significant factor and effective environment for growing up as "digital natives". Following digital threads of belonging in young people's everyday lives, we can trace and identify digital gaps that are not yet known. Virtual opportunity structures are claimed to disappear the restricting dimensions of distances and other material regional characters (e.g., unequal possibilities of education, employment, consumption, and leisure), but more research-based knowledge is needed in order to be convinced by this imaginary.

ACKNOWLEDGEMENT

DEQUAL-project is funded by the Academy of Finland (330574).

REFERENCES

Armila, P., Halonen, T. and Käyhkö, M., 2016. *Reunamerkintöjä Hylkysyrjästä. Nuorten elämää ja tulevaisuudensuunnitelmia harvaan asutulla maaseudulla*. The Finnish Youth Research Society, Helsinki.

Armila, P., Käyhkö, M. and Pöysä, V., 2018. On the Educational Edges of a Learning Society. The Finnish Hinterland as a Framework of Educational Choices of Young People. *The Journal of Youth Studies*, Vol. 29, No. 9, pp. 1198– 1215. https://doi.org/10.1080/13676261.2018.1453128.

van Dijk, J. 2018. Afterword: the state of Digital Divide Theory. In Ragnedda, M, & Muschert, GW (eds.) *Theorizing Digital Divides*. Routledge, London & New York, pp. 199–206.

Guo, K. and Dalli, D., 2016. Belonging as a Force of Agency: An Exploration of Immigrant Children's Everyday Life in Early Childhood Settings. *Global Studies of Childhood*, Vol. 6, No. 3, pp. 254–267. https://doi.org/10.1177/2043610616665036

Hargittai, E., 2008. The Digital Reproduction of Inequality. In D. Grusky (ed.) *Social Stratification. Class, Race, and Gender in Sociological Perspective*. Routledge, London & New York.

Halford, S. and Savage, M., 2010. Reconceptualizing Digital Social Inequality. *Information, Communication & Society*, Vol. 13, No.7, pp. 937–955. https://doi.org/10.1080/1369118X.2010.499956

Helsper, E.J., 2021. *The Digital Disconnect. The Social Causes and Consequences of Digital Inequalities*. Sage, London.

Hine, C., 2015. *Ethnography for the Internet: Embedded, Embodied and Everyday*. Routledge, London & New York.

Holloway, S.L. and Valentine, G., 2003. *Cyberkids. Children in the Information Age*. Routledge/Falmer, London and New York.

Ito, M. et al., 2010. *Hanging out, Messing around and Geeking out: Kids Living and Learning with New Media*. The MIT Press, Cambridge, Massachusetts, and London.

Jasanoff, S. and Kim, S-H., 2009. Containing the Atom: Sociotechnical Imaginaries and Nuclear Power in the United States and South Korea. *Minerva*, Vol. 47 No. 2, pp. 119–146. https://doi.org/10.1007/s11024-009-9124-4.

Jyrkämä, J., 2008. Toimijuus, Ikääntyminen ja arkielämä – hahmottelua teoreettis-metodologiseksi viitekehykseksi [Agency, aging, and everyday life: An outline for a theoretical-methodological framework]. *Gerontologia*, Vol. 4 (2002), pp. 190–203. http://urn.fi/URN:NBN:fi:ELE-1405542.

Marcus, G. E., 1995. Ethnography in/of the world system: The emergence of multi-sited ethnography. *Annual Review of Anthropology*, 24(1995), 95–117.

Manheim, K., 1928. The Problem of Generations. In Mannheim, K: *Essays*. Routledge, London.

McMillan, S.J. and Morrison, M., 2006. Coming of Age With the Internet: A Qualitative Exploration of How the Internet Has Become an Integral Part of Young People's Lives. *New Media & Society*, Vol. 8 No. 1, pp. 73–95. https://doi.org/10.1177/1461444806059871.

Meinrath, S. D., Losey, J. & Lennet B., 2013. Afterword. Internet freedom, nuanced digital divides, and the Internet craftsman. In Ragnedda, M., & Muschert, G. W. (Eds.) *The digital divide: The internet and social inequality in international perspective*. Routledge, London & New York, pp. 309–315.

Postill, J. and Pink, S., 2012: Social Media Ethnography: The Digital Researcher in a Messy Web. *Media International Australia* Vol. 145, No. 1. https://doi.org/10.1177/1329878X1214500114

Prensky, M., 2001. Digital Natives, Digital Immigrants. *On the Horizon*, Vol. 9, No. 5.

Statistics Finland 2016a; 2016b; 2018: https://www.stat.fi/index_en.html.

Talsi, N. & Tuuva-Hongisto, S., 2009. "Ei vietetty sinä jouluna tekniikan riemujuhlaa" Teknologinen imperatiivi teknologiaelämäkerroissa. *Kulttuurintutkimus*, Vol. 26, pp. 71–82. http://urn.fi/URN:NBN:fi:ELE-1551839.

Tapscott, D., 2008. *Grown up Digital! How the Net Generation is Changing your World*. The McGraw-Hill Companies, New York.

Tuuva-Hongisto, S., 2007. *Tilattuja tarinoita. Etnografinen tutkimus pohjoiskarjalaisesta tietoyhteiskunnasta*. Joensuun yliopiston humanistisia julkaisuja n:o 47. Joensuu.

VIRTUAL INDEPENDENCE: TEEN SOCIAL MEDIA USE DURING THE SUMMER OF QUARANTINE

Vanessa P. Dennen, Stacey A. Rutledge, Lauren M. Bagdy, Stephen Bunn, Daeun Jung, Casey Cargill, Catherine Cosgrove, Amber Hedquist and Shannon McWaters
Florida State University
Tallahassee, FL USA

ABSTRACT

During Summer 2020, the COVID-19 pandemic limited people's contact with others outside of their households. Teenagers experienced a great deal of disruption to their lives and found themselves reliant on their phones and social media to occupy their time and maintain peer connections. In this study, we examine the activities of 43 teens in the United States. Teens were interviewed twice and kept week-long video diaries documenting their daily online and offline activities. Findings show that social media activities were critical for maintaining friendships and provided a sense of virtual independence during quarantine. Teens also pursued independent informal learning activities via social media. However, themes of shame also arose, with teens internalizing negative messages from parents and media about social media use.

KEYWORDS

COVID-19, Informal Learning, Social Media, Teenagers

1. INTRODUCTION

Teens' social media use is a complex activity that is often poorly understood by the adults in their lives. Social media accounts, nestled into apps on smartphones, provide teens with the ability to explore networked worlds privately while sitting in the same rooms as parents or teachers. Adults may dismiss teen online behavior as a waste of time or distraction, or they may try to surveil and scrutinize it as a measure of control over teen behavior (Dennen et al., 2019; Rutledge et al., 2019). Heavy teen social media use can be associated with poor mental health outcomes (Woods & Scott, 2016), and also with fear of missing out (FOMO) (Barry et al., 2017). In this study, we look at how teens used social media platforms and their personal networks to foster virtual independence and satisfy a variety of personal needs. The study is situated during the Summer of 2020, when the COVID-19 pandemic slowed or curtailed most in-person social, educational, and work activities. This time frame offers a unique perspective on teen online life because it represents a period of increased reliance on online interactions for most teens (Dennen et al., 2021) and decreased reasons to experience FOMO.

2. RESEARCH QUESTIONS

The purpose of this study was to examine teens' online activities during the COVID-19 pandemic to see how social media helped or hindered their independence during this time. The study was conducted during summer, when school was out of session and great uncertainty loomed about the school year ahead. This study was guided by the following research questions:

1. How did teens use social media and networked technologies during the Summer of 2020?
2. How did teens use social media and networked technologies to support virtual independence and interests?
3. How did age and other factors inhibit or encourage virtual independence?

We use the term *social media and networked technologies* (SMNT) in this study to be inclusive of the broad array of tools, platforms, and communication channels frequented by teens in this study. In other words, we were just as interested in their networked gaming interactions as we were in their Snapchat streaks.

3. METHOD

The participants in this study are 43 teenagers, aged 13 through 18, recruited from a midsize city in the United States. Participants were recruited via a survey. In selecting the sample, we attempted to distribute participants across age groups and include representation across zip codes and schools to ensure socioeconomic diversity. We also sought to balance gender and mirror the city's racial demographics to the extent possible. There were 25 female and 18 male participants. Table 1 provides an overview of the sample by age, race, and grade level. The study was approved by the Florida State University Human Subjects Committee. All participants provided consent or assent, and parents provided consent, as appropriate by age.

Table 1. Overview of participants

Age	*N*	Grade	*N*	Race	*N*
13	7	7	5	Asian	2
14	4	8	5	Black	13
15	8	9	10	Latinx	1
16	10	10	6	Mixed Race	3
17	10	11	11	White	24
18	4	12	6		
TOTAL	43		43		43

Data collection included interviews and solicited diaries, which are helpful for capturing information about daily activities as well as reflective commentary about those activities (Bartlett & Milligan, 2015). Each participant was interviewed twice, with 8-10 days between the interviews. Interviews were conducted by videoconference and lasted between 30 minutes and an hour. Between the two interviews, participants were asked to submit a diary record of their activities and their experiences using social media that day. The diary consisted of two parts: a form to systematically document social media use, activities, and happiness level each day, and a 3-5 minute video. Participants recorded diary entries for 5-7 days between interviews and were offered a gift card incentive for their participation. All interviews and video recordings were transcribed. Analysis involved thematic coding using inductive and deductive coding approaches. The deductive codes were derived from previous research (Dennen et al., 2020; Rutledge et al., 2019), while the inductive codes were derived from the interview and video recording data. Data analysis on the larger project is ongoing, and this paper reflects initial findings.

4. FINDINGS

4.1 SMNT Use During Summer 2020

Not surprisingly, most teens in this study described SMNT as their connection to the outside world during Summer 2020. Although their city was no longer under a stay-at-home order during the study, many teens were at home with parents every day, with nowhere to go. SMNT became a means of passing time, which manifested through passive activities such as streaming media and active ones such as interacting with close friends. A 16-year-old girl described this change in terms of her Snapchat use:

> Before quarantine I guess I used to send streaks. Like I had an 800-day streak with somebody who I didn't even necessarily talk to that much. We just sent streaks back and forth every day, and then that ended and I don't even – like I don't even have a streak with my boyfriend anymore. Like I just don't – I just don't really care. I mean, I'll look at people's stories, and I guess like I'll post something on like my private story every once in a while, but I mean, I don't really send streaks anymore.

Similarly, a 15-year-old boy shared how his choices about SMNT use reflect the desire to connect to specific people. He opted to not use Facebook because, "there were no people that I actually like knew on there. There was just like – I mean, there were people I knew, but not people that I would like – that I want to see their posts really." He went on to explain how his SMNT experience during Summer 2020 was focused on interacting with "friends that I have in real life. There was somebody I met online that I played [a networked game] with once, but after that I never talked to them again. And then there are some friends that I've made through other friends online, but they also live in [hometown], as far as I'm aware."

Although social media connected teens to friends, it was not necessarily a panacea. A 17-year-old boy shared, "When you don't have anything else to do and you sit at your house and you just pretty much are on it all day it can like really affect your happiness." Toward late summer 2020 this boy got a job and felt happier to be leaving the house. This teen and others expressed that social media alone could not satisfy their needs for human connection, but rather functioned as a temporary proxy during a difficult situation.

4.2 SMNT, Virtual Independence, and Interests

The teens relied heavily on their smartphones and computers to connect to their friends and entertain themselves during Summer 2020. However, the role of SMNT in fostering virtual independence was broader than just providing private spaces for social interaction, although that form of virtual independence is developmentally appropriate and its importance should not be underscored. SMNT enabled independent explorations of hobbies, entrepreneurship, identity, and values, as can be seen in these examples:

- Hobbies: A teen interested in makeup design occupied herself by accepting makeup "challenges" from her network that she would then recreate and share.
- Entrepreneurship: Three teens (unconnected) started their own businesses and marketed their products over social media, creating their own revenue streams.
- Identity: A transgender teen used SMNT to be his true self among friends, whereas with his family he was still maintaining the identity (e.g., name and gender) given to him at birth.
- Values: A teen whose mother would not allow her to attend local BLM protests learned about them via SMNT and made the choice to participate online.

Of these activities, only entrepreneurship involved parents. Parents were needed to set up bank accounts and procure supplies (e.g., parents controlled the household Amazon.com accounts or planned shopping trips). Otherwise, these activities were teen-initiated and in some instances done without any parent awareness.

4.3 Age and Other Mitigating Factors

In a time when physical distancing and isolation was encouraged, teens used their phones to maintain independent connections with friends and affinity spaces. Teens might be at home for days under the direct or indirect supervision of parents, but they still could have private conversations with close friends and congregate in adult-free spaces. Network size affected the types of activities that teens engaged in. Those who had smaller local friend networks pre-pandemic had fewer local network connections to maintain during the pandemic and were less likely to feel the social void created by staying at home.

Older teens expressed a greater sense of independence than younger teens both online and in the physical realm. Older teens reported that amid the pandemic they were still able to see friends, although they were doing so in smaller groups or 'pods.' Additionally, they would go to stores or restaurants to pick up items for the family. A common theme was transportation. Teens who were old enough to drive went out more frequently. A 14-year-old girl shared, "My mom definitely keeps me in the house. If it was my way I'd be out everywhere with my mask, and not – I'll take all the precautions, don't get me wrong, but I cannot be in this house." Because she could no longer go to the mall and cheer practice with friends, she spent time Facetiming and texting them and watching videos on TikTok.

Younger teens tended to have more constraints on their social media access and smartphones imposed by parents, although some parents of younger teens relented on prior rules considering the pandemic. For example, a 14-year-old boy said, "some of my friends, since they didn't have social media before, I think their parents let them get it during COVID. These friends like. Say, they didn't have a phone but they had a laptop or something." This connection between age and independence was observed in the data collection process, too. In most instances, we contacted teens directly to schedule interviews and provide reminders, but parents were intermediary contacts for some younger teens. We observed parenting differences by age in a pair of siblings. The older teen (age 16) appeared to have great freedom, going out with her friends and recording her video diaries in a number of locations where she was either alone or had off-camera friends nearby. In contrast, the younger sibling (age 14) always had parents in her vicinity when participating in interviews or video diaries.

Despite the positive independent activities that teens shared and the unusual circumstances imposed by the pandemic, an interesting emotion emerged: shame. Teens expressed anxiety that they were spending too much time online and were dismissive of the value entertainment-focused activities. For example, a 13-year-old girl declared herself "ashamed" of spending two hours watching TikTok videos one day, and later said she followed too many people. Another teen shared how she monitored her online time so she would know when it was too much. Upon probing, these teens had internalized and were repeating the words and judgments of adults who shamed them. In practice, they thought they should feel bad but were unlikely to change their behaviors. Adults not only modeled the shaming discourse, but also acted to prevent the shameful behavior. One 13-year-old participant lost phone privileges during the study period for spending too much time online. This punitive action demonstrates how critical phone access is for teens and how phones survey as a form of currency for achieving virtual independence.

5. CONCLUSION

The independence themes seen in this study echo other studies of teen online life. In a survey conducted during Summer 2020, a sample of 4762 teens reported using social media to connect with friends and entertain themselves, but a decrease in posting about themselves (Dennen et al., 2021). Other studies similarly noted an increase in screen time (Campbell et al., 2021) and identified friendship maintenance as an important way for teens to manage stress (Ellis et al., 2020). However, in contrast, Ellis et al. (2020) also found connections with depression and loneliness. The teens we spoke with missed seeing friends, but overall reported that they were happy. They were not conflicted about friendship maintenance over social media. The difference in findings may reflect the passing of time. Whereas Ellis et al. (2020) collected their data in April, when COVID-19 was a relatively new phenomenon and people were under stay-at-home orders. Another study conducted at that time found that teens were also driving less than usual, and primarily for employment (Stavrinos et al., 2020). In contrast, our data was collected in July and August, when people were used to taking COVID-related precautions, were venturing outside in the summer weather, and were more likely to gather in small, in-person pods.

In terms of independent online activities, our findings show that teens' online worlds extend beyond the social and entertainment functions most often ascribed to their social media use. Our study shows that students were able to construct virtual independence through their social media usage, showing how social media can serve as a space for developmentally appropriate differentiation from adults. Other studies have shed light on the complexity of teens' online activities. boyd (2014) discussed how teens engage in identity exploration online and civic engagement is another theme found in studies of teens online (Way & Malvini Redden, 2017). Additionally, social media activities integrate an element of informal learning via SMNT, whether intrapersonal, interpersonal, or content-focused. These active forms of social media use have been associated with positive wellbeing outcomes for teens (Thorisdottir et al., 2019) and enable a sense of virtual independence.

Parents play a role in how teens construct their virtual independence. When parents control teens' access to devices and social media, their virtual independence is inhibited. Parent and media messages about the perils of social media activities and screen time lead teens to feel shameful about, diminish or hide their online activities, even when the activities represent important developmental milestones and lead to positive outcomes like learning. This finding is similar to another study that found that awareness of time spent online can trigger shame (Prasad & Quinones, 2020). However, our findings suggest that teens are not just wasting time in their SMNT worlds, but instead blending entertainment with friendship maintenance and informal learning. The increased time spent online during the pandemic reflects having additional time to fill, and a shift in acceptable ways to connect with others.

These findings have implications for how adults interact with teens and monitor and discuss their SMNT use. Although the perils of online life cannot be denied and should not be understated, to ignore the important role that online worlds play in teens' lives for friendship maintenance and informal learning is short-sighted. Furthermore, shaming their activities is not productive. Teens navigate complex social media landscapes daily. They may not do so perfectly or without any negative moments, but they learn from their experiences, and their experiences managing their SMNT worlds during the pandemic shows that they can merge these pieces of virtual independence with their physical worlds.

ACKNOWLEDGEMENT

This study was funded by a COVID-19 Seed Grant from Florida State University.

REFERENCES

Barry, C. T., Sidoti, C. L., Briggs, S. M., Reiter, S. R., & Lindsey, R. A. (2017). Adolescent social media use and mental health from adolescent and parent perspectives. *Journal of Adolescence, 61*, 1-11. https://doi.org/10.1016/j.adolescence.2017.08.005

Bartlett, R., & Milligan, C. (2015). *What is a diary method?* Bloomsbury Academic. https://doi.org/10.5040/9781472572578

boyd, d. m. (2014). *It's complicated: The social lives of networked teens*. Yale University Press.

Campbell, K., Weingart, R., Ashta, J., Cronin, T., & Gazmararian, J. (2021). COVID-19 knowledge and behavior change among high school students in semi-rural Georgia. *Journal of School Health*. https://doi.org/10.1111/josh.13029

Dennen, V. P., Rutledge, S. A., & Bagdy, L. M. (2019). Social media use in high school settings: Rules, outcomes, and educational opportunities. In *Proceedings of the 10th International Conference on Social Media and Society* (pp. 205-213). ACM. https://doi.org/10.1145/3328529.3328561

Dennen, V. P., Rutledge, S. A., & Bagdy, L. M. (2020). (Dis)connected: The role of social networking sites in the high school setting. *American Journal of Education, 127*(1), 107-136.

Dennen, V. P., Rutledge, S. A., Bagdy, L. M., Bunn, S., Jung, D., Cargill, C., Cosgrove, C., Hedquist, A., & McWaters, S. (2021, April 8-12). *Teenage social media use in the time of COVID-19: Resilience, connection, entertainment, and learning* [Conference Poster]. American Educational Research Association, online. http://aera21-aera.ipostersessions.com/Default.aspx?s=6C-5D-EC-AD-C6-F2-B8-14-3B-70-E6-3C-62-67-53-69

Ellis, W. E., Dumas, T. M., & Forbes, L. M. (2020). Physically isolated but socially connected: Psychological adjustment and stress among adolescents during the initial COVID-19 crisis. *Canadian Journal of Behavioural Science / Revue canadienne des sciences du comportement, 52*(3), 177-187. https://doi.org/10.1037/cbs0000215

Prasad, A., & Quinones, A. (2020). Digital overload warnings: The right amount of shame? International Conference on Human-Computer Interaction,

Rutledge, S. A., Dennen, V. P., Bagdy, L. M., Rowlett, J. T., & Burnick, S. (2019). Exploring adolescent social media use in a high school: Tweeting teens in a bell schedule world. *Teachers College Record Yearbook, 121*(14).

Stavrinos, D., McManus, B., Mrug, S., He, H., Gresham, B., Albright, M. G., Svancara, A. M., Whittington, C., Underhill, A., & White, D. M. (2020). Adolescent driving behavior before and during restrictions related to COVID-19. *Accid Anal Prev, 144*, 105686. https://doi.org/10.1016/j.aap.2020.105686

Thorisdottir, I. E., Sigurvinsdottir, R., Asgeirsdottir, B. B., Allegrante, J. P., & Sigfusdottir, I. D. (2019). Active and passive social media use and symptoms of anxiety and depressed mood among Icelandic adolescents. *Cyberpsychol Behav Soc Netw, 22*(8), 535-542. https://doi.org/10.1089/cyber.2019.0079

Way, A. K., & Malvini Redden, S. (2017). The study of youth online: A critical review and agenda. *Review of Communication, 17*(2), 119-136. https://doi.org/10.1080/15358593.2017.1293838

Woods, H. C., & Scott, H. (2016). #Sleepyteens: Social media use in adolescence is associated with poor sleep quality, anxiety, depression and low self-esteem. *J Adolesc, 51*, 41-49. https://doi.org/10.1016/j.adolescence.2016.05.008

SUPPORT FOR COMMUNICATION WITH DEAF AND DUMB PATIENTS VIA FEW-SHOT MACHINE LEARNING

Grigorii Shovkoplias, Mark Tkachenko, Arip Asadulaev, Olga Alekseeva, Natalia Dobrenko, Daniil Kazantsev, Alexandra Vatian, Anatoly Shalyto and Natalia Gusarova
ITMO University, Saint Petersburg 197101, Russia

ABSTRACT

Improving healthcare quality and patient safety for patients with disabilities is one of the most important goals of e-Health. A large percentage of these patients are persons with disabling hearing loss, i.e. partially or completely deaf and dumb. In our work, we discuss the opportunity of fast Sign Language processing having only a small number of examples. We investigated the possibility of classifying datasets with an extremely small number of samples of electromyograms of deaf and dumb gestures using few-shots learning methods. Several such methods have been considered - Matching Networks, Model-Agnostic Meta-Learning, and Prototypical Networks. The developed methodology makes it possible to train electromyogram classifiers using an extremely small amount of data for other deaf and dumb sign languages. To do this, it is enough to collect a small dataset for re- or additional training of these models for the classification of another language, which is easy to accomplish in practice by means of a small session of recording the gestures of several deaf-mute people - speakers of a particular sign language. In our study, we selected three main few-shot learning approaches and compared them on small sign language dataset. Based on our results, one can choose the best models and their modifications to adapt to the practice task.

KEYWORDS

Sign Language, Machine Learning, Marker Method, Neural Networks

1. INTRODUCTION

Improving healthcare quality and patient safety for patients with disabilities is one of the most important goals of e-Health. A large percentage of these patients are persons with disabling hearing loss, i.e. partially or completely deaf and dumb. According to World Health Organization, they represent more than 5% of the world's population - 466 million people (432 million adults and 34 million children). The main means of communication for the deaf and hearing-impaired people is sign language, which, apparently, most medical personnel do not know. Translation from sign language into a usual, sound language, requires a human sign language interpreter; this is not only expensive, but also slows down the pace of communication, which is especially important while providing emergency medical care. In addition, such an approach fundamentally violates medical secrecy and the requirements for personalizing medical information. Therefore, a promising way is the development and widespread introduction into medical practice of IT tools for sign language processing, that is, computer sign language interpretation systems that convert a sequence of gestures (sign speech) into text in a spoken language.

There are two ways to recognize gestures using technical means: markerless and marker (see review papers [Agrawal, Bragg, Kamal]). The markerless method realizes recognition of human gestures using video cameras and infrared transmitters that allow tracking movements, with subsequent processing of the video stream. The marker system assumes that a person is put on sensors that take into account the movement of muscles and points on the person's body - special gloves, devices on the wrists, bracelets, etc.

The markerless method involves the use of a stationary set of equipment and a high complexity of video stream processing, which makes such technologies expensive and inactive. In addition, very few of the published markless developments [Ee, Guo, Huang] are aimed at recognizing a continuous flow of sign language, rather than individual gestures. Today they do not go beyond the scope of research and development and are hardly promising for mass use in e-Health systems.

The marker method is fundamentally simpler, and many companies are working in this direction, already declaring their products as commercial [O'Connor, Song, Zhou]. In medical practice, it is enough to put on the patient a set of equipment for taking EMG in the forearm area [Myo]. The patient (a native speaker of sign language) spells the words in his usual way, each gesture is classified in accordance with our proposed model. The resulting sequential set of letters is converted into words and then displayed on the screen of the doctor's mobile phone or converted into audio speech. However, in this case, too, there are signal processing difficulties associated with the need to take into account the current context when processing specific tokens, i.e. with the implementation of the sequence-to-sequence transformation, as well as with low noise immunity of the received signal. As a result, the quality of real computer sign language interpretation systems remains low, which is especially important for organizing full-fledged communication in the provision of emergency medical care.

Artificial Intelligence (AI) and machine learning technologies, in particular Deep Learning (DL), are the mainstay for the problems of this kind. But attempts to use AI tools in the situation discussed come across, in addition, small volumes of available datasets for training, especially for sign languages other than English Sign Language (SL), as is the case in most underdeveloped and developing countries around the world.

In our work, we discuss the opportunity of fast SL processing having only a small number of examples. There are several methods for working with small amounts of data. In particular, in solving the problem of small datasets in AI, the few-shot approach [Wang] is considered to be promising. In our study, we selected three main few-shot learning approaches and compared them on small SL dataset. Based on our results, one can choose the best models and their modifications to adapt to the practice task.

In our work in Section 2 we provide an overview of few-shot learning techniques and their shortcomings for on-line marker SL recognition, in Section 3 we present our problem-oriented modification of few-shot learning techniques. Section 4 presents the results of our experimental verification of the proposed modification in relation to the three most advanced implementations of the fu-shot approach. The Conclusion briefly presents the results and further directions of our work.

2. BACKGROUND

Human intelligence can recognize new forms of a viewed object from a few examples leveraging the knowledge obtained from the previous learning experience. For the existing architectures of DL, it is a complex problem to extract previous knowledge from the "memory" and use them in the new task. DL methods often require massive data for discriminative tasks. In most models, each task is treated independently and the parameters learn from the ground up without integrating task-specific prior knowledge.

Methods that are aimed to incorporate previous knowledge and address low data problems are named few-shot learning. The focus of recent few-shot learning [Wang] research has been on the development of learning methods that can quickly adapt to unseen tasks with small amounts of data and low computational cost. To do this, there are two main approaches - Optimization-Based and Metric-Based.

Optimization-based few-shot learning frameworks use gradient descent-based methods as the optimization process in the meta-learning. Optimization based-methods propose to share knowledge across all tasks. In order to obtain optimal initial stage model-agnostic meta-learning method is proposed [Finn] learning to predict initial parameters of convolutional neural network for each task. Some methods are proposed to learn the task-specific knowledge too [Lee]. The main drawback of optimization-based approaches is a high degree of consistent and the ability to obtain an optimal initial optimization state. Besides, optimization-based methods are computationally expensive and require a large number of similar tasks for optimal performance.

Metric-based methods for few-shot learning are based on the similarity between samples. The trained model can classify samples based on the distance between them. The basic metric-based approach is a Siamese Network [Koch] where two neural networks with the same architecture are trained to learn the similarity between support set and query sample through L1-distance. Different metrics can be used to calculate the similarity between embeddings, for example cosine distance, squared Euclidean distance, L1-distance. Compared with other approaches, metric-based approaches are efficient for few-shot learning and work faster as they do not require the backpropagation process. The advanced technique for the metric-based few-shot learning is prototypical networks [Snell] that compute squared Euclidean distance between the embedded test samples and all prototypical feature vectors.

The few-shot methods are claimed for the classification of datasets containing a small number of examples in each class. But their high accuracy (up to 96%) [Ahmed] in experiments is achieved only on large datasets such as American Sign Language [Vaezi] and drops sharply with a decrease in the size of the dataset (74.7% for Flemish Sign Language corpus [De Coster] and even less, up to 48,6% [De Coster, Pigou]).

Thus, the problem of experimental evaluation of the effectiveness of various few-shot methods in relation to small-volume datasets, typical for medical practice, arises. To solve it, in our article we carried out:

- Improving few-shot techniques for practical application.
- Testing and analyzing few-shot techniques on SL recognition datasets.

3. PROPOSED MODIFICATION AND MATERIAL USED

Few-shot learning techniques discussed above are based on the concept of episodes, that is, they classify within a subset of classes, which allows the model to work more accurately. This limitation makes such an approach irrelevant for the problem of marker recognition of SLs. In this case, we need a method of online processing of the input stream of gestures, which, as a response, gives out a specific gesture from the entire alphabet of gestures, that is, makes a choice on the full set of classes (possible gestures), and not on a limited subset of classes considered as an episode. To do this, we propose a problem-oriented modification of the existing few-shot approach, detailed in the next section. Due to it, we propose a modification of the few-shot learning method shown in Figure 1 and described in detail below.

(A): Standard approach to teaching where we have access to training examples and information about to which class each sample belongs to. We train a model with an output dimension equal to the number of classes.

(B): Few-shot learning, this approach is using when there are a large number of classes and a small number of examples within each class. The dataset is divided into episodes, usually of 2-10 classes in each episode. Episode consist of examples (train) shots and queries (test) shots. Based on examples, the model "remembers" how each class looks like and, when receiving some queries (test) shots it is able to carry out a classification. The task of the machine learning model in this setting is to learn to distinguish different classes by remembering how each class in episode looks like.

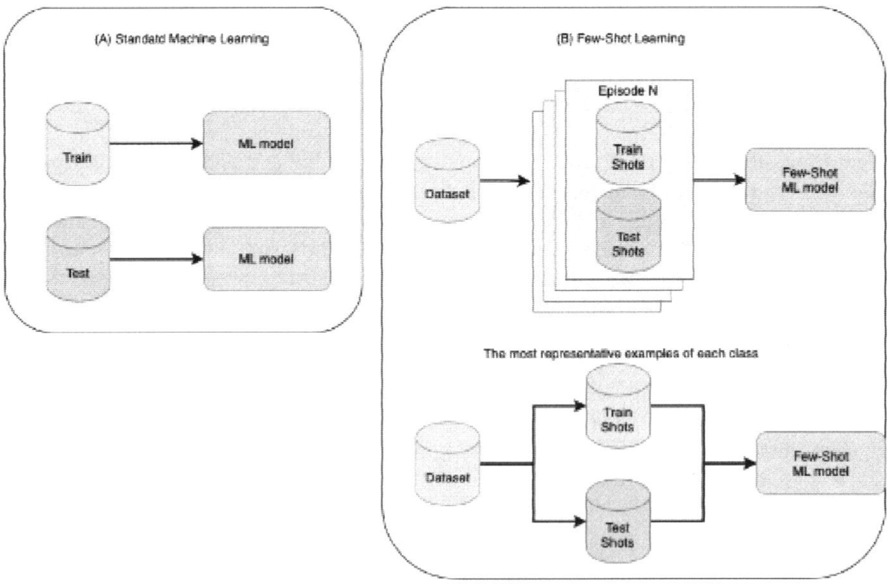

Figure 1. Examples of different approaches to model training

(B) bottom image: our modification, where we do not use splitting into episodes, but select the most representative examples from the dataset and train the model to "remember" them, then when model receive the test shots model decides which class each sample belongs to.

In order to make a method work online we propose to put k-way equal to the full size of the alphabet, so in our settings we consider all evaluation as one big episode with a most representative samples chosen as examples of class. Thus, the pipeline for processing the input stream of gestures is as follows: (1) The number of classes in the episode is set equal to the number of classes in the dataset (2) We train the number of models using few-shot learning techniques (3) the best of trained models can be used in practice.

For investigations, we used a dataset for automatic SL recognition compiled from Surface Electromyography (EMG) and Inertial Measurement Unit (IMU) [Pacifici]. This dataset contains 26 gestures of the Italian SL alphabet. For each gesture, 30 data acquisitions were executed, composing a total of 780 samples included in the dataset. The gestures were performed by the same subject (male, 24 years old) in lab settings. EMG and IMU data were collected in a 2 seconds time window, at a sampling frequency of 200 Hz.

4. EXPERIMENTS

To test the effectiveness of the proposed modification as applied to on-line processing of sign language, we have selected three models, covering all types of few-shot learning presented in Section 2, namely: Model-Agnostic Meta-Learning [Finn], Matching Networks [Vinyals], and Prototypical Networks [Snell]. The first one is optimization-based, the last two are metric-based. All models chosen are the most common in the field.

We used the following notation. In general, in standard machine learning each model is provided with a set of m'' labelled samples from 'C 'classes. Within few-shot learning 'C 'is traditionally called a 'k-way', and 'm' is called a 'n-shot' inside each episode. In addition, to configure models, additional parameter Q is introduced - the number of examples per class. We evaluated the models by categorical efficiency (CA), i.e. the frequency of the correct class definition. We left all the parameters of the models architectures unchanged. The only modification was changing the size of the input space of neural networks, which was adjusted to our dataset and was equal to 400 * 8. The experimental results are presented in Table 1.

Table 1. Categorial accuracy for different few-shot learning models

MAML [Finn]				Matching Networks [Vinyals]			Prototypical Neworks [Snell]			
k-way	n-shot	Q	CA	k-way	n-shot	CA	k-way	n-shot	Q	CA
5	3	1	0.66	3	3	0.919	26	1	1	0,655
5	3	5	0.739	5	3	0.947	26	5	1	0,649
5	3	7	0.993	8	3	0.807	26	13	1	0,653
26	3	5	0,18	13	3	0.664	26	13	5	0,649
26	3	7	0,21	26	3	0.549	26	13	10	0,647

Comparison of the data in the table shows that with a small episode size (k-way = 1-5), the accuracy of all methods is quite high and corresponds to analogs. At the same time, if the episode size is chosen equal to the total number of classes in the dataset (k-way = 26), then metric-based approaches still provide sufficient classification accuracy, comparable or even superior to analogs, while the accuracy of the optimization-based approach drops to unrealistic low values. Thus, our experiments provide a good basis for constructing classifiers for SL languages having extremely small datasets, as well as demonstrate the advantage of metric-based few-shot methods over optimization-based few-shot methods for solving the problem.

5. CONCLUSION AND FUTURE WORK

We investigated the possibility of classifying datasets with an extremely small number of samples of electromyograms of deaf and dumb gestures using few-shots learning methods. Several such methods have been considered - Matching Networks, Model-Agnostic Meta-Learning, and Prototypical Networks.

The developed methodology makes it possible to train electromyogram classifiers using an extremely small amount of data for other deaf and dumb sign languages. To do this, it is enough to collect a small dataset for re- or additional training of these models for the classification of another language, which is easy to accomplish in practice by means of a small session of recording the gestures of several deaf-mute people - speakers of a particular sign language.

Despite the results obtained, our research is still in the process of development, the accuracy achieved by the proposed methods can be significantly increased. First of all, we plan to use various augmentation techniques for this. The possibility of pre-training on data similar in distribution to the existing dataset is also being considered. In addition, in the future, it is planned to use active learning techniques to find the most representative samples from the dataset.

ACKNOWLEDGEMENT

This work was financially supported by Russian Science Foundation, Grant 19-19-00696.

REFERENCES

Agrawal S.C., Jalal A.S., Tripathi R.K. A survey on manual and non-manual sign language recognition for isolated and continuous sign, Int. J. Appl. Pattern Recognit., vol. 3, no. 2, pp. 99–134, 2016.

Ahmed M.A., Zaidan B.B. et al. A Review on Systems-Based Sensory Gloves for Sign Language Recognition State of the Art between 2007 and 2017. Sensors (Basel). 2018 Jul; 18(7): 2208.

Bragg D., Koller O., Bellard M. et al. Sign Language Recognition, Generation, and Translation: An Interdisciplinary Perspective. arXiv:1908.08597v1 [cs.CV] 22 Aug 2019.

De Coster M., Van Herreweghe M., Dambre J. Sign Language Recognition with Transformer Networks. Proc. 12th Conf. on Language Resources and Evaluation (LREC 2020), pp.6018–6024.

Ee L.W.S., Ramachandiran C.R., Logeswaran R. Real-Time Sign Language Learning System. J. Phys.: Conf. Ser. 1712 (2020) 012011.

Finn C., Abbeel P., Levine S., 2017. Model-agnostic meta-learning for fast adaptation of deep networks, PMLR, Int.Conv. Centre, Australia. pp. 1126–1135. http://proceedings. mlr.press/v70/finn17a.html.

Guo D., Zhou W., Li H., Wang M. Hierarchical LSTM for sign language translation, in Proc. 32nd AAAI Conf. Artif. Intell., Apr. 2018, pp. 6845–6852.

Huang J., Zhou W., Zhang Q., et al. Video-based sign language recognition without temporal segmentation, in Proc. 32nd AAAI Conf. Artif. Intell., Apr. 2018, pp. 1–8

Kamal S.M., Chen Y., Li S., et al. Technical Approaches to Chinese Sign Language Processing: A Review. IEEE Access, V. 7, 2019. DOI 10.1109/ACCESS.2019.2929174.

Koch G., Zemel R., Salakhutdinov R., 2015. Siamese neural net- works for one-shot image recognition, in: ICML deep learning work- shop, Lille.

Lee Y., Choi S., Gradient-based meta-learning with learned layerwise metric and subspace, in: International Conference on Machine Learning. 2018

Myo SDK Beta 7. https://developerblog.myo.com/myo-sdk-beta-7/

O'Connor T.F., et al. The Language of Glove: Wireless gesture decoder with low-power and stretchable hybrid electronics. PLoS ONE 12(7): e0179766. https://doi.org/10.1371/journal.pone.0179766

Pacifici I., Sernani P., Falcionelli N., et al. A surface electromyography and inertial measurement unit dataset for the Italian Sign Language alphabet https://www.ncbi.nlm.nih.gov/pmc/articles/PMC7644570/

Pigou L., Van Herreweghe, M., Dambre J. Sign classification in sign language corpora with deep neural networks. Int.Conference on Language Resources and Evaluation (LREC), Workshop, 2016, pp. 175–178

Snell J., Swersky K., Zemel R., 2017. Prototypical networks for few-shot learning, in: Advances in neural information processing systems, pp. 4077–4087.

Song Y., Lee S., Choi Y., et al. Design framework for a seamless smart glove using a digital knitting system. Fash Text 8, 6 (2021). https://doi.org/10.1186/s40691-020-00237-2

Vaezi Joze H.R., Koller O. MS-ASL: A Large-Scale Data Set and Benchmark for Understanding American Sign Language. https://arxiv.org/pdf/1812.01053.pdf

Vinyals O., Blundell C., Lillicrap T., Kavukcuoglu K., Wierstra D. Matching Networks for One Shot Learning. arXiv:1606.04080v2 [cs.LG] 29 Dec 2017

Wang Y., Yao Q. , Kwok J., Ni L.M. Generalizing from a Few Examples: A Survey on Few-Shot Learning., https://arxiv.org/abs/1904.05046

Zhou Z., Chen K., Li X., et al. Sign-to-speech translation using machine-learning-assisted stretchable sensor arrays. Nat Electron 3, 571–578 (2020). https://doi.org/10.1038/s41928-020-0428-6

USE OF TWO TOPIC MODELING METHODS TO INVESTIGATE COVID VACCINE HESITANCY

Phillip Ma[1], Qing Zeng-Treitler[2] and Stuart J. Nelson[3]
George Washington University, SMHS, Biomedical Informatics Center
2600 Virginia Ave, NW, First Floor, Washington DC 20037, USA
[1]MD
[2]PhD
[3]MD, FACP, FACMI

ABSTRACT

COVID vaccine hesitancy in the face of a pandemic is a concern for public health researchers and policy makers who aim to achieve herd immunity. We investigated the COVID vaccine hesitancy by analyzing Twitter posts (tweets) using two topic modeling methods: Latent Dirichlet Allocation (LDA) and Top2Vec. Of the two methods, Top2Vec was able to reveal topics which directly discussed Vaccine Hesitancy and thus offered more utility for this research topic. Common reasons for vaccine hesitancy found in the dataset included concerns about recent (at the time of tweet collection) news regarding side effects associated with the COVID vaccines, and a mixture of scientific and government skepticism related to vaccine development and distribution.

KEYWORDS

Vaccine Hesitancy, Topic Modeling, Twitter

1. INTRODUCTION

Since the approval of the first COVID vaccines, their production and distribution have been expanded to meet global needs. Initially, vaccinations in many countries were limited to the most vulnerable and frequently exposed populations (e.g., nursing home residents and healthcare workers) given the limited supply. As a larger proportion of the population became eligible for the vaccine in the US, the issue of vaccine hesitancy began to draw increasing attention. People eligible for the vaccine who refuse to receive or are hesitant of vaccination pose a challenge towards achieving herd immunity. Much time and resources have been poured into determining what the reasons are behind this hesitancy, and what approaches would be most effective to deploy against it.[1]

Twitter provides a resource for researchers to explore public discourse on a wide range of topics through tracking users' interactions on the social media platform. As of 2021, Twitter had 191 million daily active users[2] and in 2012 their users produced 340 million tweets per day[3]. Although it is possible to post media such as images and videos, users still primarily tweet text; a common method deployed by researchers is Natural Language Processing to categorize, analyze, and interpret large sets of tweets. Twitter also has an easily accessible API that can be used to retrieve live and historical tweets.

Tweets are short texts that were originally limited to 140 characters, but more recently have been expanded to accommodate 280 characters; the short length poses a challenge for text analysis. Syed et al. (2017) reported finding higher quality topics with greater coherence in models trained on larger documents (full papers as opposed to abstracts). Another challenge is that tweets are not written or reviewed in the same rigorous process as academic papers or news articles. Like other types of social media data, the text of tweets often contains colloquial language, abbreviations, references to other sources, and otherwise difficult to interpret content.

[1] https://www.nejm.org/doi/full/10.1056/nejmms2101220
[2] https://www.statista.com/statistics/970920/monetizable-daily-active-twitter-users-worldwide/
[3] https://blog.twitter.com/official/en_us/a/2012/twitter-turns-six.html

Topic modeling offers a way to select and analyze a subset of tweets that are determined to be pertinent to the study.

Researchers have been utilizing social-media datasets throughout the course of the COVID-19 pandemic. He et al. (2021) ran a variety of sentiment analyses (VADER, TextBlob, Standford NLP, and Linguistic Inquiry and Word Count) and keyword filtering on social media datasets to track public discourse regarding mask-wearing during the COVID-19 pandemic. Ordun et al. (2020) trained an LDA topic model and applied it towards categorizing tweets to track discourse regarding COVID-19 over time and was able to correlate Twitter activity with specific news events such as press conferences. Importantly, the researchers decided to use. Term Frequency – Inverted Document Frequency (TF-IDF) to vectorize documents and used Uniform Manifold Approximation and Projection for Dimension Reduction (UMAP) to plot these document vectors to visualize topics. Jelodar et al. (2020) detailed a method utilizing LDA and Recurrent Neural Networks to find topics in tweets, and to classify the sentiments of tweets within a given topic.

Latent Dirichlet Allocation (LDA) is a commonly used method for Topic Modeling and has many well supported libraries that make its implementation relatively simple. LDA is a statistical model for determining underlying topics across a corpus of documents (Blei et al., 2003). It assumes a generative model where each document consists of a mixture of topics, and words from the topic distributions are chosen to compose the document until the predetermined number of words in the document is reached. LDA also assumes that documents are probability distributions over topics, θ, and that topics are probability distributions over words, ϕ.The three hyperparameters used are κ number of topics and the two Dirichlet priors, α and β. A high α implies that each document is likely to contain many topics and a high β implies that each topic contains a mixture of many words.

Using LDA to find topics in Twitter datasets presents unique challenges. Yang et al. (2014) offered an insider's view of Twitter's internal Topic Modeling system and address the shortcomings of models such as LDA in discovering topics specifically from a corpus composed of tweets due to their relative size and paucity of topics. Resnik et al. (2015) detailed various approaches to address the shortcomings of LDA in finding coherent topics in twitter datasets, including using supervised and supervised-nested LDA models which appeared to produce more coherent topics than 'vanilla' LDA. Weng et al. (2010) describe a similar problem in producing coherent topics using LDA on tweets, and employed a method combining tweets from the same user together into a single document to explore topics that individual users address often. Steinskog et al. (2017) build on that work by comparing methods aggregating tweets from single users into individual documents, and aggregating tweets that utilize the same hashtag into individual documents. Their results demonstrate promising results training LDA models on these aggregated documents. Surian et al. (2016) compare using LDA head-to-head with Dirichlet Multinomial Modeling (DMM) and report appreciably more interpretable results with DMM on their twitter dataset examining sentiment related to the HPV vaccine.

An alternative to the LDA method is the Top2Vec model (Angelov, 2020) that utilizes Distributed Bag of Words (DBOW) in doc2vec to create jointly embedded document and word vectors. Angelov assumes that the semantic space created is a continuous representation of topics. In this semantic space the document vector represents the topic of the document, with the word vectors nearest to the document vectors being the most representative of that document's topic. As such, documents that are clustered together are assumed to be of the same topic and a centroid of these documents can be calculated. Therefore, the number of 'dense' document vector areas represents the number of prominent topics. In order to overcome issues related to computational load and the probability that documents will not cluster densely enough, the model first performs dimension reduction of the document vectors with Uniform Manifold Approximation and Projection for Dimension Reduction (UMAP). The model uses Hierarchical Density-Based Spatial Clustering of Applications with Noise (HDBSCAN) to find these dense areas and calculate the subsequent topic vectors. Words that appear in many documents are necessarily placed in semantic space that is typically equidistant from all the documents that contain it, and is assumed to be in-between document clusters and not contained within them. These words are often stop words and thus, Top2Vec does not require stop-word removal. Similarly, words that are semantically similar, in that they are used in similar frequencies in their associated topics, will appear close to one another in semantic space; this includes different stems of the same word. Thus, Top2Vec also does not require stemming or lemmatizing before the model is trained.

In this study, we have applied LDA and Top2Vec to a set of tweets to discover topics related to COVID vaccine hesitancy. The results from the two methods were manually reviewed and compared.

2. BODY

2.1 Methods

The dataset consists of the full text of tweets (including hashtags) and was obtained from the COVID-19-TweetIDs repository[4] created and maintained by Chen et al. who utilized Twitter's API to stream tweets which were related to the COVID-19 pandemic and stored them in a repository as lists of tweet IDs. The researchers provided a 'rehydrator' script in order to retrieve tweets based on Tweet ID using the Twarc[5] library, which provides access to Twitter's official API through a python wrapper. Our study used a subset of tweets from January 1st 2021 to March 14th 2021. The dataset was filtered using keywords to obtain tweets related to vaccination: 'vaccine', 'moderna', 'pfizer', 'astrazeneca', 'astra', 'zeneca', 'j&j', 'jj', and 'johnson' which yielded 3,403,166 tweets. Of those tweets, the same random sample of 900,000 tweets was used to train both models; models using larger datasets failed during training due to computing constraints. Aside from timestamps, the remainder of the associated metadata was discarded in accordance with Twitter's Privacy Policies[6] regarding publicly available tweets and identifying data.

An LDA model was trained on the selected data. The data was first 'cleaned' through removal of punctuation, stop words, links, and usernames. The dataset was then run through NLTK's lemmatization method, which is necessary in LDA models so that different 'stems' of the same root word do not appear as separate words. A smaller subset of the data was used to in order to facilitate hyperparameter tuning; a grid-search was performed where 60 different combinations of hyperparameters (κ, α, and β) were used as inputs, and a set of parameters was settled upon based on which combination yielded the highest coherence score. The number of topics (κ) which resulted in the highest coherence score was 20, which was how many topics the final trained LDA model to yield. The α and β used in the final model were 0.01 and 0.31 respectively.

Calculating Coherence Scores is a feature of the Gensim Topic Modeling library[7] and allows for calculation of a variety of coherence score modalities across a selection of its supported topic models. The default model is *Cv* which acts as a proxy for topic quality and measures the semantic similarity between the top words in each topic generated by the LDA model; the assumption being that words with similar meaning tend to occur together in similar contexts, and that a topic representing this accurately would contain semantically similar words among its top scored representatives. *Cv* is commonly used as a coherence score as it has performed well in comparison to other coherence models in scoring how interpretable topics are likely to be by human readers as described by Röder et al. in 2015 and Syed et al. in 2017.

A Top2Vec model was trained on the same selected dataset which initially yielded 3918 topics. The package includes methods for reducing the number of topics. In this use case, it was helpful to reduce the number of topics in order to make inspecting the tweets more feasible. Topic reduction is not permanent; the original structure is preserved and can be queried to identify which original topics comprise the reduced topics for further inspection. The package combines topics into the semantically most similar topic until the desired number of topics is reached.

2.2 Results

We manually identified 4 topics obtained from the LDA model that are the most relevant to vaccine hesitancy. A sample of topics are shown in Table 1.

[4] https://github.com/echen102/COVID-19-TweetIDs
[5] https://github.com/DocNow/twarc
[6] https://developer.twitter.com/en/developer-terms/agreement-and-policy
[7] https://radimrehurek.com/gensim/models/ldamodel.html

Table 1. Four examples of topics related to vaccine hesitancy found using the LDA model. The first column lists labels assigned by the researchers as human interpretations of the topics. The second column lists the top 20 words in order of descending probability

Table 1	
Topic	Top 20 most probable words
AZ/Oxford Vaccine Side Effects	vaccine, johnson, covid, astrazeneca, country, biden, european, help, news, thank, suspend, ensure, blood, emergency, clot, coronavirus, dose, germany, million, france
Effectiveness vs. New Strains	vaccine, covid, variant, country, pandemic, south, africa, global, african, strain, access, need, develop, effective, mutation, coronavirus, virus, nation, world, vaccination
Side Effects/Vaccine Reactions	johnson, vaccine, covid, effective, reaction, single, severe, shot, prevent, boris, safe, report, death, coronavirus, people, adverse, allergic, disease, pfizer, case
Long-term effects of Vaccine	vaccine, covid, effect, long, mrna, term, people, chance, risk, know, catch, year, protect, short, think, death, like, virus, time, wait

We then manually identified 8 topics obtained from the Top2Vec model that are the most relevant to vaccine hesitancy. A sample of topics are shown in Table 2.

Table 2. Eight examples of topics related to vaccine hesitancy found using the Top2Vec model. The first column lists labels assigned by the researchers as human interpretations of the topics. The second column lists the top 20 words in order of descending probability

Table 2	
Topic	Top 20 most probable words
Alternative COVID treatments, rushed development	hcq, ivermectin, cheap, vitamin, treatment, cure, experimental, treat, proven, pharma, untested, drugs, eua, drug, treating, rushed, widely, pushing, expensive
Belief that vaccine is experimental/untested	traditional, guinea, genetic, technology, mrna, rna, gene, untested, experimental, cells, modified, vector, liability, proven, injected, therapy, toxic
Low Personal Risk	survival, rate, experimental, chances, yourself, subject, chance, untested, unknown, catching, liability, term, higher, mortality, pose, therapy, gene, protect, healthy, injuries
AZ/Oxford Vaccine Side Effects	clots, clot, blood, suspended, clotting, astrazeneca, suspends, denmark, suspend, norway, reports, netherlands, european, temporarily, france, halted, evidence, fears, germany, italy
Skepticism based in semantics over FDA Approval vs EUA	fda, approved, authorization, emergency, drug, authorized, use, eua, johnson, approval, liability, approves, licensed, trials, authorizes, cleared, single, regulator, prevent, regulators
Side Effects related to autoimmune reactions	autoimmune, trigger, disease, protein, cells, immune, causes, mrna, clotting, rna, mmr, lung, cause, diseases, spike, cov, anaphylaxis, evidence, condition, sars
Belief that vaccines are a bioweapon	realise, ffs, bio, weapon, sound, transmit, yourself, lockdowns, mutates, eliminate, toxic, logic, forever, humans, cure, unknown, gonna, understand, biotech, viruses
Belief that vaccine is experimental/untested	guinea, pigs, poison, thailand, indians, trial, traditional, spreads, theirs, adverse, clinical, netherlands, experimental, omg, southern, forced, rushed, untested, covaxin, trials

2.3 Discussion

In this study, we demonstrate the use of two different topic models in order to identify topics related to vaccine hesitancy on a Twitter dataset. Our results demonstrate that Top2Vec is able to extract more relevant topics from a Twitter dataset which meet the needs of this particular study.

The LDA model revealed four topics (Table 1.) determined by the researchers to be relevant to vaccine hesitancy. The first of these topics references the AztraZeneca/Oxford and the Johnson and Johnson vaccines, their supposed side effects, and subsequent suspension in some countries[8]. The second of these topics addresses the effectiveness of vaccines against emerging strains of COVID[9]. The last two topics are concerned with side effects: in the short and long term respectively. Although the topics identified could all address reasons for hesitancy among Twitter users, the topics did not appear to represent overt hesitance or hostility towards vaccination; they may represent discussion on news topics. Notably, the 4th topic includes the word 'wait' as the 20th most probably word in the topic which may suggest users being hesitant to receive a vaccine because of long term side effects, but is not as obviously about hesitancy as topics discussed later.

[8] https://www.bmj.com/content/372/bmj.n699
[9] https://jamanetwork.com/journals/jama/fullarticle/2777785

The Top2Vec model revealed eight topics (Table 2.) determined by the researchers to be most relevant to vaccine hesitancy. One of the topics found a similar topic to the LDA model, referencing the AstraZeneca/Oxford vaccine side effects and suspension. The remainder of the topics were determined to represent tweets which were more overtly hesitant towards COVID vaccination. One topic (Alternative COVID treatments…) contains words such as "untested", "experimental" and "rushed" in addition to mentioned "ivermectin", "hcq" and "vitamin". This was interpreted as skepticism of vaccines due to their expedited approval process and offering alternative treatments for COVID. Two topics referenced "guinea", "pig" and "experimental" which was interpreted as a feeling that Twitter users would be used as experiments to test safety or efficacy by receiving the vaccine. One topic (Low Personal Risk) appeared to reference survival rates or low mortality rates of COVID infections and appear to believe that because of their perceived low risk, that receiving a vaccine was not necessary or not worth the risk. There were multiple topics (only one is shown in Table 2.) which reference the approval status of the vaccines; claiming that an Emergency Use Authorization (EUA) does not constitute FDA approval and therefore are hesitant to receive the vaccine. One topic (Bioweapon) appears to level the accusation that vaccines are "Bioweapons" and are "toxic".

2.4 Limitations

The collected dataset was a customized subset of the COVID-19 Tweets dataset. It would have been more ideal to stream tweets directly using the Twitter API using a custom filter. Twitter began censoring tweets related to covid vaccine skepticism starting in December of 2020[10,11]. As a result, there is a difficult to quantify number of tweets and twitter traffic surrounding COVID vaccine skepticism that was likely not collected and possibly lowers the proportion of vaccine skepticism represented in this dataset. Additionally, the topics which represented negative sentiment on COVID vaccination were manually selected and were limited by the subjectivity of human interpretation.

3. CONCLUSION

Top2Vec offers a novel method of topic modeling which can aid researchers in particular use cases. In this instance, Top2Vec was able to provide appreciably differentiated topics when compared to LDA and was able to identify the topic desired by this researcher. Additionally, Top2Vec offers a simplified data-cleaning pipeline by obviating the need for stemming and stop-word removal. Vaccine uptake is an important factor in combating the COVID-19 pandemic, but concerns remain about populations who are hesitant to receive the vaccine even when it is available. By using Topic Modeling on a large Twitter dataset, the study was able to identify tweets which were most likely to express vaccine hesitancy, and to explore the topics that most closely represented those tweets. Common reasons for vaccine hesitancy found in the dataset through examination of negative appearing topics included concerns about safety, skepticism about the development and approval of the vaccines, vaccine efficacy, and judgements of personal risk from COVID infection. Efforts aimed at building trust around COVID vaccination may do well to address these concerns.

ACKNOWLEDGEMENT

We would like to acknowledge the leadership and staff of the Biomedical Informatics Center at the School of Medicine and Health Sciences at George Washington University.

[10] https://blog.twitter.com/en_us/topics/company/2020/covid19-vaccine.html
[11] https://blog.twitter.com/en_us/topics/company/2021/updates-to-our-work-on-covid-19-vaccine-misinformation.html

REFERENCES

Angelov, D. (2020). *Top2Vec: Distributed Representations of Topics*. http://arxiv.org/abs/2008.09470

Blei, D. M., Ng, A. Y., & Jordan, M. I. (2003). Latent Dirichlet Allocation. *The Journal of Machine Learning Research*, *3*, 993–1022.

Chen, E., Lerman, K., & Ferrara, E. (2020). Tracking Social Media Discourse About the COVID-19 Pandemic: Development of a Public Coronavirus Twitter Data Set. *JMIR Public Health and Surveillance*, *6*(2), e19273. https://doi.org/10.2196/19273

He, L., He, C., Reynolds, T. L., Bai, Q., Huang, Y., Li, C., Zheng, K., & Chen, Y. (2021). Why do people oppose mask wearing? A comprehensive analysis of U.S. tweets during the COVID-19 pandemic. *Journal of the American Medical Informatics Association*. https://doi.org/10.1093/jamia/ocab047

Jelodar, H., Wang, Y., Orji, R., & Huang, S. (2020). Deep Sentiment Classification and Topic Discovery on Novel Coronavirus or COVID-19 Online Discussions: NLP Using LSTM Recurrent Neural Network Approach. *IEEE Journal of Biomedical and Health Informatics*, *24*(10), 2733–2742. https://doi.org/10.1109/JBHI.2020.3001216

Ordun, C., Purushotham, S., & Raff, E. (2020). *Exploratory Analysis of Covid-19 Tweets using Topic Modeling, UMAP, and DiGraphs*. http://arxiv.org/abs/2005.03082

Resnik, P., Armstrong, W., Claudino, L., Nguyen, T., Nguyen, V.-A., & Boyd-Graber, J. (2015). Beyond LDA: Exploring Supervised Topic Modeling for Depression-Related Language in Twitter. *Proceedings of the 2nd Workshop on Computational Linguistics and Clinical Psychology: From Linguistic Signal to Clinical Reality*, 99–107. https://doi.org/10.3115/v1/W15-1212

Röder, M., Both, A., & Hinneburg, A. (2015). Exploring the Space of Topic Coherence Measures. *Proceedings of the Eighth ACM International Conference on Web Search and Data Mining*, 399–408. https://doi.org/10.1145/2684822.2685324

Steinskog, A., Therkelsen, J., & Gambäck, B. (2017). Twitter Topic Modeling by Tweet Aggregation. *Proceedings of the 21st Nordic Conference of Computational Linguistics*, *May*, 77–86. http://cran.uvigo.es/web/packages/stm/vignettes/stmVignette.pdf

Surian, D., Nguyen, D. Q., Kennedy, G., Johnson, M., Coiera, E., & Dunn, A. G. (2016). Characterizing Twitter Discussions About HPV Vaccines Using Topic Modeling and Community Detection. *Journal of Medical Internet Research*, *18*(8), e232. https://doi.org/10.2196/jmir.6045

Syed, S., & Spruit, M. (2017). Full-Text or Abstract? Examining Topic Coherence Scores Using Latent Dirichlet Allocation. *2017 IEEE International Conference on Data Science and Advanced Analytics (DSAA)*, 165–174. https://doi.org/10.1109/DSAA.2017.61

Weng, J., Lim, E.-P., Jiang, J., & He, Q. (2010). TwitterRank: Finding topic-sensitive influential Twitterers. *Proceedings of the Third ACM International Conference on Web Search and Data Mining - WSDM '10*, 261. https://doi.org/10.1145/1718487.1718520

Yang, S. H., Kolcz, A., Schlaikjer, A., & Gupta, P. (2014). Large-scale high-precision topic modeling on twitter. *Proceedings of the ACM SIGKDD International Conference on Knowledge Discovery and Data Mining*, 1907–1916. https://doi.org/10.1145/2623330.2623336

AUTOMATION: AN ESSENTIAL COMPONENT OF ETHICAL AI?

Vivek Nallur[1], Martin Lloyd[2] and Siani Pearson[2]
[1]*School of Computer Science, University College Dublin, Ireland*
[2]*Just Algorithm Action Group (JAAG), UK*

ABSTRACT

Ethics is sometimes considered to be too abstract to be meaningfully implemented in artificial intelligence (AI). In this paper, we reflect on other aspects of computing that were previously considered to be very abstract. Yet, these are now accepted as being done very well by computers. These tasks have ranged from multiple aspects of software engineering to mathematics to conversation in natural language with humans. This was done by automating the simplest possible step and then building on it to perform more complex tasks. We wonder if ethical AI might be similarly achieved and advocate the process of automation as key step in making AI take ethical decisions. The key contribution of this paper is to reflect on how automation was introduced into domains previously considered too abstract for computers.

KEYWORDS

Abstract Domains, Artificial Intelligence, Automation, Ethics

1. INTRODUCTION

In this paper we examine ways in which abstract concepts, previously thought to be the preserve of human thought have been increasingly subject to automation. We take a journey through computing capabilities step by step towards complexity. We reflect on these examples, painting a vision in Section 5 of how automation in the ethical field might progress in future and offer a suggestion for what the first step could be.

2. AUTOMATING THE SMALLEST VIABLE SE PRACTICE

Software engineering (SE) has advocated the use of testing, and formalised code reviews as a means of increasing software quality for a long time (Fagan, 1976). However, as engineers who created and deployed software in 1980-90s can attest, even though it was a good idea, there was very little implementation. This is because writing good, elegant code was (and still is) considered to be an art form. This implies two things: a) some people (the artists) are a cut above the others; b) there are no rules that can make all code elegant (it's not engineering, it's an art). SE practices therefore focussed mainly on understanding the customers' requirements and being able to produce designs and code that met those requirements. This changed drastically with the introduction of automation.

The introduction of automated unit-testing, via SUnit, and subsequently jUnit by Kent Beck (Beck, 1997) allowed developers to add tests to their code, as they were writing the functionality, and not as an after-thought. This simple idea of automatically testing a small piece of functionality with well-defined entry and exit criteria increased the amount of testing being done by developers drastically. Critically, now unit-testing is seen as a first-class programming artifact that is checked into version-control, along with the code that it tests. Development methodologies such as TestDrivenDevelopment and ExtremeProgramming use unit tests as a critical part of the software development process. Automation of unit-testing has been almost universally accepted as a good practice, so much so that several programming languages, such as Go, Matlab, Python, Ruby, Rust, etc. support unit-testing directly within the programming language, while almost all widely used programming languages have extremely good testing libraries/frameworks. In systems that need testing for certification as per the IEC 61508 systems safety standard, unit-testing of all functions and all possible branches is mandated. This is only possible in modern systems through the introduction of automated testing.

Code-reviews are another example of a software engineering practice that was considered as requiring abstract skills. The practice of other team-members critiquing changes to the codebase is acknowledged to be a good way to catch bugs, provide feedback, and increase software quality. However, this requires software teams to invest time and energy in understanding the *intent* of the code, as well as its impact on the rest of the system, even parts that have not been built yet. Again, we see the recurrent pattern of the ideal activity taking a lot of time and human expertise to do well. This leads to a high cost of performing the activity, and a consequent reluctance within teams and organisations to invest in it, which leads to poor software quality (McIntosh et al, 2016). While code-review is a complex, cognitive task, some of the burden was eased with the introduction of automation. The use of automated style-checkers, linters, static analysis tools in software systems reduces the burden of the human reviewer who can now focus only on the most difficult parts of bug-finding, sharing design intent and knowledge transfer (Bacchelli and Bird, 2013).

Modern software systems are often composed of heterogenous micro-services, built by multiple teams from different enterprises. Composing these into a cohesive application that can service a user's needs requires human thought and ingenuity. Even in this domain, there are attempts to automatically create applications built from micro-services (Cabrera, C et al. 2017) and repair/adapt them dynamically in the face of perturbances (Song, H. et al. 2015; Nallur, V.et al. 2016). The field of software engineering has embraced automation as a way of making complex, cognitive tasks readily repeatable, as well as reliable.

3. AUTOMATING MATHEMATICS

Up to about thirty years ago many mathematicians would claim that there is something special about human insight, and that computers could never come up with the kind of 'eureka' moments that can occur in finding a mathematical proof. A formal mathematical proof is a finite sequence of sentences, each of which is an axiom, an assumption that follows from the earlier sentences by a rule of inference. Verifying a formal proof is purely mechanical, but it is often hard to formulate rules to find the proofs.

There are different ways in which AI has been used to contribute to the automation of mathematics. Some of these produce an interactive system in order to suggest ideas to the user, to allow description and manipulation of proofs and also to automate trivial steps which would be tedious to do by hand: for example, verification theorem-provers like Isabelle (Paulson, 1994). Others take the ambitious goal of creating an 'artificial mathematician'. This can involve detection of general patterns of proof and provision of maximum possible automation of proof. A computer following a purely algorithmic approach can consider many more approaches than a human, and look for consequences further ahead before deciding how promising each potential approach would be. Once faster computers became available, initial inefficient symbol-crunching approaches were improved by normalisation procedures (Gilmore, 1970), and by further refinement of standard procedures in the form of resolution (Robinson, 1965), then by advances in high-level tactical reasoning such as CLAM (Bundy et al, 1990).

Some very large mathematical proofs have been verified using interactive theorem provers, where humans and machines collaborate. Long computer-assisted proofs have been produced, including for the four-colour problem, Kepler conjecture and Boolean Pythagorean triples problem. The automated theorem prover EPQ in 1996 proved the Robbins conjecture. In summary, there is much progress in tackling what used to be thought as the human preserve of mathematical intuition.

4. AUTOMATING CONVERSATION

The Turing Test (originally called the Imitation Game) was proposed as a test of a machine's intelligence (Turing, 1950): a human evaluator observes a natural language conversation between a machine and a human via a textual/online communication channel (to omit other clues) and has to decide whether s/he can distinguish which entity is the machine. In 1966, Joseph Weizenbaum's program Eliza was the first to pick up the challenge, being a simple keyword-based program that mimicked a human psychiatrist (Weizenbaum,

1966). This was the start of natural language processing (NLP), which progressed from symbolic to statistical and neural approaches (Zakaria Kurdi, 2017). In 1971, *Parry* a computer program that simulated a person with schizophrenia, was the first program considered to have passed a modified Turing Test, (Colby, 1972). Various other developments followed until 2010, when Apple launched Siri, after which virtual assistants and chatbots have widely expanded in development and application.

Many of these chatbots use AI, thereby being able to respond to the context and structure of the information being provided and provide a more realistic conversation experience. They may use: Machine Learning (*ML)* to identify patterns in user input, make decisions and learn from past conversation; *NLP* to understand the meaning and context of natural language, deal with human error in the input and respond naturally; *sentiment analysis* to help a chatbot understand users' emotions. The current state-of-the-art is is OpenAI's GPT3 (Generative Pretrained Transformer), which uses ML to automate a variety of NLP tasks like text translation and answering questions (Floridi and Chiriatti, 2020).

5. AUTOMATION IN ETHICS

Ethical behaviour from AI-assisted machines has been in the news, mostly due to problematic cases that have come to light, such as bias in judicial decision-making[1], bias in recruitment[2], chatbots that started to use racist language[1], etc. These incidents have highlighted a weakness of the current techniques employed in AI-based systems, i.e., the tendency of the machines to reproduce historical bias or other infirmities in the learning data. More fundamental questions have been asked about whether any AI could ever be trusted with decisions that impact human life (Krishnan, 2009; Misselhorn, 2018). We think it is important to distinguish between ethics *inside* AI-based systems, ethics of businesses *developing* AI-based systems, and ethics of AI *deployments*. Although it is important for all three aspects to be ethical, we posit that the ethical problems involved in these three aspects may be solved using different techniques. For instance, the question of ethics *inside* AI seems more abstract, and current efforts fall short of expectations (Nallur, 2020). On the other hand, ethics of people *developing* AI and the ethics of *deploying* AI may be more amenable to being solved using currently available techniques. There are already some techniques that have been recommended to develop AI in an ethical manner (Anderson *et al*, 2019; Gebru *et al*, 2020).

Deployment of AI-based systems requires analysis of development techniques, social contexts, as well as the deploying organisation's own practices. This is currently done through an exhaustive investigation of physical and digital artefacts by human beings. In our opinion, there will be increasing efforts to automatically identify digital artefacts that could be used to infer ethically problematic practices. Initially, these might be in the form of a bot that is limited to generating reports, which are then evaluated by a human. However, in the same manner as automated testing, theorem proving, and NLP, we might be able to automate small tasks that build on each other to perform a complex operation. This may result in more sophisticated tools that may eventually be able to perform deeper analysis on a company's artefacts to infer ethical values, in the same manner that the ISO 9000 series of certifications allows us to infer product quality from process quality. Correctness-by-Construction (White, 2017) recommends this very same philosophy: By taking small steps, each step-by-step verification activity is correspondingly small and manageable. By using precise notations, each verification step can be trustworthy and amenable to automation, and there are no gaps for defects to hide in. By doing tool-supported verification, we reduce the element of human error.

Arguments against Automating Ethical Reasoning: Care needs to be taken that the automated process itself does not introduce new ethical problems, including lack of transparency and human control (Hagendorff, 2020; IEEE, 2019). Another concern is that the presence of automation tends to make humans shed their cognitive engagement. This has been flagged by some ethicists as potentially leading to a situation where we abrogate our responsibility to act in an ethical manner. A third concern is how intrusive such technologies would need to be, and whether such intrusion is warranted or trusted.

[1] https://www.propublica.org/article/how-we-analyzed-the-compas-recidivism-algorithm
[2] https://www.reuters.com/article/us-amazon-com-jobs-automation-insight-idUSKCN1MK08G

6. CONCLUSIONS

In this paper, we have considered several tasks that were previously considered to require human ingenuity, and capacity for abstract thought. We have also outlined how these domains have seen progress over a few decades such that current tools/systems are perceived to be functioning at human levels of competence or better. There is no known physical/informational limit that precludes the domain of ethical evaluation of actions from such efforts. We would speculate that simpler tasks such as checking whether datasets have been de-biased would be the first milestone in this endeavour, with other practices following suit. Automation thus functions as a marker of human ingenuity, where we are able to *dissociate* the task from the intelligence required to do it, by breaking it down into simpler objectively evaluated parts.

REFERENCES

Anderson, M. et al, 2019. A value-driven eldercare robot: Virtual and physical instantiations of a case-supported principle-based behavior paradigm. *In Proceedings of the IEEE*, Vol. 107, No. 3, pp. 526–540.

Bacchelli, A. and Bird, C., 2013. Expectations, outcomes, and challenges of modern code review. *In Proceedings of the 2013 International Conference on Software Engineering*, San Francisco, CA, USA, pp. 712–721.

Beck, K. 1997. (ed.), Simple Smalltalk Testing. *In Kent Beck's Guide to Better Smalltalk: A Sorted Collection*, Cambridge: Cambridge University Press, pp. 277–288.

Bundy, A. et al, 1990. The Oyster-Clam System. *In Proc. 10th CADE*, Springer Verlag, Kaiserlauten, Germany.

Cabrera, C. et al., 2017. Implementing heterogeneous, autonomous, and resilient services in IoT: An experience report. *In IEEE 18th Intl Symp on World of Wireless, Mobile and Multimedia Networks.* doi: 10.1109/WoWMoM.2017.7974341

Colby, K., 1972. Turing-like Indistinguishability Tests for the Validation of a Computer Simulation of Paranoid Processes. *In Artificial Intelligence.* Vol. 3, pp. 199–22.

Fagan, M.E., 1976. Design and code inspections to reduce errors in program development. *In IBM Syst. J.*, Vol. 15, No. 3, pp. 182–211.

Floridi, L. and Chiriatti, M., 2020. GPT-3. *In Minds & Machines*. Vol. 30, pp. 681–694.

Gebru, T. et al, 2020. Datasheets for Datasets. *In arXiv:1803.09010* [cs]. Available at: http://arxiv.org/abs/1803.09010

Gilmore, P, 1970. An examination of the geometry theorem-proving machine. *In Artificial Intelligence*, Vol.1, pp.171-187.

Hagendorff, T., 2020. The Ethics of AI Ethics. *In Minds and Machines*, Vol. 30, No 1, pp. 99-120.

IEEE Global Initiative on Ethics of Autonomous and Intelligent Systems, 2019. *Ethically Aligned Design*, v2.

Krishnan, A., 2009. Killer robots: legality and ethicality of autonomous weapons. Ashgate Publishing Ltd.

McIntosh, S., et al, 2016. An empirical study of the impact of modern code review practices on software quality. *In Empir. Softw. Eng.*, Vol. 21, No. 5, pp. 2146–2189.

Misselhorn, C., 2018. Artificial morality. Concepts, issues and challenges. *In Society*, Vol. 55, No. 2, pp. 161–169.

Nallur, V. et al, 2016. Clonal plasticity: a method for decentralized adaptation in multi-agent systems. *In 11th IEEE/ACM International Symposium on Software Engineering for Adaptive and Self-Managing Systems (SEAMS)*. pp. 122-128.

Nallur, V., 2020. Landscape of Machine Implemented Ethics. *In Science and Engineering Ethics*. Vol. 26, pp. 2381–2399.

Paulson, L., 1994. *Isabelle: A Generic Theorem Prover.* LNCS, Vol. 828, Springer-Verlag Berlin Heidelberg.

Robinson, J.A., 1965. A machine oriented logic based on the resolution principle. *In J. Assoc. Comput. Mach.*, Vol. 12, pp. 23-41.

Song, H. et al., 2015. On architectural diversity of dynamic adaptive systems. *In 2015 IEEE/ACM 37th IEEE International Conference on Software Engineering*, pp. 595–598. doi:10.1.1.960.5924.

Turing, A., 1950. Computing Machinery and Intelligence. *In Mind*, Vol. 236, pp. 433-460.

Weizenbaum, J., 1966. ELIZA—a computer program for the study of natural language communication between man and machine. *In Commun. ACM.* Vol. 9, No. 1, pp. 36–45.

White N, et al., 2017. Formal verification: will the seedling ever flower? *Phil. Trans. R. Soc. A* 375: 20150402. Available at: http://dx.doi.org/10.1098/rsta.2015.0402

Zakaria Kurdi, M., 2017. *Natural Language Processing and Computational Linguistics*. Vol. 2. ISTE-Wiley.

DIGITAL PLATFORMS AS MEDIATOR OF PUBLIC COMMUNICATION

Leonid Smorgunov and Olga Ignatjeva
Saint Petersburg State University, 7-9 Universitetskaya Emb., St Petersburg 199034, Russia

ABSTRACT

Research into the impact of information and communication technologies (ICT) on the field of public communication has a big importance nowadays. This article is aimed at studying the influence of lay epistemics on the formation of judgments in the course of communication on digital platforms between government officials and the citizens. To study the functioning of the process of forming judgments on digital platforms of communication between the authorities and citizens, we have worked out a new methodology of discourse analysis based on theory of lay epistemics. We stem on communication on the 'Our St. Petersburg' platform. The descriptive and regression analysis of judgements with the aid of the programming language R allows us to reveal that this platform is belonged to informative type of communication based on the behavioral principle of "stimulus-response". It was also found that the criteria of the parametric model have a different effect on the formation of a certain type of judgment in the framework of public communication on digital platforms.

KEYWORDS

Digital Platforms, Public Communication, Lay Epistemics, Judgment, Epistemic Authority

1. INTRODUCTION

Studies of the role of public communication and digital technologies in modern politics form a significant layer of literature in political science, which is actively replenished in various directions. The theory of communication studies is being developed in Russia and the processes of influence on political communication of new media are being investigated. A number of works reveal various aspects of the growing influence of new ICTs on politics and communication processes (see: Akopov, 2015; Bykov, 2013; Volodenkov, 2018, etc.). Some researchers directly argue that digital platforms are not politically neutral, and their architecture directly affects the results of political campaigns (Bossetta, 2018; Lukito, 2020). D. Kreis and S. McGregor provide evidence that during the 2016 US presidential election. IT giants were involved in election campaigns not on commercial but on political grounds (Kreiss., McGregor, 2018). Modern public communication is no longer limited to the traditional exchange of political information between people, it is moderated by very sophisticated methods in digital platforms, which opens up almost limitless possibilities for covert manipulation of public consciousness not only in authoritarian but also democratic countries (Computational ..., 2019; Howard, 2010; Morozov, 2011). The aim of the study is to examine the impact of digital platforms on the production of communication judgments. The city platform "Our St. Petersburg" was taken as an empirical object of our research. The study was conducted in 2020.

2. DISCOURSE ANALYSIS OF JUDGMENTS ON DIGITAL PLATFORMS

Digital platforms of communication between citizens and authorities are becoming part of the implementation of public governance in the modern world. They can be differentiated into four types: platforms for citizens' appeal, portals for urban (regional) problems, portals for assessing initiatives, portals / platforms for public participation. These portals (platforms) have different architectures and, accordingly, a set of affordances, which in a certain way affect the nature of communication and the formation of the prevailing type of judgments. In the process of research, the judgments formed on the platforms were classified into three types: information, general deliberative, and cognitive deliberative. Information judgments are judgments that express information about any observable facts and can contain logical connectives (what, if, because, therefore, therefore). The other two types of judgments are deliberative, and to identify such judgments it is necessary to focus on the discourses that may contain them. General deliberative judgments - judgments containing text, open for further discussion and finding a common position. Cognitive deliberative judgments are judgments containing text, aimed at finding additional knowledge in the process of discussion.

To analyze communication processes on the 'Our St. Petersburg' platform, a toolkit was developed taking into account six criteria that influence the formation of human judgments, based on the concept of lay epistemics and the parametric model of judgments by Ari Kruglanski (Kruglanski et al., 2010. P. 939-950; Kruglanski et al., 2007. P. 255-303), which has undergone a certain modification. A scale of discussion intensity from 0 to 3 and the three above-mentioned types of judgments were introduced into the toolkit.

The first criterion - *informational relevance (criterion A)* - characterizes the importance of the topic for the communicating parties, which increases from information to cognitive deliberative type of judgments. The second criterion - *the task demands (criterion B)* - determines the level of complexity of the derivation of the syllogism based on the general and particular premise. In general, deliberative judgment, there is a syllogism with a probabilistic or incomplete conclusion. And only in the case of cognitive deliberative judgments is there maximum intensity when a syllogism with a completed and affirmative conclusion is present in the judgment. *Cognitive resources (criterion C)* is the third criterion and characterize the degree of concentration of attention as the intensity of discussion of a topic / problem. The degree of intensity of this criterion increases with the movement from information to cognitive deliberative type of judgments. The fourth and fifth criteria refer to the type of motivation (Kruglanski, 1999). *Non-directional motivation (criterion D)* is determined by the degree of effort spent on determining the subject of discussion, its general nature. *Directional motivation (criterion E)* determines the level of readiness for a specific / non-specific closure and expresses the desire to continue or stop communication in connection with the certainty of the issue being addressed. Both non-directional and directional motivations gain intensity from information judgements to cognitive deliberative judgements. *Epistemic authority (criterion F)* is used to legitimize the results of the cognitive process.

Hypothesis. The digital communication platform of the population and regional authorities "Our Petersburg" affects the intensity of the use of the corresponding capacities of ordinary epistemics, which generate chances to produce informational judgments.

To test the hypothesis proposed in the study, a new method of discourse analysis was developed on digital platforms of communication between the population and government authorities. Assessment of judgments based on the modified six criteria and the scale of intensity of lay epistemics made it possible to classify judgments formed within the framework of platform interaction, as well as to determine the effectiveness of a particular criterion.

3. DESCRIPTIVE AND REGRESSION ANALYSIS OF JUDGMENTS ON THE PLATFORM 'OUR ST. PETERSBURG'

The sample size of judgments on the 'Our St. Petersburg' platform was 10993 messages, of which 83.9% were information judgments, 9.1% were general deliberative judgments, and 7% were cognitive deliberative judgments. The distribution of mean and standard deviations in judgments by criteria is shown in table. 1. The mean describes the intensity of epistemic criteria, characteristic, respectively, for information, general deliberative and cognitive deliberative judgments. The standard deviation records the scatter of judgments around the average for the respective types of judgments.

By calculating the averages and the spread of the data around the mean (standard deviation), we estimated how accurately our attribution of judgments to a particular type was obtained. Based on the calculations performed, we came to the conclusion that the standard deviations are not so large for our data. Large values of standard deviations indicate that cognitive judgments require careful assessment. The smaller the discrepancy, the more significant is the criterion for the appropriate judgment.

Thus, information judgments have the smallest average in the region of unity for five criteria (criteria A, B, C, D, E) out of six. They are characterized by a smaller spread of values (standard deviation within +/- 0.5), which means that a more accurate result is presented. Intensity in the region of three units has cognitive deliberative judgments in two cases out of six (criteria A and E), corresponding to the principle of coding by seniority (determining the type of judgment based on the degree of deliberation). The standard deviation range for cognitive deliberative judgments is in the range of two units, which indicates the diversity of the form and content of this type of judgments and, possibly, the difficulty of their identification for evaluators. Average in the region of two units have common deliberative judgments,

Data demonstrate the distribution of judgments for each type of criteria, which may indicate the different significance of the criteria in the formation of a particular type of judgment. The distribution of judgments according to criteria for the information type is presented more or less uniformly. This is due to the predominance on this platform of the traditional behavioral model of communication between the authorities and the population according to the 'stimulus-response' type. A slight decrease in the mean value for information judgments is characteristic of the F criterion 'Epistemic authority' (mean value 0.49), which may indicate some distrust of the population in the ability of state authorities to properly resolve their issue.

You can notice some heterogeneity in the distribution of judgments by criteria. So, criteria A 'Informational relevance' and E 'Directional motivation' to the greatest extent affect the formation of a cognitive deliberative judgments. It should be noted that the distribution of types of judgments according to criteria A and E is identical for both general deliberative judgments and for cognitive deliberative judgments, that indicates the corresponding regularity and significance of the influence of criteria on the types of judgments.

The situation with respect to criteria B 'Task demands' and C 'Cognitive resources' changes somewhat. They have less influence on the formation of cognitive deliberative judgments and more influence on the formation of general deliberative judgments. This indicates that the judgments posted on the 'Our St. Petersburg' platform are not always complete and correspond to the laws of logic or contribute to the launch of a lengthy discussion. The corresponding trend, but with a lower intensity, demonstrates the distribution of judgments according to the criteria D 'Nondirectional motivation' and F 'Epistemic authority'. This means that the platform 'Our St. Petersburg' either accepts a common theme without raising additional questions, which is typical for general deliberative judgments, or the topic of discussion is taken for granted without specifying it, which is typical for information judgments. According to criterion F 'Epistemic authority', the significance of the criterion falls for all types of judgments, but especially for cognitive deliberative judgment.

A logistic regression model was used to determine the relationship between the dependent variable (the probability of using information judgments) and the corresponding six criteria (predictors). The calculation results are shown in Table 1.

Table 1. Results of constructing logistic regression for information judgments

Predictors	Estimation coefficient	Standard mistakes	Wald Z-tests[1]	Level significance
Intercept	11.41243	0.25710	44.390	<2e-16 ***
Criterion A	-1.94983	0.06640	-29.365	<2e-16 ***
Criterion B	-1.70144	0.07609	-22.362	<2e-16 ***
Criterion C	-1.08143	0.09003	-12.012	<2e-16 ***
Criterion D	-0.77266	0.06629	-11.656	<2e-16 ***
Criterion E	-1.73362	0.06164	-28.124	<2e-16 ***
Criterion F	0.18189	0.06873	2.646	0.00813 **

As follows from the data obtained, all six criteria turned out to be statistically significant, and they definitely affect the dependent variable 'Probability of using information judgments'. Based on the data shown in Table 1, a logistic regression equation was obtained. The resulting logistic regression equation (1) demonstrates the inverse relationship between the predictors (criteria A-E) and the dependent variable (the probability of using information judgments).

$$\textbf{logarithm of the odds ratio} = 11.41 - 1.95 * \textbf{criterion A} - 1.7 * \textbf{criterion B} - 1.08 * \textbf{criterion C} - 0.77 * \textbf{criterion D} - 1.74 * \textbf{criterion E} + 0.18 * \textbf{criterion F} \quad (1)$$

If criterion A increases by one unit, the odds ratio of using informational judgments increases in 0.14 times, criterion B - in 0.18 times, and criterion E - in 0.18 times, that is, the odds of using informational judgments decreases slightly. When criterion C increases by one unit, the odds ratio of using informational judgments

[1] Wald's Z-test is an analogue of the Student's t-test for testing parameters in linear regression models.

increases in 0.34 times, criterion D - in 0.46 times, i.e., the odds of using informational judgments decreases significantly. When criterion F increases by one unit, the odds ratio of using. informational judgments increase in 1.2 times, i.e. the odds of using informational judgments increase insignificantly.

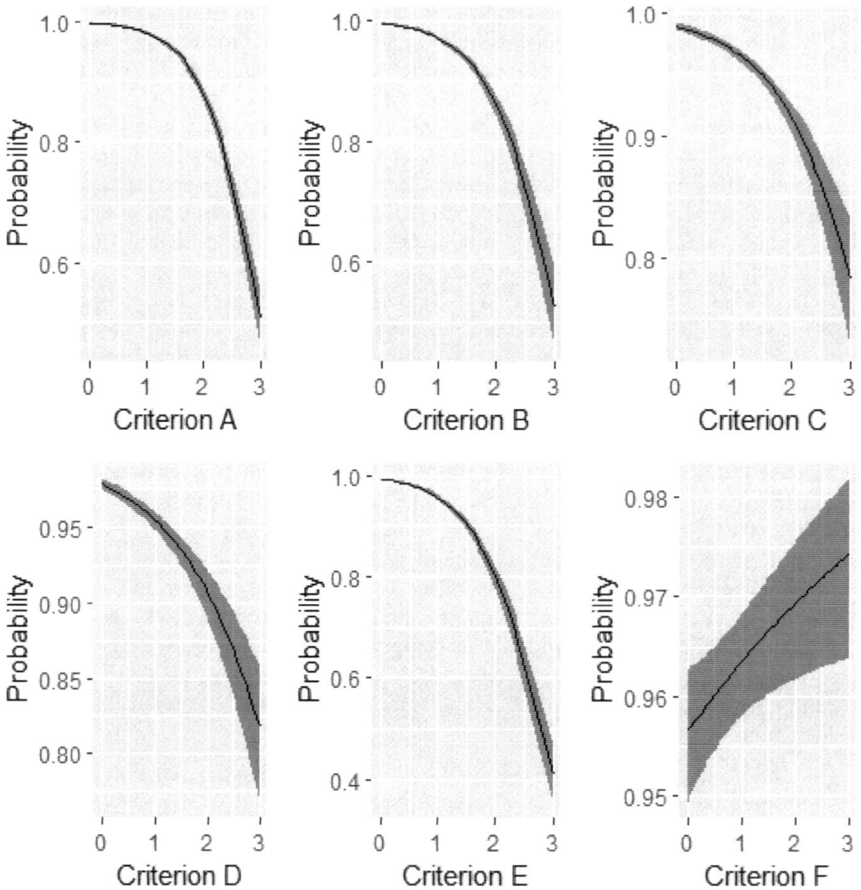

Figure 1. Dependence of the probability of using information judgments on the application of criteria A-F

The graphs in Figure 1 reflect the tendency of a sharp drop in the probability of using the information judgments in the case of using a higher intensity of epistemic criteria, which is characteristic of general deliberative and cognitive deliberative judgments. For example, in the case of criterion A, the informational relevance of the topic for communication participants using the information judgments is neutral. If the topic acquires a special personal meaning for the sides of the interaction, then the intensity of deliberation increases, and we move from an information judgment to a general deliberative or cognitive deliberative judgment, which can be seen in Figure 1 in relation to criterion A. Similarly, it is possible to trace the relationship between the probability of using information judgments and criteria B, C, D, E.

Thus, this platform favors the epistemic abilities of communication participants related to informational relevance (criterion A), task demands (criterion B), and directional motivation (criterion E). These abilities are more significant for the formation of information judgments than the engagement of cognitive resources (criterion C) and non-directional motivation (criterion D). The latter, apparently obeying the logic of the platform, are discreetly used by participants. On the platform, there is a direct relationship between the epistemic capacity responsible for epistemic authority (criterion F) and the dependent variable, which indicates the importance of confirming the response by a representative of the authority through recourse to expert knowledge in the informational type of communication. The formation of platforms suitable for deliberative communication should help to activate the relevant criteria of everyday epistemics that influence the formation of general deliberative and cognitive deliberative judgments.

4. CONCLUSION

Analysis of judgments on the platform 'Our St. Petersburg' allows us to assert that we have a platform dominated by the information type of communication, built on the behavioral principle of 'question-answer' and does not involve extensive deliberations. A descriptive analysis of variations within the information judgments shows a slight decrease in the mean values in relation to criterion E 'Directional motivation' and criterion F 'Epistemic authority', which confirms the limited ability of citizens to develop public communication and influence decisions within this platform. Analysis using logistic regression shows the presence of a direct connection between the criterion of 'Epistemic authority' and the probability of using information judgments in the process of communication on the platform 'Our St. Petersburg'. We acknowledge that future research should include analysis of these types of judgements on other types of platforms mentioned above in order to develop deliberative type of communication.

ACKNOWLEDGEMENT

This work was supported with a grant from the Russian Foundation for Basic Research (grant #20-011-31361 'Outsourcing of Political Judgment: A Critical Analysis of the Information Paradigm of Network Public Communication').

REFERENCES

Akopov, G.L., 2015. *The Internet and Politics. Modernization of the Political System on the Basis of Innovative Political Internet Communications.* Moscow: ConRus;

Bossetta, M., 2018. The Digital Architectures of Social Media: Comparing Political Campaigning on Facebook, Twitter, Instagram, and Snapchat in the 2016 U.S. Election. *In Journalism & Mass Communication Quarterly*, Vol. 95, No. 2, pp. 471-496;

Bykov I.A., 2013. *Network Political Communication: Theory, Practice and Research Methods: Monograph*. St. Petersburg: Publishing house SPGUTD;

Computational Propaganda: Political Parties, Politicians, and Political Manipulation on Social Media, 2019. / Ed. by S. Woolley and P. Howard. Oxford: Oxford University Press;

Fetzer, J., 2004. Disinformation: The use of false information. *In Minds and Machines*, Vol. 14, No. 2, pp. 231–240;

Howard, P., 2010. *The Digital Origins of Dictatorship and Democracy Information Technology and Political Islam.* Oxford: Oxford University Press;

Kreiss, D. and McGregor, S., 2018. Technology Firms Shape Political Communication: The Work of Microsoft, Facebook, Twitter, and Google With Campaigns During the 2016 U.S. Presidential Cycle. *In Political Communication*, Vol. 35, No. 2, pp. 155-177;

Kruglanski, A. W., Pierro, A., Mannetti, L., Erb, H., and Young Chun, W., 2007. On The Parameters of Human Judgment. *In Advances in Experimental Social Psychology*, Vol. 39, pp. 255–303;

Kruglanski, A., 1999. Motivation, Cognition and Realty: Three Memos for the Next Generation of Research. *In Psychological Inquiry*, Vol. 10, No. 1, pp. 53-58. Available at https://doi.org/10.1207/s15327965pli1001_8;

Kruglanski, A., Orehek, E., Dechesne, M. and Pierro, A., 2010. Lay Epistemic Theory: The Motivational, Cognitive and Social Aspects of Knowledge Formation. *In Social and Personality Psychology Compass,* Vol. 10, No. 4, pp. 939-950. Available at https://doi.org/10.1111/j.1751-9004.2010.00308.x;

Lukito, J., 2020. Coordinating a Multi-Platform Disinformation Campaign: Internet Research Agency Activity on Three U.S. Social Media Platforms, 2015 to 2017. *In Political Communication*, Vol. 37, No. 2, pp. 238-255;

Morozov, E., 2011. *The Net Delusion: The Dark Side of Internet Freedom.* New York: Public Affairs.

Volodenkov, S.V., 2018. *Internet Communications in the Global Space of Modern Political Governance.* Moscow: Prospect;

GOOD FRIENDSHIPS IMPROVE OUR LIVES. BUT CAN VIRTUAL FRIENDSHIPS BE GOOD?

Nick Munn and Dan Weijers
University of Waikato
Gate 1 Knighton Road, Private Bag 3105, Hamilton 3240, New Zealand

ABSTRACT

Good friendships improve our lives. But philosophers, psychologists, and other social scientists disagree about the nature of friendship and the value of virtual friendships. Recent technological advances and global crises highlight the importance of answering the question: can virtual friendships be good? We argue against accounts of friendship that suggest virtual relationships are necessarily deficient, focusing on rejecting the requirements of physical proximity and complete authenticity for friendship. We propose a more inclusive account of friendship that focusses on positive intentions and experiences. We also discuss examples of virtual friendships that highlight their advantages in modern times, especially their ability to promote intercultural cohesion. Finally, we suggest implications to help guide individual and collective decisions about friendship in a way that improves wellbeing.

KEYWORDS

Friendship, Virtual Friendship, Authentic, Physicality, Intention, Wellbeing

1. INTRODUCTION

Philosophers (Helm, 2009; Telfer, 1970), psychologists (Bayer, et al., 2018; Hojjat, et al., 2017), and others (Amichai-Hamburger, et al., 2013; Dunbar, 2018; Greco, et al., 2015) agree that friendship is an important contributor to wellbeing. But there is considerable disagreement about whether friendship is a central or peripheral component of wellbeing (Badhwar, 1993) and about what kinds of friendship are valuable (Anderson & Fowers, 2020; Badhwar & Dadlez, 2018). This disagreement is particularly noticeable for technologically mediated friendships (Danaher, 2019; Jeske, 2019; Munn, 2017).

Having the right kind of friendships is important for living a good life. So, understanding whether the increasing availability of virtual friendships is an opportunity or a threat is vital for making the right individual and collective decisions about the kinds of friendships to seek and encourage in modern times. Recent events have made the importance of friendship even more obvious. COVID-19 forced governments to balance the costs and benefits of physically isolating their citizens. A widely-discussed potential cost was that physical isolation would entail social isolation, or at least the degradation of social interactions to the point at which people's mental health was at risk (Courtet, et al., 2020; Marston, et al., 2020). Making the right decisions about enforced physical isolation depends on understanding both the importance of friendship for wellbeing and in what ways, if any, virtual friendships are less valuable than in-person friendships. For example, if virtual friendships are about as valuable as in-person friendships, then longer lockdowns combined with the facilitation and promotion of virtual communication technologies may be preferable to shorter lockdowns with the associated risk of higher infection rates.

In this paper, we argue that we can and do value virtual interactions and virtually mediated friendships. In the process, we propose an inclusive definition of friendship that is at odds with many recent views on the topic, highlight the benefits of virtual friendships and discuss the implications for individuals and societies.

2. THE NATURE OF FRIENDSHIP

Both philosophers (Leibowitz, 2018; Nehamas, 2016) and psychologists (Apostolou, et al., 2020; Johnson, et al., 2011) argue about the nature of friendship. Many philosophical accounts of friendship follow from Aristotle's conception of friendship (Annas, 1988; Sherman 1987; Thomas, 1989). These point to the difficulty of establishing higher order friendships and claim that in virtual spaces, such friendships are more difficult or even impossible to establish (Cocking, et al., 2012; McFall, 2012; Sharp, 2012). More recent philosophical accounts (Elder, 2017; Laas, 2018; Turp, 2020), and some psychological accounts (Rawlins, 2016; Schønning, et al., 2020), argue that, while they may have some value, virtual interactions cannot be a foundation for *proper* friendships. This claim is most often supported by stressing virtual interactions' lack of authenticity or physicality (e.g., Fröding & Peterson, 2012), features usually present in in-person interactions. We will argue against these restrictive accounts of friendship and the view that virtual interactions are necessarily deficient.

Certain kinds of physicality, such as supportive hand-holding and loving embraces, may be a basic human need (Nussbaum, 1995). The importance of positive physical interactions seems to be most obvious during the developmental phase from infancy to adulthood (White, 2018). For example, in a study of 53 mother-infant pairs, maternal touch was found to reduce infants' physiological reactivity to stress, reducing their cortisol levels (Feldman, et al., 2010). But notice that positive human touch can be important for our wellbeing or development without it being a necessary part of the nature of friendship. Humans have long had important friendships with people they have never met in person. Long before anyone conceived of the internet, people regularly wrote letters to their pen pals in distant lands. It is reasonable to believe that some pen pals were good friends despite never interacting in person. Therefore, it is clear that physicality is not necessary for friendship.

Fröding and Peterson (2012) argue that the people we interact with regularly online cannot become genuine friends because we cannot build authentic relationships with them. They claim that the temporally and modally restricted kinds of interactions we have online do not allow us to know the other person completely. If there are aspects of the other person we do not know about, Fröding and Peterson (2012) argue, then we cannot be friends with them. Rather, we would be under a kind of digitally enabled illusion. The person that we think we are friends with does not exist—they are a mere fragment of the complex whole of the real person you are having incomplete and inauthentic online interactions with. Fröding and Peterson's (2012) argument is based on an Aristotelian account of friendship that requires complete honesty between two virtuous agents. Both complete honesty and the high bar Aristotle sets for who can claim to be a virtuous agent, make this account of friendship entirely unrealistic. If we took these requirements seriously, then there would be very few, if any, genuine friendships. Very few of us are fully virtuous—excellent in all the important human capacities. Similarly, the vast majority of people find it difficult to be honest with ourselves, let alone others (Nuzzo, 2015). So, the argument that online friendships cannot be authentic fails because it sets the bar too high for authenticity—so high that very few if any in-person friendships would count.

Thinking more carefully about inauthenticity, it seems that our biggest worry is our friends maliciously deceiving us. Lying to a friend so as to not ruin their surprise party seems like a beneficent lie, and certainly one that the friend would not chastise us for after the party. Malicious lies, on the other hand, would cause us great distress to hear about. The friend that lies about their intentions to be a reliable house-sitter would likely lose your friendship and the opportunity to sit your house if you overheard them telling others about the raging party they are planning for at your house while you are away. So, we might not know everything about a potential friend, but as long as they have positive intentions toward us, our lack of knowledge doesn't appear to be a problem.

Working the above arguments into the general understanding of the nature of friendship, we propose an inclusive definition of friendship: Friendship is a relationship constituted by a clear majority of positive interactions between parties with positive intentions toward each other. On our view, friendships can be non-physical and even inauthentic, but only if those features do not lead to more negative interactions or negative intentions between the parties to the friendship. Our conception of friendship is distinct from others in the literature (Annas, 1987; Elder, 2017; Laas, 2018, Fröding & Peterson, 2012) both in that it allows for shared activity via online (as well as in-person) interaction and in that it relies on intention, rather than physical interaction, to instantiate the appropriate friendship-relations.

3. THE VALUE OF VIRTUAL INTERACTIONS AND FRIENDSHIPS

The risks of virtual interactions are discussed frequently, often at the expense of the potential benefits. For example, commentators frequently worry about the exposure of [usually young males] to violence via online gaming (Furlow, 2017; Huesmann, 2007) But they do not consider the opportunities such gaming can provide for leadership, friendship formation, exposure to people of different cultural and religious backgrounds, and so on.

In person, it is hard for teenagers to reach beyond their immediate social circle. A 14-16-year-old will have very few opportunities, if any, to interact in person with adults outside of their immediate family. They may talk to teachers, but the teacher-student relationship is an explicitly unequal one. Online, by contrast, the importance of age is diminished as it is often unknown. So, in many online endeavours, such as playing World of Warcraft with other guild members (Munn, 2012), these teenagers have interactions as equals with people from outside their age cohort. As age becomes irrelevant, positive virtual interactions can lead to friendships between teenagers and adults.

Virtual friendships do not rely on physical cues, and they draw from a much wider pool of potential friends than do in person friendships, which are of necessity restricted to those in physical proximity to oneself. In addition to the broader age cohort outlined above, virtual friendships also offer the benefit of exposing those engaging in them to unfamiliar cultures, beliefs, and religions. There is evidence to suggest that a major component of reducing prejudice is exposure to other cultures, so online interactions are then valuable in making us better people (Turner, et al., 2007; Vezzali, et al., 2014).

4. IMPLICATIONS

As virtual friendships become ubiquitous, the diversity of the average friend group is likely to expand, and in doing so, the frequency and intensity of prejudice against unfamiliar others in society will decline, simply because more people are exposed more often to others of more divergent backgrounds, than was or is the case in predominantly physical interaction. The benefit to society of this is clear. A society in which people develop a more diverse range of friendships with a heterogenous cohort of friends will be more accepting of difference than one which is restricted to traditional social structures.

If our analysis of the value of online friendships—that they are just as valuable as physical friendships, and have additional advantages which physical friendships do not—is correct, then by embracing online friendship, and by enabling and encouraging others to do so, we will lay the groundwork for a stronger, more resilient society, both in general, and in particular in times when physical interaction is curtailed by forces beyond our control. Furthermore, worries about virtual friendships taking time away from in-person friendships can be viewed as unfounded, not because it won't happen, but because it won't matter. Virtual friendships are not inferior, they are just a convenient kind of friendship.

REFERENCES

Amichai-Hamburger, Y., Kingsbury, M., & Schneider, B. H. (2013). Friendship: An old concept with a new meaning? *Computers in Human Behavior, 29*(1), 33-39.

Anderson, A. R., & Fowers, B. J. (2020). An exploratory study of friendship characteristics and their relations with hedonic and eudaimonic well-being. *Journal of Social and Personal Relationships*, *37*(1), 260-280.

Annas, J. (1977). Plato and Aristotle on Friendship and Altruism. *Mind, 86*: 532-54.

Apostolou, M., Keramari, D., Kagialis, A., & Sullman, M. (2020). Why people make friends: The nature of friendship. *Personal Relationships, 28*(1), 4-18.

Aristotle, Ross, W. D., & Brown, L. (2009). *The Nicomachean Ethics*. Oxford University Press.

Badhwar, N. K. (Ed.). (1993). *Friendship: A Philosophical Reader*. Cornell University Press.

Badhwar, N. K., & Dadlez, E. (2018). Love and friendship: Achieving happiness in Jane Austen's *Emma*. In E. Dadlez, (ed.) *Jane Austen's Emma: Philosophical Perspectives*. Oxford University Press.

Bayer, J. K., Mundy, L., Stokes, I., Hearps, S., Allen, N., & Patton, G. (2018). Bullying, mental health and friendship in Australian primary school children. *Child and Adolescent Mental Health*, *23*(4), 334-340.

Furlow, B. (2017). Media violence and youth aggression. *Lancet Child and Adolescent Health*, *1*(2), 91-92.

Cocking, D., van den Hoven, J., & Timmermans, J. (2012). Introduction: One thousand friends. *Ethics and Information Technology*, 14(3), 179-184.

Courtet, P., Olié, E., Debien, C., & Vaiva, G. (2020). Keep socially (but not physically) connected and carry on: preventing suicide in the age of COVID-19. *The Journal of Clinical Psychiatry*, *81*(3), 0-0.

Danaher, J. (2019). The philosophical case for robot friendship. *Journal of Posthuman Studies*, *3*(1), 5-24.

Dunbar, R. I. (2018). The anatomy of friendship. *Trends in Cognitive Sciences*, *22*(1), 32-51.

Elder, A. M. (2017). *Friendship, Robots, and Social Media: False Friends and Second Selves*. Routledge.

Feldman, R., Singer, M., & Zagoory, O. (2010). Touch attenuates infants' physiological reactivity to stress. *Developmental Science*, *13*(2), 271-278.

Fröding, B., & Peterson, M. (2012). Why virtual friendship is no genuine friendship. *Ethics and Information Technology*, *14*(3), 201-207.

Greco, S., Holmes, M., & McKenzie, J. (2015). Friendship and happiness from a sociological perspective. In Demir, M (ed.) *Friendship and Happiness,* 19-35. Springer, Dordrecht.

Helm, B. W. (2009). Friendship. In E. N. Zalta (ed.), The Stanford Encyclopaedia of Philosophy (Fall 2009 Edition). Retrieved from http://plato. stanford.edu/archives/fall2009/entries/friendship/.

Hojjat, M., Moyer, A., & Halpin, A. M. (eds.). (2017). *The Psychology of Friendship*. Oxford University Press.

Huesmann, L. R. (2007). The impact of electronic media violence: Scientific theory and research. *Journal of Adolescent Health*, *41*(6), S6-S13.

Jeske, D. (2019). *Friendship and Social Media: A Philosophical Exploration*. Routledge.

Johnson, H., Lavesson, N., Zhao, H., & Wu, S. F. (2011). On the concept of trust in online social networks. In L. Salgarelli, G. Bianchi, & N. Blefari-Melazzi (eds.), *Trustworthy Internet*. Springer, 143-157.

Laas, O. (2018). Questioning the virtual friendship debate: Fuzzy analogical arguments from classification and definition. *Argumentation, 32*, 99-149.

Leibowitz, U. D. (2018). What is Friendship? *Disputatio*, *10*(49), 97-117.

Marston, H. R., Musselwhite, C., & Hadley, R. A. (2020). COVID-19 vs Social Isolation: The impact technology can have on communities, social connections and citizens. *British Society of Gerontology–Ageing Issues*. Retrieved from https://ageingissues.wordpress.com/2020/03/18/covid-19-vs-social-isolation-the-impact-technology-can-have-on-communities-social-connections-and-citizens/

McFall, M. T. (2012). Real character-friends: Aristotelian friendship, living together, and technology. *Ethics and Information Technology, 14*(3), 221-230.

Munn, N. (2012). The reality of friendship within immersive virtual worlds. *Ethics and Information Technology, 14*(1), 1–10.

Munn, N. (2017). Friendship and modern life. In T. Shackelford & V. Weekes-Shackelford (eds.), *Encyclopedia of Evolutionary Psychological Science*. Springer.

Nehamas, A. (2016). *On Friendship*. New York, Basic Books.

Nussbaum, M. (1995). Human capabilities, female human beings. In M. C. Nussbaum & J. Glover (eds.), *Women, Culture and Development: A Study of Human Capabilities*. Oxford University Press, 61-104.

Nuzzo, R. (2015). Fooling ourselves. *Nature*, *526*(7572), 182.

Rawlins, W. K. (2016). Foreword. In A. Moyer & M. Hojjatt (eds.), *The Psychology of Friendship*. New York: Oxford University Press, ix-xiv.

Schønning, V., Hjetland, G. J., Aarø, L. E. and Skogen, J. C., 2020. Social media use and mental health and well-being among adolescents–A scoping review. *Frontiers in Psychology, 11*, 1949.

Sharp, R. (2012). The obstacles against reaching the highest level of Aristotelian friendship online. *Ethics and Information Technology, 14*(3), 231-239.

Sherman, N., (1987). Aristotle on Friendship and the Shared Life. *Philosophy & Phenomenological Research*, 47: 589–613.

Telfer, E. (1970). Friendship. *Proceedings of the Aristotelian Society, 71*, 223-241.

Thomas, L., (1987). Friendship. *Synthese*, 72: 217–36.

Turner, R. N., Hewstone, M., Voci, A., Paolini, S., & Christ, O. (2007). Reducing prejudice via direct and extended cross-group friendship. *European Review of Social Psychology*, *18*(1), 212-255.

Turp, M.-J. (2020). Social media, interpersonal relations and the objective attitude. *Ethics & Information Technology, 22*, 269-279.

Vezzali, L., Hewstone, M., Capozza, D., Giovannini, D., & Wölfer, R. (2014). Improving intergroup relations with extended and vicarious forms of indirect contact. *European Review of Social Psychology*, *25*(1), 314-389.

White, K. (2018). *Touch: Attachment and the Body*. Routledge.

A TEST CASE FROM NORWEGIAN RURAL AREAS WHERE STRUCTURED USER PARTICIPATION BUILDS SAFER COMMUNITIES

Anna Maria Urbaniak-Brekke[1], Ivar Petter Grøtte and Øyvind Heimset Larsen

[1]*PhD*

Western Norway Research Institute

Røyrgata 4, 6856, Sogndal, Norway

ABSTRACT

Paneda in Selje, Norway is among the foremost DAB technology companies in the world and works with warning systems for citizen evacuation. Their alert technology will be part of the national warning system, but first research, testing, evaluation and adjustment must take place. The case here is about the first test of the method, which has been used in large ICT projects. In this first stage of the project pupils from a local school in Selje at the west coast of Norway are involved in the development and implementation, with advice and direction of Western Norway Research Institute and Paneda. The results also suggest that the structured and staged testing framework may also provide a framework for local mobilisation, learning and implementation for new digital services.

KEYWORDS

User Experience, Experience Design, Evaluation, Public Warning Systems

1. INTRODUCTION

Warning of citizens and society in emergency situations has become increasingly important, due to many factors occurring in everyday life. Danger of terror attacks in large urban centres, effects of climate changes, such as floods, avalanches, fires, and many more threats, make societies in Norway, as well as all over the world, very vulnerable (Gentry & Gordon, 2019; Rød et al, 2019). It is therefore essential to develop resilient and robust systems to be able to avoid consequences of unexpected events setting human life in danger. Those systems are needed both in order to try to predict and avoid the events, but also to minimize potential losses if the emergency already occurs. Public warning technologies are being developed in order to inform citizens who can be in danger and guide them to a safer place when an unexpected and dangerous event takes place (Bean, 2019; Toyoda & Kanegae, 2014). Paneda, a company situated in Selje, in Western Norway is a pioneer in creating new public warning technology. Together with partner-companies, they prepared a highly innovative system for informing people about a dangerous situation (like a terror attack or natural disaster) and helping them to get to a safe place. However, this new technology that is being developed needs structured and iterated testing and evaluation before it will be introduced to a broader market. Structured technical testing and user testing is a necessary procedure before any system or innovation can be accepted and used publicly. Real-life tests cannot be replaced by other types of studies, marked research or data modelling (Drucker, 2007). Pilots and prototype-testing should be conducted for all new technologies despite the field, but are common especially for ICT, energy and health (Eide & Ljunggren, 2018). Testing is important for the development and learning of the company behind the technology. Eide and Ljunggren explain that a test can be conducted with both internal and external participants, and in many different forms: a prototype or pilot testing, reconnaissance or exercises, observations and feedback, as well as evaluation interviews and questionnaires (2018). Testing a technology before introducing it to the public should be especially important when it comes to developments that can have a crucial influence on human health and life.

This paper's main goal is to present a testing method and its use as a framework for both testing and introducing a public warning technology. The test of the method, which has previously been useful in large ICT projects, is organized as a case where 9th grade students from Selje are involved in local installation and evaluation of the technology, with the advice and direction of Western Norway Research Institute (WNRI) and the Paneda company. The test group involves students from 1st to 10th grade. The test case is the following: A major gas leakage in the nearby area. How to manage the risk of disasters, public warning and citizen evacuation in small communities near large transport systems? What are the good methods for user mobilization and involvement in service development? Will the new technology we introduce work and which parts of it need improvement? And finally will the testing framework in itself work as an efficient method for introducing the technology for the local population? As the test was conducted in June 2021, and not all results are deeply analysed, this is a work in progress.

2. BODY OF PAPER

Below we first present the theory, then briefly introduce the Public Warning System project, and describe the Selje-test that is a part of it, together with the method used, and preliminary results. The application of this testing method is innovative in itself, mobilising and involving the local society, and what is more young school pupils, in conducting the test both as the ones being evacuated and the ones responsible for leading the evacuation and evaluation of it.

2.1 Theory

In this research project, with the technology companies, we use an action research approach. We are participants in the development, and we expect to ground our conclusions in this action research (Greenwood and Levin 2007). Case study research is a key element as "the study of the particularity and complexity of a single case, coming to understand its activity within important circumstances" (Stake 1995). Our study is a single case where we look into a specific local community. According to Yin (1981) the strength of the case study is that it both covers a contemporary phenomenon and its context. Our findings will be from a single case, but we claim that these findings also can be a "force of example" (Flyvbjerg 2006) for other communities facing similar challenges related to emergencies and population evacuation. Greenwood and Levin (2007) define action research as collaborative social research carried out by a team of action researchers and members of local organizations who are trying to improve the local situations. Together, the researcher and the actors "define the problem to be examined, cogenerate relevant knowledge about them, learn and execute social research techniques, take actions, and interpret the results of actions based on what they have learned" (Greenwood and Levin 2007).

2.2 PWS Project

"Public Warning System" (PWS) is a national-range project which aims to research, develop and test a new and complete future population warning and evacuation system built on the DAB network (digital radio broadcasting network) (Vestlandsforsking, 2020). The project is co-financed by the Norwegian Research Council. The system shall alert and evacuate the population at critical incidents in a defined area and regardless of language and nationality. The warning will be given via audio, image, text, video, sirens, roadblocks/barriers, start/stop of machines etc, as shown in Figure 1. The need has been clearly demonstrated through many acts of terrorism, extreme weather and environmental disasters. Authorities lack good enough alert systems, while the EU sets requirements for population warning. Norway has the same requirements through the EEA Agreement (European Union, 2018).

The need for an innovative solution is clear, as existing systems have several problems. The mobile network is often out of service when it is needed the most and many people do not listen to the radio, have their mobile phone with them or do not use mobile phones at all. In addition, there is a significant problem with distance/time-factor before the emergency services arrive, and how to evacuate large crowds immediately.

During the project's lifetime (from 2020 to 2023) research work related to multiplatform and management systems will be carried out, technical testing (verification) and user testing (validation) activities will be prepared and implemented for a set of pilot services, and finally various dissemination activities will be carried out. A good networking practice for knowledge-based development should identify the correct balance between business, research and government. (Larsen et. al 2018) The publicly funded network initiatives and innovation projects like this one, in Norway, typically encourage the triple helix actors (Etzkowitz and Leydesdorff 2000) within a region to collaborate and thus bridge the gaps between the actors.

This paper describes a structured and staged test of the technology, performed in June 2021 at Selje school in Western Norway, together with thoughts around the topic from both a representative of the company developing this DAB solution and authorities responsible for disaster management in the region.

Figure 1. The elements of the Public Warning System (Vestlandsforsking, 2020)

2.3 Description of the Test

The test described in this paper was supposed to be carried out in March 2021, but due to a Covid-19 outbreak in the region, it was postponed to the middle of June 2021. The primary goal of the test is to check the operation of the proposed hazard warning system based on the DAB technology for a local school. This exercise was conducted in close cooperation with the Selje school, which gathers pupils from the 1st to 10th grade in Norwegian school system. An inspiration for this special test came with a request from the school regarding the 9th grade having a 'hands-on' experience with working with technology. Since Paneda, this rapidly growing, innovative company has its headquarters just a few hundred meters from the school, they were contacted and responded positively. The idea was then to test the warning system in the school premises, using DAB signal to turn on specific equipment giving light, sound, texts and picture effects in order to warn about an emergency and support an evacuation action. Since Vestlandsforsking leads the evaluation work package of the PWS project mentioned above, our task is also to develop testing scenarios and evaluation schemes for conducting the tests. In the Selje-test we decided to use a modern method to involve the end users and society, in this case the pupils and teachers, in performing the test and evaluating it. The scenario idea, a major gas leak close to the school, was accepted and the equipment for the test, such as screens, lights and speakers, were prepared, as well as the evaluation tools were defined. The public warning system with the equipment and technology mentioned above was installed, technical testing (verification) was performed also involving the 9th grade project group of pupils, acceptance of the total integrated system was signed out and the user test (validation) was ready to start. Then an evaluation scheme was distributed by the 9th grade pupils among the other pupils, and the user test was ready to start. An alarm went off, informing pupils and teachers being outside the school premises about a hazardous emergency and a need to seek a specific safe place inside the school. Pupils and teachers responded to the alarms and warnings and reached their planned destinations. After finishing the test the pupils of each class had to fill out the user test forms and each class had a de-briefing. Furthermore, the teachers were also interviewed about their experiences of this test-evacuation by the researchers.

2.4 Preliminary Results

The reflections of the representative for the company developing this unique DAB technology concentrates around the fact that the current public warning system in Norway is based on SMS, which means dependence on the mobile phone coverage and people's relation to using it. This is why they suggest including DAB-network and taking over of electronic equipment as a supplement for the current technology. However, the company notices that reaching public authorities in Norway with this idea has been difficult, and because of that a cooperation with a school in order to test the system was very welcomed. Another reason for it is that schools play an important role in each society, and through them, information about the det system and evacuation exercise can be spread. Also, close cooperation with other companies, police, fire department and local and regional disaster management authorities is sought. Nevertheless, there is an acknowledgement of a clear need for more tests in the future, before the technology is introduced on a national level. New tests are already being planned in other Norwegian regions where natural disasters are threatening the communities.

An interview with the disaster and emergency manager of the Vestland region confirmed the need for the new services. No modern integrated citizen alert and evacuation system exists and the need for improved services are very much needed. The role of local schools as a local HUBs for mobilisation, learning and implementation of this type of general citizen services are seen as an interesting case for further study and research.

Our preliminary results are gathered from the questionnaires evaluating the warning and evacuation of Selje school that were filled out by the students at the school in Selje (1st to 10th grade) and invited guests (teachers, authorities, journalists), a discussion after the test, and participating observations of the researchers. It turns out to be very important that the warning system and its elements are adjusted to the needs of different arenas where members of the society are present: schools, welfare units, industry, public places. At the same time it has to cover several scenarios: flood, gas leakage, avalanche, tsunami. The system must also be tested often and kept updated, so that when the need comes, it works immediately. The students of the 9th grade (usually 15 years old) seem to be a group that can easily get engaged in an exercise like this, from development of scenarios, test of the technical equipment, to the evaluation. However, it turns out that they are most interested in the technical and 'hands-on' tasks, and less in the theoretical part of it. This gives us a hint on how to develop such exercises in the future so that they can successfully involve the younger representatives of the society. From the technical point of view, we can confirm that sound plays a bigger role in warming than pictures and text, as it was the information coming from loudspeakers that was most important for both the students and adult guests. Nevertheless, the text and pictures on the screens must be customized, so that they are understandable for most people despite age, level of education or country of origin, such as internationally used pictograms and information in several languages (e.g. in Selje-test the text on the screens and from the loudspeakers was in three languages: Norwegian, English and Arabic, due to the fact that students in this school are using those languages).

3. CONCLUSION

The PWS project represents research in progress where the first field trials were run in June 2021. We gathered the first feedback on the effects of the structured testing methodology used as the key framework both for verification and validation testing in itself, but also as a method for local community mobilization and involvement in the citizen evacuation procedures. The test was successful, showing the possibilities of improvement and adjustments. Students turn out to be a group that can easily get engaged in such exercises and learn through them. Interestingly, different societal groups (students in different ages, teachers, researchers, technology developers and other guests) shared similar experiences, which shows that such a system can be developed to serve all. Finally, this test showed the potential of DAB-technology for public warning, and the way in which it should be further developed and tested.

The new prototype services will continue to be evaluated against the user requirements defined during the early stages of the project. In particular, the objective of evaluation will be to optimize the interaction between end-user feedback and technical implementation. And in addition this structured and staged testing framework might also prove to be an efficient framework for the introduction and the mobilisation for new digital services in a local community. The local schools might become the local HUBs for introducing new general digital services where the schools provide the needed infrastructure as well as learning facilities and related human resources.

ACKNOWLEDGEMENT

The authors have no conflict of interests.

REFERENCES

Bean, H. 2019. *Mobile Technology and the Transformation of Public Alert and Warning*. ABC-CLIO, LLC, Santa Barbara, Denver.

Drucker, P. F. 2007. *Management Challenges for the 21st Century*. Elsevier Ltd, Oxford.

Eide, D. et al, 2018. *Testing som metode i innovasjonsprosesser – Et verktøyhefte med eksempler fra opplevelsesbasert reiseliv*. Sourced from: https://docplayer.me/100186619-Testing-som-metode-i-innovasjonsprosesser-et-verktoyhefte-med-eksempler-fra-opplevelsesbasert-reiseliv-av-dorthe-eide-og-elisabet-ljunggren.html.

Etzkowitz H, Leydesdorff L. 2000. The dynamics of innovation: from national systems and "mode 2" to a triple helix of university-industry-government relations. *Res Policy,* 29(2):109–123.

European Union. 2018. Directive (EU) 2018/1972 of 11 December 2018 establishing the European Electronic Communications Code. *Official Journal of the European Union.* Sourced from: https://eur-lex.europa.eu/eli/dir/2018/1972/oj.

Flyvbjerg, B. 2006. Five Misunderstandings About Case-Study Research. *Qualitative Inquiry,* 12(2), 219-145.

Gentry, J.A. et al, 2019. *Strategic Warning Intelligence: History, Challenges, and Prospects*. Georgetown University Press. Washington DC.

Greenwood, D. J. et al, 2007. *Introduction to Action Research 2nd edition. Social Research for Social Change*. Sage Publications, Thousand Oaks, CA.

Larsen, Ø.H. et al, 2018. The Public Sector's Role in Norwegian Network Cooperation: Triple Helix or Laissezfaire? *Triple Helix*, Springer Open, DOI: 10.1186/s40604-018-0052-x.

Rød, J.K. et al, 2019. Er norske kommuner klare for en farligere fremtid? *Plan*, 4(51) 6-11. DOI: 10.18261/ISSN1504-3045-2019-04-03.

Stake, R.E. 1995. The Art Of Case Study Research. Sage Publications, Thousand Oaks, CA.

Toyoda, Y. et al, 2014. A community evacuation planning model against urban earthquakes. *Regional Science. Policy & Practice*, 6(3), 231-249. DOI: 10.1111/rsp3.12036.

Vestlandsforsking. 2020. *Public Warning System (PWS)*. Sourced from: https://www.vestforsk.no/en/project/public-warning-system-pws.

Yin, R. K. 1981. The case study as a serious research strategy. *Knowledge*, 3, 97-114.

AUTHOR INDEX